RETAIL (r)EVOLUTION

WHY CREATING RIGHT-BRAINED STORES WILL SHAPE THE
FUTURE OF SHOPPING IN A DIGITALLY DRIVEN WORLD

DAVID KEPRON

AIA, LEED BD+C, RDI

CINCINNATI, OHIO

ISBN: 978-0-944094-73-0

Published by:

ST Books, a division of
ST Media Group International Inc.
11262 Cornell Park Drive
Cincinnati, Ohio 45242
USA

Tel. 866-265-0954 or 513-421-2050
Fax 513-744-6999
E-mail: books@stmediagroup.com
Online: www.stmediabooks.com

Book and jacket design and layout, Kimberly Pegram
Front cover design, David Kepron
Editorial intern, Dylan R. McCracken
Proofreading intern, Allison Wisyanski

Printed in the United States of America

10 9 8 7 6 5 4 3

CONTENTS

PART 1:   Trade Routes, Stories and Stars

CHAPTER 1   **More Than Getting Stuff – Shopping as a Social Paradigm**................... 15
- Boyhood and Believing
- Trade Routes, the Agora and Mall-ing of America
- Ideas and Commerce – A Convenient Connection
- 3P's – Product, Price, Place – and People
- The Social Contract

CHAPTER 2   **'Space' vs. 'Place' – Experience Making** 29
- Great Un-Expectations
- Closets vs. Kitchens

CHAPTER 3   **Rituals – I Shop, Therefore I Am**.. 39
- The Rites of Purchase
- Shopping is an Embodied Experience
- Participating is Key
- The Media and The Message
- Sacred Ground
- Ritual Objects
- Open for Business – Crucial Times
- Cast Members – Animators – Mirroring Receptivity

CHAPTER 4   **Bedtime Books and the Importance of Story** 61
- The Hero Shopper
- Departure – Something Missing
- Initiation – Adventures in Shopping
- Return – Bringin' Back The Goods
- Stories and Mental Models
- Single Words
- Simulations – As If
- Emotional Stories
- Telling Stories In-Store
- Visual Stories as a Strategy
- Stories vs. Data Dumps

CHAPTER 5   **Play Time – Shopping and Having Fun**..................................... 83
- "Homo Ludens" – Man the Player
- Shopping and Play
- The Essential Features of Play and Shopping

CONTENTS

PART 2: Brands, Brains and Buying

CHAPTER 6   **This is Your Brain on Shopping** 101
- The Decade After the Decade After the "Decade of the Brain"
- The Emotional Brain
- Just Who's 'Minding the Store' Anyway?
- Superhighways, Country Roads and Cow Paths
- Getting to Know You

CHAPTER 7   **Three Pounds of Tofu** 121
- "Brainametrics" – Brain Facts 101
- Evolution and the Developing Brain
- How Brain Cells Communicate
- Fire Together-Wire Together
- From Synapse to Stores
- Growing Up Digital
- Your Brain on Google
- Are College Students Less Empathic Than Their Predecessors?

CHAPTER 8   **The Shopping Brain – It's All a State of Mind** 141
- Consciousness in the Shopping Aisle
- The Shapeable Shopping Brain
- The Brain is a Complex System
- Retailing is a Complex System, Too
- The Shopping Mind

CHAPTER 9   **Please Me** 161
- The "Pleasure Chemical" – Dopamine
- Places, Patterns and Perceptions
- Learning…It's All a Big Mistake
- The Pleasure Rush of Getting a Good Deal

CHAPTER 10   **Shopping: The Agony and the Ecstasy** 177
- Why Credit Cards Hurt So Good
- Using the Card Even When You Know It's Not Good For You
- Mirror-Mirror
- Reading Faces and Feeling Emotions
- This, That or The Other Thing – Why Choice is Highly Overrated

CHAPTER 11   **Left Brain – Right Brain** 203
- Life Before Written Language: Communicating in Pictures, Emotions and Gestures
- The Rise of Rationality – Plato and Domination by Reason Alone
- The Split Brain
- Left and Right Hemispheres – Which Side Does What
- The Language of Texts, Emoticons and Communicating Ideas

CHAPTER 12   **Your Shopping Brain in an Omni-Chanel Digital World** 219
- Continuous Partial Attention and the Re-wiring of Your Brain
- 10^n Screens
- Faces vs. Facts and Figures

CONTENTS

PART 3: Technology and Transcendence

CHAPTER 13 Shopping-A-Go-Go 239
- Shopping in an Age of Distraction
- Smartphone Adoption – Who's Got 'em?
- Keeping Up with the Jones'
- Apps and Traps
- Smartphone Adoption – What Are They Doing with 'em?
- Shopping on the Go – On the Mobile Device
- Mobile-Enabled Customers in the Store

CHAPTER 14 Mysterious Millennials 259
- Who, What, When, Where and Why?
- Self-Expression
- Techsters
- Loyalty, Trust and Value
- Push-me, Pull-you
- TMI OMG ;)! – Information Sharing and the Relationship
- The (Anti-)Social Network - 140 Characters, Emoticons
- Chatter That Matters – Communicating with a Millennial
- Millennials Like Going to the Store

CHAPTER 15 The Shopper's Mind Extended 287
- Connected World - Connected Brains
- "Technempathy"
- Augmented Cognition and Adaptive Interfaces
- The Shopper Ecology and the "Buyosphere"

CHAPTER 16 What's the Big Deal with Big Data? 301
- Digital Life-stream
- Predictive Analytics and the Predictive Power of Dopamine
- Sensors Everywhere – The Sentient Shopping World

CHAPTER 17 Blurring Boundaries – Digitally Driven Sensory Experiences 313
- Kiosks, Video Walls, QR Codes and the "Holodeck"
- QR Codes, Augmented Reality and Avatars
- Wearing Our Tech
- Feeling Through the Screen – Haptic Technology

CHAPTER 18 Creating Right-Brained Stores in a Digitally Driven World 335
- 'Making' is Intrinsic to Us All – Engaging Our Need to Create
- Creative Collaborative Consumerism
- The Market Segment and Brand of 'Me'
- The Brand Performance Place
- Retailing on the Right Side of the Brain
- The Store Will Never Go Away

Bibliography / Works Cited 358

To my Mother who,
taught me perseverance in the face of adversity,
nurtured my creative spirit and was always in the stands at every game.

To my Father who,
fostered my fascination with the future, by example taught me the virtue of making
with one's hands and that if a job was worth doing it was worth doing well.

To my sons Nick and Ben who,
who have grown me up, and who inspire me with their unbridled creative energy,
and who will live the future of shopping that this book envisions.

To my wife Lu who,
has opened my heart and mind by unconditionally sharing hers
for more than thirty years.

Author's Note to the Reader

Retail (r)Evolution is a book for retailers, designers, sales associates, store managers and anyone else for whom shopping is part of their everyday life. It's a provocative glimpse into the relevance of shopping and the places created to do it, and crosses centuries and continents, wireless networks as well as the human brain's intricate landscape.

Retail (r)Evolution integrates topics and themes including:

- The profound role of shopping as a social paradigm in understanding ourselves in a larger context, through ritual, storytelling and play.
- How customer experience is not 'out there' in the architecture, merchandise assortments, graphics and in-store technology, but rather in the customer's mind and created in a dynamic relationship between customers' brains and the environments they inhabit.
- New developments in neuroscience and how the brain plays a role in decision-making as well as the pleasure (and pain) we experience when shopping.
- How the rise of digital technology, the adoption of mobile devices, and the influence of online social networks are not only changing the way we communicate with each other, but rewiring our brains as well.
- Why digitally enabled, socially networked customers will be more informed, and become expert marketers in their own right, as pervasive use of social networks makes individual shoppers into their own brands.
- How the nature of the store will change to be a Brand Performance Place that allows for customers to engage in "Collaborative Creative Consumerism" and where retailers will implement "Technempathy" as a way to engage customers with technology in the service of building empathic relationships.

In three sections, I will draw on my more than twenty years of experience as an architect, artist and teacher, hopefully to provide a meaningful look at the nature of shopping places in the past, present and future. Promoting the idea that shopping is first and foremost a social paradigm, I'll look at how we as customers all need shopping, not just for dry goods and sundries but also for belonging to a larger whole.

I'm going to explore how the connections brands make with their customers become cemented through empathic extension – truly understanding their customers' needs and aspirations. Providing relevant places to engage customers will require a new understanding of what will drive them to continue to visit stores in a world where everything can be found through the smartphone or other wearable digitally connected device.

I'll take you on a shopping journey, from a look at the historical relationship between people and the shopping experience as a method to connect to the cultures they live in, to some discoveries in neuroscience and how they can help us understand what happens when making a decision in the shopping aisle…to the world of possibility when retailers and customers co-op the task in integrating technology in the store and collaborating on making shopping places that are more relevant for an increasingly savvy customer.

What does the availability of technology mean for the longevity of retail stores as a meaningful place to exchange goods and services? How does the store remain relevant when we can buy everything from our mobile phones or other digital device? In the end, despite all of the potential dystopian views about the rise of our digitally driven culture, the store will not go away. As environments change to adapt to a digitally enabled customer, it will, undoubtedly, be different than anything we have known to date. The core of customer experience, however, will remain – engaging with people, building community, and understanding ourselves and how we fit into a larger context.

Customer experience, after all, is not so much about what we carry home in our shopping bag as it is about what we carry home in our hearts *and* minds.

THANK YOU FOR READING, AND FOR YOUR INTEREST
AND CURIOSITY ABOUT THE RETAIL (R)EVOLUTION.

LET'S GET STARTED…

Acknowledgments

Writing this book – my *first* book – has been a massive undertaking, fascinating journey and a life-changing process. Throughout this process, the running narrative under my research, writing, and efforts to tie the whole together, has been the story of how this book came to be. But more than that, it has reminded me, often daily, of how I got here, how my ideas have been formulated, how none of us grows in our careers and our lives without those pivotal relationships and people whose guidance, support and inspiration serve as a kind of GPS on the long and winding road. Without them this book would not have been possible.

My interest in retail design as a combination of art and science was cemented while working with the visionary **Joe Weishar**. Joe's book, *Design For Effective Selling Space* was my first 'text book' on the practice of merchandise presentation. I thank Joe for the years under his excellent tutelage.

To **Jackie Glanz**, who has offered her unwavering support for twenty years of my involvement in the industry, I extend my immeasurable gratitude. She has taught me the value of never burning a bridge, how to sustain and grow customer relationships, and has always been there as a steadfast supporter along my career path.

To **Jay Austrian**, tireless fixture manufacturer and problem-solver, I express deep thanks for his work ethic and professional values. I learned how to design with mindfulness towards cost without compromising utility and beauty.

From **George Homer**; Brazilian born, New York native, visual merchandising consultant who I have shared *tuk-tuk* rides in Bangkok, BBQ in Sao Paolo, and a slice of a tatami mat while visiting a Japanese monastery, I gained and awareness of merchandise as a design element.

Ron and Nancy Jackson have been long-time industry friends as well as being suppliers of exquisite specialty materials to the retail and hospitality industry. They are true experts in their field, and have opened the doors to their innovative New York showroom to me over the years, invited me into a special group of retailers and other designers, and have demonstrated that strong personal relationships are a key to return business.

When I arrived in New York in 1995, my first influential connection to the who's who of the visual merchandising industry came through **Tom Beebe**. A brilliant creative spirit who wears a tangle of rubber bands around his wrist, listens intently, always makes time for you, and tirelessly binds people together in the retail world. Thanks to Tom I had the special honor of meeting the late Gene Moore in his 5th Avenue studio at Tiffany & Co. and having tea with the late Peter Glen in his Sniffen Court apartment in New York.

Thanks also go to **Bill McHenry**, **Ken Albright**, **Nicola Evoli**, and **Andreas Kussner**. leaders in the store fixture and display industry who offered their time for an interview and opened the doors to their manufacturing facilities so that I could deepen my understanding of how mannequins and merchandising units go from concept to sales floor. In this group, I also include the inimitable **Joe Baer**, who, through his yearly "Iron Merchant" challenges at IRDC, taught me that great ideas can come in a flash and be built in sixty minutes.

To my wonderful retailer friends **Bevan Bloemendaal** and **Sharon Lessard**, thank you for the time you shared early in this project to talk about retail place-making from the point of view of the retailer. From our conversations over the years, I have a stronger appreciation of the power of design to express the essence of a brand and make meaningful shopping places.

I thank the ingeniously forward-thinking entrepreneur **Bill Crutchfield** for giving me an opportunity to completely re-think the way we can create for a new retail paradigm. Working with Bill put the theory of 'thinking different' into practice to challenge the status quo and create a store concept where technology lead to a "Discovery Store" and learning was as important as selling.

Asif Kahn cemented the idea for me that mindfully integrated digital-out-of-home technology would not lead to a dystopian future. Instead, my point of view changed from grave concern to hope with a realistic awareness of the pitfalls of technology. I thank Asif for his extraordinary, cutting-edge presentation that changed my mind about how digital technologies and location-based marketing will profoundly shape the shoppingscape.

For years, I watched other designers lead firms, create great projects and speak at conferences. Unbeknownst to them, they have also been my mentors. I studied them and learned the best practices of retail design. Thanks to industry giants **Denny Gerdeman**, **Elle Chute**, **Andrew McQuilkin**, **Lee Peterson**, **Brian Shafley** and **Kathleen Jordan** for inviting me into their offices and offering their precious time to share their passion for retail design, their tireless commitment to supporting the industry's professional associations and their deep insights into the future of the business.

Other industry leaders and friends have offered their support of this project by reviewing the text and providing a sage comment that has found its way onto the cover or back pages. To **Richard Lebovitz**, **Peter Dixon**, **Ignaz Gorischeck**, **James Bellante**, **Todd Taylor** and **Dan Butler**, my profound thanks for your support and praise.

To **Eric Feigenbaum** I owe a debt for sharing his love for teaching, visual merchandising and writing a good article. With Eric, I have walked stores in foreign countries as well as the halls of schools in New York. He has been colleague with whom I have shared a love of growing the next generation of designers and visual merchandisers.

In writing this book, I often found myself with more questions than answers. There has been no other individual who has both helped me answer the questions that were gnawing at me and posing questions I hadn't considered than **Bruce Barteldt**. My endless thanks goes to Bruce whose creative mind and intellect have expanded my ideas and points of view. He has introduced me to authors and new ideas and shared my passions for the future of retail design.

Understanding that the customer journey in a digital world extends beyond the narrow vertical of stores, has been a discussion topic with my great colleague friend **Daniel Montano**. Thank you for growing my understanding of customer experience-mapping and how the relationship shoppers have with brands is broader than it has ever been.

Since 2004, I have had an association to **Little**, the company at which I am now a Creative Director (a title I share with Daniel Montano and James Farnell) in the Brand Experience Studio. I am proud to work at Little, to contribute to the extraordinary culture of authentic people who are passionate about great design, thought leadership, and have an enthusiasm for innovation.

I extend a huge expression of gratitude to ST Media Group International. To President **Tedd Swormstedt** and my editor and Director of Books **Mark Kissling**, thanks for agreeing to support this undertaking, for your flexibility and patience while I wrote this book while also teaching at FIT in New York, travelling to conferences around the globe, and meeting client deadlines.

Thanks also go to **Steve Duccilli**, Senior VP of Content at ST Media Group, and **Murray Kasmenn**, Publisher of *VMSD*. ST Media Group invited me to be a part of the *VMSD* Editorial Board years ago, putting me in the mix of both design professionals and retailers who are passionate about making effective, relevant, and emotionally connected shopping places

To my amazing sons, **Nick and Ben**, whose unbridled creative spirits have helped me understand the power of play, the significance of story and the traction of technology on a new generation of shoppers. I thank them for forts in the Magic Forest, bedtime stories, and years of making art. They have been patient observers of the process...and yes, I have finished the book now!

And finally, but perhaps most importantly, my extraordinary wife **Lu**. Along my path of discovery, there has been no individual from whom I have learned more. Her uncanny right-brain insight, creative open spirit, passion for understanding the brain and her get to-the-heart-of-the–matter way of communicating have been profoundly influential in shaping my own thought process, insights and ways of seeing the world. I truly would not be who I am today had I never crossed paths with her at summer camp way back in 1982. From a place beyond apt expression, Lu, you have my deepest gratitude for being my partner in all the changing circumstances of life.

PART 01

Trade Routes, Stories and Stars

CHAPTER

More Than Getting Stuff — Shopping as a Social Paradigm

01

Boyhood and Believing

Growing up in Montreal, my childhood friend Jeff and I spent our boyhood summers in search of adventure. Every weekend the Super Bowl took place on his side yard. The long bomb with the Nerf football was over the roof of his house and, if we timed it right, it came down in the right spot as you turned the corner around the fishpond.

We *were* Frodo Baggins and Samwise Gamgee when leaping onto the red wagon in his driveway to escape the Ring Wraths chasing us across his front lawn just as Sam and Frodo did when leaving the Shire.

We both were in love – with the same girl – and we rode our bikes back and forth in front her house a thousand times, hoping she would come out and see us. (She never did.)

We joined the diving team at the pool and learned to do back flips as well as belly flops. We bought guitars when we were sixteen and made tapes of ourselves playing the Eagles.

And, we taught ourselves how to juggle.

We spent hours juggling. We juggled against walls and off the floor. We learned tricks such as eating an apple and tossing it around your back or under your leg. And the thing we learned about juggling was that at a certain point you had to stop *thinking*.

Once you got the idea that one ball went up, and as it was coming down you tossed the other one up, and as that one came down you tossed the other, and so on – you had to stop thinking and start relying on your peripheral vision and muscle memory of where your hands would be so that they could catch and toss the balls.

In fact, you didn't even look at the balls as they traced arcs up and down in front of your face. We had to trust ourselves and the knowledge that our bodies knew what to do. We learned by repetition and the actions became encoded into our system.

While looking *through* the flying balls you had to *feel* your way forward trusting your body memory, intuition and perceptual senses.

Decades later, when presenting at the retail tradeshow, GlobalShop, I stood in front of more that 300 hundred people with three yellow balls in my hand. Over the next 60 minutes I was prepared to deliver a talk about the brain and making relevant and emotionally engaging customer experiences.

The presentation was to focus on what makes, and would continue to make, great shopping places. And, as I prepared, I looked for a way to describe the power of the relational, emotional, intuitive right brain and why it was so important for us as shoppers, retailers and designers of retail places. My goal was to have the audience understand that the world of shopping was in the midst of a paradigm shift. Fundamental change was taking place in our culture and the nature of shopping places was about to undergo a dramatic transformation so that a few years from now we might hardly recognize it.

I was about to assert that when creating engaging shopping places in the future, it will not be enough to continue on a path that has held price point, overwhelming product assortments, and the linear logical sequential approach to doing business, in positions of prominence. These things would no longer serve as differentiators between retail businesses. In a world where shoppers would not have to go to the store because the modern emergence of digital technology allows for convenient shopping any place any time, what would drive customers to go to the store would not be something new but something that we have held at the forefront of our collective human development for a few million years.

What customers will really want will be for products and service to be imbued with both utility *and* significance. The design – of products, services and entire experiences – will become a critical factor in making shopping places relevant in a world of ubiquitous access and abundant choice.

But beyond the fact that products, services and experiences will have to be beautiful and transcendent, shoppers will desire, as they have for centuries, the feeling of connection, relationship, being valued and that they can find meaning in the shopping aisles as well as the dry goods and sundries.

In a thin slice of 60 minutes I was going to try thoughtfully to cover the relevance of shopping and the places we create to engage in the activity. My slides would lead the audience across centuries and continents, wireless networks as well as the brain's intricate landscape. All the while I would assert that, even though we have been designing and building stores for years, we are not as aware of the fundamental – brain-based – drivers to buying decisions as we should be, that an understanding of neuroscience is increasingly a prerequisite to creating truly engaging customer experiences *and* that shopping, as a social paradigm, would not change despite the upheaval that digital technology is inducing throughout cultures of the world.

Shopping as it turns out would remain one of the key social experiences of our culture. However, how we do it a few years from now will look and feel like something we have only been able to imagine as something out of a science fiction movie. Future shopping places might in fact be stranger than fiction.

Juggling it seemed was an apt metaphor. By juggling I could demonstrate the issues at hand and talk about intuition – our gut feeling – that we have long held with a certain suspicion. Not our fault. We have inherited a long tradition of not trusting our emotions and even blaming them when things don't go the way we want or expect. Plato, Descartes, Freud and a host of other left-brain rationalist advocates have had us relying on our ability to reason our way to nirvana for a few millennia.

But this was not always the case. The truth is we have, in all of human history, relied more on our emotions and desires to engage in social relationships to move the machine of evolution forward, than reason alone.

We are social beings, bound to the innate need to come together in community, cooperate, share, and use our imaginations to create. Over the years these parts of us have not changed, but the ways we satisfy these needs have been in continuous evolution. Advances in technology have modified the speed of change, moving it from generational evolution in incremental steps to something more akin to revolution. The ways all generations now enlist technologies to communicate are changing, ushering in new 'languages' and all the while our brains are adapting.

The ways shoppers see the world and their role in it are at a transition point. Through the chapters of this book we will look at the nature of shopping as a social paradigm and the challenges that creators of shopping places will face in a world where the way we socialize is under rapid and profound change.

So, with a deep breath and a prayer, the balls flew.

I believed that my hands would adjust to find the balls as they dropped through the air. And, I believed that my message would find an accepting audience of retailers and designers who would apply it to creating more effective and relevant shopping places.

To better understand where we are today and the forces that are diving change in the creation of shopping places, we need to take a look backwards into our shopping past.

Trade Routes, the Agora and Mall-ing of America

Over twisting trade routes across continents, through sprawling bazaars, across the counter at the general store, or through the mail after making a purchase with your smartphone – shopping has given us a way to make meaning of who we are, how we interact, and how we live.

The shopping experience has always been about more than simply getting stuff. Historically, shopping has at its core exchange, forging trusting relationships and connecting to a world beyond us. The Greek Agora, the suburban mall, the laptop and the smartphone, have all connected us to our families, communities, nations, and our world. In doing so, they have each added to the intricate weaving of our personal, cultural and human tapestry.

While trade between individuals, tribes and nations certainly traces back to the early days of organized social groups, the silk trade route is best known for the establishment of organized trade across vast geographic areas. Along the ancient silk trade routes, selling and buying brought interested parties together in exchange. Twisting their way across the landscape, trade routes connected the Eastern Mediterranean to Central Asia and another connected Central Asia to China. In doing so, worlds merged as traders shuttled all manner of goods across barren deserts, over mountain passes and across vast continents.

As caravans laden with goods moved from place-to-place, more than spices and silk changed hands.

In the social transactions between merchants and buyers, people bartered and traded one thing for another. Cattle, agricultural products, shells, coins, beetle legs and even dead rats served to get 'this for that.' Bartering as a system for commercial exchange meant you had to be able to find someone who needed say, a cow, to be able to get what you wanted. Furthermore, herding cattle or any livestock across miles of desert was a terribly inefficient way to get things done. Eventually coins and paper money replaced the barter system and retailing has never been the same.

The impact of the developing trade routes on local as well as national economies was profound. Countless people were employed in the production of silk and spices. Economies grew in support of the transport of goods and towns flourished along trade routes providing the amenities for travellers ferrying products across the continents.

The transport of goods from great distances also brought with it other consequences, such as the spread of the bubonic plague from the east to the west in 534, 750, and 1346 C.E. The last incidence, referred to as the Black Death, was responsible for one of the largest decimations of population in human history, wiping out approximately two thirds of the population of London and killing nearly half of all other Europeans in a four-year period.

On the other hand... great things happened, such as the spread of ideas. The stories travellers told fostered cultural mythologies as well as the sharing of ideas about foreign politics, mysterious religions, and emerging technologies.

It is not surprising that Buddhism, specifically Mahayana Buddhism, became one of the great traditions of the world as it spread along the trade route from India to Asia. Merchants along the trade routes became supporters of monasteries, which in turn became convenient stopping points for caravans. Monks would pray for merchants venturing out along the 'Silk Road' and silk eventually found a place as one of the central materials used in Mahayana rituals.

Seldom did one individual travel the full length of the route. Instead, a multitude of caravans crisscrossed the continent, sometimes boarding sailing vessels that ventured across the Mediterranean towards Rome or the Pacific Ocean towards Japan.

As they traversed the landscape and open waters, traders formed networks upon which rich oral traditions grew as a means to carry out commercial transactions and share experiences between cultures. People forged mutually beneficial relationships that supported trade and shopping places grew at the intersections in a growing web of ancient social network connectivity. The ideas they shared changed individuals and nations.

The centerpiece of socio-cultural and commercial life for ancient Greeks was the Agora. The Athenian Agora sat at the base of the Acropolis, and was both literally and figuratively at the center of the Greek city. Three roads passed through its center including the main thoroughfare of the city, the Panathenaic Way, which led from the city gate, the Dipylon, to the foot of the Acropolis. The Agora housed courts, fountain-houses, public office buildings, the mint, a library, concert hall, temples and in 150 B.C.E., the Stoa of Attalos.

This ancient two-story arcade could arguably be classified as one of the first shopping malls. Its direct physical relationship to the other civil offices and religious structures that were the foundation of Greek society is a critical point connecting commerce to social-cultural ideologies. Early on, the act of shopping was connected to the city's administrative, political, judicial, commercial, social, cultural, and religious activities.

These aspects of citizenship all found a place together in the heart of this ancient city and did so in relationship to the shopping trip. If you were not going directly to the library after buying some eggs, it is likely that by happenstance or sheer proximity you learned about the goings on of the city, about the politics of the state or a court case. By being in the social mix you learned the news of the day, drew inferences about its relevance to you and became connected.

The Agora was an ancient version of a social networking site.

As the centuries passed, shopping places continued to grow, both in size and importance, in every corner of the planet. Outdoor trade fairs, seaport commercial districts and covered bazaars became focal points of cultural life and commerce. For more than a thousand years, shopping centers, combining all manner of goods and services, continued to provide jobs, growing local industries as well as national economies that had become reliant on international trade.

Over time, shopping areas migrated from seaports and city centers to places somewhat disconnected from everyday life in the cities. 'Going to the mall' would become a purposeful journey, a destination, rather than a daily activity to the local merchants to get the dry goods and sundries. While buildings housing multiple merchants existed in Europe that could have been considered precursors to the shopping center we know today, it wasn't until the 1920s in the United States that shopping centers got their start.

The idea of creating a shopping place away from the hustle and bustle of the city center has been credited to J. C. Nichols of Kansas City, Missouri, who built Country Club Plaza, as the business area for a large residential development. A differentiating feature of this new form of shopping was that multiple forms of retail were brought together with a unified architecture, parking lots (since the automobile had become entrenched in American culture as the form of transportation), and that it would all be managed and operated as a single unit.

Throughout the '20s, "Strip Centers" would continue to pop-up on the outskirts of cities, providing shoppers with multiple convenience shops, a large grocery and drug store, and of course plenty of parking. When Grandview Avenue Shopping Center opened in Columbus, Ohio in 1928, it boasted 30 shops and parking for 400 cars.

By the time the 1930s came around, the idea of shopping centers was becoming more prevalent across the U.S. When Highland Park Shopping Center was built in 1931 by Texas developer Hugh Prather, the mall was beginning to turn inward with storefronts facing away from main thoroughfares. This was a significant departure from traditional street level retailing where malls would become their own entity referencing only themselves, having their own architectural personality, public services and utilities, providing consumers with self-contained places to shop. Throughout the '30s and '40s the 'mall-ing' of America continued.

Post-World War II America was ready to shop and malls grew in size and number. In the 1950s new malls were anchored with full-line versions of major downtown retailers. The turning inward of shopping centers continued with Northgate in Seattle (opened in 1950) and Shoppers' World in Framingham Massachusetts, which signaled the first incarnation of an American mall with two levels (opened in 1951). Five years later the idea of the two-level mall was moved a step along the mall's evolutionary path by enclosing it with a roof. The opening of Southdale Center in Edina, Minnesota marked a turning point in mall development, boasting the first fully enclosed mall with air conditioning and two department store anchors bookending the building.

By 1964 the number of malls in America had grown to 7,600.

In the eight subsequent years, the number of malls in the U.S. doubled, topping out at 13,174 properties. And, a number of new formats were being developed to satisfy a growing suburban population as well as reconsidering city center opportunities. Notable among these were Faneuil Hall Marketplace in Boston, which was the first of the "Festival Marketplace" genre, and the country's first vertical mall, Water Tower Place in Chicago. Water Tower Place has since been considered one of the county's most successful mixed use developments combining retail, offices, condominiums and, of course, parking.

The '80s were the American mall developer's heyday with more than 16,000 locations built between 1980 and 1990. Not only did malls become more plentiful, but they also grew to enormous formats with "super-regional" centers becoming popular with shoppers. And then, the saving and loan crisis set in, making it extremely difficult to get credit to build new properties. Leading into 1993, a sharp decline in building starts resulted a 70% drop in shopping center development.

Throughout the mid to late '90s mall development slowly recovered and new formats began to emerge. Factory outlet centers were quickly becoming all the rage. Looking for a bargain on name brand goods, shoppers would flock to the outlet center for the day and load up on discounts on the brands they typically shopped at full price. Over the past 14 years the number of outlet malls has almost doubled from 183 in 1990 to more than 225 today.

Malls have become entertainment venues. Gigantic malls such as the Mall of America in Bloomington, Minnesota and the West Edmonton Mall in Edmonton, Alberta, Canada cover millions of square feet offering everything from ice-skating, to roller coasters, to submarine rides. Filled with themed dining, movie theaters, play areas, churches, municipal offices, libraries and museums, the American super-mall is a reincarnation of the Greek Agora for contemporary society.

As the Greek Agora was the epicenter of early Greek culture and commerce, the mall is a revenue-generating powerhouse. In many towns they have become a key source of economic development and tax revenue. "In 2012, shopping center-inclined sales were estimated at $2.4 trillion, an increase of 2.8% from the previous year. In 2012, state sales tax revenue from shopping center-inclined sales totaled $136.2 billion, up from the $131.6 billion collected in 2011."[1] Shopping centers are big employers with more than 9% of the country's workforce performing shopping center-related activities.

As the U.S. climbs out of the "Great Recession," shopping mall development is increasing slightly. Mall related employment was up 1.3% in 2012 over 2011 and as of May 2012, there were 112,874 shopping centers, up from 112,620 in 2011.

Shopping centers now cover more than 7.47 billion square feet of gross leasable area (GLA) in the U.S.

Total shopping sales in 2012? $2.4 trillion!

It's safe to say that Americans love shopping and the 'mall-ing of America' has given American consumers compelling places to do it.

Ideas and Commerce – A Convenient Connection

"A MAN MAY DIE, NATIONS MAY RISE AND FALL, BUT AN IDEA LIVES ON. IDEAS HAVE ENDURANCE WITHOUT DEATH." — JOHN F. KENNEDY

Early in the development of commercial exchange it became clear that the spread of ideas was connected to the selling of goods and services. Today, companies with a social conscience use their national and international networks to promote ideas within their brand platforms such as sustainability and compassionate capitalism. Kohl's, Timberland and Starbucks have robust sustainability programs that are integral to their brand platforms that are a win-win-win benefitting the retailer, customer, and environment.

Frequenting these retailers implies support of their programs. Using your "Kohl's Cash" to buy your back-to-school supplies is a vote for producing clean energy through solar power. Buying "EarthKeeper" footwear from Timberland is saying "yes" to reducing landfill sites and planting trees in deforested areas of China. And, investing way more than you should on a cup of coffee at Starbucks is worth it because 75% of all new company-owned stores are to be certified under the LEED® green building standard (not to mention Starbucks' other extraordinary efforts in ethical sourcing and community involvement).

These companies have it embedded in their corporate DNA that *people* drive businesses and that business promotes ideas and ideals.

With future generations of shoppers' growing cynicism towards the world of corporate governance, it has become critical to understand that for a brand to remain relevant it's not just what you sell, but what you stand for that is most important.

So, there is meaning attached to the stuff we buy. It says a great deal about who we are and how we feel about social or environmental policy. Sharing that message starts with a smile, a genuine welcome, a good pair of boots and maybe a cup of coffee.

One of the keys to the success of every positive exchange of goods or services is the experience born out of the social interaction between seller and buyer. The face-to-face interaction between two or more people and the body's corporeal connection to the world around it are profound components of the experience. What we take away from a shopping outing is far more than the dry goods and sundries but a profound, and yet intangible, element of the interaction - 'experience.'

Today's consumers expect the companies they love to do more, be more and offer more than good products or services at an acceptable price. For the customer, shopping environments are more than a space to carry out a transaction between two parties; they are the three-dimensional embodiment of the brand and a venue for interaction with the people who act as its ambassadors.

How customers 'feel' about the time they committed to shopping a retail place is the best indicator of whether or not they make a purchase and becomes a committed adopter of the brand. In the end, it's not the stuff they get, but the positive feelings they hold about the people they interacted with that helps to make shopping experiences memorable.

Positive customer experiences are more about interactions between people and the exchange about life stories than they are about the stuff we get while shopping.

People.

It may sound simple, but this crucial element to creating great shopping experiences can be the most disappointing aspect of a trip to the mall, a main street store, and even a company's website. The emotional takeaway often determines whether or not the one-time shopper ever becomes a long-time customer.

3P's – Product, Price, Place – and People

When I started in the industry, my employer, Joe Weishar of New Vision Studios in New York, was one of the leaders in teaching the 'why' rather than the 'how' of effective visual merchandising and store planning to retailers across the globe. He would continually reinforce the idea that it was the product that was the star of the show and that the architecture of the space was playing a supporting role.

As a young architect new to the world of retail design, schooled in believing that my role was to save the world from itself through creating "A"rchitecture, this was a good, albeit hard lesson to learn.

It is essentially true that great merchandise displayed in an effective way can lead to increased sales, despite the aesthetics of the 'architecture' that act as its wrapper. Not to discount the value of good design – after all my career has been dedicated to creating effective and aesthetically pleasing selling places. But, my appreciation for what 'design' meant in the service of retail's prime objective of selling merchandise, has been necessarily reshaped over years of walking sales floors, moving fixtures, watching customer interactions and discovering what really drove customers to buy.

I can now tell you that it isn't the design of the display table that makes a stack of sweaters sell out.

I would have loved to believe that it was all about the store design, but I was often reminded that pretty designs may win awards but don't insulate the retailer from bankruptcy due to poor merchandising, over ambitious buying, not being able to tell their story in a relevant way or bad customer service.

I was schooled in retail to believe that product is the leading lady. You can sell merchandise off of milk crates, fold-up tables or a colorful blanket splayed on the sidewalk like street merchants in New York. Or, even out of the back of a car on a college campus as Phil Knight did when growing Nike. Any of these can be effective places to bring your goods to market. It's what's on the table or in trunk that matters.

If product is the star then the merchant is the promoter, director, producer and stagehand. If shoppers don't have great social experiences with the merchants, they may just have some good-looking stuff in the back of a car, or on a table, a rack, or a wall.

But is simply having nice stuff the goal?

For some, it most definitely is. Nice stuff does make us feel good and if you are selling commodity items, nice may be enough. The problem with 'nice' is that it is swept by fashion, temperament, culture and all things transient. There is no anchor in the soul of a customer with 'nice.'

If, however, you are connecting customers to a deeper set of brand ideologies and building experience memories that become part of the fiber of the customer, then the social paradigm that has always been part of the shopping experience must be held in the foremost position among the intricacies in creating great retail places.

While we may have considered the 3P's – the right 'Product,' at the right 'Price' in the right 'Place' – as the basic tenets of successful retailing, there is an element that is missing in this equation. When we think about opening the doors to success in retail place making, the traditional three pillars of successful retailing leave the applecart unstable without the fourth P – 'People.' Without customers, 'Product,' 'Price' and 'Place' don't accomplish anything.

With the increasing influence of the Internet, crowdsourcing and the growing idea that more and more things are becoming 'free,' we will see that 'Price,' as a differentiator in the creating of great experiences, will fade. You can commoditize almost everything, but putting a price tag on experience and the connection born out of a truly empathic relationship is both more difficult and potentially priceless.

The social aspect of the shopping experience will grow to be ever more important as the creation of shopping places morphs in response to the world of social media, downward pressure of manufacturing and supply costs, and the ability to buy anything, anytime, anywhere through a smartphone.

If we can buy anything, anytime, from the palm of our hand, why would we ever go into a store?

We go because of the people and the experience of connection.

This mere fact, as we will see in later chapters, is at the crossroads of reinventing the shopping experience of the future.

The very core of all shopping experience faces a dilemma. In a world that allows for communication in disembodied ways and shopping at arm's length, people are losing their ability to truly engage in empathic relationships.

- If we believe that the foundation of great shopping experiences has for millennia been based on the social aspect of the exchange, how then can the store as the place of connection between customers, brands and the products they sell stay relevant in a digitally driven age?
- If shopping places exist at all in the future beyond the virtual portals to unlimited goods and services, what type of interaction will be found there?
- How does the 'social interaction' aspect of shopping take place when customers are not in the store?
- What roles do product and its presentation through display and effective visual merchandising play in environment?
- In a world of abundant choice and downward pressure on price, will the products we buy become less relevant as part of the shopping experience?

The Social Contract

Merchants and customers they serve enter into a relationship that relies on an implicit set of rules. It's a sort of social contract. When customers buy products or services, there is an implicit dialogue that goes on in their heads that might sound something like, *'I am going to buy this thing, and in exchange we will have an agreement of sorts that extends beyond the product. From you I will learn a host of relevant and sometimes inconsequential facts about the news of the day, fashion trends, how to prepare a meal and information about far off lands.'*

The social aspect of the shopping experience has always been a fundamental part of the exchange. The expectation of connection with the retailer or brand is an aspect of the shopping experience that is far more profound in shaping the memory of a shopping trip than the things customers carry away in their shopping bags. Relationship can drive sales more than cutting prices. Build a bridge with a customer and they will cross a raging torrent to get to the store.

Customers rely on the relationship with merchants and they will often go out of their way to go back to places that simply make them feel good. The idea that the experience has to 'feel good' is not new in the world of creating great shopping experiences. It's the intangible nourishment of their relational right brain through personal connections that helps to promote the likelihood that customers buy what the store is offering.

In fact, we rely on the feeling of satisfaction after a shopping experience to determine our sense of loyalty to a brand or retailer. The sense of satisfaction and the experience being 'complete' depends on how the social aspect of the engagement played out.

If the product or service does not deliver on expectations or on the basic functions it was purchased to accomplish, of course there is a problem. But, the residual emotional feeling associated with the experience trumps everything else. Those products or services that are paired with exceptional service are perceived as exceptional because the emotional connection to the people selling them fosters a relationship between buyer and seller.

The late Peter Glen, customer service advocate and contributor to (then) *VM&SD* magazine, would rail on retailers who overlooked the very idea that they were first in the business of providing great service.

His columns about his incredulity and indignation with those who failed to deliver on the basic tenet of retailing being primarily a social paradigm were amusing, enlightening and a wakeup call for those who opened their doors every day to customers. Assuming the brand's product delivers on the basic functions it purports to offer, building on the social aspect of the engagement weaves the ties that bind customers to brands.

Before the days of buying books on Amazon.com, Barnes & Noble completely changed the way customers thought about a bookstore. When going to these massive literary strongholds you didn't just have an opportunity to buy from an extraordinary assortment, but also to be in a 'place' that was crafted to allow you to linger, curl up in a big cozy chair, read magazines at will, and have a warm cup of coffee and pastry as you pored over the pages of a favorite novel. There seemed to be little pressure to buy and more of a promotion to stay and experience the social nature of the store.

There are few retailers who understand the profound dynamics of engaging customers and social interactions, as does Starbucks. No matter where you go in the world, each of these environments is crafted specifically to engage customers to be in a place that is both unique and also referential to the locale in which it is placed. Delivering more than a good cup of coffee, these places seem to go out of their way to provide an emotional connection to other people as well as the brand.

Apple stores have been the benchmark against which retailers, retail architects and designers, and even customers, compare what it means to be shopping for consumer electronics. Apple stores are exquisitely detailed with beautiful materials and clean contemporary geometries. The stores are well executed, but when you get beyond the details of architecture or environmental graphics, what you notice more are the shoppers. Yes, of course these stores have product, but your perception of even that is dwarfed by one's appreciation of the number of people engaging in conversations with each other and sales associates and playing with merchandise for as long as they want. Apple stores have become a landmark for tech-community interaction. Upon entering you're always asked if you can be helped and your name is recorded on a list so that when it is your turn, a sales associate can focus on you as individual with specific needs rather than just another customer. Most people will wait because a social connection has already been made. If time pressed, customers often make an appointment to come back later.

The underlying message? 'You are important and we understand that time is a significant consideration for you on the shopping trip, let's not waste it and get right to solving your needs.'

Shopkeepers who appear genuinely interested and grateful that customers have made the effort to come to their store, welcome customers and invite them to enter a relationship. In doing so, they open themselves to all the things that make relationships rewarding and disappointing, enlightening and disillusioning, a challenge and a walk in the park, a soft place to fall and to be viewed with skepticism.

Retailers who understand that shoppers are often times looking for more than the products they sell, let customers know they have their interests at heart. That they are good listeners and have appropriate answers to customers' questions and concerns.

They talk to shoppers and ask questions. Respond to Tweets, blog comments and customer calls. They are inventive about how their offering can satisfy a shopper's needs. They 'know' their customers both because of their ability to collect data from previous shopping trips and customers' connections to social networking sites. And, despite the fact that customers are more informed today than they have ever been, retailers often teach shoppers something they didn't know about the brand, its products and maybe even the customers, themselves.

Too much to ask of a retailer? I don't think so.

The lyrics to the opening song of the popular '80s TV show *Cheers* had it exactly right:

> "SOMETIMES YOU WANT TO GO
> WHERE EVERYBODY KNOWS YOUR NAME,
> AND THEY'RE ALWAYS GLAD YOU CAME."

Connecting to customers in relevant and emotional ways remains the underpinning of the relationship between the customer and merchants today and into the foreseeable future. Our drive to engage socially has been built into our collective human DNA over millions of years.

We are social beings, driven to connect, collaborate and coexist despite what the six o'clock news tries to make us believe. Violence towards each other has always been a part of human history, but we would have wiped each other out of existence long ago if it were not for the fact that we are hardwired for empathic connection.

Shopping places are the links, the connective fiber, between the nodes of customers on a vast consumer network.

Shopping places are playgrounds that provide frameworks that support interaction between customers and brands. A store is the three-dimensional-ization of all that a brand is.

Despite the emergence of online shopping opportunities, the store will remain a crucial place to create customer community and a brand experience. It is a gathering place to tell stories and share in a common social experience between like-minded individuals.

'Space'
vs. 'Place' —
Experience Making

CHAPTER

02

Great Un-Expectations

When I was studying to be an architect at McGill University, the curriculum included a course in landscape architecture. In one of our design projects we were given the challenge of choosing a space in Montreal and creating an environment that responded to the surrounding conditions in a manner that was respectful of its historical background, while taking into account the present-day activity. The objective was to shift the perception of people occupying the 3-dimensional 'space' from empty, leftover and underutilized to one that engaged, had purpose, created profound memories and was a destination – a 'place.'

I chose a little crack of a space between two buildings in the Vieux Port of Montreal. The space was really more of a circulation route between the waterfront and the cobblestone streets a block into the old port. It was one of those leftover, interstitial spaces, the kind that held no significance and was overlooked as the city grew up around it. It was a space bounded by a building on one side and high brick wall on the other. The inlet and exits were narrow and the view from inside was a slice of blue sky. Definitely not a destination. However, at a certain point it opened as if taking a breath, and offered up the opportunity to create a place of repose. This leftover space became a study in transformation and my understanding of the elements that define the characteristics of 'space' versus 'place.'

Something then, as it still does now, intrigued me about the in-between places, the back alleys, the gardens behind walls and the narrow spaces that act more as circulation corridor than a place to be in for any period of time.

When shopping in foreign cities, I prefer the markets, twisting roads, and covered passages leading to hidden courtyards. These less traveled areas of the city delight you with novelty and the discovery of something you might feel was hidden from everyone else's eyes but yours. They are rich in textures, smells, colors, and have individual site-specific qualities that enhance a sense of place. They elicit your emotions with sensory experiences and they are better when shared with other people.

In Miami, I walked along Collins Avenue looking for places such as these. I was ready to turn around and walk back to a spot I had arranged to meet some friends, when instead I turned to peer into a shop window.

Beautifully appointed mannequins and a blue horse with a rich brown leather riding saddle drew me into the foyer. Blue painted ceiling fans spun silently above, creating a welcome breeze. Large glowing orbs suspended in rope netting and oversized tassels hung as pendant lighting. While fully captivated, I had not yet entered the store.

I paused to take in a single mannequin display at the end of the long room and while I could have just enjoyed the entryway and walked out, the environment invited me to explore further. I moved through the archway into the store, leaving the street behind. Casually moving through merchandise presentations on tables made of large steel chain links, I found my way to the back where my search for something different was fulfilled.

A doorway led to a walled courtyard. Deep blue furniture sat upon red terra cotta tile. Tropical plants softened corners and in a powder blue wall across the courtyard, another door. Without thinking, I was on my way through the 'in-between' space of the courtyard to a place beyond.

This out-building at the rear of the lot was the boys' and girls' department. With whitewashed rustic wood planking for wall cladding and ship window portals for mirrors, this place reinforced my feeling of immersion. I felt as if I were in some other place. Not on Collins Avenue. Not in Miami. This was some other location that I could fill with imagination.

The ceiling was painted blue with floating clouds. It was as though the roof had been peeled away and you stood looking at a postage stamp-sized clip of the open sky framed only by the outline of the painted wooden walls. This was a 'place.' This place was unique, imaginative, and mostly, *unexpected*. It was Tommy Hilfiger.

The goal of great retail place making is to be remarkable – 'worthy of being noticed especially as being uncommon or extraordinary.' And, while every store visit offers the opportunity for customers to share a story of their experiences with others, they often go without remark. Many places we shop seemingly don't bother to capture our attention with memorable moments and captivate our creative imagination. Those that do seem to understand the value of making shopping experiences that touch us in an emotional way and have us chatting up a storm about what it was like to be part of the place. Nobody remembers average. However, something worth commenting on can now reach a multitude both by word of mouth and across social media networks that lace together individuals into a global community of shoppers.

I have had similar, remarkable experiences to the Tommy Hilfiger store elsewhere: the stair in the Anthropologie store on Regent Street in London with its living wall, the hawker stalls creating outdoor food markets in Singapore, being under the diaphanous tree-graphic ceiling of Globetrotter in Cologne, Germany, and climbing the stair in the Hollister Co. store in SoHo New York with its deep shadows and illuminating screens showing real-time video feeds from Huntington Beach. There have been many of these places that I have come upon on my shopping journeys. And, there have been an abundance of shopping environments that don't move the needle on the emotional connection scale. Place making is an emotions game. It is a body-memory experience and mission critical for any shopping place.

In most of my remarkable shopping moments, I didn't expect the discoveries that I now so vividly recall. And, I remember them not just as vivid images in my mind's eye, but in the way my body felt as I walked through them. The unexpected element is a key feature of creating memorable places that delight our senses. The experience of something new within a context of those things we expect heightens the memory of place. Our brains love the unexpected, and they are able to pick up small anomalies in the patterns we perceive in the environments around us. In fact, we learn through being exposed to novelty. The pleasure centers of our brains are set up to respond to the unexpected by releasing neurochemicals that can make us feel good. We don't, however, need to stumble upon an oasis to get this sense of pleasure by the experience of a new place. Novelty can come in very small packages too. Small changes in the shopping places we are used to such as a change of color, new signs and other graphics, new merchandise, or the change in an arrangement of a group of fixtures are noticed by our perceptual systems. Not much in a store goes without being noticed by the customer's brain. What the customer pays attention to, however, has everything to do with where, and how, these interruptions occur as they move through a space or flip through the pages of a website on their mobile phone.

We are very good at understanding patterns. In fact, we rely on pattern recognition to help us make sense of our world. Patterns in the places we go help provide scaffolding for understanding our environment, giving things in it context. Expecting the patterns to remain consistent is a hallmark of how our brains process the world. When the unexpected occurs our brains take note. In future chapters I'll explain why our brains crave unexpected rewards, how these rewards create pleasure and why I think we must incorporate these moments of delight into retail places.

Customers who go to the same shopping places on a regular basis – call them 'brand loyalists' – expect both consistency *and* change. That is, they need the structure, or a base line, for understanding the brand experience in the store. Structure is provided by factors such as architecture, an approach to merchandising, the way sales associates engage customers, the graphic content of the environment, music, scent, and product adjacencies.

So while we recognize the aesthetic of re-used/re-purposed/re-imagined eclecticism of Anthropologie stores, they are all different – and the same. Starbucks stores rely on three different design concepts, which are re-imagined using the same palette of design language, materials, and graphics approaches. Regardless of where in the world the store is, it draws on recognizable elements that are consistent with a well-established brand story.

They are the same in principle but unique in each location. Each of course responds to a different set of site-specific requirements, which will always require some inventive thinking since there is invariably a column in the way, a change in level or some other peculiarity to the space. However, the conscious effort to make each location different in design fosters an atmosphere of creativity for both the retailer's in-house store planning teams as well as design firms. Furthermore, it has the added benefit of the portraying a point of view about being relevant to the local community. And, it gives the customer a new look, novelty within a structure, whether they are in different areas of a single city or shopping across a network of international locations. These variations on a theme create customer experiences of novelty within the familiar.

Remember 'cookie cutter' store rollouts? They were very popular in the past but lacked a sense of 'place.' No one particular location differed from the next. While this created a quick and easy reference point for customers to connect to the brand, it didn't speak to our need for novelty.

These places delivered the same products, in the same environments, in the same ways in multiple locations. This of course greatly simplifies the logistics of product manufacturing, delivery and store build outs, but it worked contrary to our proclivity towards the desire for something new. Customers want *their* stores to be unique to them, even when they are shopping an international brand.

Stores that don't reflect the local surroundings lack a sense of place because they can be, well… *any place.*

Place making is not about creating environments that seem to have landed here on earth from some other corner of the galaxy. Those environments may be trendy and cool but verge on being disconnected from meaningful integration into the communities they serve. Customers need the store to be both recognizable to provide some sense of consistency *and* they need it to change, evolve and accommodate the growth of the relationship between themselves and the brand. When brands build strong relationships with brand loyalists, there are constants on which the relationship is founded *and* the implicit understanding that change is inevitable.

In a world where rapid change is a foregone conclusion, how the store accommodates the evolving needs of the customer is in the midst of an unprecedented upheaval. As in any good relationship, as one partner grows, the other faces a challenge, to change as well or go it alone in the pursuit of the status quo. Retailers who do not stay in lock step with the change of their customers run the risk of disconnect and being replaced by others who are more attuned to the customer's needs.

Each of the great shopping places we visit is designed to create experiences that are about more than just selling products. The goal is to create a sense of belonging that resonates with the customer. Either because it summons old memories, conveys a sense of community, engages the senses or simply feels familiar. The dance between retailer and customer in the store is an intricate bit of footwork.

Objective: don't step on your partner's toes.

As an architect whose specialty is the design of retail places, I want people to 'dance.' I want customers to buy of course, and the shared responsibility between the retailer and me, the architect/retail designer, is geared toward creating a place that motivates buying behavior. The best that I can hope for is that I create environments that enhance that likelihood.

But, I learned a long time ago that it is not entirely about me the architect/ designer, my personal design agenda, or my definition of beauty. I had to put those things aside, both to lead *and* learn to follow in the dance. In the world of creating 'retail dance floors,' the customer and brand are stomping out the tempo. My job is to give them a flat floor and help keep the music playing.

A customer coming to the store does not necessarily guarantee a purchase. Often the store design, merchandising and attitude of sales associates seem to be counter-productive to selling anything. We've all got stories of shopping experiences that were not enjoyable.

What can a retailer do to make it better?

Create places for engaging the creative emotional brain and promote genuine connection.

Craft in-store merchandising strategies that consider online buying behaviors.

Tell stories that support the key brand principles. Grow a culture of knowledgeable and truly engaging sales associates.

And, make experiences that are relevant, allowing shoppers to 'dance' in the way they want instead of making them follow numbered footprints on the floor.

It becomes complicated, quickly.

Generally, the customer doesn't have a clue of what it takes to make shopping places come alive. They show up. The rest is up to the retailer. The job of delivering quality places to engage the brand, and the products it sells, requires the same tireless commitment each time the front door swings open.

Closets vs. Kitchens

There is a difference between the closet that holds my shoes and the kitchen in my parents' house.

My closet is storage space. It holds all my stuff. It is organized (well, mostly), utilitarian, and lacks any sort of emotional connection or aesthetic that promotes feelings and memories. Interestingly, when I take the jacket I really like off the hanger and hold it up in my room, it is as if that garment metamorphoses from a weaving of thread to a vessel of memories, a suit of armor, a conversation piece and a display of my sense of well-being.

The jacket in the closet is simply a jacket; it has no inherent meaning. Off the rack, the jacket takes on a role, a personality. Taking it from my closet to my room I experience it in a different way. The context of being in a 'place' gives it qualities that are not about thread count, color, and whether or not it is the right look for the dinner party, concert or office meeting.

My parents' kitchen, unlike my closet, has the unique character of holding every memory of Thanksgiving dinners and the stuffing my mother makes, the over-cooked broccoli and her pumpkin pies. It holds the conversations with my brothers when we used to laugh over childhood adventures. It holds the memories of discussions of school, girls, the exam next day, and plans for the future. It holds the memories of baking Christmas cookies, making art, and sound of my dog's feet racing across the floor to his bowl, which he always ran into and spilled in the corner.

This area of my childhood house has the unique ability to echo with emotions. It connects to me in a profound and embodied way. My body remembers.

There are fundamental differences between 'spaces' in which we simply carry out a transaction and 'places' that engage us in embodied experience making. The success of shopping places is hinged on retailers' understanding that connections to their stores and their brands, are cemented with more than just the products they sell and the price points they provide them at. Positive shopping experiences promote connection through building trust and delivering on expectations in an environment that supports the emotional connection between people.

When teaching a design course at Inter-Dec College in Montreal I had students arrange their desks to create a space in the middle of the room, creating a sort of corral. I then asked a student to stand in its middle, stretch out her arms and turn slowly while walking about and then, when she was ready, to stop and be still. I then asked her to report what she felt, how she experienced herself in relation to the space and its perimeter.

Alone in the circle, individuals reference themselves and the bounding edge. They talk about how they feel about being close to the edge – safer, further away – not as much. When in relation to something or someone else, a dynamic evolves. Relationships build and one thing influences the other.

When one person is in the space the energy occurs in a straight line – between the individual and the edge. When another enters the space the energy connects the two of them with the edge as well and a new bounding box occurs. The large open space is segmented to create a space between people.

After a short pause, I asked another student to get in the corral, hold out his arms and spin slowly while moving through the space. When he came within a few steps of the other student I asked him to stop and report what he felt about his relationships to the bounding edge and the other student. What ensued was an intriguing conversation about objects in space, how proximity to other things created context and tensions, both literal and figurative, and how the proximity between two objects energizes the space making it more than an area of floor marked off from the rest of the room by a row of desks.

Another student climbed in spinning and stopping. Then another. And another, until the entire class was in the ring. Asking everyone then to sit on the floor, the desks became walls instead of waist-high fencing. The rest of the room disappeared. With our focus on relationship to each other we had created 'place.'

'Places' are more intimate, and I would contend, more profound, due to the relationships built between people not walls. Places are imbued with emotion that creates the experience of being connected.

Cavernous stores, those that are measured in the tens or hundreds of thousands of square feet, are so out of human scale that they have a challenge creating a sense of place. Huge volumes packed with merchandise are a recipe to overwhelm, not only because our brains can't process all the visual, auditory and other sensory information, but also because the sheer size disconnects the customer from experience on a human scale.

So while department planning helps break down the assortment into digestible chunks of similar products and adds clarity, enhancing our ability to take it all in, it has the other benefit of making places out of spaces. Departments, shops within shops, allow for connection in a more personal way than if you were simply to provide a labyrinthine space with row upon row of merchandise.

When shoppers scan a store environment and its densely packed sales floor, it often becomes awash with visual patterns. Groups of individual products begin to blend into a sea of sameness and the connection to a branded 'place' begins to fade. As the size of a shopping environment grows, promoting abundant choice as the key business strategy, the proportion between the numbers of people versus products reverses. Fewer shoppers within a defined area put more space between them, replacing opportunity for personal connection with rows of stuff. Shopping trips become more of a search for commodities and deeply engaging experience takes a back seat to loading up the shopping basket and moving on to the next task on the to-do list.

The enormity of vast mountain ranges, wide open planes, enormous city squares or even stores that measure in the hundreds of thousands of square feet can indeed be awe inspiring. However, their impact is more about giving us a feeling of our diminutive size in relation to the world (or universe) around us. Though there may be a transcendent feeling to experiencing such places, we always 'come back to earth' as it were, to engage in relationship with people.

Walk some of the largest shopping places in the world, like the bazar in Istanbul with its seeming endless corridors of shops, and you discover that beyond the initial impact of its scale, the memory goes next to the interaction you had with a shopkeeper. In remembering my shopping trips through bazars, the twisting alleyways loaded with products have blended into a visual pastiche that are an echo in comparison to the vivid memories of bartering with individual store owners and the excited exchange between the man trying to make the sale, my interpreter, and me.

Times Square in New York is both enormous and a visual delight. But, if you emptied it of people, it wouldn't have any of the impact when throngs of people fill the area to welcome in the new year or simply come together to take pictures on the corner amidst its digital backdrop.

The experience of memorable places is made more profound in their sharing with others. I would suggest that the experience of place is less about architecture than what happens *between* people. The place between people is magical because in it, the energy of connection is shared. We will look at the idea of a 'concept of mind' later in the book, which suggests that our minds exchange information and energy binding us together in a collective experience. Connecting to the hearts and minds of customers happens in the experience *between* us, in our face-to-face connection.

Great shopping experiences find their way into the customer's emotional memory, creating lasting body memories built on participation. One actively needs to 'do' something. You can't just passively shop. You have to go into the store, walk the sales floor, try on or pick up merchandise, and have an exchange. This of course is a challenge in a digital world were one can access the full breadth of any retailer's assortment from a home computer, laptop or handheld device. These new digital shopping methods seem to be in direct conflict with the idea that we need to engage in shopping with our physical bodies, among others who share in the experience, in order to be memorable. There are indeed challenges to engaging shoppers in an embodied and meaningful way through a screen. That is of course if we assume that experience exists *only* in the shopper's body. We will see later that it is a mind-body relationship that drives experience. Our bodily connection to the physical environment is a driving force in the making of experience, but without the brain and shopper's mind we have nothing.

In the future of a digitally driven shopping world we may well see experiences that require less bodily interaction as augmented reality and virtual constructions take us places in our minds alone. Given that we have a few hundred million years of human development behind us, where we physically interacted with the world, I don't think the need for direct physical engagement will disappear. Purely digitally driven experiences, such as virtual reality shopping environments, will certainly be available. But, these virtual 3D 'places' are still a challenge for most of us who find the body's connection to what we see through a VR headset to be slightly disorienting and, for some, have the after effect of making one feel nauseated.

As we move through space we learn about the environment. Our bodies understand the difference between walking on wood, concrete or a moss-covered forest floor. We understand these surfaces differently when we are in bare feet, in socks, boots or sneakers. Our skin knows the difference between a sharp winter wind and a humid breeze after a summer rainfall. We understand our environment, and indeed ourselves, from the feedback we get from our bodies.

When we enter stores we are adapting to a host of changing sensorial inputs. Our eyes are adjusting to different lighting, calibrating to fluorescent, tungsten or LED luminaires that replace the natural sunlight. Our faces and skin are reacting to changing humidity, temperature and registering if there is a light breeze in the space.

Our ears are taking in the change of auditory stimuli from the street or mall concourse. Taxis and the roar of busses leaving the stop are replaced with the sound of air conditioning, cash registers, music, and people talking. Even our noses and taste buds are picking up scents either intentionally manufactured to perfume the space or incidentally because the person you walked by just had chicken with garlic sauce at the food court.

I often find myself walking through stores touching everything. Tabletops, merchandise, wall surfaces, and floor fixtures don't escape my desire to touch and *feel* my way through the aisles.

There are a host of physical attributes of shopping spaces that come together in this intricate dance to create a 'place.' Architecture, lighting, materials and finishes, colors, textures, product adjacencies, visual merchandising and display, graphics, etc., are all part of the retailer designer's toolbox to make great environments to shop. This sense of place can be found in the grand bazaar, main street or malls, the general store, bakery or café.

Shopping trips have not been just some utilitarian pastime. Beyond the exchange of goods and services they have always served some other emotional value. Whenever we engage with some shopping place, we are connected to them with both our bodies and minds. These two aspects of who we are come together in the making of experiences. Memorable shopping trips are built on a series of enactments that require the codependent relationship between the customer's body moving through three-dimensional space and the customer's mind, which makes meaning from it all.

Rituals — I Shop, Therefore I Am

The Rites of Purchase

Every morning, customers file into their local Starbucks coffee shop, order their beverage with the impossibly long name and go on their way to work. While it seems rather simple, this repeated process is full of activities that make coffee drinking a ritual in their daily lives. Even in countries like China, trips to buy a steaming cup of coffee are beginning to replace a long-standing tradition where tea was the 'drink of choice.'

The purchase of the drink is only a small part of the chain of events that make the experience so popular. The scents, sights, textures, standing in the queue, idle chatter with other customers, reading the menu board (even though you already know what you will order), how the baristas welcome you (with your first name if you've been there enough), waiting for the hot cup to be placed on the counter, adding your milk and sugar, and then heading on your way — are all part of a process that is coded into your memory as what defines the morning ritual of getting coffee. The whole sequence of events is crucial because it sets up your day triggering a recognizable order that you come to rely on to help the day make sense. Not just because the drink warms your core or because the caffeine finally jolts you awake, but because the repetition of the experience puts the work week of Monday to Friday in a context that differentiates it from the weekend.

The time of the day, place on the street, people you see and talk to, objects you see and hold, the smells and sounds all coalesce to create sensory patterns that make the experience meaningful.

Starbucks understands the 'power of place' and that a customer's embodied participation in the experience is key to cementing the relationship between the brand and those who buy its product. In fact, a campaign a couple of years ago drove the message home with window graphics that encouraged customers to "Take comfort in rituals."

Ritual, and our participation in them have been fundamental to the development our culture for millennia. Through participating in ritual we come to understand ourselves in relation to a greater context. I have heard it said that 'repetition is the mother of skill.' In the case of ritual, 'repetition is the mother of understanding.'

As shopping has become a key feature in our socio-cultural development, it has in many ways taken on many of the key features of ritual. Getting your morning coffee is a ritual that many of us can relate to, but the idea of shopping trips being like a ritual transcends coffee to all sorts of goods and services. Great retail stores have become profound ritual experiences because they are in part built on lasting body memories of places we shop.

In this chapter we will look as the elements of ritual experience and how they are part of most shopping trips. Participation in ritual shopping activities can enhance customer experience and in doing so, enhance connections in the retailer-customer relationship. As stronger bonds grow between people and the places they shop, a sense of loyalty and commitment develops that in turn promotes return visits, which every retailer wants. Rituals we participate in become part of the fabric of our lives. They are roadmaps that plot the course of how shopping experiences should unfold and what they mean to us as we travel along the customer journey.

One of the challenges in discussing the idea of ritual is the natural tendency to see it through the filter of religious studies. While I don't want to suggest that getting a cup of coffee and participating in religious ceremonies are the same thing, they do nevertheless share common principles that make the experiences we have while shopping important to us and meaningful in our lives. As we investigate underlying principles of ritual we will begin to see how the concept can be broadened beyond our immediate perception of it as religious practice to incorporate the things we do every day, such as shopping.

The notion of ritual first appeared as a formal term of analysis in the nineteenth century to identify what was believed to be a universal category of human experience.[2] Theories abound about whether ritual requires one's direct participation or that you can, through mere observation, be engaged in ritual. In fact it is both. Participants and observers are co-creators in the ritual, each playing instrumental roles in its propagation. Whether we watch or directly participate, we learn about the culture in which the ritual is enacted.

Participants of rituals 'act'; those who observe, 'think.'

In a simple way, we can think of our culture as being composed of essential and discrete performances that can be displayed to others outside our community. When others are exposed to these demonstrations, they alter or reinforce their thoughts and feelings about our culture and how they should act or think in relation to us. When we repeat these activities at specific times of the day/month/year they become embedded not simply as routine, but as acts that have more significance to our understanding of our world and ourselves.

Through their enactment, these performances become a sort of script to be used by performers and observers to enhance their understanding about the group's key systems of beliefs and practices and what it means to be a part of the society.

For the outside observer who watches these enactments unfold, these performances are sometimes the most real and observable units of the cultural structure. Their performance "has a definitively limited time span, a beginning and an end, an organized program of activity, a set of performers, an audience, and a place and occasion of performance."[3]

If we think of ritual as performance, something that is enacted by someone, then it follows that ritual performances produce feelings not just in the minds but also in the bodies of their performers. What is important to remember about the body's connection to understanding is that we don't, for example, understand religion by simply having knowledge of the religious doctrines, but by going to church/synagogue/temple every week. We go and engage in the performance of the rites.

If we apply the idea of direct participation in ritual acts as generating meaning in the individual, we might also say that we don't really know the potential pleasure of shopping or buying something by having a friend tell us of their experience in a store, but from doing it ourselves. When we begin to see rituals as performances we get a better understanding how important our body's involvement is in understanding experience. As we physically engage in the performance of the ritual acts, we can come to more fully appreciate concepts that are otherwise inaccessible.

In a digitally driven culture, social networking is changing the way we communicate, promoting the 'performance' of life moments as video or photos uploaded to the Internet for mass consumption. If ritual is a cultural performance lending meaning to the participants or observers, then the nature of ritual may also be in the midst of change. Handheld digital devices are moving key context establishing ritual enactments from performances at specific times in specific places, to happening anytime, anywhere we can capture digital images and present them to the world. This is going to have a significant impact on how shopping as ritual unfolds.

A few years ago I bought shoes at Nordstrom. While they looked great in the store and seemed to fit just fine, when I got them home they were simply un-wearable. They sat in a closet for almost a year until I took them back. No questions, no guilt just a quick and pleasant return by a sales associate who was all too happy to make my experience something that I would in turn share with others.

I had heard about Nordstrom's legendary customer service but not actually ever had the first-hand experience. The stories were always impressive, but it turned out that actually shopping at Nordstrom was the only way to fully appreciate what was otherwise only hearsay. Having direct experience allowed me to fully understand their policy about putting the customer first.

In this case 'doing' was 'believing.'

"Ritual does not simply represent the belief that it references, but it instead communicates and transmits important cultural knowledge that is called into existence by the very performance of ritual."[4] The Nordstrom brand culture is driven by a set of ideologies that put customer service first. It is probably outlined in a customer service manual someplace at the corporate headquarters, but it is played out on the sales floor (as well as the Internet) in the interaction between customers and sales associates. Brand values and culture are made real by their being enacted.

This of course points out the critical role of sales associates and how they interact with customers. Through their actions during an exchange on the sales floor, website or social network, customers come to understand what the brand stands for. Sales associates play important roles in the performance of brand rituals. How they do what they do conveys a message about what matters to the brand and what value the brand places on the customer.

Through participation in shopping as ritual both consumers and sales associates take on identities that are embedded in the rites. The scripts that brands weave into their brand presentation and the acts we follow when shopping in their stores are parts of ideological stories. Through our participation in shopping activities we adopt them as our own. In this way, shopping helps to create our identity.

I am more aware than ever about the nature of shopping as a ritual. Shopping's ritual qualities are not to be relegated just to Christmas, or other special occasions for that matter, but to virtually every day we engage in the practice.

Shopping, as ritual, is not defined by gender, cultural, economic, religious, or racial boundaries. Shopping's ritual qualities cross all of these boundaries and join us together in communities of collective understanding about what it means to be an adopter of a brand, to shop one retailer over another or to be a member of community, a culture and the cosmos.

Shopping is an Embodied Experience

While we experience stores in large part with our eyes, our bodies fill out the understanding of what it means to be in a retail place. We are three-dimensional beings in a three dimensional world and our bodies 'remember' what it feels like to be in different places.

The idea that our bodies participate in the experience of shopping should not be considered lightly since it is through our bodies that we come to full understand ourselves in relation to our world.

Far from simply being a mode of transportation for our head, our bodies are instrumental to the experience. 'Doing' shopping is a key component determining 'being' part of the experience. You don't simply *think* about shopping, you get up and '*go*' shopping. And, while it is only a poor approximation of the full-bodied experience of being in at the mall or market, you still have to 'go' to you computer to shop via the Internet. Even while shopping via your smartphone, you are still someplace, actively engaged in some sort of physical movement, more or less.

An ancient adage attributed to Confucius some five hundred years ago claimed:

> "I HEAR AND I FORGET.
> I SEE AND I REMEMBER.
> I DO AND I UNDERSTAND."

As a strongly visual-spatial learner, I completely appreciate this as a mode of learning. I understood drawing more deeply when, standing at the easel, I would take on the pose of the model myself, shifting my weight from one foot to another or tilting my torso this way or that.

It wasn't until a tutor made me assemble 3D models and draw the engineering problems of my architecture education, that I fully began to understand the relationships between the mathematical algorithms and anything in my world. The problems of steel design, structures or electricity were taken out of the conceptual world of my thoughts, into a built world that I created.

Both thoughts *and* actions are involved in shopping. Fully understanding what it means to be an adopter of one brand over another, or engaging in one shopping place over another is not something that you do at arm's length. You get in there and get involved playing both roles of participant and observer. We are both the makers of the experience and the beneficiaries of things well made.

Participating is Key

"Just Do It" is arguably one of the best slogans created in contemporary branding as well as being the cultural mindset of Nike. It is also a call to action, to participate. To get up, get out and get with it.

Repetitive patterns of 'doing' can be considered simply to be humdrum 'routine.' As innately creative beings, we tire quickly of those activities that are simply repetitious in nature. And so, it is not so surprising that innovative technologies have often been turned towards alleviating us from the repetitive, time-consuming activities such as household chores and industrial production. Vacuums, dishwashers, washing machines, lawnmowers, and a host of other household appliances help out at home so we may engage in loftier pursuits.

Ritual, while often having repetition as a key component to the rites, is something more profound. "Not every pattern constitutes ritualization, but every instance of ritual presupposes a process, a dance-like quality of interaction between an ecosystem and people" that has meaning grounding the participants in context to the world around them.[5]

"The most widespread [ritual] actions are spectating, purchasing, and consuming. They are done partly out of necessity but mostly for the sake of participation."[6] Shopping as a collective series of enactments gives meaning and context to all of our lives.

It is important to note that we do not have shopping done *to* us.

While we may be simply observers of shopping behavior as we walk through stores at the mall or discover our way through an open-air market, we also help to create our experience by actively participating in its making. The degree to which we actively engage in the experience of a shopping trip is proportional to how profoundly the experience becomes part of us. The more we take part in the experience with our bodies, the more it is embedded in our emotional core.

This will become important in the future of retail place making, as an entire generation is becoming a cohort of digital content makers. Today's digitally enabled youngster will likely find future retail places to be a mix of 'old-school' embodied experience combined with opportunities to engage with interactive digital interfaces. The ritual performance of shopping experiences will have a completely different look when we consider the emergence of a shopping culture whose personal performance is an every-moment opportunity that is published to their social network via the Internet. We will look at the implication of this paradigm shift and the creation of in-store customer experience in Part 3.

There is a part of all shoppers that loves to be served; that likes the doting waiter, the overly attentive sales associate, the reliable doorman. It feels good to be treated with a little extra care. Every customer wants to feel appreciated, and to know they are of value to the retailer. The less they have to do, and more others have to do, the better.

On the other hand, there is also a part of all of us that loves making stuff. If shoppers can disengage from the social pressures of 'ought to's, do's and don'ts, the self-consciousness of adult group decorum slips. These moments reactivate the childlike enthusiasm to engage in making the experience one's own.

Retail places such as Make Meaning, The Paint Bar, Build-A-Bear Workshop, and the trendy burger joint on midtown Manhattan's east side, 4Food, incorporate the notion that when customers engage in the making of their experiences and co-author the narratives they have of a shopping trip, they not only buy a heft of merchandise but they also really have fun doing it.

In today's retail marketplace, many stores are created with the too-simple assumption of a one-size-fits-all approach to shopping. Of course that's at odds with the idea that we generally want to feel ourselves as being individuals, with needs, wants and aspirations that are unique to us. In a digitally driven world that continues to promote the idea that posting personal details on social network sites is a definition of who we are, we will continue to see specification within product categories into subsets of subsets of demographics until the individual is the epicenter of a retailer's marketing focus.

The degree to which retailers and brands can personalize products and services, will be an indication of their ability to keep in pace with the dynamic nature of digital world. Customers will come to accept that everything changes in so far as the changes suit them, personally.

The "NikeiD" program, while having been available for some time, is a step by an international brand and retailer in the direction of allowing customers to customize their own shoes. By engaging customers in creating the color, graphics and other details of their running shoes, they allow them to be a part of an international brand-mindset at the same time they are presenting their own individuality to the world. Mass-customization will go from being a trend to being the status quo, where production times are reduced from months, to weeks, to days to hours – when 3-D printing eventually goes mainstream.

In a world where we are both looking to support our long-held social imperative of wanting to belong to a group, we work equally hard at making our experiences 'unique.' Ownership of property is an important factor in self-determination. Our perceptions of experiences become our reality and as we participate in making them, we also fashion our identity.

A significant part of 'buying in' to one brand or retailer over another is our desire to incorporate the brand's ideologies into our own belief systems. We want our brands to *belong* to us as much as the products we buy from them. You have likely described a store you often go to as 'my store.' Not just because you mean to describe it as the one that is close to where you live in the physical sense, and not that you actually 'own' it, but that it has been included into your set of relationships, things you are deeply connected to and that in some way have made it part of who you are. A sense of ownership develops that 'gets you where you live,' emotionally.

People who adopt brands or retailers into their lives actually defend their choices of buying products or services from them. They need to; it would be like not standing up for a family member. Being a brand loyalist says a lot about our beliefs and values. And so, it is not surprising that once we adopt a brand or retailer into our lives, we commit ourselves to living by what it stands for because it has in a way become equally part of our character.

I've seen people argue over whether *their* store is better than someone else's. They'll say that 'my store has the best… *whatever*,' and they'll drive a country mile to get what they need there. What they 'need,' however, doesn't fill just their pantries, but also satisfies their hunger for an emotional connection to something greater than themselves.

Part of the idea that customers connect to brands or retailers in a sort of personal relationship comes from their direct participation with retailers at multiple touch points along the customer journey. In the service of satisfying the prime objective of retailing – to sell goods and services – customers engage in sorts of activities while they are both in and out of the store. All of these brand connection moments become part of the process of shopping. Today we understand that these are spread across geography and digital form factors. You can be both in your home and on the go, on your mobile device or in relation to some other interactive digital device. Each of these touch-point fits into the ritual of a branded customer experience.

I believe that given the opportunity, people generally like to get involved with their stores. There are some retailers who take this idea directly to the sales floor where the entire concept is built around customers making the products they'll buy. Beyond making art, candles or stuffed bears, there are companies who developed retail concepts that extend beyond the sole purpose of displaying and selling of products to becoming more actively engaged in the building a sense community with customers. They do so by offering opportunities for connection through in-store activities that involve direct participation.

The Home Depot, WYSH-Wear Your Spirit for Humanity, and Lululemon, get customers into their stores to make things, participate in seminars and do yoga.

Retailers that actively engage the customer in more than simply making a purchase in the store see the long-term benefits of increased dwell time. The store becomes more than a place that has stuff; it has heart. It becomes a meeting place for like-minded people who choose to be engaged and show their loyalty through being return customers and brand advocates.

So, The Home Depot has adult customers crafting wooden dump trucks on a Saturday morning with their children, WYSH invites customers to educate themselves about parenting, journaling and to customize T-shirts, and Lululemon has people vowing to be more Zen-like while bending themselves into a pretzel. Customers learn more about themselves and build a bond with the brand through fostering an emotionally connected community.

And, by the way… these are all done outside of what we would call traditional store hours. Customers get up early, or go after the kids are asleep, to participate. They are motivated by doing/making/enacting and if they happen to pick up some hardware, buy a t-shirt or a yoga mat while they are there, then, all the better for them and the retailer.

Both the participant and the observer are engaged in the experience. Each takes part in the enactment of certain myths but does so from different vantage points. Because you are an observer of ritual doesn't mean that you are apart from it. As we walk the mall or shopping places we are both observers *and* participants. In either case, each individual is vital to the unfolding of the shopping ritual.

While it is true that the prime objective in creating great shopping places is a commercial transaction, successful merchants understand the power of ritual. They create customer experiences that are about lasting memories built on well-crafted ritual enactments of their brand platforms.

So what about the idea that some find shopping to be likened to a religious experience? Do we really attribute that much gravitas to shopping?

Recent work by Martin Lindstrom proposes that not only do customers have strong feeling about their relationships to major brands, but also that exposure to them results in lighting up the same areas of their brains that are activated when exposed to images of religious icons. [7]

In a study conducted by Lindstrom, people were shown images of strong brands and religious icons and their brain activity was measured in an fMRI (Functional Magnetic Resonance Imaging) machine. When people viewed images associated with strong brands such as the Apple iPod, Harley Davidson motorcycle or Ferrari automobile "…their brains registered the exact same patterns of activity as they did when they viewed religious images…" According to the Lindstrom study, "… there was no discernable difference between the way subjects' brains reacted to powerful brands and the way they reacted to religious figures." [8] "In fact, the reactions in our volunteers to brands and religious icons were not just similar, they were almost identical." [9]

So despite the original assertion that we would try to disconnect ritual from the idea of religion, it seems that while shopping for major brands, the customer's brain, in the end, is apt to light up as we experience images of Budweiser, Beckham *and* the Bible. From the point of view of brain activation, the processes that we embed into our shopping rituals imbue them with special meaning in a similar way that we have come to perceive significant spiritual or religious icons or activities.

The Media and The Message

When rituals are thought of as performances, the enactments can be seen as the ways in which the cultural content, unique to a particular group, is organized and shared on particular occasions through some specific media. The sharing of content can be done in a number of ways including dance, song, procession, theatrical performance, presentation of images or any combination of all of these. Looking at retailing through the lens of ritual, it is easy to see how a brand's culture is spread among the shopping population. While we expect the foundational principles of a brand's culture to remain constant, the way they are being performed today are in the midst of transformation. More than ever before, brands and retailers have multiple distribution channels for their messages. Participation in brand/retail rituals is no longer relegated to the store alone but occurs within an intricate, three-dimensional web of customer-brand/retailer interaction.

In our technologically enhanced and socially networked world, the way in which a brand's culture is shared – or performed – is multifaceted. The store as the single medium for retail ritual is morphing and shopping is becoming multidimensional.

Permanent stores, pop-up shops, websites, mobile applications, social media networks, public events and appearances by brand ambassadors, as well as multiple channels for advertising, marketing and PR, all contribute to the distribution of the brand message. Each of these customer touch-points offers the opportunity for people to engage in a part of the brand's ritual performance.

Throughout the ritual retail performance, there is of course, directly, or indirectly, the selling of products or services as well as a brand's cultural identity. Retail rituals engage customers who are sometimes active participants and at other times simply observers. In either case, individuals become aware of core messages that the brand wants customers to understand.

If we think about the multitude of distribution 'media' that brands put to their use in selling both products, and by association, ideologies, we can appreciate Marshall McLuhan's now famous saying: "the medium is the message."[10]

McLuhan asserted that the medium affects the society in which it plays a role, not only through the content that it delivers but also by the nature of the medium itself. Take mobile phones as an example; it would be very hard to argue that the cellphone revolution has had no impact on society. And so, it is not just that brands or retailers can distribute messages on handheld devices, but that the devices themselves are fundamentally changing the way the message is conveyed – and thus the message itself – as well as society.

Mobile devices are changing communication methods and creating 'new' languages such as texting. A new world of digitally enabled communication is pushing rapid change upon societies and cultures around the world and in turn revolutionizing how customers and brands communicate. Each of the 'form factors,' be it desktop computer, cellphone, tablet, or digital screen, engages customers in new way of participating in retail rituals. Each of them has different levels of effectiveness in reaching the emotional center of the customer and in their combined uses, we as a shopping culture are being affected.

With the emergence of new media to convey brand messages and engage in shopping ritual, things will get complicated since the message is linked with, and changes with, the medium carrying it. This means that retailers and brands are likely to be challenged with adapting core principles to multiple platforms. Not all screens are alike in their ability to engage and 'sell.' Furthermore, this change of brand messages to fit a particular form factor is not going to be a one-time thing. The world around us is in dynamic change that is moving at an unprecedented pace.

It stands to reason then, that brands need to find ways to both distribute 'culturally specific' messages that stay true to core beliefs while being re-shaped by the medium they employ as a delivery system. Not all messages are the same at every point of interaction along the shopping journey. They can't be if they are being carried by different mediums. In-store and on-screen messaging of brand ideology are, at their cores, from the same wellspring, but at the point of customer interaction, different.

In a dynamic digital environment, customers will come to expect rapid change as a given and those responsible for content creation will need an infusion of support. We will see in later chapters that this is likely not to come from advertising and marketing agencies but from the customers themselves who will actively participate in making content. This type of direct interaction with shopping places will re-shape the paradigm of retail ritual entirely.

Sacred Ground

We have looked at the idea that 'spaces' and 'places' are different in the previous chapter and that 'place making' is a key differentiator in making shopping experiences more profound. From the point of view of places being fundamental to the ritual nature of shopping, we can look at the types of places we create as either being supportive of ritual or a distraction from it.

According to Ronald Grimes, "Space which is empty, uniform and abstract, is given shape and life so it may become a ritual place such as a burial ground, dancing ground, or cathedral. All of these are curiously vacant and even haunting, when the actions of ritual are not occurring in them. Ritual place is a matrix of ritual life."[11]

If you have ever been in a restaurant, store or theater when they are closed, you'll understand the feeling in the Grimes statement. Without people, these spaces are slightly eerie. The feelings of how important other people are to our experience of places become very acute when they are missing. In many instances, we rely on others to round out our experiences with emotional content and the sense of connection to a place.

Shopping can of course occur inside and outside, in places that are specifically designed to support it, and in those that can spring up over the weekend and disappear by Monday. But to what degree does the design of the place have an influence on how a shopping ritual unfolds? Well, if shopping is a ritual activity, then everything in the process is specifically crafted to move the ritual forward. Everything is 'designed' to heighten the impact of the performance. In this way, you might say that every element a customer sees, touches, smells, hears, and does in a shopping environment is crucial to the feeling shoppers have about the place and brand. But, this is not always the case. Often there are things that designers think are important, but go entirely unnoticed by the shopper.

A focus on architectural expression is often a misappropriation of time, energy and money that seeks to satisfy some architectural imperative rather than really understanding what customers notice as they walk the sales floor. This is not to discount the deeply influential roles architecture and design have in the creation of place, but more of a call to always see the making of shopping places through the eyes of customers walking the sales floor. This customer-centric point of view comes from fully understanding customers by seeing them through both demographic and 'psychographic' lenses. Understanding the customer from the point of view of their psychology also requires an understanding of the customer's neurobiology.

As a retail architect with this point of view, I have spent years creating retail store concepts that are required to be efficient and beautiful places for customers. I have not yet had a client who has asked me to produce a design concept that was over budget, unattractive and that couldn't accommodate the merchandise making up the assortment. All retailers want places that motivate customers to act – to make a purchase. Acting in retail ritual performances results in experiences that lead to the adoption of a brand and its products, with the eventual end result often being a sale.

The architecture of shopping places has always been fundamental to the experience. 'Architecture' though, is not necessarily a base requirement for ritual since spaces may be also defined through actions alone. Ceremonial dances around fires, for example, may mark out circular boundaries simply by the movement of the dancer's feet through the dirt. There is no architecture that facilitates the enactment of the dance, but there comes into existence with each step a clearly defined ritual space nevertheless.

So in creating store concepts, retail designers are always balancing brand, customer, merchandising, *and* design.

What is important with regard to architecture and ritualizing is that the built environment *supports* the enactment of the ritual and propagation of ritual ideology. Cathedrals, in their glorious architectural expression, have for ages, been designed to support Christian ritual and through them feelings of transcendence. However, uplifting and profoundly spiritual experiences can also come from standing on a mountaintop. Architecture is a key factor to the experience but it is not necessarily a prerequisite to the enactment of ritual. Everything that the store designer puts into the store, however, must support the telling of the brand story and its enactment in the ritual of shopping.

You can build almost anything these days allowing architecture to push the boundaries of the laws of physics. What is important is that the store architecture emerges from a clearly defined set of brand truths/ideologies. This set of rules can be said to act as a retail experience platform upon which all of the decisions about the shopping environment are cross-referenced. The experience platform serves as an ideological outline that helps to chart a path for design decision making in the same way that liturgy does for the enactment of religious rites.

Seeing through ritual space is partly how we orient ourselves and define the sequence of the ritual. So it is with understanding shopping places from the point of entry. We have already discussed the number of sensorial changes that ones body is adjusting to when walking into a retail place. There is no difference when entering a place of ritual.

Immediately we understand that we are 'in' as opposed to being 'out.' What we see from the vantage point of this transition zone is key to the unfolding of the ritual. Sightlines from the entry point lead us into the space. The body follows the eyes.

Boundaries between individual classifications of merchandise within the shopping environment and those between one brand's storefront and the others in the mall, or on the street, need to have clear identities. These points of entry/exit may be permeable allowing customers to flow between one area and another. They should at the same time define a zone of activity and distinguish the nature of the interaction between itself and the adjacent space.

Storefronts are particularly important in distinguishing ritual shopping place. They signal a clear demarcation between the space of the 'profane' – outside – and the 'sacred' inside world of the brand.

Passing through the entryway should signal an arrival in a new world apart from the collective social place of the street or mall concourse. This happens by introducing a number of perceptual cues. Looking back to the Tommy Hilfiger store experience in Miami, all of the elements of the entry sequence served both to highlight the differences between the street and the interior as well as this particular retailer from anyone else on the block. They played with my senses, not in any Machiavellian way, but by consciously addressing customer emotion through sensory responses to the changes in environment. The store set up the ritual process by defining entry into the space as a remarkable moment.

Regular customers are like a congregation. They have member status that affords them certain privileges. They move freely through shopping places, with a familiarity of the assortment and store layout. They have a deeper sense of belonging to the brand (or the brand belonging to them) than those casual shoppers who by happenstance find themselves in the store because a window display caught their attention or that they are part of a group ambling around the mall for the afternoon.

The regular customers, from time to time, are rewarded for their commitment. Their 'membership in the club' affords additional perks as such as greater discounts and gifts. For example, I have preferred status with my airline of choice. This status allows me to check in, get through security and upgrade to first class when a seat is available. Average customers, while part of the retail ritual entourage, usually have lesser sets of perks than those who have demonstrated brand loyalty by loading their closets or pantries with a retailer's merchandise. 'Loyalty programs' are a good illustration of how being a committed follower of a retailer or brand is promoted through dispensing rewards in the form of added value and discounts.

Shopkeepers or company owners, store managers, sales associates and other employees play roles higher up the hierarchical ladder. As a result, boundaries in the shopping place are more permeable to them. In the end, the way in which one crosses boundaries in ritual places is an indication of who you are and the role you play in the ritual process.

Delineation between men's and women's areas, the front and back of houses, or in front of the altar as opposed to behind it, exist within an established hierarchy. Boundaries might only be implied but we have learned by observation (and direct experience) the decorum necessary to allow for the appropriate rituals to unfold. Through multiple shopping trips we all have become exceptionally good at picking up and understanding the cues to how a space is used.

You don't climb behind the altar and you don't get behind the cash wrap counter unless you are a religious leader or a store employee.

From the entry area, sightlines leading along strong axes either to merchandise presentations, display points, graphics, etc., elevate the importance of these elements in the space. They also help in the establishment of hierarchies informing the customer about what is important. Whether it is a new arrival, seasonal display, text-based message or lifestyle graphic, or a sales associate happy to help you find what you need, these elements of customer experience are key to the unfolding of the shopping ritual. Terminations of these axes, as in one's view down the nave of a church, need to culminate in things that matter rather than in featureless dead ends. If the retailer is going to get customers to look there, and they will, what they visually focus on in this view has to be an important element of the ritual.

Ritual Objects

Think of a famous clear green cola bottle with an hourglass shape. The Coca-Cola bottle is known worldwide.

Whose perfume bottle is square? Chanel.

Which chocolate bar comes in a triangular-shaped golden box? Toblerone.

Andy Warhol made whose soup can label famous? Campbell's.

How many of you have kept the box that your iPhone came in?

Or the "Little Brown Bag" from Bloomingdales to carry lunch in, until the handles wore thin?

Think diamonds and a turquoise blue box and Tiffany & Co. is, inescapably, the image we see in our mind's eye.

Products, and packaging, too, become part of the ritual. Created to make products more visible on the shelf and occasionally beautiful in its own right, the wrapper has come to signify the brand and that we, as consumers of its products, are believers. Often product packaging, apart from the actual contents in the box, can become iconographic, taking on, and projecting outwards, the essence of a brand. Our re-use of product packaging is another way to demonstrate group belonging and a sense of well being to society at large.

Packaging is like retail ritual residue.

Often associated with ritual enactments are objects that are called into service to represent some part of the story. Goblets, bowls, knives, statuary, tapestries, furniture, pipes, masks, animals and clothing are but a small selection of items that have traditionally found their way into ritual enactments.

Ritual objects are meaningful not because there is necessarily anything intrinsic about them that makes them sacred but because we infuse them with significance. They are reminders of sacred personages, texts, and events and as such are revered by those participating.

The ritual object's power may be everlasting and it may be kept under lock and key with someone to look out for its well being. It may also be transient, only in effect when being used in ritual, but not lasting beyond the ritual itself – being burned, eaten or tossed into the water. The value of ritual objects is that they are able to distill a whole complex of meaning into a single item that projects meaning to others who are either participating in the ritual or watching it happen.

Stores are loaded with ritual objects called merchandise. The striking difference between ritual objects in the case of shopping places, and those used in more traditional ritual enactments such as religious ceremonies, are their number in shopping places. While there may be only one chalice, perhaps a few statues, or one sacred cow, ritual objects in stores can number in the thousands. And, they are not only used by a selected leader of the ritual but by all those who are engaged in the shopping activity. All participants have free access to the objects of retail rituals. Unlike a small selection of objects that help define the ritual process in religious enactments, a plethora of products (and the qualities of their design, manufacturing, and in-store display) come to signify the brands that stamp their logos on them.

In the case of a store, every piece of merchandise has meaning, even when there are twenty of the shirt in five color ways on a rack. In a sense, there is a democratization of the ritual object in retail stores. Even though you and a few thousand other people across the country will buy that little black dress, all customers inherit the same level of brand DNA by wearing it.

By wearing, using, and consuming merchandise, we take home a piece of the ritual. The value we attribute to the things we buy is both a function of what it does as well as what it 'says.' You could equally carry the items jammed into the bottom of a luxurious handbag in a paper lunch sack. But when they are loaded into a $4000 Louis Vuitton shoulder bag, who cares if the cap is off the lipstick and there is a bunched up Kleenex at the bottom of it all? You are telling others that "it's good to be me and oh, by the way, I'm better off than you."

In fact, should you be a consumer of Louis Vuitton products at all, you are truly buying an object of a high rite since no LV product is sold other than in its stores or through its company website. If the handbag doesn't sell, it is eventually destroyed, thus taking ritual object in the shopping sphere to a more sacred level. These practices control the brand quality and promote the ideology of luxurious exclusivity, driving the pricing structure of a purse to be on par with a work of art – sacred art at that.

In this way, merchandise becomes an extension of the ritual space. Both figuratively and literally, a little bit of the store goes home with us every time we make a purchase and take the merchandise out the front door.

Open for Business – Crucial Times

Ritual is also bound by time, both in the sense of having a beginning, middle and end and as being specific to a time of the day, week, or year. "Ritual is formative of the ways we bide our time. In ritualizing we concentrate, and thereby, consecrate, time."[12] Shopping experiences unfold with specific timing and there are those who will attest that time disappears altogether when they are in the midst of a great shopping experience.

As rituals, shopping trips have historically had well defined beginnings. They usually started with a customer's arrival in the entryway of the store. In the contemporary digitally driven world, however, the beginning of the engagement is being redefined. The start of a shopping experience is no longer thought of as starting at the front door but more likely via a mobile device or home computer. In fact, this retail ritual 'beginning' is now in a state of dynamic change. Shopping experiences can start almost anywhere and customers can begin the process whenever and wherever they want, not just when and where the doors swing open at the start of the typical business day.

Every customer experience has a rhythmic tempo, or structure, that aids in its unfolding similar to the way the timing in a piece of music takes a listener from beginning to the end of a song, or the way a theatrical performance has scenes, acts and closing numbers. We experience stores with storefronts or homepages – opening scenes – we shop various merchandise groupings and displays – acts two and three, and we hand over the cash at the cash-wrap counter – closing number.

While we can see the same general structure to the sequence of events in almost all stores: enter, shop, buy – the tempo, length of acts or how frequently the chorus returns can also be distinctive between brands and various retail places. Stepping into a fast food restaurant, ordering your meal from a menu board then eating it in fifteen minutes on hard plastic tables or counters is very different than fine dining at an upscale restaurant where you might linger with a cocktail in a lounge, go through multiple courses, each with a palette cleanser of cold sorbet, then dessert and coffee.

Changing the timing of retail ritual influences how customers feel going through the process. Some retailers have changed the way in which customers shop an assortment, such as IKEA, who changed the way we shop for furniture and home goods. Their stores lead you on a choreographed sequence of product vignettes. The path of travel is deliberate, and it takes time to follow it from various showrooms to checkout in the warehouse.

Sephora, which revolutionized the cosmetics category with an 'open sell' approach, also changed the timing of the ritual process. They broke down old department store paradigms of selling cosmetics behind counters by allowing customers to shop at a pace that allowed them to discover on their own. Self-directed discovery and trying products prior to buying them set customers on a path that satisfied their need for novelty, and self-determination at a pace that *they* could control.

In these two cases, retailers changed the ritual timing of shopping their stores, making it the process unique to them. Despite being just one of a multitude of retailers in the categories of home furnishings or cosmetics, they have crafted customer experiences that are recognized the world over for not just changing the way a store looks, but for how it functions in the service of a brand's ritual performance.

Ritual time can also be considered in the sense of being a series of moments, something that people anticipate and which can be defined apart from the regular flow of events. The sequence is recurrent and something that is planned for. This sense of ritual time is 'circular' and over time has been played out in the form of seasonal ceremonies and sacrifices. This is the way many who talk about ritual time conceptualize it. We all know this type of retail ritual timing in the form of shopping trips that are part of Christmas, Valentine's Day, back–to-school and other seasonal events.

Retailers have calendars filled with the arrival of seasonal merchandise and visual display programs. Holidays and other times of celebration are opportunities for retailers to sell merchandise that is in synch with secular religious rituals. So, try as we might not to consider shopping as a religious experience and to see it as a ritual practice independent from liturgy – it isn't so easy. For as long as animals have been sold to sacrifice at a shrine or temple, it seems that religious celebrations have always been intertwined with shopping.

Other seasonal shopping events such as Black Friday (the day after Thanksgiving in the U.S.) and now Cyber Monday (falling on the Monday after Black Friday) are pure fabrications (referencing each other). They establish crucial ritual times that serve their commercial enterprises under the guise of a cause for celebration. If it is repeated seasonally, then this pattern of behavior establishes a new ritual for customers to follow.

So, while kids generally don't celebrate going back to the rigors of school in late summer, retailers have turned it into a crucial ritual time that has become a rite of passage and an indicator we rely on to forecast the health of the economy.

These two views of ritual time frame it as an event occurring at predetermined moments or as a sequence/tempo in the unfolding of the enactment.

A significant question to ask at this point is, what happens to ritual time when the world of e-commerce essentially does away with boundaries imposed by the ticking of the clock or the changing of the seasons?

Events such as online retailers' 'flash sales' can be considered in the context of this cyclical retail ritual timing. It is interesting to note, that even though these types of ritual events become expected from online retailers, the frequency and time that they will happen are often a mystery. In this way they play on the brain's love for the unexpected and novelty, at the same time as keeping customers hooked on the expectation that something is about to happen that they don't want to miss.

When we are increasingly using the Internet as a method for shopping, where everything is available *all the time*, does the idea of ritual shopping time disappear?

It used to be that the hours were posted on the door and a little card was flipped saying "closed" when retailers were done for the day. Now, the shop is never closed. 24/7, 365 days a year, most brands are open for business. The Internet never sleeps.

The emerging 'always on' generation of young, digitally enabled shoppers will change the game with regard to the idea of rituals being carried out at particular times. It can't always be Christmas, despite the basic message that we should be carrying the joy of the season in our hearts all year round. We know it comes but once a year, and like most significant holidays, we have developed particular shopping rituals around these crucial times. So, despite the fact that we do not always have the seasonal overlay of a Christmas celebration to influence the look and feel of the store or online website, significant shopping events now can happen anytime.

If ritual time is a crucial point to understanding what the event means and how people place themselves within the context of a larger cultural structure, what happens when the time you go shopping is no longer an issue because you can go online and buy anything at any time?

We might also ask whether or not the sacred nature of the retail ritual experience is diminished if we can do it whenever and wherever we want.

Do we become any less aware of the brand ideologies or become any less connected to the community of brand adopters by shopping more frequently from a smartphone or desktop computer?

The time that people set aside for their participation in or observance of rituals makes them more important. This time 'off the grid' is important because it allows people to focus on the nature of the ritual experience. These concentrated moments in time become like otherworldly experiences that have a transcendent quality and take people beyond themselves and connect them to a larger whole.

When we think of the influence of digital technologies and shopping from a mobile device, laptop computer or tablet while sitting in an airport, the back of a taxi or one's back yard, there are distractions to those shopping moments, which make it inherently more difficult for the customer to focus and be fully present and invested in the world of the brand.

It is likely that when we are not setting aside time to focus on ritual we risk having the sacred conflict with the ordinary or instrumental. It is also likely that in 'multitasking' we are in a state of partial attention and simply less engaged in the process and, as a consequence, less affected by the enactment.

A significant challenge for retailers and brands in a digitally driven world is finding a way to connect customers to ritual time that is apart from their daily activities. With ritual time extended to 'any time' and ritual objects and ritual place being disconnected from embodied experience through the digital interfaces, retailers have a significant challenge to maintain profound body memories as part of the customer experience.

In our high-tech, social-networked world, the ritualizing of shopping experiences is not confined to specific places or times of the day. Ritual nature of shopping may still have a predetermined seasonality when in conjunction with established religious and secular holidays. Key components to ritual experience such as participation – the place, ritual objects and crucial time set apart from the rush daily life – cannot be found through a handheld device or other digital interface. Not until we are able to inhabit virtual environments that call into action all of our perceptual senses, will the store be replaced as a profound place for building community and participation in the embodied experience of the brand.

Even in the face of increased, anytime access to products and services through the Internet, the in-store experience is inherently more valuable as a place of ritual enactment. In a digitally driven shopping future, creators of retail places will have their work cut out for them as they compete for customer interaction with online experiences and digital environments that may be considered 'better than real.' A component to great shopping experiences has been, and will continue to be, the relationship customers build with sales associates *in* the store.

Cast Members – Animators – Mirroring Receptivity

I have already suggested that shopping is far more than simply the stuff we get, the tangible things we wrap up and take home. As a social paradigm, shopping builds relationships between people and brands. As a ritual, shopping relies on the people who are involved in its enactment.

To be involved in ritual requires that participants, and observers, give themselves over to the process and allow for the flow of the ritual to take place. Information, knowledge, emotions and understanding, all move between participants. Being receptive is a two-way street. Both participants and those charged with the responsibility of leading the rites need to share a willingness to lay themselves open to being seen.

The more profoundly people get involved in the process, the more they become connected as a congregation, a culture, a social network, or customer. Products and services we buy can come and go, but the memories of our experience built on the relationships we have with people in the store make customers for life.

Humans thrive in relationships and have, over years, evolved to incorporate the remarkable ability to understand each other simply by looking at each other's faces and body language. First impressions can say a lot. A sales associate's body language and facial gestures serve to prime customers with expectations about how the rest of the shopping experience will unfold.

Subtle gestures in our faces project to others whether we are receptive to relationships and to what degree. It doesn't take much for us to sense if people are open or closed just by looking at them. Most of us have walked into stores where we feel welcome and in others where we are looked at as outsiders who don't fit the customer profile. This of course instills great importance to the facial expressions of sales associates when they are greeting those crossing the threshold. The degree to which the sales associates project receptivity is a large part of the customer journey 'starting on the rite foot.'

The second section of the book will look at the roles of 'mirror neurons' and 'facial action coding systems' in projecting the right emotional tones to customers since, "for most of us, our face is the exterior area by which presence is mediated to others. It is the tangible surface by which vulnerability is exposed or withheld.."[13]

The more skillfully retailers manage the unfolding of ritual in their stores the better the experience will be. Enhancing the experience will reinforce the meaning and value of the ritual. In turn, it will enhance connection, loyalty and commitment and in the end, enhance return visits. Simply put, to make shopping trips more enjoyable and relevant in the face of a digitally driven shopping culture, we need to understand the ritual nature of shopping and how, for the customer, the experience is a profound demonstration of who they are or want to become.

Shopping rituals establish meaning beyond the product and give a transcendent quality to being a customer who connects to any particular brand. When customers immerse themselves in the ritualized space of the retailer, engaging in co-created experience, they move from simply the routine behavior of commodity shopping to something they deem more sacred.

Bedtime Books and the Importance of Story

Stories are powerful. They are among the engines of culture and we have relied on telling them for millennia as part of our human socio-cultural and spiritual development. Stories are crucial to our empathic development as well as providing context to our lives. As with our participation in ritual, we also use stories to creatively engage in making meaning of the world around us and the sometimes-unpredictable events that happen in our lives.

In the creating and telling of stories we can relive experiences in our past, and in doing so, prepare ourselves for those experiences that we have not yet had. Many of us as children grew up with bedtime stories that were magical fairy tales, or tall tales built on both our fantasies and fears. And while we might have been both delighted and terrified, stories were always meant to be meaningful, teaching morals and values, how to take care of ourselves, the ways we should treat other people, and about the way things worked in the world.

The best stories are easy to remember because they paint pictures in our minds that tap into our deep feelings. Because they often create emotional responses and evoke strong visualizations, they play into our long history of communicating through pictures. In many ways, stories are the framework by which we remember things.

We have, over time, come to better understand our lives not by carefully laying out a sequence of logical propositions, but by associating emotion with events and crafting explanations around not only *how* things happened, but *why* they happened as well.

We humans are naturally curious beings and while it has always been part of our makeup to try to understand *how* things happen – to make sure we repeat successful behaviors to ensure positive outcomes – we have also looked to understand *why* things happen. Through reflection and analysis we can put past events in context and make meaning of the ways they unfolded as well as prepare us for future events.

Stories have always served to propose explanations for those things that we could not understand. From the weather and change of seasons, to the cycles of life and death. In the absence of scientific explanations for why things occurred as they did, we crafted stories as explanations and created rituals to attempt to bring order and even a measure of control in an otherwise unpredictable and chaotic world.

More than simply a way to offer up a quick fix to explain the unexplainable, stories could also highlight the unexpected and provide information about the resourceful ways people have overcome adversity and solved problems. Stories are told because through them we share with others the wisdom we have gained through our trials and tribulations.

The Hero Shopper

All great retailers are also great storytellers. They understand their brand identities and they present them to the customers in ways that are understandable as discrete narratives. In the retail world, brand stories are told overtly through sales associate and customer interactions as well as through advertising, marketing, in-store communications, visual merchandising, architecture and through the very nature of the products they sell.

Themes to the stories we share may take on various forms. The characters involved in the plots and locations in which the stories unfold may change, but the core components of all stories are not dramatically different than those shared between us for years.

In our digitally driven world, the way people are communicating is dramatically changing. In response, retailers will have to find a way to stay connected to their customers in a way that's engaging and relevant in an environment that has shoppers immersed in an overwhelming digital information flow.

To illustrate the power of storytelling and the way it's likely to change in the future, we need to take a look at some of the basic ideas at the core of storytelling in cultures. These core components to storytelling shape the message conveyed to the customer and find their way into retail stores and now into the extended customer journey by way of handheld and other digital devices. While the core components of good storytelling may be the same, the way they are being told across various platforms is rapidly changing.

Joseph Campbell's seminal book *The Hero with a Thousand Faces* argued that all myths, across cultures and time, have contained the same basic elements and follow the same basic plot. According to Campbell, there are never any new stories; we simply recycle a universal storyline.

"Furthermore, we have not even to risk the adventure alone; for the heroes of all time have gone before us, the labyrinth is fully known; we have only to follow the thread of the hero-path. And where we had thought to find an abomination, we shall find a god; where we had thought to slay another, we shall slay ourselves; where we had thought to travel outward, we shall come to the center of our own existence; where we had thought to be alone, we shall be with all the world."[14]

Campbell believed that all stories were a recycling of a "Monomyth," a single storyline that can be broken down into three components:

"*Departure*"– in which the Hero takes up a call to action and ventures out on a quest away from the everyday world he [or she] knows, into a place of "supernatural wonder,"

"*Initiation*" – in which he faces challenges along the path that he overcomes and in doing so is changed and,

"*Return*" – in which the Hero, being essentially transformed through his trials, comes back home from his mysterious adventure with new knowledge and powers that he has acquired, which he bestows on his fellow man.

For Campbell, the archetypal story begins with an individual "from whom something has been taken, or who *feels there is something lacking* in the normal experience available or permitted to the members of society. The person then takes off on a series of *adventures beyond the ordinary*, either to recover what has been lost or *to discover some life-giving elixir*. It's usually a cycle, a coming and a returning."

If we consider retail storytelling through the lens of Campbell's "monomyth," we see that all shopping experiences have at their core the idea that customers go on an adventure and come back somehow changed. Not because of the things that they bought, but because of the brand narrative that they bought *into*.

Retail stories, regardless of the medium that they are conveyed through, all have the same basic principles of Campbell's "monomyth." Whether the brand story is told through a lifestyle graphic or visual merchandising display in the store, or a social media network, the story of a brand always references the key set of ideals that customers, through buying products and services, adopt into their own personal life stories.

Let's take a look at how each of these component pieces fit into the process of retail storytelling.

Departure – Something Missing

If you begin to see the story of the Hero in each of us on a shopping trip to the mall or the corner store, it is not a surprise that the "Departure' phase is initiated with customers feeling that "*there is something lacking*" in their lives. Of course this can simply be that they have run out of milk, bread or eggs, but there is nothing particularly mythic about racing out to buy some commodity. Most of us would agree that shopping for our basic needs is not an adventure or based on aspirational feelings, nor do they need to be. Nevertheless, even retailers who are in the business of selling everyday basics need to create stories that extend beyond the things they sell and focus on things they believe in (convenience, service, low prices, etc.).

As an example, a lot of grocery stores sell organic produce. I prefer to shop at Whole Foods Market because organic products are not just part of their assortment, but because they are part of their entire mindset with regard to the way they believe people should live. Many of my local grocery stores have bell peppers but I choose to go to Whole Foods, even though they likely cost a bit more, because their brand story is based on a message about healthy living. By shopping there I inherit a little part of the Whole Foods mindset and I feel better about my choices.

Not to undermine the profound sociocultural significance of stories/myths that are the foundations for coming-of-age initiation rites that Campbell would have described, shopping too has aspects of initiation into social groups, or can also serve as a coming-of-age ritual. As each of my sons was approaching teenage years, going to the store and buying a Swiss Army knife was not just about supporting our fun in the forest on the weekend to whittle sticks and make bows and arrows, but also a recognition of their self-mastery and their emerging maturity as young men.

Retailers also create a family of separate brands that are in sync with customers' various stages of life. This is important because as a customer grows through, and out of, using a particular brand in childhood they move into adopting something that is more appropriate for them as adults and contains the same basic brand ideologies in the story that the brand tells the customer. As we grow in age, economic and social status, the retailing world offers us an extraordinary choice of goods and services that reinforce our coming-of-age.

Sometimes the products we buy serve as signposts along the path in the telling of our life story. We occasionally hold onto the things we bought far beyond when they have outlived their usefulness because they are meaningful to us as part of our story. We also buy things whose use might have equally been served by something less expensive but that give us something ultimately more emotionally valuable. This is certainly true of the luxury goods category where products go far beyond simple utility, becoming sacred objects in their own right.

The stories brands tell about what their products will do, not just in the utilitarian sense, but the spiritual sense as well, are part of the brand mythology. 'Buy this purse, these shoes, this laundry soap, this car, this lipstick, this book,' and it will change your life. Not just because it will organize the tangle of junk that sits in the bottom of your purse, get your clothes whiter, move you faster, make you look more luscious or be a better manager/parent/teacher/artist/whatever, but it will elevate you to a different social/spiritual plane.

Often, how customers learn these messages is a result of how effectively the brand conveys the core themes in their story. Perception is everything when you go beyond the utilitarian functions of the things we buy. In a world of overwhelming abundance, we look for more than whether the thing does its 'job.' We want its design to also be beautiful and for it to have some sort of magical power that renders us more significant by our simple association to it.

When we move into the esoteric qualities that brands impart upon us as the owners of their goods or customers in their stores, we see how the story attached to products and shopping places adds a considerable, while nevertheless intangible, quality of transcendence.

Do you really need to buy a white t-shirt for $200? No, but you feel marvelous in it not just because the thread count is greater than the $10 one (often it isn't) but because a celebrity was seen wearing it and well, just look at their mythic stature. By having an association to the brand story, we are transformed (in Campbell's words) beyond the "*normal experience available or permitted to the members of society .*"

We want to believe that these products and places will give us that little something extra even if only for 15 minutes as Andy Warhol was famous for saying. The degree to which a brand story is credible is a key indicator if 'shoppers' become 'customers.' This is why brands so often associate themselves with celebrities or have customer testimonials (stories) espousing the benefits of products.

Spokespeople, whether celebrity or Regular Joe, have been to the volcano. These individuals have lived through the Hero's journey and we perceive them to be proof of the product's advertised attributes. Their lives have been 'changed' and in describing their ascension, they give others hope that they too will have the same experience. Stories that espouse the transformative power of a brand or product told by those who have 'been there, done that' add credibility and open the door to believing that the customer journey will be worth it.

Initiation – Adventures in Shopping

In the sea of sameness among retail stores, the great shopping places are those that deliver "*adventures beyond the ordinary.*" Campbell's choice of words to describe the "Initiation" phase of the Hero's journey as "adventure" is very much the way retailers need to craft store experiences for their customers.

In the Initiation phase, the Hero is confronted with things out of the ordinary that challenge and teach but also can be thought of as to 'delight.' We can think of this middle part of the journey as the shopping trip itself. It starts with leaving home ("Departure") and continues with venturing to the market, main street or mall.

The idea of going on an "adventure" has a 'feel-good' quality. It reminds me of Bilbo Baggins, when running from Bag End to catch up to his company of Dwarves, answers an inquiry from a neighbor about where he was going by calling out, "I'm going on an adventure!" Having overcome his trepidation about the potential dark side of what he will encounter on his quest, he is filled with a sense an enthusiastic acceptance for discovery and a willingness to expose himself to new experiences with wide-eyed wonder.

This sounds like a customer heading out to the mall. At least, this is what I hope for customers to feel as they get up from the couch or from in front of their computer, to leave the comfort of their homes and embark on their own shopping journeys.

But, it's often not the case for a whole subset of the shopping population – men. For many men the very idea of shopping is like crawling directly into the dragon's den. Retailers often do better at crafting stories for children, who arguably have no direct buying power, than for men for whom these days share at least half of the responsibility of generating the family's disposable income.

I have often wondered how it is that retailers, in general, have not yet devised a way to craft great shopping 'adventures' for men. This is especially curious when it was men who traditionally left the home to be full-bodied participants in rites of initiation into manhood. The coming of age was generally put upon them as they were taken from their mother's arms to go into the wilds, deep into the caves or to the mountaintop. They went out boys and came back 'men' with a psychic shift that they were now different.

When it comes to the subject of 'going shopping,' the scales of engagement are so decidedly tipped in the female direction that the euphemistic industry title for 'shopper/customer' is "she."

"He" is to be viewed as a reluctant packhorse burdened with lugging supplies throughout the trip. Strangely enough, even when we talk about Men's Wear, there is the assumption that the shopper is still… 'she.'

Where are all the men? Do they even go shopping? Apparently they do, but if you talk to them they will say that they do it with little enthusiasm. There is an enormous opportunity here; one that is more than a big ol' chair, video screen playing the game and a place to crash land when 'she' is having all the fun.

Somehow we have convinced ourselves that the man, and a place for him to sit in the store, is a necessary evil. As far as being a shopper goes, retailers have somehow come to believe that men are really basic. If men aren't enthusiastic about going shopping, perhaps it has more to do with the fact that there simply aren't more brands that tell great stories of adventure crafted specifically to the sensibilities of men.

Jean Paul Sartre was quoted as saying: *"for an occurrence to become an adventure, it is necessary and sufficient for one to recount it."* Perhaps when men have more stories they can tell about their great shopping trips, the perception of shopping as simply being a thing to get done versus an adventure to live will change. Being remarkable – having something to talk about from a shopping trip – is a key feature of successful brands.

Retailers at times seem to be incredibly adept at creating places that make it really tough for customers to have pleasant adventures. There is a fine line between store planning and merchandising that promotes a sense of discovery and confusing the customer and making it difficult for them to know where to go.

Customers don't take kindly to things that get in the way of their having a good time while shopping. It is, after all, supposed to be fun. While Campbell's Hero may not have had fun per se, the adventure and Initiation were not all doom and gloom either. When we think about creating positive shopping experiences, it is best when retailers write stories as 'adventures' in ways that are not arduous, full of difficulty and challenges for their customers. Adventure in shopping needs to be thought of as full of intrigue and novelty, fascination and delight.

Return – Bringin' Back the Goods

Think of the great movies you have seen where the protagonist 'returns.' You know the ones, those powerful stories where everyone thought him (or her) to have certainly perished in his quest, and then he arrives home to the astonishment of the others, battered but better.

The whole idea behind going on the Hero's journey is that it matters. There has got to be some sort of gold at the end of the rainbow, otherwise why do it? The quest has a motivation behind it about getting something, but the objective isn't always to bring back something tangible. In fact, many times it is the intangible fruits of our labor that are more significant. In the case of the Hero's journey, the wisdom gained through the ordeal is transformative and everlasting.

In committing to the shopping journey we do in fact get the objects we need and desire. But, as we have seen earlier, it is often the sense of belonging to a group, through which we learn about ourselves, that is the more meaningful part of the shopping experience. A sense of belonging and understanding ourselves in context of a greater whole, matters.

And so, people go to great lengths to participate in being customers of one retailer or brand. To them, buying one brand over another, matters.

The spoils of the journey are not strictly for the Hero. The typical script reads that in his (or her) overcoming the challenges of the Initiation phase, he is generous with what he has learned, recovered, or found. In their quest "...to recover what has been lost or to discover some life-giving elixir," shoppers share knowledge of their own Hero's journeys with others.

While it may be a bit dramatic to attribute "life-giving" qualities to those things that Hero Shoppers discover on their trips, the re-telling of their stories does have the ability to keep the brand story 'alive.'

There are stories about how a product literally saved someone's life, but it is most often the intangible effects of association to a product or brand that are more widely felt. We attribute successes in various aspects of our lives – for example, 'dress for success' – to the positive benefits of using one product or brand over another. By continuing to use them, we reinforce the stories we tell until they are part of who we are.

The Hero's journey is meant to be transformative. And so it should be with shopping experiences. When people buy products or services and eat them, wear them, drive them, or otherwise use them, they are continuing to re-tell the brand's stories to themselves and continue on the journey that results in the making of a mindset.

Eating a delicious meal made with organic produce does in fact have life-sustaining value, but it is also how we 'feel' about putting things into our bodies that are good for us that has a lasting effect. Wearing that beautiful dress can make you 'feel' great and driving that car can make you 'feel' invincible.

How you feel is projected into your environment and all the while your attitude affects others. In this sense, what we acquire on our shopping adventures rubs off on others. People talk, both in person and online, sharing stories about their shopping experiences. Family members, friends, colleagues, other shoppers and even casual acquaintances vicariously live the effects of our journey simply by association to us.

Stories and Mental Models

As we listen to, or read stories, we are far from passive.

To understand and remember stories, people do not just read (or hear) the words; they integrate their knowledge of the world with the information in the text. Our understanding of what is written or spoken in stories is augmented by a vast array of real world experiences and body memories.

When reading or hearing a story that describes a game of pitch and catch between father and son, we summon up information about what it is like to throw, and catch a ball, as well as the smell of the leather glove, the sound of the smack of the ball in the mitt, the feeling of the ball's stitching running across the finger tips – even if done only once before.

From an early age I read and told stories to my two boys. We created tales of fictional characters Wally the Weasel and his magic easel, and "Neuscinneum Fairy" whose specially brewed elixir made of Honey Suckle nectar enchanted a far off valley. Each night the narrative described another chapter in their lives and each night I drew on personal experience to craft another adventure. I relied on camping trips with my parents, skiing in the Laurentian Mountains north of Montreal, years standing at an easel painting – and I created imaginary lands by reassembling experiences from my past.

As we read, or listen to stories, we develop elaborate mental representations of the situations described in the text. According to Nicole Speer and her colleagues, these "…situation models arise through the integration of a reader's knowledge of the world with information explicitly presented in text."[15] In Speer's study, the researchers established evidence through fMRI scans of individuals reading various narratives, that "the neural responses to particular types of changes in the stories occurred in the vicinity of regions that increase in activity when viewing similar changes or when carrying out similar activities in the real world."

In other words, as subjects read about changes in the situations of characters in a story, their brains reacted in a manner that was similar to them personally experiencing them. So, for example, "when readers process changes in a character's interactions with an object, pre-central and parietal areas (of the brain) associated with grasping hand movements increased in activation."

These mental situation models that we create can be complex and incorporate "multiple dimensions of the situation…including the characters and objects present, the spatial and temporal layout of the narrated situation, and the characters' goals and intentions."[16]

While the elaborate descriptions of specific situations may add more nuanced layers to the understanding of something we read, they are not necessary for us to get the point. Recent theories about how we understand what we read suggest that these situation models are based "on the activity of brain regions involved in analogous perceptions and actions in the real world." If we read about throwing and catching a ball with Dad, our brain areas that were active when actually doing it, are active when we are simply reading the text. Our body's memories fill in the details and help us understand the meaning of what we read, or what we hear if the story is read aloud.

It is a wonder in its own right that our brain has the ability to paint pictures in our head and spatially locate us in the environment of the text. Being able to see mental pictures is powerful. It is one thing to say that when we read something we create mental images in our mind's eye. However, it is very different to say that when we read something, our brains are activated as if we are actually enacting what is being described by the words.

When customers experience shopping places, it's important to understand that what they see, hear and read is always triggering memories that they have of previous experiences in their lives. It is difficult to say how every customer will react to the presentation of the brand story. Who knows what present day experiences will trigger memories from their past? These memories and their associated feelings profoundly influence how a customer interacts in a shopping place.

Single Words

When talking about the idea of brand narratives and storytelling, I don't mean to imply that there are long narratives that customers need to read or be exposed to. In many cases a simple message, even a single word, can tell a story and activate certain feelings within a customer. We are all very good at reading visual messages and inferring from them intent or understanding implied meanings from images that we see. Over the course of our human evolution we have become very good at 'reading' the subtext of both written messages and things we see in our environment.

When it comes to stores, we are very good at inferring that a retailer may be out of stock by seeing low numbers of units on the shelf. Customers may understand that the store doesn't have their size, color, or style and choose to go elsewhere to shop instead. These are conclusions that customers come to on their own. They are narratives that they run in their heads, not from seeing text-based messages, but visual images that tell a story nonetheless.

Equally, shoppers also conclude that the price of a sweater is much more expensive when they see three on the table versus 300.

It is interesting to note that both text-based and visual stories seem have the ability to trigger body memories in customers that bring up feelings of previous experiences that they may have had. There are studies that provide some support for the idea that the way we understand even *single* words is grounded in our visual and motor representations of them.

Studies by Brian Pulvermüller have demonstrated that brain regions involved in reading action words (verbs) are some of the same regions involved in performing analogous actions in the real world.[17] So, if you read the word "throw" or "catch," brain regions light up in fMRI scans that are activated when moving one's arm or hands.

While this might lead us to think that presenting customers with text based signage that simply says "shop" or "buy" would lead them to load their shopping carts and open their wallets, it's not quite as straightforward as that. It might on the other hand simply activate a flood of memories – good or bad – about what they associate with the idea of 'shopping' and/or 'buying.'

We certainly know the power of the sign that says "sale," "discount," or "50%." Those single word signs (while not verbs) have time and time again caused action, sometimes as simple as an unexpected add-on purchase and other times a stampede through the front doors on Black Friday.

The challenge to using simple action words to try to initiate buying behavior is that we need to be able to understand, on a customer-by-customer basis, the associative memories, the individual experiences encoded into the situation models, for each shopper. This is of course rather difficult, if not impossible, when the flow of customers into shopping places may number in the millions.

A key take-away of the research that shows that our brains react to single action words as if we are doing it in the real world, is that it suggests that brand stories need not be long and elaborate. Concise stories might be more efficient in evoking positive experiences in shopping places than long and elaborate tales. When you consider that we are increasingly in a time-pressed world, where we are in a continuous state of partial attention, brand messages that are simple and emotional might prove to be more effective. Of course this has a direct influence not only on in-store signage, graphics and way finding but also in the presentation of merchandise stories that need to be simple, straightforward and clear.

Some Millennial shoppers, for whom communication is reduced to emoticons and messages that are 140 characters or less, call into question how profound stories about the meaning of the brand should be conveyed. Shaggy dog stories are likely to be less effective upon those who are primed for impatience through the immediacy of the Internet. Communicating with a generation that has created an emotional shorthand of smiley faces and text-based acronyms that are more like hieroglyphics than real words, will be a challenge for brand storytellers in the future.

Idiosyncrasies of the Millennial shopper aside, retailers might rely on the law of averages and assume that for a majority of customers, very short phrases, or even single words, will trigger 'good' memories and therefore positive action leading to a purchase. Simple messages are not always better, but one would think that when you have only a few seconds to capture attention and convey a salient message, you'd better get to the heart of the matter with an emotional punch line and do it quickly.

Whether short and sweet or longer and more nuanced, the telling of brand stories must have as one of its core features, a narrative whose plot is about the creation of positive and emotionally satisfying shopping experiences.

Simulations – As if

People's brains create mental simulations of what they read not just because they situate one's self in past events so that we can draw on the body memory of our previous experiences, but also because creating simulations allows us to try to anticipate what might happen in the future.

According to Buckner et al, as people read stories, they are able to both construct simulations of situations of previous experiences as well as imagine potential future ones. [18]

When it comes to customers building simulations of future shopping events, the best predictor of future success is a history of positive shopping trips. Customers will come to rely on their memory of experiences with the brand, both in and out of the store, and use them to anticipate the nature of their next trip. Building a culture of storytelling that provides customers with great moments of connection – where retailers meet customer needs for relationship and that gives them a clear understanding of what the brand is about – is a set up for future success.

While creating a mental simulation is not as profound as actually participating in the shopping experience, you might say it is the next best thing. Given that customers are *out* of the store more than they are *in*, it stands to reason that they tend to rely on mental and body memories more than being told the brand story through the in-store experience. When customers use mental simulations of shopping experiences, they are using stories they build in their mind's eye to anticipate future outcomes. When they can tell themselves a story of how a shopping experience may unfold, they are effectively managing their emotions. Knowing what is coming helps them to prepare themselves with appropriate responses.

There is no doubt, customers tell themselves stories about the brands they shop and establish sets of expectations about what future shopping trips should entail. When the characters and/or environments in brand stories change, customers take note because they have written themselves into the plot and *their* story lines have also changed. They will cross reference against old scripts to try to make sense of a twist in the plot and determine the best outcome for themselves in the new narrative.

As we will see in later chapters we are particularly good at recognizing patterns in everything around us. So when it comes to telling stories in shopping places, retailers would do well to reinforce patterns of stories by telling them consistently store-to-store, shopper-to-shopper, season-to-season.

Emotional Stories

Retailers need to establish a way of telling their brand story in such a way as to give people the best emotional connection to the plot. Setting a positive mindset predisposes the customer to want to engage while in the store and enhances the likelihood of making a purchase.

Stories have to be believable to get customers to go along on the journey. Being believable means that the elements of the plot need to be crafted in such a way as to be consistent with what customers expect of the brand.

As three-dimensional representations of the brand, shopping environments need to 'say what they do' and 'do what they say.' Parts of the story line that seem out of place will attract immediate attention and call into question the authenticity of the brand as storytellers. This is particularly true for an emerging generation of younger shoppers that is exposed to a wealth of information about a brand through their mobile devices. Millennials are perhaps more informed than any shopping generation before them. They are savvy and more aware than ever before about the influence of marketing and the selling of products. Transparency and authenticity are key drivers to the relationships that will emerge in the future as these young customers come to rely on social media networks and their friends to let them know which companies are staying true to the brand ideologies and living the stories that they promote through their advertising and marketing campaigns.

If brands or retailers are found to be behaving in ways that are counter to their projected corporate cultures, the relationships with their customers can begin to unravel. Lack of trust is likely to engender a sense of skepticism about whether or not customers are being told a tall tale or a simple straightforward message about brand ideals. In the end, retailers don't want to have their customers doubting the truth about their messages.

Adding emotion to the story line doesn't just tug on the heartstrings; it actually activates areas of the brain that are involved in certain feelings and makes customers want to be a part of the narrative. At its best, great brand storytelling gets customers to care about the 'cause' and want to engage in supporting it.

Retailers go to great lengths to create stories that reference everything they believe in. The goal of great retail storytelling is to get customers to commit to a call to action and do something, mainly to buy what the retailer is selling. More than this though, the story needs to provide incentives to carry the action beyond the store experience into the world where customers become storytellers themselves. Brand stories need to promote a willingness to act on behalf of the brand, to play a role in propagation of the brand myths. Avid and active customers can be a retailer's or brand's best marketers.

When customers make the story of the brand part of their lives, they become co-authors in the brand narrative. In personalizing the experience customers become part of the brand, actors in the play, each one playing roles that align with their own lives while following a plot established by the brand.

In the last part of the book we will look at how the Internet, social media platforms and creative applications are allowing customers to make stories every day. The nature of storytelling is changing but the core messages are the same as they have been for a long time; customers like the empowerment that comes from the creation of a story that matters to them. When they participate in its making, it is unique to them, displaying their personality and how they fit into the brand narrative.[19]

Over time we have become used to stories and have developed a sort of internal reference system for narratives that help us understand the world. "Humans are not ideally set up to understand logic; they're ideally set up to understand stories," says Roger C. Schank a cognitive scientist.[20] This very right-brained activity is about creating context, putting things in relationship to other things and drawing connections between them to infer causality. Rather than just being swept in a sea of change, customers and their mobile devices are interacting in a digitally driven world to make change happen at a pace like never before. The coming revolution in retail place-making will be deeply bound to a sense of ownership by customers who engage in making places on their own terms.

This may sound like retail anarchy, but brands will continue to move into a place where curating storylines is a large part of what they do. Shopping places will be more of a framework for interaction with the brand where customers can input content that may augment both the interactions they have *and* the physical environment.

I will not forget the stories my father told about his childhood and peeling concord grapes he had bought at the market while he walked home, or my mother's tales about growing up the only girl in a family of 11, or *Charlie and the Chocolate Factory* as read by my 6th grade teacher, Mrs. Gilmore.

The power of a well-told story can last for years. It can shape the way we think about individuals or companies. Stories can foster fears and prejudices, make meaning out of madness and fill our creative souls with imagination fuel to last a lifetime of flights of fancy.

The power of story was cemented in me in the late '90s, many years after seeing the first of the modern summer box office blockbusters in 1975. Since seeing *Jaws* – the classic Steven Spielberg film based on the Peter Benchley novel by the same name, about a great white shark that terrorized a New England resort town – I never have seen the open water the same way.

I became a great water skier because I never wanted to fall and I was sure that even in freshwater lakes, that down below my toes, there was something lurking that would certainly want to eat me for lunch. But that was 1975, and you might think that, as an adult, I would've overcome the trauma of seeing so many people swallowed up by Spielberg's mechanical great white, affectionately dubbed Bruce by the film crew.

You would think. But that's not the way it has turned out.

More than 25 years after seeing the film, my colleagues, George and Joe and I had finished a week of work with a Thai department store in Bangkok. Getting up early and staying late at the store, the days were long, and by the end of the week we were tired. Our clients, a successful Thai family who had grown a family business into one of the largest department store chains in in Southeast Asia, also happened to own a hotel in Ko Samui and offered a weekend stay to recharge.

Flying into the 'airport,' which was nothing more than a long patch of grass nestled in the cleft between mountains, was exhilarating. With our bags gathered, we passed under the grass-thatched roof that served as the open air terminal. We then were packed into taxis and on our way to the hotel.

The dusty road split open a path through the dense jungle forest. After a gated entry we came upon an oasis amidst bamboo thickets and the sounds of animals that had owned this spot of green long before Westerners thought it quaint as a getaway.

The first day was dedicated to detox; the second would be one of adventure.

My gregarious Brazilian colleague George, a great visual merchandising consultant who loves exploring, eating great food and, for whom life is simply to be enjoyed by being well lived, had the idea to defy gravity. First activity of day two? Parasailing.

It was only fitting then that he was the first to strap into the harness. The idea was that the boat driver would gun the engine, George would run down the beach towards the water and the parachute would lift him into the air. George was confident that this would be fun and seeing the turquoise bay from 200 feet above the water would be a thrill to remember.

George was also a few pounds heavier than me. Well okay, maybe slightly more than a few.

The boat shot forward. George ran. And ran, and ran until he was hurdling through the water.

One step, two steps, three steps and no lift off.

Things were not going as planned.

Unable to get airborne, the harness jerked him forward as the four Thai boys on the boat waved with broad smiles and shouts of encouragement. The rope connecting George to the boat snapped taut and George was airborne – for a moment – before going face down into the water, arms spread out from his sides.

He wasn't moving. I was thinking the worst.

Running down to the water, we lifted George up and thankfully he was fine. Banged up, he sat on the sand, gingerly turned to me and said, "your turn."

The boys strapped me in, and reconnecting the rope to the clip on the front of the vest, we were poised for round two. My turn, and I was none too excited about the whole thing. George was still sitting down, head lowered.

The boat engine roared and I took one step and then about a half of another – and I was aloft. Screaming all the while, I shot into the air and George receded into the background as a little dark spot on a big white beach.

A long loop into the bay followed and at the top of the curve, while returning to the shore, the boat began to slow. I was curious about this because as an architect, I know a little about the laws of projectile motion, gravity and a few other laws of physics that require the boat to keep moving to keep me up in the air. With the boat slowing even more and then coming to a full stop, I started my descent.

Into the middle of the Thai ocean I was falling and the only thing I could think of was the shark music from Jaws. Scanning for shadows in the water I was cursing Steven Spielberg until splash down, my red parachute trailing me.

Slightly tangled in the lines, I was lifting my feet while pulling myself as close as I could to the boat, but it had run out of gas! I had to get out of the water while trying to equally not signal every shark in the ocean that it was lunchtime.

One of the boat boys told me they had to get back to shore and get a refill for the gas tank, and for me to just stay put while another guy on a jet ski went back for it.

Yeah, right. Just stay in the water. He had no idea what he was asking me to do...

The gas was refilled and I wasn't eaten, but the power of story was made clearer to me at that moment than it had ever been before. Close to *thirty years* after seeing the movie, my fears of being lunch for a great white shark were very much alive.

Telling Stories In-Store

When I started in the retail design business, a serendipitous sequence of events lead me to Singapore where I took a position as the Director of the Visual Merchandising program of LaSalle International Fashion School. After a year abroad, I moved to New York to continue in a career that seemingly found me rather than my ever having made a plan to be in the retail world.

Working four years with Joe Weishar at New Vision Studios, I was the resident architect in a small group of visual merchandising specialists. While we designed retail stores, a large part of the business involved training retailers in effective visual merchandising practices. Travelling from Istanbul to Bangkok, we took apart (and put back together) both specialty and department stores to teach our clients how better to tell stories with product.

Joe believed that once people understood the reasons 'why' we were visually attracted to a certain display or turned to the right upon entering a space, the 'how' of creating effective selling spaces would be brought to the store level by the creativity of the sales associates, visual team, and the department and general store managers – those who were on the floor every day.

In teaching the 'why' of effective merchandising and display we believed that the 'how' would change from place-to-place, retailer-to-retailer or category-to-category. We brought the message of why customers behaved the way they did by teaching retailers about foundations in art and design as well as psychology and neuroscience while wearing the hat of a merchant. Joe was fond of characterizing us as "merchant designers" and I still use the term today. New Vision Studios started with storytelling at the product level. The product was the protagonist. The store and fixtures were the stage, set for the unfolding of retail narrative.

When we talk about storytelling in three-dimensional spaces, the narrative is done at the product, graphics, signage and architectural levels. The power of great visual merchandising and display is that product presentation can tell extraordinary stories to customers, often with very little capital expense. The product has been bought and allocated throughout the sometimes-vast store footprint and it should be used as one of the key features to the projection of what the brand stands for. Messages can be conveyed about price point, a brand's level of exclusivity, the depth of the assortment and whether the retailers will have a particular style, simply through a relationship of product density to the overall space. This type of storytelling has nothing to do with architecture and design and everything to do with the product being the star of the show.

While merchandise has been the leading lady of the storyline for some time, a new world of digitally based Internet shopping is changing the relative importance of products over providing a performance space for the brand. With products now being available any place any time through a customer's mobile device, retailers will continue to face increasing challenges with telling visual stories with products in stores. This is not to say that the importance of merchandise in the store will be eclipsed by digital customer experiences, but rather when you are likely to have less of it in the store, because you can shift assortment depth to an online distribution channels, what you do have hanging on racks or sitting on shelves becomes increasingly important. How you display a significantly curated assortment needs to be done in a compelling and engaging way that adds to the drama and theater of the store experience.

Looking back at visual merchandising's coming of age, creative types generally had a few resources to spend and, often, a location in the basement of the store. They frankly didn't get the respect they were due as creative visionaries, priming the motivation to buy through 3D storytelling. Retail executives relied on the numbers and profitability was demonstrated through areas of the business such as operations, logistics, technology and sourcing rather than the emotions, storytelling and art of product presentation. It was, after all, more difficult to quantify the ROI of visual merchandising and a display than the cost of a light bulb or how much it would cost to ship goods across the country.

In more recent years, visual merchandisers have become integrated into the storytelling framework of brands and are now indispensible parts of the management team. Virtually every major brand has a senior position for the visual merchandiser. Much more than simply being 'window trimmers' who add the icing to the cake, visual merchandisers are the key storytellers in stores.

Colleges now offer Bachelors degrees in visual merchandising. While having a college degree is not a prerequisite to landing a job as a visual merchandiser, the fact that accredited colleges are providing three-year degrees in the field highlights the point that visual merchandising has come of age as a serious business and as a *bona fide* career path.

Visual merchandising also has a number of professional associations such as The Planning and Visual Education Partnership (PAVE) whose core mission is "*To support students studying in the field of retail design and planning and visual merchandising through its annual design competitions for college students. PAVE also seeks to encourage* retail management, store planners, visual merchandisers, architects and manufacturers to interact with and support design students." Through PAVE's efforts, thousands of dollars are raised and distributed to both students and schools to ensure that the education of students with a focus on the retail world continues.

Visual merchandising need not talk about price *per se*, though signage and graphics that depict how much things cost are certainly part of the visual palette. The role of visual merchandising is to talk about passion, emotion, dreams, and desires. These are all right-brain intangibles that nevertheless add substantially to a retailer's bottom line. They motivate shoppers to become long-term customers by catering to their desire for three-dimensional pictures that organize and clarify, demonstrate and educate, and help guide them along the narrative.

Great visual merchants are consummate storytellers. Whether it is simply to attract attention and excite, point the way to a new arrival, or use humor to convey a message or lifestyle attitude, the visual merchant punctuates space with 3D exclamation marks.

Visual Stories as a Strategy

Having the product, price and place equation figured out no longer assures success in retail place making. Customers want a little romance. A strategy that proposes to capture the attention of today's fickle customer with 'everyday low prices' is not going to continue to be a winning game plan when prices are being driven down by online retailers and 'fast fashion' companies, who speed product to market with new trends in two weeks or less. Not long ago, online purchases required a few days' wait for the merchandise to be delivered to your home. Now, online retailers are delivering next day (even same day or within the hour) and are setting up distribution centers in increasing numbers to satisfy a growing digitally enabled marketplace.

Still, shopping online lacks most of the visual merchandising finesse, which in stores, adds much-needed romance to retailing. If you are buying a gift for someone special, the in-person experience of the details makes it memorable. There is still no substitute for seeing, touching or smelling the gift, and the certainty afforded by carrying the wrapped gift out of the store – as well as what's said while doing so – that makes memorable moments. Visual merchandisers are the curators of desire and bring the skill of three-dimensional storytelling to retail place making.

As the 'silent seller,' visual merchandising is the Marcel Marceau of the sales floor. Continually changing to accommodate new arrivals, seasonal promotions, sales, and simply to reinvigorate or animate the sales floor, visual merchandising needs to be incredibly agile as it supports telling the brand story without ever actually saying a word. Better at conveying messages than even the single action words discussed earlier in the chapter, great visual stories convey a wealth of both functional and emotional information to the customer.

It is important to remember that visual merchandising *includes* 'display' but is much more than that. The relationship of product to the space, its arrangement on store fixtures and walls, and how the customer 'reads' the assortment, as well as the integration of environmental graphics, digital signage and lighting, are all under the purview of the visual merchandising team. When all of these elements are considered in relationship to the architecture of the space and coordinated in their execution to deliver a consistent image of the brand, the visual merchant leads the customer through the space both visually and physically unfolding chapters, acts, verses and choruses.

Some stores are designed to be like theme parks, literal translations of stories into built environments. Disney and Warner Brothers Studio Stores in the late '90s ushered in an era of themed entertainment stores based on the stories of their superheroes and cartoon characters. Restaurant chains such as Rain Forest Café and the Hard Rock Café were leaders in the themed food-service category.

There is nothing subtle about sitting in the rainforest eating with elephants, monkeys and simulated rainstorms, or being in a stage set by Disney, or having Superman pushing the elevator up through the space as in the former Warner Brothers store on 5th Avenue in New York. All of these were well-executed and entertaining environments. The brand story was made real and the success of the shopping trip was dependent on the overt theatrical nature of the place.

Urban Brands – Anthropologie, Urban Outfitters and Free People – embraces the power of creative visual merchandising. This retailer empowers the visual team to be instrumental in creating the store interiors. Rather than just following a planogram from the corporate office and placing product in predetermined locations, they are actively involved in the store build-out. Often these environments are rich in texture, visual interest and extraordinarily inventive in their use of found objects.

Neiman Marcus has one of the best art collections in the world and their visual strategy puts it front row and center for their customers to enjoy. Sculptures and paintings are spread throughout the store, adding visual delight and an air of sophistication to the upscale specialty store chain. Neiman Marcus' enclave for the more contemporary set, CUSP, retains the sophisticated slant with environments that are both fashion-forward boutique and contemporary art happening. Art objects may not directly lead to sales but they contribute to the story. They have a history and an authenticity that customers gravitate to more and more.

The late Gene Moore started an artistic tradition over fifty years ago at Tiffany & Co., telling fantastic stories with beauty and wit in store windows that were no more than twenty inches across. He made products that could sit on your fingertip, bigger than life.

Linda Fargo's windows at Bergdorf Goodman were like great novels with complex plots and rich characters. Seeing them over and over again during the Christmas season was like picking up a book you loved and discovering new details you missed in previous readings.

Simon Doonan's cheeky irreverence and controversial wit stunned, amused and beguiled, pushing the envelope in the telling of stories, but nevertheless won him, and Barneys New York, worldwide acclaim as fashion mavens.

Stories vs. Data Dumps

Stories are not simply about conveying information between people. Sharing data and facts is not storytelling. A reliance on trying to infer the success of experiences only on spreadsheets and analytics is often void of truly understanding the emotional content of the customer experience.

Business leaders will not ignore the value of gathering data, nor should they. 'What the numbers say' gives us part of the picture, but often denies the subtlety of the emotional drivers behind the success or failure of an initiative. Unless we are talking about purely automated processes, there is a subtext underlying the spreadsheet that tells of the human experience on the retail sales floor or the website. Information sharing without emotion is a data dump. It is not a story.

We are able to capture the most minute details of customer's interactions in stores. Whether they are male or female and of what age, how they move, how long they dwell in front of a display, what they touch and where they go, are just small portions of data we can collect in real time as customers move through the front door and peruse the aisle ways.

Outside of stores, as customers interact with their mobile devices, tablets, touchscreens, home computers and other digital devices, data is continuously streaming across the Internet, being captured and archived. Augmenting what we know about customers' behaviors in stores, what we're now able to learn about customers' behaviors *out* of stores is increasingly important. Retailers believe that "Big Data" – the collection of details about customer's social networking activities, online buying behaviors, website visits, blog posts, etc. – is going to be a powerful tool to predict customers' needs, wants and desires, and to provide the right products at the right price in the right place.

All this data presumably helps retailers craft better experiences by personalizing the journey to match customer demographics and preferences. Collecting the data isn't difficult; we are getting amazingly adept at providing technology tools to retailers to 'learn' who is shopping their stores and how they can be better served. On the surface, this has the ability to be positive for both retailer and customer.

Interestingly though, we are beginning to rely more and more on parsing data streams to help us understand people. This reliance on left-brain processes that are linear, logical, sequential and numeric in nature is attractive to business, as it has been for some time. The tendency to look for crystal clear definitions, absolutes and specific answers is born out of our propensity to marginalize non-quantifiable emotions – the prevue of the right brain – in favor of things we can *rely* on. The numbers don't lie, but they don't tell the whole story either.

Corporate retailers who look at data to understand customers are disengaging from the face-to-face interactions with shoppers that shopkeepers traditionally experienced first hand in years past. When shoppers become data points, the emotional factor begins to disappear. The personal connection wanes and people are points on a graph. Understanding the whole story of a store is an integrative exercise that requires understanding facts and figures along with feelings and fantasies.

Play Time — Shopping and Having Fun

The forest at the end of my street has become one of the greatest play spaces for my sons and me. Nearly every weekend we make a short jaunt to the edge of imagination and jump in.

A hallmark of my relationship with my boys has always been play. This shared activity has been bonding, educational and a collective act of creativity. In our playing, we have learned how better to communicate with each other and with strangers through role-playing. Our countless hours of play over the years have helped us foster a sense of empathy by putting ourselves in the shoes of the fictional characters we created.

When my boys were younger, our family's play adventures took us to local parks, apple orchards and pumpkin patches, theme parks, outdoor plays, music festivals and children's museums. Museums with interactive opportunities were best and hours would slip by as we played. Two of our favorite places to visit, the Garden State Discovery Museum in Cherry Hill, New Jersey and the Please Touch Museum in Philadelphia, had shops. I don't mean gift shops, though they had those, too. I mean 'play-stores'… as exhibits.

In these pint-sized shopping places, the world is scaled down and children can play shopkeeper and customer, fill mini shopping carts, ring up sales at the cash register and pretend to bring home the week's groceries. That play-stores exist at all in children's museums is worth noting as an indication of how deeply rooted shopping is as part of our culture. So as children play in museums and learn about biology and building, the stars and the seas, dinosaurs and dump trucks, they also learn about how shopping works as a daily practice and as cultural social paradigm.

When creators of children's museums include shopping exhibits as part of the offering, it validates the idea that as a cultural construct, playing and shopping are intimately connected and are supposed to be both educational and fun. For many people, their childhood activities linked 'playing' and 'shopping.' Early in our lives we learned that shopping should be like play. When cultural institutions such as museums engage young visitors in exhibits about shopping, they teach them both how to shop and how shopping fits into larger social construct of things that are important in their lives.

There are qualities of the shopping experience that are almost directly synonymous with the nature of play. To better illustrate how play and shopping are closely linked, let's turn our attention to a brief explanation of how our culture evolved through play and how the basic tenets of play align with the shopping experience.

"Homo Ludens" – Man the Player

The Age of Enlightenment (1650-1800) had big thinkers usher in a cultural movement that espoused the power of reason over all else. The Enlightenment period found the Swedish botanist, physician and zoologist Carl Linnaeus crafting the modern approach to taxonomy. Entirely consistent with his time, and thinking of humans as superior to the rest of living things by way of our obvious ability to reason, Linnaeus bestowed the moniker "*Homo Sapiens*" – 'Man the Wise' – in his system of classifying organisms.

We are, of course, at the top of the evolutionary ladder due to our relatively huge prefrontal cortices and the ability to think far beyond other species. The title *Homo Sapiens* has stuck, despite the fact that we are more than simply 'wise.' We humans also have an extraordinary gift for creativity and making. We often pride ourselves on the things we do, looking to our accomplishments and the products of our industrious nature to validate and define us.

After the Age of Enlightenment philosophers continued to search for meaning in our human existence as well as trying to create definitions that would encapsulate all that we are. We are smart, or 'smarter' than other creatures, to be more exact, but we are so much more than that. Our intelligence gives us the capability to create and manipulate our environment. True, other animals also make things, but our ability to make things that make *other* things is something unique to humans.

The idea that we could also be defined as *Homo Faber* – 'Man the Maker' – was a philosophical concept articulated by Hannah Arendt and Max Scheler. Arendt and Scheler's concept of 'Man the Maker' refers to humans as controlling and manipulating their environment through the making of tools.

In his 1907 book (translated from French) *The Creative Evolution*, Henri Bergson sought to define intelligence, in its original sense, as the "faculty to create artificial objects, in particular tools to make tools, and to indefinitely, its makings." The term *Homo Faber* did not supplant *Homo Sapiens* as a label distinguishing us from the other beings on the evolutionary tree, but suggested that 'wisdom' or 'intelligence' was born out of our ability to make objects and put them to use in our lives.

It's not surprising that philosophers were engaging in discussions with a focus on our skills at 'making' because at the time, Europe, and eventually the United States, were deep in the throes of the Industrial Revolution (roughly 1760-1840). During this period of remarkable innovation, coal and steam power sources fueled growth at an unprecedented rate. Manufacturing experienced an overhaul from manual to machine labor. *Homo Faber*, Man the Maker, was in his element.

Since then, we have indeed accomplished astounding feats, but still, we are more than simply the things we make. What creates our culture is also 'made' of things that seemingly have no direct material 'product' but nevertheless seem critical to the development of society. That we humans also '*play*' is one of these.

One of the most influential books on the subject of play, *Homo Ludens* by Johan Huizinga, argued that play came *before* culture. For Huizinga, "The great archetypal activities of human society are permeated with play from the start...genuine, pure play is one of the bases of civilization."[21] For this reason we might consider '*Homo Ludens*' – 'Man the Player' – as an apt title among those that hope to explain our multifaceted nature.

Play is not so much a simple element *in* culture, another thing that we *do*, but more related to the development *of* culture.

Distinguishing between the view of play as an activity in culture versus the idea that culture grows from the stuff of play, is significant because it implies that play, while required to be fun, is also serious business. As Huizinga puts it, "play is older than culture, for culture, however inadequately defined, always presupposes human society, and animals have not waited for man to teach them their playing. We can safely assert, even, that human civilization has added no essential feature to the general idea of play. Animals play just like men."[22]

Play is primal.

All play means something.

As a socializing function, there is something in the activity of engaging in play that teaches us, grows empathy, provides context, explains, and creates meaning much the same way that the enactment of ritual does. Sound like our discussion on shopping? It should, because the non-materialistic outcomes of play are so much a part of who we are, that we might say that play is woven into the very core of our empathic beings.

Through playing, we become better connected to ourselves, others and a larger societal worldview. In the end, the expression: "It's not whether you win or lose, but *how* you play the game" has particular significance, because it's in the *playing* that we come to understand what it means to be in the game at all.

In our moments of play we can hold multiple realities in our minds. We can be either the Good Guy or the Bad Guy. Taking on these personas we are also able to keep in mind an awareness of the limits to which these roles can be enacted within the context of the game. In play we don't get so consumed with role enactment that our rationality, morals and ethics get thrown out the window. We can *be* someone else while we play, but we always know that it is a game and whom we revert to being when we are done. The overall objective, in the end, is to have had a joyful interaction. It's meant to be fun.

In his book *Affective Neuroscience*, Jaak Panskepp explains that, "the same brain circuitry that prompts play also stimulates joy and is found in all mammals."[23]

You might say that we are hardwired for joyful, empathic interactions with our fellow humans and that play is but one way we achieve the biological directive. In that sense – for shopping to be engaging and effective in delivering on the theme of being a principal form of social activity built on empathic connection – it must be fun.

Shopping and Play

Granted, it would be a bit of a stretch to assert that *every* time you go out to buy something, it should be a playful experience. Some commodity purchases just don't lend themselves to being playful, nor should they necessarily have to. In general, shopping experiences should be a pleasure, though that is not always the case. When you get beyond a refill on the milk and eggs, going to the store, mall or market should be a 'play date' whether you are eight or eighty.

When thinking about shopping and play, we are likely to imagine stores such as FAO Schwarz on Fifth Avenue where Tom Hanks danced across the floor-piano in the movie *Big*, or the Toys"R"Us in Times Square with its Ferris wheel and animatronic T-rex. While these two environments are indeed playful, not all shopping environments need to be an amusement park for customers to enjoy themselves. Understanding the basic tenets of play and its relationship to the development of culture, even brand culture, allows us to see how we can create playful moments of engagement throughout the shopping process and at multiple points along the customer path to purchase.

There are great examples of creative retailing that take even commodity purchases such as groceries into the area of play and fun. Tesco's "Home Plus QR Code Subway Store" introduces shopping fun into the subway system of Seoul, South Korea.[24] Life-size illuminated images of refrigerated cases and grocery store shelving allows shoppers to use their smartphones to scan QR codes and have their groceries delivered to home before they return from the daily commute.

In a busy metropolitan area where digitally enabled commuters have easy access to Wi-Fi systems and the Internet, this creative solution to providing shopping fun during the drudgery of a commute home is an excellent example of how retailers will engage customers in the future. We could argue that this solution works well for an inner-city condition and that in rural areas it would be less appropriate, but in our digitally interconnected future, there will no place in the world without access to the Internet.

We have already looked at the idea that shopping, at its baseline, is a profound social experience built on empathic connections fostered through rituals and storytelling. We now add play to the equation as one of the cornerstones of the profound sociocultural nature of shopping experiences.

Because play often requires the imaginative adoption of roles, it provides opportunities to 'put yourself in someone else's shoes.' Taking on someone else's perspective helps foster the capacity for empathic extension. Play is therefore fundamental to the development of empathy *and* has a direct tie-in to shopping. If the one of the goals of making great shopping places is to provide opportunities for people to build relationships, it stands to reason that making the customer engagement playful helps get us closer to the 'endgame.' As people play in retail stores they become connected. Engaging in the retailer's play space, customers come to see the world through each other's eyes and through the eyes of the brand as well, because when engaging in play, they necessarily take on roles within the context of the brand story.

Psychologists, anthropologists, sociologists, teachers and a host of other thinkers on the subject of play have looked at its relevance to our individual lives and the development of societies in general. Earlier we discussed the basic ideas of ritual and saw that its foundational elements could also be applied to shopping experiences. Play also has, at its core, a number of components that have direct connections to the activity of shopping and the places that are created to do it.

The Essential Features of Play and Shopping

In looking at the essential ideas of play in the following paragraphs, we'll discover that the stuff of play is synonymous with shopping.

In fact, seeing the connections between ideas on play and how the shopping experience unfolds, it's a wonder that not every experience we have in the store is packed with playful moments regardless of the type of product or service customers are buying. If Tesco can make shopping for groceries fun in the subway, then any retailer should be able to engage their customers in playful interactions.

- **Play is deeply participatory in nature – an embodied experience.**

When shopping, we find ourselves in places open to an experience, engaged in doing something, as opposed to being held by inertia. We have arrived at the mall, market or main street having defied Newton's first law of motion.

At both the mall and the playground, we play with other people and in doing so, we develop an empathic sense about what the other players are feeling. When we extend ourselves inside of the play experience, our ability to put ourselves in the other person's shoes and feel what the other person is feeling comes from the fact that we engage in adopting roles. If we play the same games repeatedly, very likely we will share roles, sometimes playing one character then switching with our play partner on another occasion.

As we learn the 'rules of the game' at a specific retail store we are at once players in the game, characters in the story and participants in the ritual. These three key features of shopping experiences begin to blend.

"The social bonding that comes from play favored the evolution of the human sense of empathy," says American physician and neuroscientist Paul MacLean.[25] So when little boys and girls play dress-up, cops and robbers, or doctor, they are practicing a very real sense of pure empathy. When we play with each other, we place ourselves in contexts that allow for us to truly feel, think and behave as if we are the other person.

As we are shopping in a particular retailer's store we are also practicing empathy. While it seems counter intuitive, we are participating and learning how to deal with others despite the fact that we left home thinking that we were just going out to get a little something for ourselves. If we fully participate in the experience, we share a sense of community with others who are having fun while walking the aisles, trying things on, interacting with technology and handing over cash or credit card at the wrap counter.

This type of role-play is transformative, since for many of us, directly experiencing something for ourselves in a full-bodied way, is truly how we learn. You can be told about someone else's experience and intellectually get it, but it is not until you live it, with your mind and body, that the emotional content of the experience is deeply felt. We may say, "yeah, I know how you feel," when talking about a positive or negative shopping experience, but in actuality we don't. Not until we have lived it. The interpersonal process is at work in the way customers share their experiences with each other in both one-to-one relationships *and* one-to-thousands in online social media circles. But, we need to do more than simply see or hear about an experience to fully get it. In the end, *feeling is believing*.

One of the greatest challenges to the idea that shopping and play are connected, and that each requires participation with our bodies to fully appreciate the experience, comes when we consider the pervasiveness and continued growth of shopping through digital devices. If play requires two or more individuals, and shopping, as a social experience, implies connecting with others, then buying from a phone is about acquisition, not developing relationships.

The power of buying things with a computer at home or your phone while on the go can't be denied. Retailers or brands not exploiting this avenue for selling products and services seem backward in our present day society. These 'channels' are of course a huge business, but the nature of the experience as a social enterprise is diminished unless you have live video chat, or some social network connection, though that still is a poor approximation for real, face-to-face interaction.

It is not surprising that social networking sites, having virtual foot-traffic in the millions, are able to sell products or advertising space amidst the social content created by their members. We are brought together socially through technology and offered products in the periphery of the web page. Seems we can't disconnect the idea that social engagement and shopping are inextricably linked.

The divide between shopping experience through the Internet and embodied experience in the store will only continue to increase in our digitally driven future. It may be that there are those products and services whose commodity-based nature will put them firmly in the world of the Internet and others that are impossible to fully appreciate unless they are experienced in store. In either case, creators of shopping places, whether they are on the Internet or a physical environment, will have the challenge of infusing each of them with aspects of play.

- **Play is made possible by expressing a sense of shared vulnerability, which is allowed by an implied covenant of collective trust.**
When we are playing, each of the participants allows the activity to unfold and does so in cooperation with one or more other people. A defining feature of play that makes it different from fantasy is that it requires interaction between individuals. Even when we are playing by ourselves, we engage an imaginary friend, or give human qualities to stuffed animals or some other inanimate object so that we can make playing into a social experience. We cooperate and engage in creative feats to make wondrous things whether we are playing with imaginary or real friends. The engagement is a means by which we enter into relationship, and in doing so we expose a certain degree of vulnerability through which we begin to develop empathy for others. Being vulnerable is a demonstration of being open to the other players. You can't both be open in spirit and hold others at arm's length.

The degree to which customers will allow themselves to be vulnerable in a shopping place is a sign of their level of trust with the sales associate, retailer and the brand. There are categories of products or services that inherently require customers to be more vulnerable as they shop. The easiest of these to think of, of course, is intimate apparel.

As customers shop this category they are understandably sensitive and exposed to feelings about body image, social stereotypes and sexuality. Whether the result of surveys, studies or anecdotal data, retailers who sell intimate apparel estimate that about 80% of women wear the wrong-size bra.

These kinds of statistics lead one to question whether or not customers are just poorly educated about what makes for a good fit or whether the nature of the shopping experience exposes a high level of vulnerability that makes customers uncomfortable. This would lead them to rush through the process or to be too embarrassed to ask the advice of a sales associate. This of course leads to the idea that both the fitting process and sales associate's sensitivity are important in supporting an enjoyable shopping experience in the intimate category.

Another category that requires a similar feeling of sensitivity to shopper's vulnerability is that of the 'plus-size' woman. After designing store concepts for the leading North American plus-size women's brands Lane Bryant and Addition Elle, I can attest that, for some shoppers, vulnerability is a serious and prevalent issue. From the moment a plus-size shopper enters the mall she's confronted with stereotypes that don't fit her persona. By the time she has reached the store, she has been bombarded with a number of images and messages that don't reflect who she is, how she feels or how she likes to shop. Even entering a store for plus-size women involves the public admission of being plus sized, which is often at odds with our cultural affinity for seeing beauty as a size 2 not 22. When finally in the store she loves, it's as if she's in an oasis. She is welcomed for who she is and knows that she can truly trust the sales associates to understand her feelings and needs.

It is equally important to understand that customers can feel vulnerable when they're buying edibles, not just wearables. A growing awareness for how our food is processed and the effects it has on us, has allowed retailers such as Whole Foods Market to develop a customer base that trusts the label. Based on that trust, customers rely on them to nourish their health and vitality, and in doing so, become part of their customers' lifestyles and sense of wellbeing.

While not all products in Whole Foods Market stores are organic, the company has a brand platform built on the promise that they "… feature foods that are free of artificial preservatives, colors, flavors, sweeteners, and hydrogenated fats." And that they "… are committed to foods that are fresh, wholesome and safe to eat." While it might generally cost more to shop there, I implicitly trust that what I'm buying from them is better for me. When I shop at Whole Foods Market, I spend less time reading labels and more time loading the cart. [26]

Those relationships that are successful, profitable, and enduring are those which hold in high regard the vulnerability that is intrinsically tied to being open and accepting while at play.

- **Openness and acceptance are necessary parts of a play environment.**

Can a store environment convey an open and accepting sensibility before the customer begins to walk the aisle and load up a shopping cart? Ask the happy greeter at Walmart, or the bare-chested surfer dude with the six-pack abs at Abercrombie & Fitch (or Hollister & Co., A&F's more junior brand). The *greeter* has become a staple at Walmart and A&F/Hollister alike. Granted the two retailers have a different take on the idea, but they nevertheless serve the same function. Whether they are an affable elderly woman in a blue tunic or a bikini-clad teenager doused in a signature fragrance, smiling faces open up the opportunity for the shopper to feel more accepted and comfortable when in the store.

The greeter has become somewhat ubiquitous. Everyone gets the premise. This person's job is to be nice to you as you enter the store. But the power of a smile at the point of entry can affect a customer's motivation and demeanor.

The idea of the greeter is wholly different than say, the bouncer who guards the entryway to a popular club. The bouncer restricts, limiting entry generally based on appearance or known status.

Being welcomed as you enter a store is a means of getting your shopping trip started in the right direction and setting you up for fun. To those who are open to engagement, a genuinely pleasant greeting can open up the lines of communication in the transaction and pave the way for a positive state of mind that promotes additional sales. If misplayed, by being disingenuous or simply lacking an authentic sense of appreciation that the customer has made the effort to come into the store, the shopping trip is potentially doomed before it has started. A welcoming salutation and big smile feeds our sense of connection and opens us up to wanting to play.

There are, of course, retailers whose greeters occasionally forget that they are ambassadors for the brand. Since we are incredibly adept at reading faces and inferring intent from facial gestures, a simple look may be all it takes to let customers know that they should be shopping elsewhere. The 'looking down the end of the nose' approach to greeting a potential customer is neither 'open' nor 'accepting' and is never an auspicious start to a long relationship and certainly does not bode well for promoting loyalty and trust.

- **Play tends to be open-ended – its world is a timeless realm.**

I have always loved going to the movies. By the time the trailers end, I am fully in the world of the film. People beside me disappear and I am part of the unfolding story on the big screen right up to when the credits roll.

The same happens when I play. Hours can pass when I am fully engaged and I often look up when playing ends as though I am re-entering the real world.

The experience of shopping can often have the quality of a time warp. Many people welcome shopping as a respite from everyday life. They enjoy the brief escape from the routine of their lives. For many, shopping is a play date, where the experience is an end in itself. The shopping event is just another way to socialize. It's about feeling good, joyful and playful, and people appreciate the subtle subtext of the story that shapes the customer journey and the emotions that arise along the way.

When people engage in activities that deeply connect them to their imagination, they often have an experience of time being held in suspended animation. Often while playing, time seems to become less relevant. In the context of play, we dive deep into imagination and time slips by.

To fully engage in play, we need imagination. Without it, we are stuck in the present, unable to take on roles fully and create new worlds. These flights of imagination are critical. They are the journeys away from ourselves that allow us to experience the point of view of others. "What makes play such a powerful socializing tool, then, is the means by which imagination is unleashed."[27]

Shopping experiences require us to suspend disbelief long enough to enter the world of the brand or retailer. In the stores we love, anything can happen. We willingly allow ourselves to be swept away in the experience of shopping. Both play and shopping support our aspirations to extend beyond ourselves, reaching out and connecting to the world. Great shopping places can be environments in which retailers engage our imagination by creating alternate realities. In doing so, the store is a powerful force that draws the customer, like Alice, through the looking glass to play in Wonderland for a period of time. During play, time seems infinite and sometimes, great shopping experiences can transport us to a place that time forgot. As Jeremy Rifkin says, "Through play, we incorporate parts of these other imagined realties into our being. We become connected."

The idea and sensation of timelessness relate to increased dwell time in a store. As customers get lost in the play of shopping, time passes and shoppers are more exposed to products, services and brand ideologies. All retailers want customers to stay in their stores longer; more time spent generally implies an increased probability of more sales. The challenge for the retailer is to make sure that as customers linger in a playful shopping experience – that they are engaged.

Getting time to stand still in the shopping aisle has a lot to do with creating an atmosphere of wonder. However, attracting and holding the customer's attention is increasingly difficult in a world driven by digital distraction.

- **Play takes place in a space that is symbolically marked off from utilitarian space.**
When I grew up in suburban Montreal, there was a playground a hundred feet from

my front door. My parents' house sat on a block that encircled an open area. There were no merry-go-rounds, teeter-totters, or monkey bars. It was simply an open field. We called it "The Circle."

My friends and I had clubhouse the size of a toolshed. We had a fort under some twisted bushes and one in my parents' basement under the stair.

My neighbor's driveway became 'center ice' at the Montreal Forum and we reenacted epic hockey games as we tumbled about with plastic blades on old hockey sticks and foam from pillows taped to our legs as our 'pads.'

We played 'kick-the-can,' tag, and 'hide-'n-go-seek' until our mothers stood in their doors, calling us in for a bath before bed.

The Circle, park, driveway, side-yard of the house, or under a bush – were play spaces. Despite being used over and over again, these places were made new each time we played. Sometimes the boundary was reset or the rules adjusted to fit the number of players or accommodating boys *and* girls, and each time the 'playground' was alive with magic. If you were in it, the real world was left behind.

One of the defining features of play space is that for the duration of play it is symbolically marked off from the space around it. Whether delineated by walking the perimeter, laying down markers, or defined by its volume and geometry, the place in which play unfolds becomes a world unto itself.

When we played as kids, each of our playgrounds was a safe haven. There was no danger other than the man-eating creatures, 'bad guys,' or the pit of fire that we brought into being through our imagination. "Step over that line and you fall into the lava!" we would say. Of course there was no lava, but for the duration of the game you believed that there was and acted as if you could feel the heat. The boundary was set and you held to it. The worlds we created were set apart.

Shopping places are also set aside from instrumental space. Traditional stores of course, are unlike the play spaces that develop spontaneously and then live for only a few hours. Just a few years ago, stores were designed, built and considered rather permanent. They had to last at least 3 to 5 years (though retailers would always hope that they wouldn't have to renovate until a few years after that). At the end of that timeframe, a retail refresh was in order and the stores would get a new look to keep up with the customer's need for novelty.

Now they are expected to change regularly.

As we become increasingly tied to the pace of change in a digitally driven world, customers expect stores to be fluid, frequently changing and adapting to the needs of a customer for whom change happens at the click of a mouse or swipe of a finger. Stores, as a retail play-space, are also expected to change more frequently and customers are becoming familiar with pop-up environments that exist for a few days. Far from being a fad, the ephemeral store is in sync with the way we grew up understanding that an opportunity for play could happen in a moment and be gone shortly after our interest waned or the story played itself out. In the case of pop-up shops, they are never designed to last forever. They are conceived in the same way that play spaces are, to last for the duration of the fun; then they "go away and come again another day."

In the context of a world that seems to be spinning ever faster, the time between a new store opening and its first refresh is decreasing. Flexibility is a key feature built into many store designs. The more elements of the store that can move, the more retailers feel that they can adapt to the preferences of their customers. Given the dynamic nature of the digital world, things can come and go quickly.

This ephemeral quality is redefining the very nature of what it means to be a store – a place bound by walls, ceilings and floors. The store as play-space is changing to be something you can carry in the palm of your hand. However, it should be no less engaging when customers are interacting there. Enabled and empowered by mobile technology, the store as a sacred space symbolically marked off from surrounding instrumental space can now be *any place*.

A shopping place can be a megamall or fold-up table on a street corner. It can be an extremely expensive piece of real estate on Fifth Avenue in New York, to which customers make a pilgrimage, or... a truck that roams the city streets going wherever the customers are. The space can be millions of square feet or a tent at a flea market. Whatever the case, for the period of time that the play unfolds, these places are special, apart from the rest of the world. In the moment of the transaction, the space contracts yet again to encircle two people who engage in relationship.

Regardless of the duration of stores' physical existence, they are imaginative worlds apart from the practical, utilitarian spaces of everyday living. In stores, the world of the brand comes alive with animation by customers and sales associate in the same way that play spaces are activated by players.

Without players, you have no game.

Without customers, you have no business.

Retail places rely on customers. Without them, the store, as play space, doesn't exist. We need people to play with; otherwise the activity is in our heads and is simply 'fantasy.' Likewise, we need people to shop because they animate the space, participate in the ritual, tell the story and play along with us. We become better at retail play because of them.

Because playing is done in concert with others, it is a shared act of collective trust. The play space is not owned by any one person. In some play activities, the goal might be to become the 'King of the Mountain,' but all who play in the game start out owning the 'mountain' equally. Within the context of playing a game, everyone is equal.

The market, mall and main street have permeable borders that allow the passage of people. The perimeters of shopping places are usually clearly marked and you generally know the difference between being inside and outside of a retail environment. People come and go, and for a moment in time, they live out brief parts of the story of the brand.

While it is true that people get very attached to their brands and shopping places, often referring to them as "my coffee shop" or "my pharmacy," they really only 'share' the experience. They no more own the store they are in any more than I owned the park I played in as a child. The park or any play space we created as kids was something that we invited others into or were invited into ourselves as guests to play out a part in the activity.

In playing, we set aside an enclave that we temporarily share. We come together in a zone clearly marked off from its surroundings, sometimes making other people's lives richer through the experience. And, we do so by choice.

- **Play is entered into voluntarily – you can't be forced into play.**
Play and shopping are volunteer activities.

In the end, we choose to be either involved or not and we have the right to say 'I am sitting this one out' if something doesn't feel right. We *choose* to go to the market, the mall or main street. We opt in because, for most of us, shopping is playful and fun.

It's important to acknowledge this idea of free will because when customers have shopping choices to make from multiple brick-and-mortar and online stores, and they choose to come to one particular retailer over another, it's a demonstration of their willingness to commit to a relationship. Every customer that walks through the door is an individual who is potentially willing to spend money and time. Can every retailer satisfy every customer's needs and desires? Well, we know that's impossible today. In the near future, however, computing power and an ever increasing use of the Internet by shoppers, will mean that there will be loads of data to be used in the service of predicting customer needs. But, even now, many retailers don't go quite far enough in establishing a relationship and getting to know the customer better once the customer has come to shop.

A customer's choice to engage in a retailer's store is an act of personal empowerment. That said, not all customers cross the threshold fully committed to, and feeling comfortable with, the retail stores they visit. The moment of first engagement can turn a casual shopper into a long-time customer – or not. As the customers then walk the sales floor, they're continually in a process of making choices – where to go, what to pick up, what to look at, what to try on, what to buy or whether or not simply to leave.

Just because customers walk through the door doesn't mean that they have volunteered to be hustled or pressured to buy. Sales associates need to strike an intuitive balance between appearing to be selfless and at the service of the customer, while at the same time knowing that they have an opportunity to move merchandise and make a sale.

It is a choice to support one business/brand platform over another. A customer's freedom of choice is a key driver for retail engagement.

When a retailer successfully captures the senses, piques curiosity and invites the customer into connection beyond a simple transaction, it's because they deeply understand that playful engagement is what builds memories. And, with so many choices to be made, not to engage customers in a playful way is to hasten a retailer's slide into the world of the 'unremarkable' while another ascends to be King of the Mountain.

Play is an expression of the freedom of choice. So is shopping. *"As man apprehends himself as free and wishes to use his freedom, then his activity is to play."*[28]

• **Through play we are provided with context and meaning and become connected.**

We humans love to play. We get together and participate, giving ourselves over to each other and the passage of time in places that are consecrated as play space for the duration of the activity. And, we do so willingly. We are smart, hard-working, industrious, ingenious beings that go about the growing of ourselves in society through play. Given the choice, we'd rather be playing. Play is what really brings us alive as individuals and as a society.

Any retailer who believes in its store as a place of play, whether a dollar store, specialty shop, mass merchant or luxury brand – understands our intrinsic need to socialize and that play is a viaduct to emotional connection with the customer.

More than playful, shopping places can be magical. Like the fantasy worlds of our childhood play dates and the imaginative stories we created of slaying dragons, climbing the highest peaks and always catching the bad guys, shopping mimics the basic tenets of play. When we shop, we incorporate parts of other imagined realities into ourselves during the time we are in the retailer's play space. Or at least they should be. The extent to which retailers can engage their customers in play while they are shopping their stores is an extraordinarily strong indicator (and predictor) of brand growth and success.

Make no mistake, though; making the shopping experience playful doesn't mean you're bringing customers to the circus every time they come to the store. The play aspect of shopping can be much more *subtle*.

While customers are in the store or connecting to the retailer through their phone or computer, they should be offered every opportunity to play. This means they exercise choice, ask questions, envision new sights and ways of thinking, connect with associates, try new things and ideas, and evaluate their own preferences, lives and dreams. But a playful space is more than the sum of its parts. It's the cultivation of a sense of community as well, of things you can't hang on the rack or fold on a shelf.

As customers are invited to participate in play, they become transported to the retailer's alternate reality. While there, they have a feeling of being in suspended animation. For a moment in time, they are more profoundly connected to themselves, other customers and the brand. The playful experience of shopping provides context and learning opportunities. Customers carry all of these experiences outside the store as emotional and body memories.

PART 02

Brands, Brains and Buying

This is Your Brain on Shopping

The Decade After the Decade After the "Decade of the Brain"

Ask most people to name five things under the hood of their car and they most likely would do so with ease: carburetor, air filter, oil filter, radiator, spark plugs, etc. But, ask people to name parts of their brains and most are hard pressed to come up with more than a couple that they can pronounce. Despite the fact that we can't do without it, most of us go about our daily lives blissfully unaware of the remarkable organ that is in our skull.

Our brain, you would think, would need no introduction since after all, it is in part what makes the 'You' in you. Without your brain you would have no conscious thoughts. Without your mind you are a biological entity but not a sentient being. There would be no 'Sapiens' to your *Homo Sapiens* and you and a tree would be pretty much the same.

The human brain is perhaps the most complex of all systems in the entire universe. There are more cells in the brain than there are stars. The brain deserves serious consideration from all of us if we want to live healthier lives and better understand each other and ourselves.

Just how is the customer's brain interacting with the environment when it goes – along with the rest of the customer – to the market, mall or main street?

As I'll explain in the pages ahead, the brain is far from passive on shopping trips. It's actively involved and engaged during the browsing and buying experience. There are parts of the brain working at both the conscious and subconscious levels that experience bursts of activity (or 'light up,' for short) during buying decisions.

In fact, scientists now believe that most of our 'thinking' – more than 95% of our 'thoughts – occur at the subconscious level. That means we're not consciously 'thinking' most of our 'thoughts.' The brain processes information, then makes decisions in areas that have been in place for hundreds of millions of years. And these parts of the brain tend to run more on emotions than on higher-order cognitive processing - reason or logic.

So, shoppers are largely unaware of the complex interplay between their brains and the environment while on the shopping trip. Each moment that they walk down the aisle in a store, use their smartphone or tablet, engage with digital content or with real, live people during the buying process – inside the middle of their brain, a part of their gray matter *appraises* whether or not they enjoyed the experience and will further influence whether they buy something *and* if they will repeat it.

Equally, there are those brain processes that give rise to our conscious awareness. They play a critical role in how we think and feel about the time we spend shopping. These are the internal dialogues we have in our head about the people, place and things in a store. These, too, have an impact on the associations we make with the brands we buy and the shopping places we become engaged in.

In the next few chapters I will only scratch the surface of understanding the brain and the mystifying mind. I'll share some basics about the brain, its functions and concepts on consciousness. We'll try to get our heads around the idea of mind and how the mind and the brain are not the same thing, but are very much connected in making more effective shopping places.

To get us there, I'll look at some specific functional areas of our brains that influence our reactions to our environment. I'll look at how we can engage the brains *and* minds of shoppers and explore why understanding even the very basics of the latest brain science is particularly important to the design of shopping places.

In the past few years, neuroscientists have made unprecedented headway in the understanding of the brain's biology. These days, the brain has been a mainstream topic of interest in the media. In a recent special series on the brain, Charlie Rose and acclaimed American neuropsychiatrist and Nobel Prize Laureate, Eric Kandel suggested that we have learned more about the brain in the past five years than we have in all of human history. The series offers 13 hours of some of the best discussion on the advances in neuroscience available on streaming video. [29]

Sometimes technology can lag behind our imagination and aspirations. In the world of neuroscience, we've had a bit of catching up to do. The original "Decade of the Brain," a period of intense brain study in the '90s, held some lofty goals. Making them a reality would mean that we had to wait for technology to catch up. The massive growth in digital-imaging technology over the past half decade has provided the engine to go where no neuroscientist has gone before by allowing us to see the intricate workings *inside* the brain and the remarkable complexity of the cellular connections that make up our gray matter.

The brain is made up of about 100 billion brain cells called 'neurons.' There are hundreds of other types of cells in the brain as well, but neurons are key to energy and information flow. They are the roads on which neural traffic travels. Trillions of other structures called 'glial cells' also support brain function. Think of glial cells as 'dark matter,' the stuff that is between the billions of planets in the universe that helps to keep it all together.

Each neuron links up with about 10,000 other neurons creating neural circuits that work in both distributed and integrated ways. Some parts work on their own, *and* they may also work with other parts. When all of these neurons link together, they give rise to emergent properties. Neuroscientists believe that neural activity, the chemical and electrical processes between neurons, is the basis for thoughts, feelings and perceptions.

Recent discoveries in brain science are beginning to give an inkling as to how this extraordinary network of cells, signals and interconnections is always at work. This activity is continuous during the most extraordinary and the mundane activities of our lives as shoppers, consumers and brand followers. How exactly this happens, scientists are not exactly sure, and so, they are embarking on the search to map out how all of these circuits are linked together to create – somehow – all of the behaviors we humans exhibit.

Thirteen years after the end of the original "Decade of the Brain," President Barack Obama launched the "BRAIN Initiative" (Brain Research through Advancing Innovative Neurotechnologies), an intensive focus on the brain and how it works. Starting in April of 2013, a host of scientists embarked on yet another collaborative and concerted effort to better understand the organ in our heads. Their big idea: "The BRAIN Initiative will accelerate the development and application of new technologies that will enable researchers to produce dynamic pictures of the brain that show how individual brain cells and complex neural circuits interact at the speed of thought. These technologies will open new doors to explore how the brain records, processes, uses, stores, and retrieves vast quantities of information, and shed light on the complex links between brain function and behavior."[30]

Nothing short of a Herculean task.

The idea of mapping the neural network in a brain is not particularly new. In fact, it has already been done, though on a much smaller scale. In 1963, Thomas

Brenner started studying a worm, "*C. elegans*," as a research organism. Brenner and his associates published a paper explaining that they had mapped the worm's nervous system and tracked every stage of its development on a cellular level. [31]

Brenner and his group were able to determine all 302 of the neurons in the worm as well as the 7,000 connections called "synapses" between them. I know. It's a worm. And you're thinking, we're a little far from the shopping mall and wondering how we are going to connect the neuroscience of worm to human buying behavior. But, mapping the nervous system of a little worm that measures no more than a few millimeters in length is stunning in its complexity and functions as a precursor to understanding the structure of the human brain.

As scientists continue their research on the mapping of the human brain, they hope to come to understand how it is wired and, as a consequence, develop a comprehensive model of human behavior.

To find a precedent in scientific research for something that comes close to the scale of mapping the neural connections of the human brain, we simply have to recall our search to uncover the code of our genetic blueprint, DNA, in the Human Genome Project. In April of 2003, thirteen years after the Human Genome Project started (and two years ahead of schedule) and at a cost of 2.7 billion dollars, the effort was completed. [32]

Determining a similar roadmap for the brain is a great idea but there need to be a number of intermediate steps before we can seriously consider mapping something the size of the three-pound mass we have locked up in our skulls. Thanks to emerging imaging technologies and 3D-modeling developments, however, we are now getting closer to the prize.

One of the steps to creating a neural roadmap has scientists such as Sebastian Seung at MIT, in the process of generating the "Connectome," the mapping of all neural connections…but only in a mouse's brain. [33] Seung and his collaborators, including Winfried Denk at the Max Planck Institute and Jeff Lichtman at Harvard University, are working on the mapping of each neural pathway in a brain that is clearly tiny in relation to a human's, but far more complex than that of Brenner's *C. elegans*. The end result of this research is proposed to trace, microscopic slice by microscopic slice, how one neuron connects to others. The end result will provide a three-dimensional diagram of the wiring of a mouse's brain.

Still the question remains: could the same thing be done with the human brain?

To get down to the level of the cellular connectivity throughout the human brain, scientists are finally ready to launch a large-scale, international public effort that has as its goal to develop a full record of the neural activity across complete neural circuits. To do this, you can imagine, is an enormous technological challenge. Mapping every complete neural circuit in the brain is like creating a Google map of all the highways, side-roads and foot paths on Earth then filling a galaxy with a few billion more Earths and then mapping the connections of those to each other.

The White House's BRAIN Initiative is just one of a number of such searches and it will likely be based on the "Brain Activity Map" project proposal published in *Neuron* in June 2012.[34]

Dr. Rafael Yuste, professor of biological sciences and neuroscience at Columbia University, one the authors of the Brain Activity Map project as well as one of the group of advisors to the White House on the BRAIN Initiative, spoke about the BRAIN Initiative project at the World Science Festival in New York in June of 2013. In explaining what the scientists are up against, he likened the task ahead to mapping the relationships between pixels on a television screen.

To visualize where we are today in our understanding of the brain, let's imagine the image of a large TV screen. Now, imagine that we look at only one pixel on that screen and call it a neuron – the basic brain cell. Now, imagine that we are going to explore the relationships between that individual pixel and the multitude of others that it may have connections to on the screen.

Then do the same thing for every other pixel.

Okay, great. We have one frame of the movie done.

Now, do that again for every frame, of the thirty frames that pass by every second, for the next two hours. Get the idea? Not surprisingly, the BRAIN initiative will be underway for years to come.

So, we ask, how are these complex connections between brain cells related to buying behavior in shopping aisles?

What should make the brain of interest to retailers and retail design professionals?

The main reason, of course, is that if they understand a little about what makes the brain tick, then they are in an infinitely better position to capture attention, engage emotions and motivate purchases.

If you are a retail designer or retailer and you are asked, "where does customer experience happen?," you might answer, "in the spaces we design and build, the materials we specify and the products we present to shoppers." In other words, the experience is 'out there' in environments that we walk through while on the shopping trip. The floors, walls, ceilings, lights, merchandise, fixtures, graphics, music and smells surrounding the customer are, after all, what comprise the shopping environment.

But customer experience is, in fact, only partly in the environments that we create for shopping and *almost entirely inside customers' heads*. As customers' brains go on shopping trips, there is a dynamic relationship between brain activity and the environments with which they interact. Our perceptions of the environments that we shop and the relationships we engage in while shopping have everything to do with the human brain.

The brain both makes and is made by experiences. The experiences we have cause brain cells to fashion links, and repeating them cements these neural connections, creating memories that activate feelings and actions. Customer experience and the brain are intimately tied.

They are interdependent.

From the point of view of customer experience, when retailers and retail designers better understand the brain, we will be able to better craft in-store and online experiences that are more relevant and meaningful to customers. We will be better able to understand customers' true motivators, and deterrents, to buying behavior.

The Emotional Brain

The very act of entering a shopping place is driven, mitigated and calibrated by our emotions. Have you ever walked into a store and then immediately turned around and walked out? Learning how the brain works makes us more aware of what makes us walk out – or stay and shop.

When we consider the myriad brain processes triggered by just our physical perceptions, we begin to wonder how the brain plays a role in decisions that are both conscious and subconscious. Suddenly, driving to the corner store for groceries is not such a mundane task when we imagine the billions of cells at work making it possible for us to venture out for a refill on the milk and eggs.

Learning about our own brains teaches us how we can enhance our relationships, including the ones with ourselves, which make our lives more meaningful. Self-awareness is a powerful key to personal change. Neuroscientists are now learning that when we develop a sense of mindfulness – a sense of inner awareness that grows from being more focused on our thoughts and in tune with our bodies – we play an active role in our own brain growth. When we become aware or mindful of our thoughts, actions, ritual shopping trips, frequented places and practices, we see how powerfully our actions and thoughts shape us.

What about those times you walked into a store and felt so good inside that you lost track of time, and loaded your shopping cart with all kinds of things you didn't necessarily need, but felt drawn to buy anyway? Well, our emotions, intuition and instincts are hugely powerful aspects of the shopping experience. As we will see, they are key driving forces to the things we are attracted to and how we react in the shopping aisle.

Later in this section, I'll explain how repetitive behaviors lay down and reinforce connections between neurons. Multiple exposures to certain stimuli wire brain cells together, creating thoughts, feelings and behaviors.

What we practice grows. In a neural sense we become what we think.

From the point of view of shopping, repetitively experiencing and choosing to attend to certain shopping environments lays down the neural pathways for what we come to expect from certain retailers. Some of these neural pathways are general and are applied across a wide array of retailers and shopping experiences. Others may be very specific and play a role in how we determine the differences between retailers within the same category. So, in a very real sense, patterns of experiences shape our brain by connecting brain cells together and creating a sort of code by which our brain operates. Shopping at a certain retail place over and over again becomes part of the way we see ourselves.

We don't become what we buy. But, we may buy who we are.

For many shoppers, their relationships with the brands they love hold great significance in their lives. The shopping brain is largely shaped by the brand/retailer–shopper relationship. The way it processes the experience of interactions and shopping environments has everything to do with how customers feel when shopping and whether or not they stay longer, buy more, become customers for life or, turn and high-tail it out of the store. What happens in the shopping aisle, or on a handheld device in the street, activates and actually changes the brain.

Social experience affects brain chemistry and can forge new neural pathways that may have lasting effects on all kinds of behaviors. Shopping, and its fundamental attribute of being a social activity, can be a change agent.

The key factor in the success of a shopping place lies in the fostering of relationships. Since the brain is the part of us that provides the machinery to process relationships and engage in emotional connection with others, it is a major player in how the shopping trip unfolds.

Brands, brains and buying are all connected.

It may sound Machiavellian; a retailer sets up experiences in the shopping aisle on inside knowledge about the brain, then manipulates the customer into making purchases that were never intended.

Except, it doesn't work like that.

Studying the brain won't achieve 'shopper mind control.' We need to understand that if the brain is the mechanism that processes experience and outputs action – in the shopping world that may be to-buy or not-to-buy – then it is in the retailer's or store designer's best interest to understand how to create the best conditions to engage the brain in an emotional relationship.

Think of brain as the 'social-emotional organ' of the body.

Why engage shoppers and their brains in a positive emotional relationship rather than simply offering a well functioning store, with abundantly stocked shelves and deeply discounted prices? Because a purely logical approach is not enough – the brain, at its core, is also emotional.

With this in mind, retailers and designers of shopping places should strive to create environments that activate positive emotional responses. How the brain is likely to react to certain stimuli is good to know when trying to avoid feelings of fear, revulsion, or anxiety. When retailers and designers understand how the brain reacts to conditions in the environment and creates feelings and behaviors, they can create much more customer-centric retail places.

With the abundance of choice we are now exposed to, it is becoming increasingly clear that giving customers more than 25 types of peanut butter, 50 types of jam and 40 types of bread to choose from doesn't necessarily make a better sandwich. In fact, it just gets them stuck in the shopping aisle the way peanut butter gets stuck to the roof of your mouth. Just because customers can choose from a number of options doesn't mean they will. And often, it's not because they don't want to or don't like what they see, but because they feel confused, ambivalent or overwhelmed with choices.

In the past, customers regarded choice as the key differentiator and they increasingly asked for *more*. It is important to remember that generations prior to the Millennials grew up with more of a scarcity model. Customer mindsets coming out of the experience of the Great Depression and the Second World War, where the basics of everyday living were not available or rationed, made abundance the goal. More choices provided a sense of well-being and projected a certain vitality and social status.

In today's hyper-abundant world where virtually any product or service can be acquired with the swipe or touch of a finger, choice will no longer distinguish one shopping place from another. In fact, there is considerable evidence to prove that *more choice actually makes the experience – and one's perceived satisfaction of it – worse.*

What people increasingly seek is more authentic, connected, emotional experiences that fill their lives with less stuff and more meaning. When you've filled your shelves, you turn to fill your heart.

In the years to come, understanding the customer's emotional brain, and how to engage it, will be key to success in the retail place-making game. Understanding how to create places and craft experiences that engage the customer's emotional side will become increasingly important when all the merchandise that they may possibly want is available *outside* the store. The store then, will become a place that satisfies the customer's emotional needs with relevant experiences beyond providing products at a good price. Shopping places that engage the customer's brain, getting it to *feel* more and *think* less, will have a better chance of creating long-term memories and lifetime customers. In many cases customers don't think at all in the shopping aisle and are moved to buy more based on emotion alone. Buying for our emotions, trusting our gut, comes from a more ancient group of brain structures and touches us on a profound level. Capturing customers' hearts is done through their minds.

Let's explore how.

Contrary to what love songs, movies and storybooks say, the heart itself is not where love is kindled. 'Love' has now been seen on a brain scan – evidently in the right hemisphere. Our brains are connected via a neural network to the heart, which keeps it beating *and* provides the intrapersonal biofeedback that we call 'heartfelt' emotions. Equally, if we are speaking of intuition, the brain also mediates the sensations around our intestines that we call a 'gut reaction.'

Yes, we have brain cells in our guts.

Recent studies have found that there are actually brain cells in both the heart and the gut. According to Michael Gershon, an expert in the field of neurogastroenterology, there are about 100 million neurons lining the sides of our intestines.[35] It turns out that this is *more* than what is in our spine or peripheral nervous system. So, when you get that pang in your stomach as a result of an intensely emotional interaction with a loved one or butterflies before some big event, you are literally 'feeling the connection' between your brain and these brain cells in your heart and gut. Further research suggests that about 90% of the fibers in the primary visceral nerve, called the vagus, are carrying signals from the gut to the brain, not from the brain to the gut.[36]

Though we often discount these sensations, we would do well to pay attention to these feelings. They are the best biofeedback we could ever have and they are reliable indicators of what matters to us.

We often quiet the rumblings of our emotional-intuitive selves, believing that if only we can reason our way through a problem, taking full advantage of the cost-benefit analysis that the intellectual part of our brain has to offer, we will come to the best decisions. In fact, as I'll get to in later chapters, we can get stuck in our rational left-brain and the higher order cognitive functions of the pre-frontal cortex, the most recently evolved part of our brain, and as a result make poor decisions when we would have done better to have simply *thought* less and *trusted our gut* more.

On the other hand, solely relying only on our emotional right-brain and intuition for how to interpret and react to the experiences we have would of course prove to be disastrous since our left-brain, and more developed pre-frontal area, have a lot to offer when we need to pay attention to details.

The brain, with its capacity to influence our decisions, is not an either/or, rational/emotional, left-brain/right-brain, processor. Our hearts and minds are connected and each affects the other, resulting in our feelings, behaviors and choices. For the brain to work well, it requires coherent, well-functioning and integrated processing, across a complex network, which spans both sides of our heads.

So how do we appeal to customers in their 'head space'? Know this: customers *want* to be in relationships with their brands or retailers that 'get them.' They want to be understood and know that the retailers or brands they buy know who they are. Not necessarily by name, of course, though that also helps, but by creating experiences that speak directly to their individual needs, their unique sensibilities.

While customers' sensitivity to price might be something to pay attention to, how customers 'feel' about the brand or retailer is what ultimately matters. Price-point may play a role in a buying decision, but a feeling of emotional connection may overcome a hesitation to buy something that seems too expensive. With the validation that comes from feeling seen and heard, the buying decision leapfrogs over the wallet and lands directly in the heart and mind.

So, creating relationships with customers is not accomplished through their credit cards, cash in their pocket or in their wallets. It's not done in their handheld devices, tablets or home computers. It's not, actually, even done in the store. The relationship between customer and retailer can happen anyplace. Relationships between the retailer and customer, on many levels, transcend the functional three-dimensional space of the store. The store, the computer, tablet or handheld device is simply a vehicle that facilitates the connection. Customers and retailers grow the relationship in their minds. And that, as far as we know, has no specific location in our heads, but is rather in our bodies and in the exchange of energy that flows between people.

When retailers and their store designers set out to create great shopping places, they need to take an *empathic leap towards the customer*. What does that mean in practical terms? When we create stores that are designed through the 'mind's eye' of shoppers, the focus must be on what matters to customers and their emotional needs. We glean knowledge and insight about customers on shopping trips by putting ourselves in their shoes, imagining how they feel every step of the way. What will welcome them? What will they likely see when they enter the store? How will they make sense of it all? By understanding the brain, we better understand how to develop and exhibit customer empathy.

Reaching out to connect with the customer on an emotional basis does not preclude product offering, clarity in merchandise presentations, and price-points, all of which influence the shopping experience. But it's the connections that are made with the customer on an emotional level that linger long after products are paid for. The extent to which these retail planning staples – along with store architecture, environmental graphics design, packaging, and other branding efforts – reach the emotional centers of the customer's brain, determine the residual feelings of having had a positive experience, an openness to keep coming back for more, and spreading the word to others.

I remember walking the streets of SoHo in New York and coming upon a sales associate on the street giving out samples of soap. Before you knew it, I was going through the hand washing ritual that is a hallmark of the Sabon store experience.[37] As I stood over a stone basin, I was instructed to gently massage sea salts with fragrant oils into my skin. While exfoliating, hydrating and massaging each digit, the sales associate led me through a series of fine points about the products that I was using. My hands had never felt that good and my olfactory senses were alive with the scents of the hand scrubs that we used. Did I buy something? Of course. Did I share the experience with everybody that would listen to it? You bet. I even dragged my two boys there when we were on a weekend walkabout in the city. And they loved it too. The experience was physical and emotional, and established memories I easily recall.

Just Who's 'Minding the Store' Anyway?

The human brain is remarkable for its physical complexity and mysterious metaphysical mind. It's estimated that approximately 90% of what the brain does is outside of our conscious awareness – meaning that on its own, the human brain is making thousands of decisions every day and we are not even aware of them. Many of these are channeled through the autonomic nervous system, the part of the neural network that keeps our heart pumping, our lungs filling with air and many other body functions happening without faltering.

Our brain processes information with remarkable speed. It makes us jump away from a rustle in the tall grass before we consciously think, "*it's a snake!*" Our brain functions faster than our ability to think consciously and even faster than our physical ability to act on conscious thoughts. We can sense a threat even before we are consciously aware of what it is. Our brain is constantly appraising our environment, looking for cues and clues.

Should we be scared that we are most often on autopilot? Not really. We have thousands and maybe even millions of prewired preferences for performing various actions and making a host of decisions. After all, the human brain has had hundreds of millions of years to develop the intricate wiring that now gives us the ability to do the things taken for granted. Many of our emotions and physical abilities are hardwired into our system. And despite this fact, we humans continue to think we are in complete control.

As we go about our daily lives, we think that the little voice in our head, the one that we hear talking to us as we are thinking through a problem, is calling the shots. The 'voice' I am talking about is our conscious self, the part of us that percolates to the surface of our awareness, floating above our brain's subconscious activity.

Because we are aware of our 'thinking,' we tend to believe that our brain has a sort of corporate headquarters, a specific place from which these thoughts originate and are distributed, like orders, to the different areas of our bodies to make us feel and behave the way we do. Except, there is no such place in our head. There are indeed certain functional areas of the brain that process vision, speech, motor activities and other body functions, but there is no 'center of thought.' What is amazing about the human brain is that thoughts are generated over a distributed network of functional areas. The human brain, more than any other creatures' on the planet, draws its remarkable cognitive capacity from the connections of billions of brain cells across the entire organ.

Don't be misled into thinking that the brain is on the loose, running rampant. There may not be a central locus of control, but the systems that are responsible for enabling everything we do, think or feel are, nevertheless, very structured and staggering in their levels of complexity.

Our search for how the brain works has been underway for some time. In the late 1700s Austrian anatomist and physiologist Franz Josef Gall came up with the idea that different parts of the brain were responsible for different aptitudes and personality traits. This was a pretty good hypothesis for a guy who lived in at a time when medical practitioners still cut holes in people's heads to let evil spirits out.

Gall is considered the founder of *phrenology*, the study of the skull, specifically the bumps on the skull as they related to aptitude prominence. He related a number of human faculties to the size of the organs he believed existed in our heads. Gall suggested that the brain was made up of twenty-seven separate "organs." If one aptitude was more prominent than another, Gall theorized that the organ associated with it would grow and become evident by creating bumps that could be felt under the scalp.

Unfortunately for Gall, the religious powers in Austria had him run out of the country for promoting ideas that were considered against the prevailing religion. Acting against the will of the church in those days could cause a scientist some problems likely leading to one's demise. So, he moved to Paris thinking it to be a safe haven and fertile ground to grow his theories *and* a new business.

Despite the fact that he had essentially started the scientific community on the path to the idea that the brain worked as a series of localized functional groups, he displeased Napoleon who had him investigated to determine if he was a fraud, if not, at least, just a poor scientist. It turns out that Napoleon's skull didn't have right bumps showing the characteristics of nobility that the future emperor was sure he had. You would have thought that Gall might have invented a couple of 'Napoleon bumps' to make good with the little man with enormous aspirations of European domination. Gall being a scientist rather than a savvy politician, did not make it into the Academy of Sciences in Paris as he had hoped. His application was scuttled after an investigation was done at the request of Napoleon by the physiologist Marie-Jean-Pierre Flourens, who found that the theories were not founded on good science.

Even though Gall's ideas did not attract universal acceptance, his investigations inspired others to find out what areas of the brain did what and just where the thing we call consciousness might be hiding after all. Other scientists continued to study the brain, and years later, in 1861, French physician Paul Broca located the part of the brain responsible for production of spoken language, later known as Broca's area. The German physician, Carl Wernicke, then located the area responsible for understanding written and spoken language. Neuroscience was finally on its way to understanding what areas of our brains were responsible for which faculties.

Whereas Gall was concerned with the surface structure of our skulls, the scientific community was going deeper into the brain itself and determined that the brain is in fact highly localized. Meaning that there is a multitude of what you might think of as microprocessors. Harvard researchers Alfonso Caramazza and Jennifer Shelton postulated that, "the brain has specific knowledge systems – 'modules' – for animate and inanimate categories that have distinct neural mechanisms."[38]

Likely developed millions of years ago, these different functional areas served to ensure the survival of the species by giving our distant human ancestors the mental machinery to determine just what it was that was moving slowly in the tall grass. "These domain specific knowledge systems aren't actually the knowledge itself, but systems that make you pay attention to particular aspects of a situation."[39] These different functional areas of the brain are important to consider when thinking about customer behavior because they process sights, sounds, smells, shapes and textures and also the emotional responses that customers generate while in the midst of a shopping trip.

Over time and with repeated use, visual cues for example, were encoded into our brains so that we took notice of the motion of things. We became good at distinguishing between a branch bending in the breeze and the motion of a snake slithering through the grass, or the difference between harmless mammals such as warthogs, and predatory cats with powerful claws and sharp teeth, prowling near by.

Woven together to create an integrated web, all of these modules function both independently *and* together to run the show. If you're a computer-minded individual, you can think of the brain as having both serial *and* parallel processing systems. Each of them is up and running all the time. We have "myriad cognitive abilities that are separated and spatially represented in different parts of the brain, each with different neural network systems."[40] As it turns out, our brains have multiple control systems all making 'decisions' and working together – not a central-command post.

So, the brain on a shopping trip is buzzing with cognitive processes – things we are actually aware of thinking about while walking the aisles, and subconscious processes – those things that are happening in our brains without our thinking about them at all. There are buying decisions we will come to that are the result of experiences in our recent shopping *past* and those that are, in a way, 'hardwired' into who we are as a consequence of human evolution.

There are decisions we will make to buy something based on a well-considered set of comparisons and careful cost-benefit analysis, and those purchases that are founded in emotional reaction.

Then there may be some purchases that come seemingly out of nowhere but which seemed, in the moment, like a good thing to do and you found yourself handing over the credit card before you knew it.

We can thank a few million years of brain evolution for allowing us humans to not have to pay attention to everything around us all the time. You can imagine that if we had to, we would be on overload every second of every day. In this way, the brain is extraordinarily efficient. It creates memory packets that chunk objects and experiences with similar characteristics for easy retrieval.

If you hear the word 'shopping' or the name of a favorite retailer, your brain would call up images and pictorial representations of those words. The right brain would search, instantly, for the autobiographical data and stories associated with those words for you. It would bring together a holistic view of your experiences of that particular retailer and the subtle differences between it and other retailers within the same category. The right brain would be able to infer whether or not it was a luxury or mid-priced brand. The right brain would have a series of intuitive feelings about the retailer, as well as interest in the novelty of experience and the search for what is unknown.

The left brain would string together the words used to describe these representations. The left brain would tend to put the store within categories that are cataloged in memory, and consider details such as price points and the specifics of the various merchandise classifications. The left brain would reference something that it already knows, so that it could make easy classifications of objects called to mind.

You would likely come to conclude that there is a certain number of components that make a shopping trip or a visit to the specific retailer what you know it to be. Through our exposure to certain shopping experiences, the brain creates a set of *patterns* that establish *expectations* about how the next trip should unfold. We take note of unexpected events in the patterns we have encoded regarding our previous shopping trips. A number of our personal interactions and perceptions of the environments we walk through are coded into long-term memory and result in behavior and emotional reactions that are triggered by the activation of neural networks laid down last week or long ago.

While we think we are consciously in control of ourselves, and the world around us, the *subconscious* is often running the show. What percolates up into our conscious awareness is built on a multitude of individual processes that never see the cognitive light of day. When we think about the implications of understanding the shopper's mind, we are better able to understand the cognitive and emotional triggers to customer behavior. We develop a greater appreciation for how we can craft shopping environments that are more emotionally engaging and that foster relationships in a more profound way.

Our brain's ability to process much of our environment at a subconscious level allows us to focus on 'higher function' pursuits. We couldn't possibly attend to everything in our environment all day long, making decisions about the most minute details of our lives. That would overwhelm and burn us out. So our brain has developed as a remarkable system that attends to everything by *categorizing those things that need our conscious attention to make decisions* about what behaviors are appropriate, and those things below the radar which the subconscious takes care of on its own.

Many retailers and store designers don't realize this. A little brain science 101, and we could avoid burdening customers with trying to make too many decisions, asking them to make comparisons between price points and various brands of merchandise that line shelves. Huge product assortments, multiple signs, different lighting conditions, multiple materials and finishes, music, video and throngs of other customers can put a shopper into cognitive overload.

If we understand what the brain is likely to process sensory input automatically, without our conscious attention, then we can also intentionally modify shopping places and immediately draw the customer's attention to aspects of the store environment of which we really want them to take note.

Retailers can make it easy for customers to choose. But that also involves understanding how customers' brains are likely to process all of the information that's in front of them.

Once we've captured the customers' attention, functions including perceptual processes, long-term memories, innate emotions, *and* conscious decision-making kick into gear so that they investigate further, try a little bit more and maybe, if they feel inclined to, buy.

Retailers, brands and the creators of shopping places ought to consider who's really 'in charge' on a shopping trip, what's winning that conversation in the customer's head. It's important because a considerable amount of the time, retail places are *not* selling to the conscious mind, but the subconscious, "the man behind the curtain." Many times we are selling *past* the conscious to their subconscious emotional centers within the customer. We will discover that, in doing so, retailers and designers naturally connect to the customer on a more profound and memorable level.

Superhighways, Country Roads and Cow Paths

You may say, we aren't *really* under that much control of what has been encoded into our DNA through our biological development, are we? The nature-nurture argument has to have *some* place in this discussion. And it does. We are neither entirely driven by behaviors encoded in our human DNA, nor are we simply the sum total of all of our experiences since birth.

There have been a number of theories put forward by neuroscientists over the years about the degree to which behaviors are genetic or learned. The idea that we are born as a blank slate, and all that we are is a result of experiences we encounter, has long been overturned with a preference for the view that our brains are wired both genetically *and* through experience. There are behaviors we exhibit that result from a few million years of evolution, and those that may result from your reading this paragraph.

Perhaps one of the best ways to appreciate what is going on at a genetic versus experience level in the customer's brain is to imagine the complex network of neural connections described in the earlier paragraphs as roads and traffic.

Neuroscientist Cornelia Bergman of the Howard Hughes Medical Institute explains it this way: "...you can think of neural connections as roads in a traffic pattern...the highways in everybody's brains are the same – the big pathways that link thousands of cells together are very orderly and have very precise genetic instructions that tell the brain how to lay down those pathways in different places. Then, there are the smaller roads that are partially genetic... and then you have the little cow paths – the smaller connections, the more local connections – those are controlled by experience."[41]

As an example, color vision is genetically encoded – *nature*. With regard to seeing color, you have no say in the matter. This would be taken care of on the superhighways of our neural network. We all have the same genes that tell our brains how to deal with what we see and there are only a handful of them responsible for seeing colors. If you happen to have a deficiency in one or more of these genes, you may have one of the various forms of color blindness.

On the other hand, the language you speak, English, Chinese, French, or Portuguese and the particular dialect of each of these, is determined through experience – *nurture*. These aptitudes might be seen as being part of the country roads of our neural network. You may learn any or all of these depending on what languages were spoken in your childhood home, where you grew up or what school you went to.

Personal preferences that dictate why a customer likes to shop at one mall over another, chooses one retailer over another, buys one brand over another, or has a certain fashion sensibility – can be connected to direct personal experiences – the cow paths in our neural network.

The degree to which customers are genetically wired versus the sum of their individual experiences is a key factor in how they behave around other people and in environments such as stores.

Does brain science's nature-nurture discussion follow us into the shopping world? You bet. How could it not? The key issue for retailers and creators of shopping places is to figure out which triggers, be they built into a customer's mind from years of evolution or the direct result of personal life experiences, impact how people shop in the store. This information about what drives customer behavior at the brain level should then impact design and merchandising.

The feelings we have and behaviors we exhibit in shopping places are created by those parts of our brains that are genetically mediated at a subconscious level *and* by those thoughts and emotions that are partly created by direct, in-the-moment, experience.

Getting to Know You

Imagine trying to understand the specifics of every customer's personality, motivations, needs and desires.

This used to be possible when customers and shop owners knew each other personally. Customer/retailer relationships were different when your local merchant knew your and your kids' names, when your birthday was, could tell you your favorite color, and could serve up your 'usual.' The personal touch spoke to our need for validation, a sense of community, and connection.

There are a few retailers whose present-day practice of serving their customers harkens back to the old-school days of building personal relationships. I suspect that it happens more frequently in smaller towns, where independent shop owners run main-street, rather than big-name brands. At my local coffee shop they know my name and they have learned what I will most likely order. But in many of today's shopping places that sense of intimacy has long since disappeared.

At this point in the design and development of shopping places, retailers rely on a law of averages, providing environments that capture a large number of people with similar characteristics and cater to them the best they can. I suppose the approach is very 'democratic'; everybody gets the same treatment. With national brands or retailers, the customer interaction protocols are delivered the way a quarterback in football calls an audible. Everyone on both teams hears the same message. While it means something to everyone on the retailer's team, there are likely people on the customer's side of the line of scrimmage who don't understand it and are left thinking that since they don't understand the message, it can't possibly have been meant for them personally. The same message is supposed to serve everyone, despite individual differences.

Aggregating customers into groups based on demographics is about to change.

With increased use of the Internet to shop, retailers are able to collect an enormous amount of data about customer preferences and shopping history. By extrapolation from the data they collect, they are able to better predict buying behaviors that are based upon the 'country road' and 'cow path' parts of the customer's brain – those parts of our brain that mediate feelings and behaviors which have been built on cultural and individual experiences. There will come a time in our shopping future where the influences on buying behavior based on individual personalities or preferences will not be such a mystery.

If we take into consideration emerging technologies and our ability to capture very specific data as customers shop online, on the street or in the store, we are getting closer to being able to have environments that might well address *every* customer – by their first name – while shopping.

The increasing use of smartphones with GPS systems is enabling retailers to identify more customers who come into their stores because the phones emit digital signatures that locate the user anywhere on the planet.

Along with the identification of the individual phone is a host of content that describes its owner. Virtually any amount of data can be tagged to a smartphone device. This is potentially invaluable to brands and retailers, assuming they are able to parse the ones and zeros into meaningful chunks and use them to better define relevant experiences for the shopper.

As retailers and brands become more aware of the particular information on an individual shopper, there are opportunities to do things as simple as pushing coupons to the customer's phone for in-store use. Retailers could also provide more complex digital interactions, such as allowing customers to control digital content throughout the store to meet their specific desires and shopping habits.

User-generated content is becoming increasingly popular. We're not yet at the stage of user-generated *stores*, but the idea is not so far-fetched as you might think, and it is very much in the digital future of retail place making.

In the meantime, an enormous amount of time is spent culling down customer data into demographic and psychographic profiles, to better identify potential needs and wants. Presumably the more we know, or think we know, the better we are able to create experiences that are crafted to quicken the transition from individuals being shoppers to committed customers. If the goal is to enhance the likelihood of someone making a purchase, then catering to his or her individual personality type is a step in a positive direction. Customers like the validation that comes from being recognized as a valued part of a brand's business.

In the creation of retail concepts, it is not unusual for brands to *create* customer profiles. The understanding of new and developing opportunities in particular markets, puts most retailers on a creative path to imagine who they believe to be the ideal shopper for their stores. Given a certain number of personality characteristics, store environments are designed to resonate with the target customer. A lot of work goes into creating fictional personality types that are most likely to find the store, products, presentation and sales associates a perfect fit to who they are and what they need or want. This makes perfect sense; create places that make the customer feel at ease, connected and validated, and they are likely to stay longer and buy more.

But, there is a downside to creating shopping places that focus on the sensibilities of manufactured personalities. If we consider the highway/road/path analogy, to focus on the minutia of personality, we can get caught in the long grass on the sides of the cow path and potentially miss the more direct route to emotional connection with the customer by taking the highway. When we focus too much on the details, we leave out the broad brushstrokes. Often designers of retail places get mired in the things that customers never really notice or appreciate.

Personality traits are one thing, but the innate drivers to behavior are things you can most always count on. While retailers are becoming increasingly adept at determining the specific nature of an individual shopper, virtually all shoppers share many fundamental feelings and behaviors about the experiences they have. Individual personality characteristics tend to be more fluid depending on a host of factors such as whom people may be with while shopping, or demographic factors such as gender, age, race or economic standing. Personality can be a moving target.

We can't discount the value of understanding behaviors born of the characteristics of a person's personality. But, we need to be aware of more direct and reliable responses to the environment that are not based on the fickle idiosyncrasies of a person's personality type. There is a baseline of human behavior that applies to all individuals regardless of where they grew up or what language they speak.

It's what makes us human.

While understanding the specifics of customer personality is good, underpinning the shopping experience is a set of traits that are shared by all. Motivation giant Edward Deci suggests we all need to feel competent, autonomous, and connected. The desire for empathic connection, the avoidance of pain, and 'hardwired' brain systems for sensory perception are absolutes that cannot be overlooked when creating effective shopping places.

So, it's critical for retailers, brands and designers of shopping places to understand the core drivers of customer behavior. Many of these are built in to every shopper's brain thanks to a few hundred million years of human brain development. Others are expressed as emotions and behaviors that are likely to be triggered by culture and more individual experiences.

In the first case retailers can turn to a wealth of brain science that is pulling back the curtain on the mysteries of how our brain works as an integrated network of various functional areas.

In the second case, they can continue to look into more thoroughly understanding customers by developing better personal relationships with them. This may come from increasing authentic one-on-one interaction with them in-store (or online), which, in many retail environments, is woefully lacking.

Within the digitally driven economy, retailers increasingly will learn from the details that come from following the Hansel-and-Gretel-trail of digital breadcrumbs left behind every time the shopper interacts with the retailer or brand at digital touch-points along the customer journey.

07

Three Pounds of Tofu

"Brainametrics" – Brain Facts 101

We have started our primer on brain science and its relationship to shopping by looking at how functional areas might work in the brain and very broad ideas around a concept of mind. In this chapter I'm going to shift to a more focused look at some specifics of the brain and how they may directly influence the design of shopping places and customer engagement. With growing understanding of what areas of the brain do, we can better estimate with greater certainty what reactions we are likely to get when customers are in the midst of shopping activities.

First, a few brain facts that will serve to influence your thinking about how it goes on a shopping trip.

Energy use:

- Your brain is about 3% of your body weight, but uses about 20% of your body energy.
- 20% of the blood flow from the heart goes directly to the brain and the brain uses about 20% of the oxygen that you breathe.

Development in childhood:

- A process called "synaptic pruning" starts at birth and continues into teenage years as the brain trims away unused or less efficient neural pathways.
- Measures of brain activity indicate that in the second half of a child's first year of life, the prefrontal cortex is making connections between neurons at a rate such

that a child's brain consumes twice as much energy as an adult brain. This hyper growth rate of wiring between neurons continues until about the age of ten.

- During the first month alone, the number of connections increases from 50 trillion to 1 quadrillion. If a baby's body grew at this rate, the body weight would skyrocket from around 7.5 pounds at birth to about 170 pounds by the age of one.

Numbers of neurons:

- There are about 86 billion neurons in the brain, though typically the literature has suggested the round number of 100 billion, which makes for easier math. (By the way, an octopus brain has 300 million neurons and a jellyfish has none.)
- Each of those neurons is connected to about 10,000 other neurons, making about a quadrillion connections.

Brain usage:

- Raw computational power of the human brain is between 10^{13} and 10^{16} – about 200 billion operations per second.
- A supercomputer has 60,000 miles of wiring. The brain's equivalent of interconnectivity would be about 200,000 miles of wiring.
- We do not only use 10% of our brains, as is often said. We use all of it almost all of the time.
- The right side of the brain controls the left side of the body and the left side of the brain controls the right side of the body.
- All thoughts, actions and feelings are the result of electrical and chemical reactions in the brain.
- The brain is 'plastic,' meaning it can repair itself and even generate new neural connections in response to new learning. Under certain circumstances, the brain can even create new cells through a process called 'neurogenesis.'

Evolution and the Developing Brain

The first time you get a look at the human brain, what you see is a wrinkled mass of folds and overlapping structures. The idea that the brain is made up of a number of functional areas is somewhat hard to understand when looking at the structure as a whole. The best way to envision the brain is to think about it from the point of view of how it developed through human evolution.

The "Triune Brain" theory developed by Paul McLean constructed a model of development from the most primitive spinal cord evolving to the oldest structure, the 'Reptilian Brain,' leading to the 'Limbic Brain' and finally to the most recent area to evolve, the 'Neocortex.'[42]

The Reptilian Brain appeared about 500 million years ago first in fish, then developed into the structure we see in most of today's reptiles about 250 million years ago. The reptilian brain is pretty simple and includes the 'brain stem' and the 'cerebellum.' It is particularly good at determining threats and discomfort. One of its claims to fame is the 'flight-fight-freeze' response. It is rigid and compulsive though it keeps brain arousal levels in check as well as basic functions such as the heart beating.

The Limbic Brain showed up in mammals about 150 million years ago. This part of the brain sits 'on top' of the reptilian brain and is responsible for recording memories of behaviors that resulted in agreeable or disagreeable experiences. Today we think of this area as the seat of our emotions.

The limbic area of the brain works with the older reptilian brain to motivate behaviors that are more automatic and not particularly flexible. The limbic system often is involved in the *value judgments we make*, that are often unconscious, though no less influential on behavior.

The Neocortex expanded greatly about 2 to 3 million years ago as the genus *Homo* emerged, continuing to evolve significantly until about 100,000 years ago. The neocortex developed into two hemispheres that are responsible for the functional capacities that we consider the essence of modern humans. The neocortex has four lobes.

- **The Occipital Lobe** is located at the back of the head. It is the main seat of *visual functioning*; form, color and movement are all analyzed by this area. By comparing visual perception with memories of things you have been exposed to, the visual cortex allows you to recognize the things you see. The occipital lobe passes this information to the limbic area for immediate evaluation about what behavior may be an appropriate response to a particular set of visual stimuli.

- **The Temporal Lobe** is related to higher processing of *visual functions*, recording *memories*, processing information about *sounds*, and the conversion of sounds into *linguistic representations*. This area allows us to speak and understand language. More *complex, non-reactive, decisions* are mediated in the front part of the brain that is good at performing crosschecks and cost-benefit analysis. The right temporal lobe is related to laying down *visual memories* and the left is more involved in *verbal memory*.

- **The Parietal Lobe** is the *spatial orientation area* and combines information from multiple senses, including vision, hearing, and touch. The parietal lobe takes in auditory and visual information and associates them with memories to help give them meaning. The parietal lobe formats motor commands for the muscles that allow the body to be oriented in space. Without the parietal lobe, you would not be able to understand written or spoken language.

- **The Frontal Lobe** is the most 'evolved' part of the cerebral cortex in humans. This is the part of the brain that is responsible for making us 'human.' It is often thought of as being responsible for what are typically referred to as *executive functions* – higher order thought processes.

In addition to reasoning and planning, the frontal lobe modulates your emotions and helps to give you personality. The pre-frontal cortex (PFC), the most forward area, located behind the eyes, has nine key functions associated with it.

- Regulation keeps the heart, lungs, and intestines all coordinated and in balance.
- Attuned Communication is our capacity to be in relationship with other humans and to be able to be attuned to their subjective experience.
- Emotional Balance keeps emotions in equilibrium – not too emotional as to be manic, and not too low or depleted to be rigid.
- Response Flexibility allows you to mediate consciously how to respond to outside stimulus. It can act as a buffer to mediate emotional responses, so that you don't always act on impulses and are able to choose the best course of action in a situation.
- Fear Modulation is part of the older limbic area in a structure called the amygdala, but the PFC has fibers that connect the 'executive function' areas in the more recently developed part of the brain with those in the amygdala so we are not always jumping out of our skin at every loud noise or the sight of every large object.
- Insight is responsible for the ability to be an active participant in the unfolding of your personal story. This is the ability to see yourself in the past, present and future and behave in a way that creates the narrative of your life.
- Empathy is the ability to put ourselves in other persons' shoes and to be able to see the world from their point of view. Structures called 'mirror neurons' and 'Von Economo' neurons wire the brain in a way that allow us to 'feel' what someone else is feeling.
- Morality helps you have a bigger picture of the world and not just to act on your primitive brain stem impulses. That you can think about the larger social good, reason imaginatively about acting morally, is part of the PFC's function.
- Intuition results from feedback from neural networks connected to your intestines and heart that give you the ability to be bodily aware of how the environment is making you feel. We referred to this earlier as 'gut feelings' and 'heart-felt' emotions. While they are not 100% reliable, we should pay attention to them, since they are among the body's ways to send us messages about the environment.

From the point of view of evolution, the largest and most recent part of the brain's development has come in the growth of the neocortex, the wrinkly part we all envision when we hear the word 'brain.' This part of the brain has developed the most in humans. Furthermore, the pre-frontal cortex has developed disproportionately in relation to other structures.

Since mammals arrived on the scene about 200 million years ago, the cerebral cortex has become larger in importance than the other, more ancient structures of the brain. The older parts of the brain didn't go away during the evolutionary process – they had become too important to our basic functioning – but they were added upon with the development of structures that would allow for higher-level behaviors.

The increase in size of the neocortex seemed to go hand-in-hand with the evolution of more complex social groups. Many of the functional areas in this part of our brain help in processing things such as language, reasoning skills and morality, all of which were a crucial part of forming cooperative societies.

There was, of course, a practical matter at hand with the increasing size of the brain, namely, the resulting larger size of heads. It would seem natural for the heads of primates to have continued to increase in size as the brain developed, and they did, to a point about a 100,000 years ago when human brains (and therefore, heads) simply couldn't get any larger.

Had the brain continued to evolve larger in volume, the size of the skull would have had to increase as well, making it rather impossible to pass through the pelvis during childbirth – unless women's hips also evolved to be about three feet wide. This would have had a disastrous effect on activities such as, say, running, which was pretty important when trying to flee from animals with teeth the length of your forearm.

From an energy consumption point of view, the brain is a gas guzzler. Even though it only represents about 3% of the body's overall weight, it consumes about 20% of the body's energy. Had the human brain continued to get any larger, it would have required too much in terms of energy resources, simply to carry out the most basic behaviors to survive. Thinking would have literally been exhausting.

In a fascinating twist of evolutionary design prowess, instead of continuing to get larger, the brain began to *fold in on itself*, giving us the crenulated structure we have today. Instead of simply increasing in volume, development occurred to increase the surface area of the most recent part of the brain. It turns out that if you unfolded the left and right sides of the neocortex, you'd have a couple of large pizza shapes. All of that is densely packed into our skulls.

There is a commonly held idea that the cerebral cortex is the pinnacle of brain evolution, owing to the fact that brain size is greater in what we consider intelligent species. "There is a long tradition that ascribes properties to humans that are supposedly not found in other animals...It is assumed that animals with larger brains are more intelligent than those with smaller ones."[43]

According to studies done in the past few years, we shouldn't get too excited about holding on to this dogma. Bigger (cerebral cortices) does not necessarily mean 'better' *or* any 'smarter.'

When you look at the size of the cerebral cortex across animal species, there is indeed an increase in its size in relation to the whole brain going from about 40% in mice to 60% in capybaras. In primates it increases to 67% and in humans it comprises a whopping 80% of the entire brain.

However if you go searching beyond primates to other mammals that have big brains to see if the idea of big brains means more smarts, we find that whales and elephants have brains that are about 4 to 5 times larger than ours. Most of us would agree that despite their relatively bigger brains, their behavior is much less complex than that of humans.

For years, scientists have believed that humans' unparalleled abilities for planning and abstract reasoning came from having a more developed cerebral cortex, particularly the front part of our brain in the prefrontal cortex. It turns out that this is not entirely true. When you compare the size of the human brain to that of our closest evolutionary relatives, the great apes, ours is just about what you would expect for a primate of our size.

So, bigger brain size does not directly account for intelligence.

In addition to thinking that there are direct correlations between brain size and intelligence, scientists have also thought that a bigger brain would naturally mean more neurons. More brain volume, you would think, implies more brain cells to process information. One might also expect that as the cerebral cortex grew in size that you would find a larger proportion of these additional neurons 'up front' in the most recently developed areas of the frontal lobes of the brain.

Wrong again.

In comparing our brain size to that of chimps and gorillas, scientists have found that while we do indeed have bigger brains, humans *do not* have relatively more neurons.

The magic number of 100 billion neurons that is often used to describe the brain is somewhat overstated. It turns out that the number is closer to 86 billion, give or take about 8 billion in the average human male brain.[44] What is more curious about the fact that we have been off by about 15% in the overall estimation of how may neurons we have in our brains, is that *there are not more in the frontal lobes as we might have expected* (or hoped, so that we could find some explanation for what is so special about the human brain).

Despite the fact that the most evolved part of our brain occupies 81.2% of the total area, it contains only 19.1% of the brain's neurons. The cerebellum – the part of the early reptilian brain that is the seat of motor control, coordination, and motor learning, by comparison – occupies only 10.3% of the total brain but is jam-packed with 80.2% of the neurons. The entire neocortex, the area thought to be the engine responsible for human thought and culture, doesn't have as many neurons as the little caboose bringing up the rear.

If there aren't more neurons in the most recent area of the brain to evolve, what's going on at the front of the train?

The frontal lobes and the prefrontal cortex are the parts of the brain that are considered to be involved in memory and planning, response flexibility, abstract thinking, language formation and comprehension, initiating appropriate behavior, learning rules and sifting through the myriad of perceptual information coming into our bodies through the sensory systems and imagination. That's a load of responsibility, since these are functions we often consider as being those that make us human.

How could it be that relatively fewer neurons in the frontal areas of the brain can be so masterful at handling all of those tasks? So here's the deal: While there are fewer neurons in the cerebral cortex than the other parts of the brain, what has been determined is that there are *better connections* between them. "What is larger in the frontal lobes than in the rest of the brain... is the '*arborization*' of the neurons – that branching of the dendritic tips of the neurons with the possibility of increased connections."[45]

Each neuron has structures called dendrites that are like little branches that *reach out and connect to other neurons*. These dendrites provide each neuron in the prefrontal cortex with greater connectivity than in the other parts of the brain. This means that each of the individual neurons in the prefrontal area of the brain is wired to a larger number, and more diverse set, of other neurons. Moreover, these connections are coming from a wider network across the brain, creating more neural chatter but essentially putting more hands on deck when solving problems. It's like your brain's very own social network.

More *connections* between the neurons in the most recently evolved part of the human brain are what seem to differentiate our brains from those of the other creatures on the planet. How the cells in our brains are able to communicate with each other is a defining feature of what makes us human.

How Brain Cells Communicate

When we consider feelings, thoughts and behaviors, and how all these things come to be, none of them would happen unless we had the neuron. The neuron is the conduit through which all of the information of the system is channeled. In the past few chapters we have described the neuron as a key feature of the complex system, but what is it made of? How does it play a role in sensory input and communication across the brain's network of superhighways, country roads and cow paths?

In addition to the cell body, neurons are made up of 'axons' and 'dendrites.'

Axons are long extensions that reach out to other neurons and are the structures through which electrical signals move.

Imagine you want to water your garden. Your house is the cell body and a single axon could be considered the hose attached to the spigot through which the water flows.

At the end of the axon (garden hose) is a 'synapse,' the connection point where one neuron communicates with another. At the terminal point of the axon a bulbous formation that holds chemicals called neurotransmitters helps to 'connect' one neuron to another. There is not a physical connection between neurons but rather a very small cleft across which chemicals flow to attach to and possibly activate the next neuron.

Dendrites look like small branches that also connect to other neurons and receive messages from other brain cells. You could think of dendrites as additional hoses all branching off the one connected to the spigot. They reach out and connect to other neurons (or go straight to the flowers they are responsible for watering in the garden).

In order for the whole system to start working, a dramatic reversal of electrical potential needs to occur at one part of the cell's membrane. A stimulus may result in a change in the cell from being negatively charged to being positively charged. When this happens an electrical signal called an 'action potential' travels down the axon at speeds up to 100 miles per hour. Travelling at this speed, the neuron can fire up to 1,000 times a second.

The spigot at the house is opened and the water comes rushing into the hose on its way to the nozzle you are holding at the end of the line.

When these electrical signals reach the end of the axon they stimulate the release of the brain's chemical messengers called 'neurotransmitters.' These chemicals float across the synaptic cleft and bind to receptor sites, which act as on-off switches for the next neuron. If the chemicals released bind to the appropriate receptors on the next neuron, the signal is transferred and passed down the neural network.

When the water fills the nozzle at the end of the hose, you squeeze the trigger, spraying water on the target plant. The plant gets the needed water and a series of chemical reactions take place that support its growth.

Billions of neurons are receiving thousands of signals every second from tens of thousands of other cells. The spikes of electricity that blast down the axons on their way to other neurons come fast and furiously. It is not just the shear number of spikes that makes a difference in things such as perception, memory formation and behavior. Instead, researchers are discovering that the *pattern and frequency* of firings likely lead to perception, cognition and memory formation. Brain cells receive inputs in different time sequences. The left and right ears, for example, are slightly out of synch since one ear may hear a sound on its side of the head before the sound travels through the air to the other ear.

We can get a better understanding of how communication between our neurons creates meaning by looking at how we process visual information in the environment. Each of our eyes has about 100 million photoreceptors in the retina that pick up changes in light patterns. As light comes into our eyes, it's processed by several layers of neurons. As we look at the world around us, cells at the back of the eyes change the visual input into a series of spikes that shoot down axons to the visual cortex at the back of the head. The signals are relayed and processed through various brain structures, giving rise to conscious perceptions of the environment. "All that you perceive of the visual world – the shapes, colors and movements of everything around you – is coded into these rivers of spikes with varying time intervals separating them."[46]

The firing frequency and the pattern of the electrical blasts down the axon create a sort of 'code.' The code has embedded in it all of the features of the visual images – the location of objects in space, shapes, colors, textures, light contrasts, and how the objects are moving. Making this more complex are groups of neurons that may be related to each of the features we perceive in objects in our visual field, and that relative firing patterns between neurons may also play a role in the encoded information.

It's not just the firing pattern in one neuron; it's also the pattern of other neurons that fire in relation to it, which transmits information. The combined activation of cells may signal to the brain to pay attention to particular environmental stimuli and an object's attributes. "Some evidence suggests that synchronized timing – with each spike representing one aspect of an object (color or orientation) – functions as a means of assembling an image from component parts."[47] So a pattern of spikes that signals 'round contour' fires in synch with a pattern that represents the 'color orange,' enabling the visual cortex to understand that what you are looking at is an orange, not an apple.

Even at a cellular level we humans are all about relationships.

Fire Together-Wire Together

"How do you get to Carnegie Hall?"

"Practice, practice, practice!"[48]

Everything that we do as customers is based on neural firing patterns. When we make a practice of coming back to a store or buying from the same brand, or creating a positive association and sense of pleasure with a product, we are experiencing the repeated neural firing that creates new wiring. The specific firing patterns that the neurons shoot back-and-forth between each other becomes significant in determining how we understand the world. Understanding, behaviors and emotions are coded into those sequences of neural firings.

The synapse is 'strengthened' when the firing of one neuron on one side of the synapse leads the neuron on the other side of the synapse to register a stronger response. The more these firings take place, the more the resultant memories, perceptions, thoughts, or behaviors are set in place and become hardwired into who you are. This is commonly known as the 'fire together-wire together' rule for how neural connections in the brain work. The more you practice something, the more it is embedded in to the neural firing patterns of the brain. As you think, behave or feel anything repeatedly, the cell firing patterns and the neural connections of the particular pathways between activated neurons get strengthened.

It seems reasonable that if perceptions and thoughts are generated by neural firing patterns, then the more you think about something, the more strength you are giving to the neural connections which are the foundations of those thoughts. Behaviors that come as a result of those thoughts are similarly strengthened. You literally can think and practice your way into doing some things or behaving differently.

As a good example of the idea of how practice makes perfect, the gold medal winner of the 2012 Olympic archery competition was considered legally blind, yet scored an impressive score of 699 out of a possible 720 points. Im Dong-hyun is said to launch upwards of 1,000 arrows a day in practice. Each time he plants his feet, steadies himself, and draws the arrow back on the bow – his brain is encoding the body memory of what it feels like to release the arrow and hit a bull's-eye.

Over and over again, Im Dong-hyun teaches his brain what the angle his arm holding the bow needs to be, where his right elbow is in relation to the height of the target, and how much stress he feels in his shoulder, forearm and fingers as he grips the bow-string and pulls it back. Once the body memory is encoded into his neural network, repetition locks it in for retrieval and success. Hopefully, neurons that have wired together will fire together and the next shot will bury itself in the center of the target 70 meters away.

So yes, 'practice does make perfect,' 'you can teach old dogs new tricks' and 'if you don't use, it you lose it.'

Now consider brand development and customer relationships. Good branding, effective retailing and enhancing customer satisfaction are all about strengthening associations through neural firing.

Still, how can retailers create fully committed and impassioned customers who repeatedly visit their stores or website? Practice, practice, practice! They need to get their customers to practice behaviors, repeatedly, that result in positive feelings that are in turn associated to memories of positive experiences while shopping in stores or online. This of course puts the pressure on them to deliver every time and every place the customer comes in contact with the brand.

From Synapse to Stores

The basic tenets of good retail place making, like the consistency of merchandise presentation, have a basis in our neurology. Continually giving the customer the same experiential cues forms a set of neural firing patterns that become encoded into their understanding of the brand, the store and what it means to be a customer.

When variables are consistent with each visit, the customer's brain quickly understands the sequence of events that is about to occur and the shopping trip unfolds with a sense of confidence and comfort. Consistency in the delivery of the shopping experience sets customer expectations and customers come to rely on these established patterns.

What about change and novelty? Changing displays, presentation approaches, and category adjacencies too frequently can keep the customer recalibrating and may lead to confusion. On the other hand, if continual change in a rapid cycle is part of the retail experience platform, then this too becomes a pattern and the customer might well say "come on, let's go to 'xyz.' It's always different and they have new things every day." Whichever the case, the idea is to *build a pattern of perceptions about the brand, the shopping approach and the environment* in which it is done. And once the patterns are set, a change signals novelty and the customer's brain takes notice.

None of these patterns is more important than those that have long been established to support the relationship between the customer and the brand/retailer/sales associate. The neurons that fire together when customers are in social circumstances have been part of our brain's evolution for millions of years. One might argue that neural pathways that have evolved to quickly identify emotions and intentions in other people's faces and body language have been crucial to our survival. The evolved brain has a quick, go-to reference set of facial expressions and body movements that we hardly have to think about, and are readily understood at a glance.

When customers form strong bonds to retail places, they embed memories and emotions into their neural networks. The more they think about the brands they love and the more they shop at stores they have an affinity for, the more these brands, retailers and shopping places literally become parts of who those customers are. Experience changes our neurophysiology.

Neurophysiological changes and new neural pathways are created that are directly related to experiences both in stores or by way of interaction through digital devices. Combined with a set of prewired neural networks resulting from millions of years of human development, the new patterns that are built through engagement in shopping become a powerful force in shaping the customer's experience along the path to purchase.

Our brain takes notice of the anomalies in our perceptions and the process of identifying new feelings, behaviors or emotions gets underway. Learning is a result of breaking old, established patterns and refocusing our attention on alterations in the patterns, or creating entirely new pathways. Once patterns are established in the brain and neurons are wired together, things that we experience which don't fit within those expected sequences are immediately felt as out of place by the brain. This can be a good thing. Interruptions in the expectations we have about how things are supposed to be, prove to be very valuable in getting customers to pay attention to the things we want them to see, places we want them to go, and buy what we want them to buy.

While the brain can grow in an additive process, making neural connections through repeated use, it is equally good at being efficient and getting rid of 'dead wood.' The other side of the coin in the 'fire together–wire together' idea of neural pathway formation is 'synaptic pruning.'

We start out as children with many more neurons than we end up with as adults. As children, we overproduce synaptic connections as our young brain grows, reaching its peak by the age of nine years old. By the time we begin to mature into teenagers, the brain goes on a process of trimming this number down. This is less a 'slash and burn' than a creation of a remarkable topiary garden. Neural pathways that are seldom used are selectively trimmed out of the network in preference for others that have become stronger through repeated use. The process is thought to continue and does not plateau after adolescence, but continues to drop off gradually until a person's late twenties. [49]

One of the largest implications to the trimming away of synapses is that cortical structures responsible for things such as empathy and our ability to engage in face-to-face embodied interaction (both crucial features of shopping places) might, if not continually used, be trimmed away during this time of maturation.

Now, think about the continual use of digital devices by today's teens. As their heads are down and their thumbs are flying across the screen, they are reinforcing neural patterns that favor that type of communication over interacting face-to-face. Long-term, multigenerational digital communication practices are setting us up to be woefully equipped to manage embodied interpersonal experiences. If shopping is a social paradigm, then retailers are facing a severe challenge as to how they'll deeply connect with their customers when they may not have as much mental circuitry to do it.

Growing Up Digital

The pervasive use of handheld devices is not only changing the way we are communicating with each other; it's also fundamentally re-wiring our brains. Repeated use of smartphones – with texts limited to 140 characters, acronyms and emoticons – is changing a few million years of brain evolution. What has taken a few million years to develop is unraveling in the most unexpected and pivotal change in modern human neurodevelopmental history. This change in the brain is happening in a way that will have profound effects on not just shopping, but everything. And, it is all happening not at an evolutionary pace over years and years, but in one or two generations.

Moving forward, the way brands and retailers will communicate with customers, and how the creation of shopping places will have to respond to remain relevant in an age of digital distraction, must be in lockstep with how the customer's brain is being re-wired.

If retail place making lags behind the changing brains of customers, a profound disconnect between brands and buyers will begin to emerge. It may manifest as a drop in customer traffic, but more likely, it might unfold as a brand being unable to reflect the needs and mindset of a changing customer. The growing chasm between what retailers have been doing and how customers will think and what they will want, will eventually require an overhaul to our thinking of what it means to connect to customers. The great challenge for retailers today is to keep up with exponential change. If they fall behind, the bridge they'll have to build will be a span to a distant shore that gets further away with every new length of deck that is built.

This change is more at the pace of 'revolution' than 'evolution.' With all revolutionary change, there are some casualties. From the brain's perspective, neural networks that support interpersonal communication through embodied, face-to-face experiences, are taking a direct hit.

In the summer of 2002 (a few short years before the advent of Facebook and other social media sites), two political science professors at Stanford University conducted a study that sought to identify the effect of Internet use on communication and sociability. Their findings indicated that, for every hour individuals spent using their computers and the Internet, traditional face-to-face interactions time with real people dropped by nearly thirty minutes.[50]

'Digital Natives,' those people for whom the Internet and digital technology is part of their everyday experience of life – are beginning to develop brains that are dramatically different than 'Digital Immigrants,' those for whom the digital information world is not as embedded in their daily lives, and who grew up in social groups that were not online, but face-to-face.

We have talked about the relationship between what is genetically encoded and what is learned. While evolution has made our brain the social organ of the body and an empathic relationship machine, much of the social behaviors we exhibit are learned along the 'footpaths' of daily experience. During the formative years of childhood, when brain change is at its peak, kids are spending increasingly more time on their computers, tablets and mobile devices. The neural structures that are developed or pruned away influence today's kids' future ability to engage in meaningful relationships.

In a critical developmental period, where it could be said that the brain is most 'plastic,' traditional neural pathways that are developed in embodied relationships are likely to be underdeveloped and risk being part of the brain's efficient gardening scheme and cut away by synaptic pruning.

A 2007 University of Texas study of more than 1,000 children found that on a typical day, at least 75% of them watched TV and 32% of them watched DVD's/videos for a total average daily exposure of 1 hour and 20 minutes. The children who were between the ages of 5 and 6 spent an additional 50 minutes sitting in front of a computer on the Internet. Many young children, 20% of young toddlers and more than 30% of 3- to 6-year-olds, also have televisions in their bedrooms.[51]

Young people can now be connected through digital media continuously, 24 hours a day. They are becoming increasingly disconnected from face-to-face interaction in a seeming preference for virtual relationships over the real thing. This of course is troubling not just because parents, who find communicating with kids in the teenage years a challenge, will find it even more difficult to talk with their adolescent children, but because the communication disconnect may well happen at a younger and younger age.

A 2010 national survey by the Kaiser Family Foundation found that the amount of time young people spend with entertainment media has risen dramatically, especially among minority youth. Today, 8- to 18-year-olds devote an average of 7 hours and 38 minutes (7:38) to using entertainment media over the course of a typical day. This adds up to a startling 53 hours a week! Given that teens are using an assortment of digital platforms to integrate into their social structures, "they actually manage to pack a total of 10 hours and 45 minutes (10:45) worth of media content into those 7."[52] Meaning, that in addition to the things they do, such as playing games and surfing the Internet to listen to music, upload and download video content – they are using digital media to communicate with each other in typical day-to-day activities. A large part of teens' social activities have been moving from face-to-face interactions to online communication through social network sites.

We are approaching the edge of a *communication chasm* and the effects on the neural structures of the brain are being revealed though scientific study. More access to digital media naturally leads to more exposure, which, of course, reinforces new neural pathways at the expense of others. But what is the increased exposure to digital content doing to the brain (especially the young plastic brains of kids and young adults)?

Is it really re-wiring the brain system as might be expected from the fire together–wire together paradigm?

If it is changing the neural circuitry, what is it trimming out? What is it helping to grow?

To answer these questions and highlight the problem facing the future of retail place making, we need to look at a couple of studies.

The first is about the ability of the brain to change, in as *little as five days*, in response simply to doing Internet searches with Google. The second is a study spanning more than *thirty years*, which presented some alarming results regarding the loss of empathy in college students.

Your Brain on Google

In 2009, brain researcher and author Dr. Gary Small wanted to look at how much impact extended computer time was actually having on the brain's wiring. Specifically he was interested in finding out how quickly the brain could build neural pathways and whether or not he could measure the changes as they occurred. [53]

Small's hypothesis was "…that computer searches and other online activities cause measurable and rapid alterations to brain neural circuitry, particularly in people without previous computer experience."[54] To test this hypothesis, he and his team studied the effects on subjects' brains after performing the simple task of something we all now take for granted: 'Googling' something.

Small and his colleagues established two groups – "Net Naïve," those who had limited Internet experience, and "Net Savvy," those who had more extensive experience. Each of the test groups read text on a computer screen that was formatted to simulate the typical layout of a printed book, and their brain activity was recorded on an fMRI machine. As Small had expected, the brain activities of both the Net Savvy and Net Naïve subjects were close to identical when reading the page of text. Each of these groups had years of experience reading books and areas of their brains that controlled language, reading, memory and visual abilities, lit up with little difference between them. Interestingly, during the book-reading test, the Net Savvy subjects also used an area of the left front part of the brain known as the dorsolateral prefrontal cortex. The dorsolateral prefrontal cortex, together with other connected areas, is thought to be important in working memory and executive function – including the regulation of thinking and action. The Net Naïve subjects showed little to no activity in this area.

Next, the subjects were asked to do a Google search as their brains were being scanned. The Net Naïve group showed a brain activation pattern similar to their text-reading task, with no appreciable difference in brain activity between the book reading and Internet searching tasks. The Net Savvy group, however, showed "significant increases in signal intensity in additional regions controlling decision-making, complex reasoning, and vision… Internet searching was associated with a more than twofold increase in the extent of activation in the major regional clusters in the Net Savvy Group compared with the Net Naïve group."

Finally, to see if he could train the brains of the Net Naïve subjects, Small had both of the groups go home and practice Googling for one hour a day for five days. At the end of this period, he had both groups repeat the Internet searching exercise while he scanned their brain activity. The findings? After just five days of practice, "the exact same neural circuitry in the front of the brain (as the Net Savvy subjects) became active in the Net Naïve subjects." With only five hours of practice Googling, the Net Naïve subjects had already rewired their brains.

Despite the exploratory nature of this study, it brings to light the question about how young, plastic brains are being changed when exposed to many hours of digital media each day. Because we know that emotions are coded into our neural circuitry through building up patterns of firings that wire neurons together, we are up against a particularly difficult challenge.[55]

Could it be possible that in the crucial years of brain development, interpersonal skills such as feeling empathy and the articulate use of language (which are key features to the success of shopping places) are being undone or replaced with neural patterns for different skills that simply get more frequent use by a younger generation glued to its smartphones and the Internet rather than face-to-face interaction?

Well…there is some scientific evidence that suggests that the brain changes that come as a consequence of early and prolonged exposure to technology are not only possible, but that they may never be reversed. Does that make you want to think twice about giving your young daughter or son their first smartphone in elementary school?

Small suggests that, while today's young brains are being wired for, and by, "rapid-fire cyber searches," the neural pathways for human communication "weaken as customary one-on-one people skills atrophy."[56]

If you believe in one of the core themes of this book – that shopping is first and foremost a social paradigm – then there is a whole lot of thunder on the horizon. If you are a retailer, a store designer or even a shopper, there are a number of questions which require thoughtful consideration:

If young shoppers are potentially rewiring their brains so that one-on-one, face-to-face interaction is unlikely if not impossible, how will we engage customers in a full-bodied, emotional way when in the future they may not have the mental machinery to do so?

Will technology continue to change our brains so that this key feature of shopping is no longer relevant? If so, what will become of the store when we will really no longer have to go there?

What will the social aspect of the shopping experience become? Will it be a series of texts, emoticons, and word phrases in 140 characters?

Can the subtlety of brand message be conveyed in a handful of handheld screen views?

How will retailers and customers communicate if they ever get face-to-face? Will digital in-store technologies trump the personal interaction?

To stay out of the front of the retail revolution, these questions really need to be asked and thought about carefully even though we may be unable to answer them today. We need to hypothesize about the future of retail places not just a year out from today but what they may look like ten years from now. As emerging technologies reshape the nature of experience making, shopping, and the ways we go about doing it, will most definitely fall in line. Changing processes will change the shopping paradigm. Those retailers who choose not to adopt a mindset of future-casting will slip quickly into obsolescence and become irrelevant to an emerging customer.

Are College Students Less Empathic Than Their Predecessors?

The second of the studies that points to the potential long-range challenge of engaging customers in an embodied, empathic way comes from the study of empathy in students graduating college. Unlike the study by Gary Small on the effect of Internet searching for a period of five days, a study led by University of Michigan researcher Sara Konrath was a cross-temporal meta-analysis published in August 2010 that looked back over *30 years*.[57]

The focus of the Konrath *et al's* research was specifically to look at empathy as a measure of how this quality in people helps them relate to others in a way that promotes cooperation and unity rather than conflict and isolation. If Konrath could determine that there was a change in people's ability, or willingness, to be empathic over time, she might also be able to draw correlations between environmental factors such as socio-economic conditions, the growing prevalence of digital technologies in people's lives, and how these are related to people's ability to relate to each other.

Determining the relative amount of empathic extension between people may provide insights into how and why people help and relate positively to one another.

In this study, the researchers examined scores on the "Interpersonal Reactivity Index," which measures a multi-dimensional theory of empathy, in American college students over thirty years. The IRI takes into account a number of factors such as 'Empathic Concern' (EC) and 'Perspective Taking' (PT).

'Empathic Concern' measures people's other-oriented feelings of sympathy for the misfortunes of others and, as such, is a more emotional component of empathy (e.g. "I often have tender, concerned feelings for people who are less fortunate than I").

"Perspective Taking" is a more cognitive or intellectual component of empathy and measures "people's tendencies to imagine other people's points of view (e.g. "I sometimes try to understand my friends better by imagining how things look from their perspective").

One might expect that increasing narcissism, individualism and materialism during the past decade would naturally have led to a decrease in empathy during this period. It is hard to be overwhelmingly concerned with your self-interests and equally empathic for others – at the same time.[58]

Konrath's research suggests that the growing self-interest among graduating college students is further reflected by the extraordinary growth in the popularity of social networking sites from (at first) MySpace to Facebook and Twitter where users publish, for all the world to see, their personal information, images, thoughts and opinions.

While it is true that social networks *can* of course include the attributes of reciprocity – sharing emotional concern and positive communal emotions such as sympathy and affection, Konrath found that young people "…more frequently remove themselves from deep interpersonal social situations and become immersed in isolated online environments."[59]

Not great news.

When the study published its results, the findings were perhaps not entirely surprising, but nevertheless startling. Empathy has *declined* over the years. From 1979 to 2009, empathic concern (EC) dropped 48% and perspective taking (PT) dropped 34%. Taken together as a representation of empathy, the results show that American college graduates have 40% less empathy than their predecessors. And, the precipitous decline began to occur around 2002.

At the Google Atmosphere Conference in 2010, Google's CEO Eric Schmidt said that prior to 2003, mankind had generated a sum total of 5 exabytes of digital content. This is equal to 5 million terabytes and is approximately 12 million times the information in all the books ever written.

Today we generate this amount of content in a matter of days.

Statistics like these, while not being exactly causal, leave Konrath and her team to "speculate that one likely contributor to declining empathy is the rising prominence of personal technology and media use in everyday life."[60]

It's not just that we are more twisted into the optic fibers of a cyber-world tapestry; it's that the information is also coming at such a blinding speed, that frequent technology users, both young and old, are in a state of continuous partial attention. We have become so used to things moving at the speed of light in the digital world that our tolerance for things that take time and patience has begun to wane.

Studies like those cited above point to a growing change in how we are communicating. The effect of these alterations on shopping is going to be nothing less than a complete overhaul in how retailers and brands reach out and connect to customers in a relevant way. *It's not just that there is more information to download into the shopper's brain. The brain itself is changing in the way it has been wired for millennia.*

When the Internet became firmly rooted as another channel to sell goods and services at the beginning of the millennium, the retailing world experienced a widespread panic that online shopping would be the end of the bricks and mortar store. It hasn't happened.

The Internet is now simply considered part of the retail landscape. To create better shopping places, we need to appreciate the complexity of brain change in response to the pervasive digital environment. Emerging technologies will force us to ask different questions about what drives customer behavior, and to understand better what is going to continue to engage the emotional, empathic brain that has been part of our human evolutionary history.

The brain will change.

Yours is doing so now… as you read this book. The way retailers respond – creating shopping environments that maintain relevance using technology as part of the experience – will restructure the channels for selling goods and services.

The store won't disappear any more in the future than it did when the Internet and online shopping began two decades ago. Shopping places will, however, evolve, maybe into environments we can only now imagine in movies.

Can retailers, brands and the designers of retail places keep up with the customer's changing brain? They'll need to. However, it will be a challenge to engage the shopping brain in a social paradigm that will be wholly different than what we have ever seen. To achieve and sustain relevance, shopping experiences will become remarkably adaptable taking into consideration what will inspire and invite buying behavior in the context of a digitally distracted culture. In addition, retailers will have to discover new ways to engage a customer who, on a neurological level, may not have the mental machinery to fully engage in empathic extension as in years past.

In a digitally driven shopping world, there will be an abundance of opportunity for customer interaction. In the next chapter, I'll explore how the emotional relationship with customers is encoded in our neural circuitry and why the shopping brain loves patterns as well as seeks out novelty.

The Shopping Brain — It's All a State of Mind

Consciousness in the Shopping Aisle

The conscious shopper – is there any other kind? Shoppers know they are out on a shopping trip, using their smartphones to locate a store, downloading an app or price-checking a product they are about to buy. They know they are calling a friend, taking a picture, talking to a sales associate, picking up a garment from a clothing rack, pulling out their credit card and paying at a cash register. Shoppers know they are shopping and they are making decisions based on the fact that they have voluntarily given themselves to the experience. They know what they want and where to get it. And, when they don't know, they figure out where to go for help.

While shoppers may be consciously aware that they are on a shopping trip, they may be unaware that emotional reactions, seemingly out of their conscious control, can be triggers to buying behavior. The motivation to make a purchase is not solely determined by idiosyncratic personality traits that come about from individual life experiences, nor are they driven solely by demographics. Customers sometimes buy things they never expected to while on a shopping trip and the reasons they do so can be based on innate feelings more than conscious decisions.

As I said earlier, most of our 'thoughts' are happening in our subconscious, which implies that most of our shopping experiences are subconscious, too. If so much is happening below the radar, why do we need to talk about consciousness in the shopping aisle? Two important reasons.

First, what we actively think about while participating in shopping places – conscious thought – still has an enormous impact in decision making. We are thinking beings who have internal dialogues that influence what we do as we look at a shelf full of products or plan a shopping trip. *'Do I go to this store or the other? Do I look left or right when I first enter a store? Do I ask for help from the sales associate or try to figure it out on my own? Do I go all the way to the back of the store or make a quick tour of the first twenty feet and turn around and leave? Do I buy this thing or that? Do I get it now or do I wait? Do I even like this place?'*

These are but a few of the internal dialogues we have as we engage in shopping. In fact we are talking to ourselves all the time while shopping. Sometimes these are reasoned discussions, and other times ridiculous arguments, but we are in dialogue with ourselves, a lot, while we are walking about the aisles.

Secondly, a consideration of consciousness is key because most of what we talk to ourselves about while we are shopping, is *primed by our subconscious.* 'So wait a minute,' you're thinking. 'We're going back to the subconscious again?' As it turns out, even though we would like to believe that what is front-row-center in our conscious mind we simply call into existence because we want to, a lot of what surfaces is pushed there from previous experience in history or from as recently as a moment ago.

Determinations of whether to buy a product based on what we think about its price – *Is it too high and out of our budget or is it just right with enough saved to get lunch at the food court?* – we would think are all based on conscious processing of the cost-benefit analysis done in the rational, intellectual part of our brain. And they are, to a degree. But then older brain systems that do things like recognize and help to avoid pain and seek pleasure come into the equation as well. Many shopping activities, it seems, are mediated by an older part of the brain that *thinks* less and emotionally *reacts* more to the conditions of the environment. As the cogs in our cognitive process set to work, the decision-making process, to-buy or not-to-buy, hangs in the balance.

Let's focus on trying to get our heads around the idea of what consciousness is, how it comes into play for the customer while on a shopping trip and how the retailers and brands can influence what shoppers think about while walking the sales floor or cruising a website. We'll begin to see how the millions of little decisions being made by the brain in the subconscious are dynamically and intricately tied to the decision-making process *and* concept of the customer's mind.

If you ask most people to describe themselves, they might offer a title, label or what they do for living. They might also answer in terms of the relationships they have. I am Nick and Ben's father, Lu's husband, Joan and Don's son. I belong to this church and play on that baseball team. It is easier to define ourselves in these ways because they are relatable representations of the way our brains have constructed our realities.

It's less common for people to talk about the sum of their neurobiological experiences. People don't talk about themselves as a human multi-verse of electrical impulses, chemicals jumping across gaps between brain cells, memories and emotions which our minds both conjure up and keep locked away for easy retrieval when needed.

Just who is the 'You' in you? And where is it actually located in that little protective shell called the cranium? Is there a specific location of the brain where 'You' reside, some little corner or organelle that is the 'You' part of the brain? No, not really. 'You' are at once no place specific and equally everywhere in the brain.

Imaging technologies are allowing views into the brain that were considered impossible only a few short years ago. Today with Functional Magnetic Resonance Imaging (fMRI) and Electroencephalography (EEG) we can see pictures of the brain in action. These technologies allow us to visualize brain areas lighting up with various levels of intensity in response to stimulation of one sort or another.

Having huge magnets whirling around your head or a net of electrodes connected to your scalp to view into the brain is a far cry from feeling around on someone's scalp for bumps related to various "organs" as Franz Gall had thought. That we can actually see in real time what is going on in someone's brain is astounding and it has given us great insight to understanding how we function.

Consciousness, however, continues to confound philosophers and neuroscientists alike. While we can't see it, we know it's there, yet we haven't been able to find a brain module whose function is to bring about conscious thoughts.

It is somewhat ironic that despite our absolute agreement that we all have this faculty, we find it so hard to explain. This conundrum of coming to consensus on exactly what and where consciousness is led British psychologist, Stuart Sutherland to write, "Consciousness is a fascinating but elusive phenomenon; it is impossible to specify what it is, what it does, or why it evolved. *Nothing worth reading has been written about it.*"[61]

Images that are available to us today through various scanning technologies may help illustrate the 'neurobiological correlates to experience,' but it is a whole other thing to understanding how the activity of brain cells make the mysterious leap to becoming human thoughts and feelings.

In the Charlie Rose special series on the brain, John Searle, American philosopher and the Slusser Professor of Philosophy at the University of California, Berkeley offers further qualities of consciousness, suggesting three key, distinguishing features:

"…it has a special *qualitative 'feel'* – listening to music is different than brushing your teeth,

it is *subjective* – it is going on inside me,

it is *unified* – multiple sensory inputs exist as a unified 'feel'.…"

So, while we are getting better at understanding *what* consciousness might be, *where* it might be and *how exactly it comes into being*, are still a mystery.

In the same way that information is not all run through one command center, we can say the same about the idea of consciousness. There is no locus of conscious control that all of our various local processors channel information through that makes us aware of subjective experiences.

As neuroscientists determine that we have specialized capacities, functional modules, in all areas of the brain, they also suggest that conscious experience is related to each of the parts of the brain associated with each of these capacities. Their emerging understanding is that consciousness is spread out, across the entire brain; it is distributed.

If I am actively participating in shopping, I am aware of the experience. The more engaging the experience, the more the sense of being aware is heightened. Memories about the experience are consolidated. As customers walk the sales floor, all of their perceptual systems are taking in information. What they hear, see, smell, touch, and even taste – are being picked up by their brains and decoded. Customers are registering the sounds of voices – not just the narrative linguistic information imparted – but the feeling associated with the message, as well. They see whether something is in the periphery of view; not just that it is moving, but how. They are conscious of the relative lightness or darkness and the lighting or shapes. They sense the temperature of the air, its smell and even taste, in the environment.

Our brains crunch all of this perceptual data in milliseconds.

In a flash, memories are recalled, innate responses are triggered, and behaviors are enacted. Memories provide information about what we should do and new experiences are stored for future reference.

But, as customers walk the shopping aisles, they aren't actually or necessarily paying specific attention to most of what is around them. Unless of course, there is something that seems out of place, a smell that isn't right, a fast-moving object in the peripheral view, bright color, a variation in the size of a group of objects, the look on a face that signals indifference or boredom instead of a welcoming smile. When our brain picks up these anomalies, it tells us to pay attention. Our awareness of these things is brought from what otherwise would have been processed solely at a subconscious level to a place right up front, so we can determine a course of action.

People walking through a store aren't thinking about all this brain activity. They are often only aware of the end of the cycle when they have conscious thoughts about their experience. Usually, these thoughts are used to weigh out the pro's and con's of a situation, and make a decision.

When creating shopping places, it's more productive to have all of these things in mind while establishing customer journeys. There is no secret formula since no one shopper is exactly like another. What retailers and their store designers do need, however, is an increased awareness of how the brain's reaction to the environment creates the customer's mindset. As shoppers decode experiences at a subconscious level, feelings arise, which, in turn, activate the decision-making processes about making a purchase.

While we think that there is a 'You' in everyone and that this sense of consciousness is unified, these feelings are created by multiple and vastly different systems. "Whichever notion you happened to be conscious of at a particular moment is the one that comes bubbling up, the one that is dominant. It is a dog-eat-dog world going on in your brain with different systems competing to make it to the surface to win the prize of conscious recognition."[62]

The idea that multiple brain systems are in a sense vying for a position at the top of the consciousness ladder has a direct influence on what we expose customers to in shopping environments. Knowing that many of the stimuli perceived in an environment go *unnoticed*, the task for retailers and creators of shopping places is to craft environments that focus customer attention by *creating interruptions in perceptual patterns*.

It is more than just beautiful architecture and great merchandise that makes for great experiences and lasting customer relationships. It is how the various elements of the store, or even the website, come together to activate the shopper's perceptual systems, which in turn trigger subconscious brain processes, leading to emotions percolating to the surface of our conscious awareness where higher-order decision making and a customer mindset about the brand are held.

The Shapeable Shopping Brain

Not only are we able to look at the brain in action in 'real time,' but we are also able to witness, at a cellular level, the transformation of the brain in response to the environment. We can now see how neural pathways are formed, maintained through repetitive use and replaced by others as we learn new ways of doing things and communicating with each other.

Our brains are changing in response to our environment all the time. Perhaps one of the greatest insights that developed out of the original "Decade of the Brain" was that the brain is not the fixed structure it was believed to be. Not so long ago, scientists believed that once development through childhood was complete, the adult brain did not change. It was thought that on the other side of puberty, the mental machinery was set and you simply had to work with what you had from that point forward. It was generally accepted that we would naturally see a decline in mental capacity as we grew older.

Naturally, a view of brain development that says the brain doesn't change drew lines in the sand between the nature and nurture schools of thought. There has been a long-standing disagreement about what degree of brain functionality was due to genetics or environment and how it played into the development of personality, aptitudes and whether or not one was more or less vulnerable to disease. If all you could be was determined by what you had when you were born, then the view of brain development would be pretty limited. A static view of the brain did not allow for many things that we know about obvious facts such as that we can, and often do, learn new ideas, skills and aptitudes well into adulthood.

The great news is that scientists are continuing to find evidence that the brain is far more 'plastic' and that it changes with exposure to experiences, growing new neural pathways. For hundreds of years prior to this exciting discovery, scientists were wrong about the brain. In discovering that the brain was actually malleable and adaptable like Plasticene, neuroscientists coined the term 'neuroplasticity.'

How does it work? Well, think of your brain as a series of roads that are activated when you do, think or feel something. Every time you perform a particular task, behave in a certain way or feel particular emotion, your brain resurfaces the roads. The brain's internal road crews reinforce and build them up for faster travel.

Suppose that we start to think about something differently, feel a different way or learn how to do some other task; we start using a new road in our neural network. This is as simple as brushing your teeth with the opposite hand. The brain takes note of anything we do that is out of our typical routine. The new route builds new brain pathways because it's a new experience. This applies to everything including things such as learning a new language or musical instrument, tasting new foods, trying new gadgets, visiting new shops and, yes, visiting familiar shops that change their environments. Changing the way you perform a certain task, the way you behave in a social situation, or the way you feel about someone or something, puts the brain on the road to creating new pathways. This is neuroplasticity in action.

If we keep on using a pathway, our brains eventually begin to prefer the route it offers, and the new way of thinking, doing or feeling becomes second nature. Signals travelling along these well pruned paths move more easily. As the old route is used less frequently, the brain in its search for efficiency simply shuts down that particular road and redirects our mental traffic along the newly created path.

Years ago at my home, we had our kitchen renovated. The sink was removed and for a short while, we had to use the mudroom laundry basin to wash our dishes. Well, where do you think we all automatically turned for the first two days? The hole in the counter where the old sink was. Once we got used to going to the laundry basin, and the kitchen sink was installed, guess what happened? Of course, we kept going to the laundry basin for a day or two.

The brain works on a 'use it or lose it' paradigm. If you are not actively using a part of your brain, that neural real estate is given over to something else.

Psychiatrist and medical researcher, Dr. Norman Doidge details the amazing powers of neuroplasticity in his book *The Brain That Changes Itself.*[63] Doidge explains that the plastic brain can change both its function and structure depending on what you do with it. Thoughts and other activities that you do with your brain actually turn certain genes on and off inside you brain cells, which make proteins, which in turn change the structure of the cells and the neural network. This is great news because, in principle, it means that we can actually think, behave and feel our way to a new future.

If the brain was considered immutable and fundamentally fixed after childhood, it also follows that human nature would also be rigid and resistant, if not impossible, to change. We know of course that this is not true because our personal experiences tell us that we can learn new tasks, behave in new ways and feel differently about other people. The beautiful 'upside' to this revelation is that 'we *can* teach old dogs new tricks.' This bodes well for everyone when we understand that we can undertake practices that help foster empathic connection, potentially repair damaged areas of our brains and better integrate areas of our brains that support well being.

How does the brain's neuroplasticity come into play within shopping places? Well, for starters it means that customers won't always believe or feel the same things about a retailer or brand.

Personal relationships take work. So do retailer-customer relations. Retailers can't assume that customers will keep coming back. They must actively engage them to get them do so. Exposure to new experiences and having them repeated over and over again will eventually create new ways of thinking and feeling. While you never have a second chance to make a first impression, the second, third, fourth, and fifth experiences can fundamentally change the way customers may have perceived the brand or retailer when they first visited a store. Once learned behaviors and feelings are in place, it isn't easy to change them, but it can be done with concentrated effort. Change what people experience and you change what they think. Change what they think and you change their brains, building neural pathways for new feelings.

The Brain is a Complex System

To fully capitalize on the opportunities of a digitally driven retailing future, one needs to appreciate the intricate relationships of all of the elements that create the retail system. The store is simply one part of the system that will grow ever more complex as multiple distribution channels and buying modalities emerge within a digitally driven economy. The customer is yet another part within the set of interdependencies.

And, customers' brains are yet another complex subsystem to the overall network that results in the making of stores and customer experiences.

To say that the brain is a 'complex system' requires a baseline understanding of what that means. There are multiple characteristics – let's call them constituent parts – and it's important to know how they bring about emergent properties that could not have arisen without one part of the system influencing another. As Jack Nicholson once said while accepting an Oscar, "Everything counts."

The idea here is to illustrate that what happens in stores is the result of *multiple* systems working together to bring about a customer's state of mind—and, therefore, their shopping experience. It's true that if you look at the entirety of the retailing system, the individual customer is a tiny piece of the retail puzzle. But – and this is big but – it's the most influential part of the system. The customer and his or her complex brain has a profound impact on retailing as a whole. Without customers, the entire system just doesn't exist.

So, now, with that in mind, let's take a look at the characteristics of complex systems to better understand where retail design and practice can influence behaviors and, therefore, the outcome of customer shopping experiences.

We have briefly explored the brain as a system with multiple areas of functionality that work both serially and in parallel. All kinds of different activity is happening in the brain as we process experiences. While there are specific areas that process language, there are other areas that light up in fMRI scans which help to infer meaning and a course of action related to what we hear.

If we want to understand how the customer's brain creates experience, we have to see it not so much in terms of single functional areas being responsible for individual behaviors, aptitudes, or emotions, but that the entire brain is connected to create the whole of experience. Multiple areas all work together to bring about that experience and, of course, the process is not linear.

Weather, traffic patterns, even termites building a mound, are all examples of complex systems. While there are several definitions for complex systems, most of them contain the following eight common elements:

1. **Composed of multiple components:** Complex systems are *composed of many (often heterogeneous) components* that are linked in a network across the system. The individual components can also be complex themselves, often having many connections among the parts that make up the component itself.

    The brain is made up of a number of component parts – functional areas – each capable of processing certain stimuli but also that work with a number of other areas to make meaning out of our environment. One of the amazing features of the human brain that differentiates it from other higher-order mammals is the number of connections between neurons distributed across the brain. Because our brain is much more connected across the neocortex, humans can do many things the great apes can't. The newest part of our brains to have evolved has more connections than the brain of any other living creature.

2. **The whole is greater than the sum of its parts:** Complex systems cannot be described by a single rule and their characteristics are not reducible to one level of description. In other words, the interactions between the parts make the characteristics of the whole system different than collective characteristics of each component.

What arises out of the interaction of the brain's component parts cannot come about from only one area. For example, we have an area of the brain, the visual cortex, which allows us to process visual information. However, the vision processing area of the brain alone cannot bring about conscious thoughts of what we see in front of us. To be consciously aware of what it is we see, we rely on other areas of the brain to crosscheck visual information with stored memories. Having then determined what something is, we then rely on the language processing areas to describe what we see in words, or the motor processing areas to draw it.

3. **Dynamic and non-linear:** The interactions between each of the parts are dynamic and nonlinear. In linear systems, the effect of an input is always directly proportional to the cause. For example, reflex behaviors, such as when a doctor hits a nerve in your knee with a little rubber mallet and it triggers a 'knee-jerk response,' may be considered linear. In complex systems, the individual parts of the systems are interconnected in a non-linear way and a change in one area may have cascading effects on the system as a whole. *A small change in one area may have catastrophic effects in another.* Another example would be a 'high striker' or strongman game at a country fair. The harder you hit the lever with the mallet, the higher the puck rises on the vertical track.

The brain, in general, does not process the environment in a linear way. It takes in a great deal of input, and what comes out as an action, thought or feeling is not always a directly proportional response.

4. **Self-organizing:** Complex systems are self-organizing and arrange themselves in intricate patterns without any particular oversight by other components. [64]

When wind blows across a desert, sand grains organize themselves into patterns of waves. Cave crystals organize themselves into patterns to form complex groupings of enormous structures.

As I discussed earlier, though the brain has no one location calling all the shots, it organizes all of the perceptual information from external and internal environments, and, day-to-day, we generally feel in control and unified in our thoughts.

5. **Emergent phenomena:** The activities of a complex system have what are known as emergent properties, which is to say that while we may determine the basic effects of a system from its constituent parts, it may have properties that can only be determined from looking at higher-level activities.

So, for example, if we look to the building of a termite mound, you can study the biology and biochemistry of the insects at one level. At a different level, you can look at the mound building from the point of view of the 'social interaction' between the colony members to enable the building of the structure. Mound building is the termites' higher-level activity.

Individually, the parts of the brain can accomplish certain functions, but when working together, the brain can create emergent properties, such as the idea of 'mind,' through the coordinated effort of multiple components.

6. **Memories:** Because complex systems are made up of dynamic elements that are always receiving input, and in turn changing as a result, the system as a whole is likely to change over time. As changes occur, prior states of the system may have an effect on present states. In a complex system, the past shapes the present.

The brain's ability to encode memories for retrieval plays a very influential role in behavior. While it can be said that 'knowing better' does not always lead to 'doing better,' we have the ability to determine a future course of action by drawing on a bank of memories of previous experiences.

7. **Feedback loops:** Complex systems are those that have within themselves the capacity to respond to their environments in more than one way. They have feedback loops that can either reduce or amplify feedback in the system. As one part of the system is affected by a particular input, there's a corresponding response – a thought, a behavior, a feeling – which then, in turn, informs the system and modifies it.

We have the ability to learn by trial and error. You might say that we essentially learn by getting it wrong. When we break from predictable patterns our brain takes note and sends out signals across the entire network that something is *different*. To get the thing right, the brain's systems re-adjust, making changes until a new pattern is learned. Success or failure of the approach is fed back into the system, and the system is changed depending on the prior outcome.

8. **Open:** Complex systems are typically considered 'open.' An open system continuously interacts with its environment or surroundings. The interactions in an open system can take the form of exchanges of information, energy or material into and out of the system's boundaries.

The brain is continually taking in information. There is evidence that the brain takes in information even in coma or semi-vegetative states where you would think it is 'off-line.' Because the system is always open for business, it is under the influence of environmental stimuli – both externally and internally – that bombard the functional areas with input cascading through the system, potentially causing changes.

Since neuroscientists started trying to understand the brain as a whole by looking at what happens in each of the parts/functional areas, the thinking has been, 'if we can get to what each part is responsible for, then we might understand the whole of the brain and perhaps uncover the seat of the conscious mind.' Well, as it turns out, the more scientists uncover, the more 'complex' the whole picture becomes. What *is* clear is that many of the important answers to how things work come not only from understanding what each part does, but how the multitude of parts works in relationship to each other to create a unified whole.

Retailing is a Complex System, Too

With multiple elements all working together to create a network of experiences, the business of retailing is a complex system as well. There are multiple components to a retail enterprise. And somehow they all get arranged to create customer experiences.

Despite the well-choreographed efforts within the retail supply chain to get goods to market, the outcome is not always as predicable as retailers would like. The structure of the retail business network is enormous and weaves together a multitude of disciplines, including branding, consumer behavior, architecture store operations, materials, finishes and building technology, design, information technologies, and product manufacturing. While retailers control the product at the shelf level, this finely tuned machine is open to all sorts of influences that can have extraordinary and unpredictable consequences. The retailing system is 'open' and under the influence of outside elements.

Retailing as a complex system has embedded within it subsystems, the same as traffic and weather patterns, social networks and let us not forget, shoppers who can, on their own, be pretty complex as well. When you fit the customer and all of their emotional and behavioral intricacies into the retail system, predicting retail success stories becomes very difficult. As part of the complex system that is the retail world, customers, their feelings, behaviors and brains, are definitely a hugely influential part.

Product launches, seasonal deliveries and promotions don't come with iron clad guarantees of success. There are examples of products that were thought to be the next best thing that remained on the shelf and had retailers scratching their heads. And, who knew that the buying public wouldn't be able to get enough of Pet Rocks, Rubik's Cubes, Furbies, and Tickle Me Elmo?

Since the retail world is part of the global economy, many retailers rely on growers and manufacturers in other countries and delivery systems that are always under the potential influence of everything from pirates to weather patterns. Try telling Starbucks that the growing conditions in South American coffee plantations, the price of coffee beans and their myriad locations are not parts of a complex system. As customers line up to get their daily dose of caffeine, they are completely unaware of the multiple influences affecting the profit margins of the company. Among these influencers on Starbucks' business is how customers, themselves, feel when they're in their stores.[65]

Changes that take place in one component of the retail system – the emergence of handheld technology or the growing pervasiveness of social networks, for example – has fundamentally put the course of shopping on a new path. These new technologies, developed completely independently of the retail world, introduced new components into an already complex retail system from the outside. Smartphones have forever changed the way customers communicate with each other and connect to the brands they love. That they are in the hands of virtually every customer has had cascading effects on not just communication and buyer behavior, but on the customer's mindset about how shopping is done. Like any model of a complex system, the shopper's brain and the retail world in which it plays a role, are continually under the influence of external and internal forces.

Looking into the future of retail place making, the personal technology revolution will fundamentally change customer's brains and their mindsets towards shopping environments. Keeping up with these neural transformations that customers will undergo, and the resulting behaviors and feelings, will be a challenge and major focus for retailers as they try to maintain their relevance. They will have to learn how to adapt quickly or be rendered irrelevant and jettisoned in a preference for new shopping paradigms – not unlike old neural pathways pruned away in favor of new ones used more often.

As the speed of change continues to increase, our brain's neuroplastic nature will also be put to the test. In a digitally driven world, the customer's brain will be under continuous re-making. The human brain has already started its largest 'roadwork' project ever, as the entire neural system is being re-mapped, top to bottom, from highway to cow path.

A new factor of 'time' will add yet another layer of complexity to this intricate web of interdependent and interconnected complex subsystems. Transitions between brain states and customer mindsets about what shopping is will compress, and evolutionary change that occurs *over* generations will happen *within* generations. Even quicker than that.

This isn't an old-school 'evolutionary' process. Like a weather system that gathers speed, creating atmospheric turbulence that eventually gives rise to a tornado, the inputs into the complex retail business system are causing the air mass around the shopping world to revolve. As the twister of ones and zeros bears down on the retail landscape, the store will be swept up and placed in a new location that may look only vaguely familiar.

There will undoubtedly be effects on how and where we shop which we cannot possibly imagine at this point. Many of these changes will only become apparent as they grow out of the new relationships between the parts of the dynamic-adaptable-emergent-interdependent complex systems that are the world of shopping and the customer's neuroplastic, adaptable brain.

Of the common features describing complex systems listed above, *'openness'* is perhaps the most important. Neither the world of retail business practice nor the customer's brain, as complex systems, is impervious to outside influence. The customer's brain, as we will discover later, doesn't want to be an island unto itself since it thrives in relationship and situations of novelty. A closed system would shut itself off from a world of new experiences. For any of us who has ever tried to change behaviors, feelings or learn a new task, we'll agree that even though change is difficult, the brain is actually built for it and is more than eager to play. Equally, if the retail business world were closed, it would turn its back on remarkable technologies that are changing both operations and the way retailers and brands need to communicate. To stay relevant in their customers' minds, retailers and brands must continue to welcome outside influences into their complex systems.

The Shopping Mind

When thinking about the brain and its relationship to the concept of mind, we need to broaden our view of where the brain begins and stops in the body. It is important to understand that the brain doesn't exist only in the skull. Well, technically it does, but the idea is that the brain developed over a very, very, long period of time, from a relatively simple spinal column to the extraordinarily complex system we have today in our heads. "The simple connection of sensory nerves from the periphery to our spinal cord and then upward through the various layers of the skull-encased brain allows signals from the outer world to reach the cortex, where we become aware of them."[66]

The brain is not disconnected from the body but evolved from it. It extends beyond the three pounds of tissue in our skull to incorporate our entire body. If we think about it in evolutionary development terms, the brain is an extension of the nervous system, which is connected to all aspects of our body, though we often think of it in reverse.

I have used the terms 'mind,' 'mindset,' 'mind's eye' and 'customer's mind' without having provided clear definitions of exactly what they are, yet we all seem to intuitively understand what those terms mean. We would likely agree that we all have a mind, but we haven't defined what it is or where it might be found. While a universally accepted definition of consciousness has stumped scientists, philosophers, neuroscientists and psychologists, differing opinions on a concept of mind have been an elusive concept for most mental health professionals as well. However, Harvard trained neuropsychiatrist, Dr. Dan Siegel, has proposed a definition of the mind that is at once simple, as well as encapsulating the intricacies of the brain as a complex system.

Siegel's definition is useful for us to understand the importance of brain not just as a passenger on a shopping trip but also as an active creator of the shopping experience and the emergent property we call 'mind.'

"THE MIND IS AN EMBODIED AND RELATIONAL PROCESS THAT REGULATES THE FLOW OF ENERGY AND INFORMATION."

In this definition there are direct relationships with the idea of complex systems we discussed earlier. Siegel explains that this definition was derived from more than twenty-five years of practice as a neurobiologist and clinical psychiatrist and from interviews of literally thousands of professionals from the neuroscience community as well as thought leaders from other disciplines.

Despite the fact that this definition has found wide acceptance, he also points out that it has not gained *universal* usage, or agreement for that matter, among the neuroscience community. That said, to see why such a definition of the mind is useful to understand the customer better and to help create more effective shopping places, let's break it down.

- **"Embodied"**
  In Siegel's definition, the mind is embodied because the information and energy flow into and out of its complex system happens, at least in part, in the body. Energy and information pass through the body from the exterior before they ever get to the high levels of brain functioning.

  The voice I hear, the person I carry on a conversation within my mind is *in* me. It is embodied. I feel as though it is part of me, not outside of me, and it goes with me wherever I go. The feeling of having a mind is a phenomenological manifestation, there is no one physical place where the mind lives per se, yet we nevertheless feel it to be apart of who we are. As such, we perceive the mind to have a body, or at least be *in* a body, and that it is directly tied to the body's perceptions, sensations and behaviors.

The brain-body aspect of the mind applies well to our discussion of shopping. Customers physically experience the places they shop; shopping, traditionally, has been an embodied experience. People go to shopping places and put themselves in environments where all of their perceptual senses are engaged. As customers' bodies connect to the environment around them, their brains light up and their minds are active. In a way, then, the shopper's mind is connected, through their brains and bodies, to the environment around them. The shopper's body acts as a perceptual filter for experience.

When we begin to consider shopping experiences that live in a digitally driven world, one could argue that the idea of embodiment might begin to play a lesser role in establishing the customer's mindset towards the retail place or brand. Connecting to a retailer through a screen engages the eyes and ears. But even in the circumstances where a customer is shopping through their smartphone, they are still, physically, in some place. They do not exist in a vacuum apart from physical experiences. Shopping through your phone, tablet or home computer while sitting by a cozy fire in your den is very different than it is while riding the New York subway or standing on the busy street corner. Those environments still influence customers and the way they *feel during that experience as it relates to the brand or retailer* they are shopping.

Seen in this way, when brands and retailers seek to connect with their customers through digital interfaces along the customer journey, environment becomes critical. Retailers cannot guarantee that customers shopping through their digital interfaces are in environments that are optimal for the brand experience. They can, however, directly control the quality of their interactive content. In this way, they can guarantee that whatever customers filter through their eyes and ears engages the emotional centers of the brain through compelling visuals and great storytelling. As we discussed earlier, stories, and even simple words, have a remarkable ability to cause 'as if' experiences in the customer's mind.

- **"Relational"**
  Since the early pages of this book I have shared ideas about shopping being first and foremost a social paradigm. People engage in shopping experiences in part for the stuff they buy as well as those things that money can't buy: the interpersonal connections they make with shop keepers, sales associates, other shoppers.

Brands are like people.

They have personalities, points of view, and personal expression in the built environment. In some ways, brands and retailers, as well as the products they sell, become our 'friends.' They are there when we need them, they help us out when we are in a pinch and make life easier and more enjoyable. Brands are incorporated into our sets of social relationships and, they too, become in a sense, *embodied*.

The mind thrives in relationship. The mind sees relationship in everything, constantly playing one relationship off another, gauging cause and effect. The mind not only takes note of relationships; it's also actively shaped by them.

As customers enter shopping places, their experience of the place and the time they spend there, is modulated by how the sensory input they are exposed to is processed by the brain (and whole body) and what the mind makes of it all. As shoppers interact with sales associates and other shoppers, they share all sorts of messages. Walking through a space, eye contact, facial expressions, intonation in someone's spoken words, as well as environmental stimuli in the architecture, color and materials, graphics and signage, lighting, and the built geometries of the space – all activate the mind. These things are inevitable.

Great shopping experiences are designed to include the optimal arrangement of all these factors in the support of fostering harmonious relationships. The famous Finnish architect, Alvar Aalto, believed that "building art is a synthesis of life in materialized form. We should try to bring in under the same hat not a splintered way of thinking, but all in harmony together."

For many artists, architects and musicians, beauty has been the bringing together elements in harmonious proportions. This does not necessarily mean symmetry or that all of the parts need to be equal. When they are combined, however, there is coherence and clarity in the message, whether we are experiencing a building, a painting or a piece of music.

Coherence in the customer's mind, as well as in the design of a shopping place, is created when there is harmony between the parts of these complex systems. At a brain-mind level, this comes with integration of the brain's various functional modules. In the store, it comes from the mindful design of *all the relationships*, in the architecture, products or people.

In an earlier chapter I described an exercise I used to do with students – placing them one after another in a space and asking them to be aware of their subjective experience as more people were added to the enclosure. This was a design-mind experiment that asked each student to be more aware of how it feels to be in relationship to the boundaries of the defined space and to each other. What we noticed was that the energy changed within everyone as more individuals were added. Some people enjoyed the close proximity to others, and others found having people in their 'personal space' quite uncomfortable. "Relationships are the way we share energy and information flow, and it is this sharing that shapes, in part, how the flow is regulated. Our minds are created within relationships – including the one we have with ourselves."[67]

The relationships that are part of the shopping places we visit, shape our minds and determine the nature of experience we have, both while in the stores and as it lingers in us as memorable moment of our day. Shopping can leave us invigorated and energized, or overloaded and depleted. How we engage the mind of the customer in the aisle, on their smartphone, or through location-based digital content, becomes an extremely important part of the design of shopping experiences.

In each of these circumstances, the flow of information and energy is different because the series of relationships in which they are being experienced is different. All of the relationships are nonetheless important in capturing the customer's mind. The relationship you can have with a retailer through your phone is wholly different than that which happens in a face-to-face encounter with a living person, helping you find the right fit for a pair of jeans. The mind prefers the interpersonal to the impersonal.

- **"Regulates"**

    The mind is an amazing regulator, like a traffic cop who spends rush hour stopping and waving speeding cars through a busy intersection. While maintaining uninterrupted flow on a busy street, the traffic cop also *monitors* the flow of cars, their speed, and the number approaching that would like to turn left or right, as well as pedestrians who are texting without looking as they step into the street.

    The traffic cop also modifies the flow of cars through the intersection throughout the day. Like the traffic cop, the mind both monitors *and* modifies the flow of energy and information across time. It keeps the energy and information 'traffic' moving both in and out of the system.

All shoppers have their own individual minds that always come along on shopping trips. Because the mind is a regulator both monitoring and modifying the flow of energy and information, it is far from a hapless passenger on the shopping excursion. It plays a direct role in, and has the ability to *change*, the experience. Through interaction with both the physical environment and the other people in the store, the shopping mind actively participates in creating customer experience.

Motivate the mind and you can move mountains.

Retailers would do well to understand the idea of 'regulation' in terms of what they expect their customers are able to comprehend in their stores, how much they can absorb and process.

While the brain is exceedingly good at processing huge amounts of information, some retail stores put it into overload by assuming it wants, and can handle, even more. It is hard to drink from a fire hose. Like the traffic cop trying to control overwhelming traffic volume, we can't expect the shopper's mind to be able to regulate and make meaning of the abundance of choices in many retail stores. Yet shopping places often assume customers can just take bigger gulps. That amounts to information overload. In energy terms, chaos, and chaos isn't good for business.

From the point of view of the retailer, the idea of 'regulate' speaks to how they set up the environment to enhance the flow of information and energy. What is often needed from the retailer is better internal 'regulation.' When thinking about aspects of store design such as assortment planning, the term 'regulate' is synonymous with what many retailers are understanding as a need to curate. So while the customer's mind may be like a traffic cop regulating the flow of information and energy into and out of the brain, retailers are more like museum directors, curating the amount of product in their collections. If retailers expect the 'traffic cop' in the customer to be able to deal with what they are exposed to while shopping, they need to become better attuned to the customer's brain and regulate what is pushed the customer's way.

- **"Information and Energy"**

   Information and energy flow among the customer, the shopping environment and the brand are two keys to success in retailing. The sharing of information happens sometimes overtly through things such as price-point and sale signs, graphics that show depictions of customers in lifestyle settings, the way sales associates talk to customers, or messages shoppers might hear on a public announcement system. They also may happen less directly between people and how they interact with each other, or the way product is displayed. The sales associate's attitude may impart a message of apathy or being open and willing to engage in a relationship. Product density in the store may impart the message of a value-oriented proposition rather than exclusivity.

   Shopping environments also have *energy.*

   Architecture, acoustics, materials and finishes, signage and graphics, as well as the products themselves, actively create conditions that have effects on people's feelings while on a shopping trip. A busy, value-oriented grocery store on a Saturday morning is very different than an exclusive by-appointment-only jewelry shop selling exquisite timepieces.

People also have energy. We can all tell when we are with 'good energy' people who enliven the room or 'bad energy' people who somehow drain the room of its vibrancy. We can't see this energy flow, but we sense it in their faces and their body language. Psychologists call this 'emotional contagion.' One person's *affect* ... affects another person, and so forth.

So you see, capturing the 'hearts and minds' of customers isn't that difficult. The heart and the mind are, after all, intimately tied. To reference Dan Siegel's statement then, when looking to find the minds of customers, we only need to look in two places: in relationship and the body.

Understanding the brain allows for better understanding of customer motivations and offers the opportunity to create better places to engage customers on a conscious *and* subconscious level. To forge more meaningful relationships and to enhance the likelihood of customers making a purchase, retailers must make friends with the customer's *mind* while it is out on a shopping trip.

From the ancient reptilian brain to the higher functioning prefrontal cortex, we are wired for responding to environmental experiences in both innate and cognitively mediated ways. We are designed not just to react to our environment, but to *create* it, actively.

If retailers and the makers of shopping places do nothing more than connect in relationship with their customers and more fully understand their brain-body experiences in the places they create to sell their wares, they will be *light years ahead of the competition*.

When retailers profoundly understand that the relationships they create and the feelings they engender in their customer's body more effectively engages their customer's brain, they will create more effective shopping places. Brands can actively create the customer's state of mind while shopping their stores. And as their minds are activated, customers find themselves interacting with the brand in a relationship that is more relevant to their lives.

Please Me

The "Pleasure Chemical" – Dopamine

Ideally, shopping feels good.

We love the excitement of a great bargain. We also love the acquisition of a coveted item that may not be on sale at all. For some people, price doesn't matter as long as the item is acquired. Every consumer has a different happiness threshold, a unique definition of pleasure and experience of satisfaction or joy. One person's deal on a used car can bring as much giddy pleasure as felt by the customer who drives a brand new Maserati off the lot. Pleasure is personal. It's also an extraordinarily fascinating process in the brain.

One thing is for sure: something very powerful is taking place during the shopping process that far transcends simple product search, purchase and ownership.

Shopping is emotional. But the pleasure principle is not all in the head. Pleasure, as I'm about to explain, is chemistry.

Buy a piece of chocolate cake, a favorite designer dress, sports watch or new computer, and the chemistry of pleasure involved is amazingly similar. Within the limbic region of the brain are structures regarded as the "reward center." And the chemical that stimulates the pleasure we feel: Dopamine.

How did we come to understand this little bit of brain biochemistry? Turns out amazing brain facts about pleasure have come about from studying avoidance and reward in... rats.

Back in the early '50s James Olds and Peter Milner, two Canadian scientists at McGill University, were exploring reinforcement processes using intra-cranial stimulation (placing a small electrode into the interior of the brain). They wired up a rat, placing a tiny electrode into the rat's limbic area. What they hoped to figure out was whether or not rats could be made uncomfortable by electrical stimulation of this old mammalian structure, deep in the brain.

The scientists hypothesized that ever so slightly zapping the rat's brain as it entered a corner of the cage would cause it to *avoid* the area. It turned out that the rats were not only undeterred, but that they kept on *returning* to the area, and getting zapped. Over and over again. The rats, it appeared, *enjoyed* being in the corner (and thereby getting zapped) so much so, that they disregarded their thirst and hunger. Given the choice between the feelings coming from the stimulation of this brain area and satisfying their basic needs, the rats *chose the stimulation*. Not a particularly good choice when eating and drinking are pretty important. But then again, they were rats.

It turns out that Olds and Milner had stimulated an area in the brain called the 'nucleus accumbens' (NAcc), which was indeed part of the limbic system, though not connected to the pain and discomfort sensation. In an ironic twist of scientific experimentation, they had unexpectedly found the 'pleasure center' of the brain.

In subsequent experiments, they allowed the rats to press a bar in order to give themselves the small electrical stimulations to the NAcc. The rats pushed the bar over 7,500 times in a 12-hour period and achieved an average of 742 bar pushes per hour![68] Soon enough, the rat's repetitive self-stimulation eclipsed everything else. Food and eating didn't matter and they essentially tripped out on dopamine until eventually they died.

The scientists didn't know the exact details of how this unexpected result was caused by an excess of dopamine overwhelming the system, but they were sure that the aversion they expected from stimulating the area deep in the rat's brain wasn't what was happening. They concluded that the phenomenon might lay the methodological foundation for further study of the mechanisms of *reward*.

As the neurochemical that promotes feeling good, dopamine plays a vital role in the 'pleasure center,' which, as it turns out, is the area that includes the nucleus accumbens (NAcc), the amygdala, the septum, the prefrontal cortex and the ventral tegmental area (VTA). Quick tour?

The **VTA** is part of the very old brain and sits at the top of the brain stem; it has neurons that reach out to the nucleus accumbens. The **NAcc** is tied to laughter, learning, and reward, as well as... fear, impulsivity, aggression and addiction. The **amygdala**, two almond-shaped organs, acts as a harm avoidance system; it's the brain's 911 center. The **hippocampus** is a particularly important limbic structure associated with forming new memories and connecting emotions and senses such as smell and sound to memories.

When the brain processes a *sensory input that signals reward*, the VTA releases *dopamine* into the amygdala, and the NAcc. The NAcc, in turn, shoots off a signal to the **prefrontal cortex**, which among other higher functions, helps to focus our attention. The prefrontal cortex, while being part of the latest area of the brain to develop, is closely connected to the limbic system, one of the oldest parts of the brain, and helps to modulate pain and pleasure responses that are generated out of the old, mammalian limbic system.

So when the brain gets a hit of dopamine in response to some pleasurable stimulus, the prefrontal cortex goes into action trying to figure out where this warm and fuzzy feeling is coming from and what we should do about it.

There are two key neurotransmitters, each playing a role in this pleasure circuit. **Serotonin** tells the brain that you have had *enough* of the chocolate cake you're eating, gives the body the impression that the cake is no longer needed, and *turns off desire*.

Dopamine, on the other hand, *increases the desire* for the stimulant (as in the rats in the Olds and Milner studies, who pushed the bar over 700 times an hour), and keeps us craving more cake.

What Olds and Milner tapped into was that dopamine is one of the most powerful neurochemicals in our brain. We now know that the addiction cycle we see resulting from use of drugs, gambling or I dare say, *shopping*, is part of dopamine's interplay with the brain's pleasure system.

The Olds and Milner study kick-started the search for how the pleasure center worked and what neurochemicals were at play in making us feel good. Further study would lead scientists to understand that dopamine is a factor in a number of emotions, but insofar as the warm, blissful, glowing feeling we all get from a pleasant experience, dopamine plays the leading role.

Twenty years later at Cambridge University, Wolfram Schultz, a neuroscientist, carried out studies with monkeys and fruit juice.[69] Schultz's approach was pretty straightforward; he started by creating a loud sound, waited a moment and then gave the monkeys a little squirt of juice in their mouths. During this procedure, he had an electrode implanted into neurons that measured electrical activity in individual dopamine-producing cells.

Initially, dopamine was only released when the monkey got juice; the loud sound didn't have any direct effect on the neurotransmitter's release into the brain. Schultz discovered that subsequent pairing of the sound and the administering of juice began to change the timing of dopamine release. With repeated trials, the dopamine previously released only *after* the stimulation of juice, began showing up *before* the monkey actually got the reward itself. What was happening? Dopamine-producing neurons were learning that there was a pattern – a loud sound indicated that a squirt of juice was about to come, so the brain's pleasure center would kick into gear.

Eventually the loud sound was all that was needed to get the dopamine flowing. Within a few tries, the monkey's brain had made the connection between the sound and the good feeling/reward. The sequence of events prior to the administering of juice (and the resulting release of dopamine) could become almost anything: a sound, a flash of light, any combination of them would work.

Once the brain got the pattern, dopamine release was guaranteed. Schultz called these neurons **prediction neurons** since they could help to foretell the arrival of juice and, in the end, they seemed to be more interested in *predicting* the arrival of juice than getting the juice itself.

Dopamine neurons aren't just about pleasure; they are part of what *allows us to make predictions*. They are really good at picking up patterns. Some of these predictions are directly connected to our motivations about interacting with our environment. Depending on how things work out when we interact with things around us, we come to be discriminating in identifying objects of vital importance versus objects that have little meaning or value to us. For example, we come to understand quickly as children that there is comfort in mommy's arms, but not from the pile of blocks in the corner of the playroom.

Other forms of predictions code for how we come to know the way things are in our environment. Physical parameters of objects, such as spatial position, velocity and weight, are also understood by the brain, and we expect them to be the same each time we encounter them.[70] This helps us determine if things are as they should be in our environment. When we see the Eiffel Tower, we come to expect that it doesn't stand on its point but on its four legs. Prediction neurons are the very basis of perception and help us determine how we move through our changing landscapes and circumstances with relative ease, safety, comfort, and, if the predictive pattern is conducive to joy.

Our brain's ability to make predictions ties into how we expect future events to unfold before they actually occur. The predicting capability of dopamine neurons allows us mentally to evaluate various strategies on how we should react to something by integrating knowledge from various experiences and determining the right course of action that leads to the increased likelihood of positive outcomes. Without this predictive capability, life would be "déjà vu all over again."

So, dopamine neurons are really good with 'if this, then that' scenarios but, what happens when things *don't* go as planned, as is often the case?

What Schultz determined through his experiments was that while dopamine neurons are good at predicting the future, *they are even more adept at raising the red flag when things don't go as expected*.

When the monkey was repeatedly getting his mouthful of juice after each sound of the tone, dopamine production began to diminish. As the task became repetitive and the reward became conditioned, the dopamine neurons didn't pay as much attention.

But when the pattern was changed, even in the smallest way, the system became *more* active again. If the juice did arrive, but on a different time schedule, say after a one-second lapse, the dopamine dropped initially, then increased again after the monkey's brain figured out that now there was going to be a short delay. The new pattern in the sound-juice system became understood after a few tries. The brain simply had to recalibrate to the new timing of the events, and all was well again in the pleasure center.

If the monkey did not get the sip of juice at all after the sounding of the tone, Schultz also noticed a drop in dopamine release. The expected pattern was interrupted again and the monkey's brain took notice. After all, the monkey's brain had just figured out the new pattern and when the expectation of getting the reward was not fulfilled, something had to be done. The monkey's brain was shouting *'hey, how about that juice... like now...I'm waiting!'*

If the monkey didn't get the promised juice after the sequence of stimuli it had become used to, the dopamine neurons stamped their proverbial feet and shut down, sending an error signal into the system: 'The dopamine neurons have gotten it wrong.'

When something went amiss and things didn't happen as expected, these neurons sent out an error signal to the entire brain alerting it to the fact that what had been predicted didn't happen. This key 'wake-up' signal, called 'error-related negativity' (ERN), is thought to be a unique electrophysiological marker that reflects changes in dopamine when people make errors in cognitive tasks. ERN is the basis for noticing changes in patterns in our environment and experiences, and therefore, learning new things.

Even though the brain loves dopamine, if you are caught in a repetitive cycle of 'if this, then that' experiences, then the brain has learned the drill and the dopamine release becomes less effective in influencing behavior.

There is no pleasure in the mundane. Some call it boredom. The brain will tolerate it, but what it really wants is the pleasure of *getting something wrong* and the dopamine release from *exposure to new experiences*. The brain wants to decipher the variations in experiential patterns. To take notice of the new and improved. It's the way our neurochemistry has kept us aware of changes in our environment, and, in a way, how we have been able to survive.

When changes occur in an experience and you switch it up a little, introducing novelty into the equation, you mess with the predictions these neurons have made about what to expect. Once the brain takes note of the error it had made in reading its neurochemical tarot cards, the brain begins to ramp up dopamine production. In these moments of recalibration or learning a new pattern, the brain is bathed in dopamine. It really likes this part of the game.

Perhaps the most important part of the Wolfram Schultz work was the understanding that while our dopamine neurons like predictable rewards (the juice following a tone), *unpredictable rewards are 3-4 times more exciting than those that can be predicted.*

This is why gambling, and specifically games like roulette, craps and slot machines, are so seductive. As the wheels in a slot machine whirl around, our brain is busy trying to determine the pattern of how many more arm pulls will finally result in the winning combination of tumblers all coming up the same. The sounds of adjacent slot machine winners shouting with delight over a big win, along with the clinking sound of coins dropping into the tray, continue to reinforce the idea that a payout is likely to come. The brain tries to read the sequences of cherries, lemons, stars and dollar signs to decode the patterns in the game and tries to predict when the landslide jackpot will happen.

And of course there is no pattern or way to predict. But the brain doesn't know that. And in fact, if it can't find one, it will get creative and begin to impose one. Because the brain can't really find a pattern and predict when it will be payday, the brain essentially gets caught in a loop until it eventually gives up.

If on the other hand the slot machine should actually pay out, the brain gets an unpredicted reward, and according to Shultz it *really* likes these types of rewards over those we can predict in advance. Should you actually hit the jackpot or see someone beside you on the casino floor win even a little bit of money, it's likely you'll pull the arm another time, and another, and another.

Store design and visual merchandising are rife with patterns (and breaks in patterns) and shopping environments are filled with the science of pattern recognition, reward and reinforcement.

Now, think about the retail world and promotions such as 'gifts-with-purchase' (GWP) or 'buy-one get-one' (BOGO). You've shopped a particular store a number of times. You loved the first experience when you didn't really know the store, or its merchandise and you thought the sales staff were great. Lately, the experience seems a little flat. You're just not getting the same rush that you did in the beginning. It has all become a little, well…predictable. You're not disappointed when you shop there, but that original level of excitement isn't happening. From the brain's point of view, it gets the drill. Been there, done that. The whole thing has become a little humdrum. Dopamine neurons have begun to drop off in their production of the pleasure chemical.

Novelty is what the brain wants and maybe the new spring collection isn't enough anymore to get your dopamine production system all fired up. Except that today, when you do make a small purchase, you find out that you get a 20% off coupon on your next purchase … or a small compact mirror with that new eye shadow, or a trial fragrance sample, or your name in a raffle to win a trip to the islands.

Guess what? You're feeling a little perked up now, and it occurs to you that there was that other little number back there in the store that might just need another look.

Now, you may or may not go back and add to the shopping trip, but your attitude is significantly changed. A small, unexpected interruption in your brain's predictions of the shopping trip with a little gift, and your dopamine neurons are back in the game. You feel good, certainly better, and you are more inclined to make a return trip because, who knows, there may be another unpredictable reward next time like the one you received today.

Places, Patterns and Perceptions

We have, over time, become exceptionally good at recognizing patterns. On a cellular level, our brain likes patterns because that's how it processes information. If you think of the brain as a machine, then it's much more like the digital processor in your computer than, say, an old analogue radio. Our brain understands the patterns of ones and zeros – the chemical and electrical spikes coursing across the neural network – and it uses established patterns of these neural firings to differentiate new experiences from the old and familiar.

As far back as one can imagine, our developing brains were putting together patterns generated from our observation of behaviors exhibited by other humans as well as other creatures, both predators and prey. Survival depended on our ability to remember them, and so, evolution provided us with highly specific modules that now need no prior experience or social circumstance to kick in. "These mechanisms are innate and hardwired…some we share with other animals; some are uniquely human."[71] Our ability to recognize interruptions in patterns is a key aspect of how we process the information our brains take in from the environmental stimuli around us. We now know that dopamine neurons are in part responsible for our ability to try to predict outcomes and to take notice when these predictions are off target. They decode patterns and we rely on them to help us to create coherence and to navigate our way through the world.

Interestingly, our brains look for patterns in everything around us. We rely on them so much that we impose them where there are often none. We see patterns in the passing of clouds through the sky or in the stars. We listen for, and think we can follow, sequenced rhythms in a jazz improvisation. We fall prey to games of chance by pulling the arm of a slot machine and hoping to see the winning combination of shapes when the tumblers settle into place.

The pattern anomalies that our brain picks up in the environment form the basis of how we learn. And how we shop.

Understanding that our brain is a pattern-recognizing apparatus is critical to appreciating how a customer perceives the shopping environment. A customer continually scans the visual field, looking for patterns in the shapes, colors, movement, and the light contrast to make sense of what's happening.

Some of these objects are already encoded in our memory, so we pay little conscious attention to them. There is no dopamine rush in simply seeing the same old environments or experiencing the same behaviors from the same people all the time. There is no reward when we are familiar with the stimuli, but rather when the *unfamiliar* signals to us that something is inconsistent with what we expect – when something alters or breaks a pattern.

Because our brain sees the world this way, the way patterns play across the visual field of the shopping place has a direct effect on how customers are led through an environment or how they might get confused, frustrated and leave.

As we saw earlier, understanding the world in terms of patterns is not just about our processing of the visual field. The perceptions associated to changes of temperature, how close or far away we sense objects to be, the sounds we hear, how we interact with technologies and the way we perceive, think and react to people we encounter, all form a series of neural patterns that get encoded, becoming *representations of our shopping world*. We therefore come to expect certain environmental attributes to be consistent with how we understand shopping in one type of store or another, one category of product over another. There may be variations category-to-category, location-to-location and retailer-to-retailer, but we tend to group similar things together and extrapolate certain attributes across a wide range of experiences.

So, when it was a matter of survival a few million years ago, pretty much all things with forward looking eyes, big pointy teeth and that stalked, came to be perceived as potentially dangerous. We figured out then that *this* particular pattern of physical attributes meant we should pay close attention, or we might end up being lunch.

Except maybe for 'Black Friday,' as deal-hungry shoppers clamber over each other to get through the door, today's shopping places are not, of course, a danger to our lives. We need not be concerned about what is lurking around the next display or what will jump out of the frozen-foods case. Nevertheless, patterns are created in the way we come to expect being greeted at the door, how certain classifications of merchandise are typically displayed or the way a series of store aisles, product adjacencies, or web pages are laid out. The consistency in how we experience these things cements understanding of what it means to shop a particular retailer and connect to the brand. Variation in those patterns – novelty – is what keeps us coming back, because variation activates the pleasure centers and initiates learning, which, while we may not all admit it, we love, at least on a brain-chemistry level.

Customers form expectations about how they experience the people, places and things in stores. They create mental models of what they want to see and where they want to see it. The goal is to *keep the pleasure center engaged*, generating good feelings while in the midst of the shopping experience. Achieving this goal is a task that requires a balancing act between providing customers with experiences that promote two seemingly divergent concepts: consistency and novelty.

Next time you are walking a shopping place, ask yourself this question: *"What does this retailer want me to look at?"* Can you tell from the entry area what they want to draw to your attention? As you walk the sales floor, are there cues to look at that guide you along a journey, or certain displays to walk up to, or some particular graphic to look at or read? Do you hear music, smell a faint aroma, feel a light breeze across the skin or meet a sales associate who is eager to engage you with a smile?

Have you ever gone into a grocery store that you have shopped a number of times, simply walking to 'aisle 6' to find coffee, hardly paying any attention to where you are going? You know the route and may even be walking head down, responding to a text. When you show up in the place you bought coffee from the last few times and discover that the store had been remerchandised the night before, you are confused and slightly disoriented.

All of these experiences are built on our understanding and retrieval of patterns encoded in our brain.

Think of the stores you shop, small boutiques to big-box retailers. Aside from the idea that assortments with products ranging in the tens of thousands are just too hard for us to absorb, the way they are arranged on walls, floor fixtures, feature presentations, in display cases or around the check-out area, has everything to do with how we decide to give them more attention.

When we walk a shopping environment, we see a wash of products, signage and screens, all vying for our attention. Often, when we walk into a store either for the first time or as a regular customer, there is no 'pattern' in the array of things we see and experience. Nevertheless, our brain continues to search for patterns, trying to make sense of the architecture in the environment and the rows of products lining the shelves without our being cognizant of this search.

As our eyes scan back and forth, we reach out with our body, feel with our skin, tilt our head to hear a sound better, breathe deeply to smell and taste an aroma. We do these things trying to make sense of our environments.

However, very often what we perceive is fewer patterns and more visual noise. To the brain, it's like listening to a radio that isn't quite tuned in to the station. Except, even at moments like these, the brain is hard at work trying to decode or find some anomaly that will get us to focus on a particular object in space, or a shelf, or a rack, or a mannequin.

Shoppers' positive emotions are rooted in the predictions of the highly flexible dopamine-producing brain cells, which are constantly cross-referencing against a bank of memories embedded in our neurology. These cells, and the networks of which they are a part, are continually adjusting their connections to best reflect a customer's reality. The beauty of evolution is that our brains are not the fixed and rigid systems that we had some 200 million years ago. The brain changes in response to new experiences and the pleasure center reinforces learning with the rewards of positive feelings that come from the release of dopamine.

Every time we encounter something new, our brain cells are hard at work trying to figure out what's going on. If no recognizable series of patterns is accessible to us from our seemingly limitless bank of encoded experiences, our neurons start forming new connections.

There isn't much that escapes the brain and its perceptual systems. The fact that we may not be fully (consciously) aware of everything in our environment doesn't mean that the environment is not on the brain's radar. Our brains are able to pick up interruptions in very complex patterns before we are able to identify the pattern itself.

Novelty, changes in the patterns of things we are exposed to, prompts new learning. Your brain loves to learn and quite ironically, from a brain-chemistry point of view, starts by 'getting it all wrong.' The brain looks for patterns, makes predictions and... misses the mark. It's not so much a mistake as a missed take. A golden opportunity for growth and new discovery.

Learning...It's All a Big Mistake

Retailers are teachers and their shopping environments are their classrooms. In order to have customers understand something, they have to learn it. Whether simply a new arrival, a promotional offering, a brand message about a point of view on sustainable building practice, what the new style or color is for that season, or more subtle lessons about why they are unique, customers can learn only if retailers 'teach.'

Teaching customers is a practice and process of delivering patterns of experience that establish expectations. Once customers 'get it,' and provided that getting it doesn't (or shouldn't) take too long, the retailer has connected to a baseline of understanding and a mental model is encoded that acts as a reference point for all future experiences.

So, how then does the customer's brain learn the shopping drill of being in this or that store, buying fresh vegetables or intimate apparel, sporting goods or a rice cooker? How is it that learning in the store is connected to the good feeling of shopping? How do shoppers understand what one brand stands for and why they don't like shopping at the other store?

Trial and error. For both the customer and the retailer.

It's not about getting the answer right, but rather stumbling, or just getting it completely wrong, that helps us learn the most.

The brain works this way with virtually everything.

Say you're sitting in the classroom or board room and the CEO says, "today we are going to talk about xyz, and remember, there are no dumb questions, and no wrong answers, so let's have lots of dialogue."

From a very basic brain perspective, this is right on the money. But we all know that there is a lot that gets in the way that often keeps us from being vulnerable enough to ask the dumb question or get the answer wrong. These are more cognitive motivators, or de-motivators, to behavior. The thoughts that run through our heads are often something like, "I don't want to look foolish" or "I can't expose my lack of knowledge to the people I am supposed to be leading."

This conflict inside of us is tied into reward systems connected to dopamine and the pleasure center. In most cases, we choose not to ask the question or offer up an answer, hoping that someone else will do it and save us the painful experience of what we might think will lead to embarrassment. We tend to be more motivated towards behavior that seeks to *avoid pain* (cognitive or physical) than to seek out positive reinforcements. I know, that seems completely contrary to thinking that only positive rewards keep us motivated.

Dopamine neurons are the guardians of expectations.

If in previous experiences we have 'learned' that the wrong answer leads to humiliation – a negative reinforcement – our dopamine neurons have encoded it into our neurochemistry. However, if we had learned from previous experiences that there *really* was no wrong answer, then there would be no negative stigma to offering one up (either right or wrong). The motivation to learn new things would not be encumbered with latent negative feelings. Dopamine neurons are both good at picking up errors – things that are out of place and don't meet our expectations – and correcting them as well.

If dopamine neurons are geared towards picking up errors in the predictions we have made in our 'first this, then that' understanding of how things are supposed to be, then they are actually more interested in the things that go wrong than the status quo. This is not to say that there isn't a good feeling to getting something right, there is, but the feeling wears off quickly and getting the answer right, when you are pretty sure of the correct response anyway, serves as a poor motivator to keep on playing the game.

Refreshing the store has a different motivation when you look at it from the point of view of giving the brain something to chew on. Sure, seasonal changes signal different assortment selections and holidays mean more sale merchandise and lovely displays. But these changes to the store landscape activate the customer's brain and aid growth and learning opportunities by creating new neural pathways – the result of experiencing the environment anew every time they shop.

It is not a matter of continually changing the entire store in order to engage the shopper's novelty-loving brain. The brain can pick up the *most subtle of changes* in floor sets, displays and graphics – and learn. Retail environments can convey a change in even a single item in a grouping of products and the brain will zero in on it, focus the eyes on the target and tell the head to turn and legs to propel towards it for further investigation. Yes, one well-placed item in an entire wall or 80,000-sq.-ft. sales floor can signal a change to the customer – and you have his or her attention.

Error-related negativity (that little electrical impulse that alerts you to something being different) is a key feature to learning. As we have seen through the Schultz studies, when the dopamine neurons are off the mark on their predictions about what they expect, the brain produces an error signal. This impulse is understood to start in an area of the brain called the **anterior cingulate cortex (ACC)**. The signal is thought to be quickly distributed across the brain by some specialized brain cells called **spindle neurons**. [72] This type of neuron is longer than the regular neuron, and only found in great apes and humans. They are 'super fast' at distributing messages across the brain. When some anomaly is picked up in predicted patterns, the whole brain is made aware that something's wrong in the neighborhood in but a fraction of a second.

When it comes to learning in general, the ACC is critically involved in figuring out particularly difficult cognitive challenges and is most reliably activated with increasing task difficulty. People can make decisions about doing one thing instead of another through a number of cognitive processes and using a number of brain areas, but insofar as the ACC is concerned, this part of the brain is the place in which the learning process starts.

The relative size of the error signal generated by the ACC predicts the degree to which people learn more about the negative, as compared to the positive, consequences of their choices. [73]

Not all people learn the same way. I am a visual spatial learner, and it took me forever to understand engineering in architecture school until I could build 3D models and make drawings of complex problems. Some people learn better with different types reinforcements. Some try simply to avoid negative consequences, and other people are motivated by seeking positive rewards.

The error-related negativity seems to help us learn by doing two things: 1) predicting errors and, 2) helping us to monitor conflict when making difficult choices, like choosing between two similarly positive outcomes. When researchers have looked at the error signal with regard to learning, they have found that rather than having an effect on getting us to make faster decisions, responding more quickly to certain stimuli, they are more associated with trying to have us avoid negative events more than to seek out positive ones.

In other words, if we have a choice, we would rather focus our attention on the avoidance of pain than actively seeking out positive rewards. In the end, this does tend to put more 'good feelings' in the day when you are actively weeding out the potentially 'bad.' There is, after all, a long evolutionary history of trying to avoid those things that might hurt us. We might put off eating until tomorrow but *being eaten* today was something that we had to learn to avoid, and quickly. Picking up the anomalies in our environment and processing them to determine the most appropriate behavioral response are well ingrained in our neural network.

The ACC monitors when mistakes are picked up in our behavior leading to positive or negative consequences, and in our brain's errors in predicting the patterns of our environment. It also 'remembers' what dopamine neurons have just learned by creating new patterns and predictions in response to the new things going on around us. If it didn't readjust the set, the ACC would keep us in a state of perpetually repetitive behavioral loops.

From the point of view of providing the customer with positive and remarkable experiences, we have a challenge: give them enough to establish comfort through consistency and engage them in neural activation through novelty.

The Pleasure Rush of Getting a Good Deal

It is somewhat straightforward to call attention to something on the sales floor by offering up novelty for the brain to decipher. To get a customer to actually buy what the retailer has drawn to the mind's eye is an entirely different matter.

The brain activates multiple functional areas to come up with decisions and resulting behaviors that support positive experiences. When the shopper is walking the sales floor, the brain is hard at work.

The pleasure center involves a number of brain structures found throughout the older limbic brain – NAcc, amygdala, ACC, VTA – as well as the most recently evolved prefrontal cortex. The PFC is like an arbitrator helping the brain wade its way through the decision-making process of whether or not to buy something. The PFC connects to the older, more reactive limbic system that might have you buying on impulse or leaving the store because the price points 'scared' you. It holds these more primitive emotions at bay while it buys time to 'crunch the numbers' about whether one purchase decision is better than another.

Customers go about shopping, blissfully unaware that they are being attracted to one display over another and helped along in making a decision by environmental stimuli that trigger both emotional and higher-order cognitive processes in their brains. Many decisions are based on emotions that are buried deep in the subconscious.

Assuming the retailer has been able to get the shopper's attention, the next step is to determine how shoppers cognitively get around the 'to-buy or not-to-buy' question.

If you are an economist or the CFO of a company you'll know that, in terms of general macroeconomic theory, what drives purchases decisions is based on a combination of the consumer's set of product preferences and sensitivity to price. It makes sense after all that when people are out shopping, the decision to make a purchase comes after considering the characteristics of the product – whether it satisfies on both utility and design quality, *and* how much it costs. But then it's not quite that simple. People may believe that even though the product does what it is supposed to do and they find design qualities of something attractive, they can find price to be a disincentive to buy. On a brain level, price tags are painful.

There seems to be a tradeoff that customers are willing to make between the potential pleasure of getting something with the pain of how much its going to cost them. Recent evidence suggests that distinct neural circuits related to our anticipation of both positive and negative outcomes provide critical input into subsequent buying decisions.

The "SHOP task" was part of a study, done by Brian Knutson and George Loewenstein at the department of Psychology and Neuroscience at Stanford University in 2006, where the researchers tried to look at the macroeconomic theory of buying decisions from the point of view of the brain.[74]

In this study, Knutson and Loewenstein tried to determine if activation of specific brain areas would be able to be predictors of a customer's decision to buy something. What they were interested in was whether or not specific neural circuits responded to product preferences versus excessive prices. So, they created a study to determine if there were certain neural pathways that were activated by how much customers preferred a product, or that were involved in the shopper being deterred from buying something because of price. They wondered "whether anticipatory activation extracted from three regions could independently predict subsequent decisions to purchase." The results of the study discovered that activation in three areas of the brain could determine, *in advance*, whether or not a person would choose to buy something based on preference or price.

We can all relate to being in a store looking at something we really want, but being turned off by the price. What Knutson and the other researchers on the team discovered, was that the relative activation of one brain area over another can shut down the buying process *or* make a product irresistible. As we stand in the aisle looking at the array of products, our shopping brain is running through a number of processes that try to anticipate a feeling of loss or a feeling of gain.

On a brain level, the 'to-buy or not-to-buy' decision involves:

• the Nucleus accumbens (NAcc) - which we have already seen is connected to the pleasure center, one's desire for things and, therefore, dopamine production. It is considered to be the neural circuitry associated with 'anticipated gain.'

• the insula – this is the area of the brain that is connected to our perception of pain in others. It is considered to be the neural circuitry associated with 'anticipated loss.'

• and a specific area of the prefrontal cortex called the 'mesial prefrontal cortex (MPFC) – this area of the brain is connected to a role in representing internal information, including emotional introspection and autonomic control. Recent evidence also suggests that parts of the MPFC region may also play a role in processing reward outcomes.

The brains of subjects (shoppers) in the study were observed in an fMRI machine while making decisions about whether or not they would buy various products. To see what areas would light up during a buying process, the shoppers were shown products first, then the price tag was introduced and they were asked to make a decision about buying the product or not.

Here's how things played out:

Initially, the shoppers were just presented with objects that could be purchased without any indication of their price.

When subjects were presented with things they could buy without any decision to be made about whether the price was too high or just right, the NAcc immediately lit up. NAcc activation relates more to our preferences about things, whether or not we wanted something and how intensely, and as such it reflected the shoppers' desire for the objects they were looking at. The degree to which the NAcc appeared to be active depended on how much they wanted the product.

At this stage in the process the brain is not thinking about the *cost* of having whatever it is being presented with; it is simply saying to itself, *'Oh boy... I can have that!'*

A moment later, when the subjects were introduced to the price tag, both the MPFC *and* the insula both lit up. It turns out that both of these areas of the brain have a specific function with regard to determining what the customers' next step would be.

Would they buy or not buy?

To understand what was at play in the decision-making process, we can look at the individual roles of each of these two brain areas.

The MPFC is connected to trying to figure out whether or not the price was too high, too low or just right. Was the deal fair or not? Immediately, the MPFC went into crunching the numbers and discriminating between the desire and price differential. If we think of the NAcc as zeroing in on 'gain prediction,' the MPFC is concerned with 'gain prediction error.' This area of the customer's brain performs the cost benefit analysis of the decision making process.

So while the NAcc says, *"I like this thing. Let's get it,"* the MPFC says – *"Hold on there a minute. Let's take a look at some of the outcomes of what getting this thing will be."*

The insula, on the other hand, is part of the old mammalian brain. It's incredibly adept at picking up signals about pain and is concerned with 'loss,' which, therefore, ties into aversive feelings. Because the insula is so good at tuning into stimuli that signal the potential for pain, it is hypothesized to play a role in loss prediction. Since most of us consider paying too much for a product or service to elicit 'painful' emotions, we are likely to move cautiously when considering jumping into a new purchase where the price point is high. And, we are likely to avoid a purchase altogether when we feel the price of the thing we want to be excessive.

The bottom line of the Knutson study was this: if the insula's activity were greater than that of the NAcc – if the perception of the price being too high led to a feeling of anticipated 'pain/loss' – there was no purchase. If the shopper wanted something but the price was too high, the insula's activity overrode the NAcc's desire for the object and shoppers were likely to leave it on the shelf, table or rack. Furthermore, the heightened insula activity *deactivated* the MPFC. It actually *shut down the process of thinking* about whether or not potential gains would outweigh potential losses. The customer simply avoided objects where the prices seemed excessive and they were willing to set aside a purchase decision despite their apparent desire for something.

If, on the other hand, the price point was dropped, the researchers found that the NAcc activation went up (increased desire and excitement), the insula's activation went down (pain and loss being mitigated) *and* the MPFC was activated (jumping in to work the numbers).

If the NAcc activation was more than the insula and the MPFC, through working out the cost-benefit analysis, determined that the combination of function and price was a good deal, then a purchase was inevitable.

Prior to making a purchase, a shopper's preferences activate the NAcc, signaling a desire for something. Excessive prices act as a deterrent to purchases by signaling potential pain and/or loss. Furthermore, when shoppers are confronted with what they consider to be prices that are too high, feelings originating in the insula inhibit the brain's use of more executive functions in the prefrontal cortex to think through the conflict of whether or not this is a good thing to buy or not.

Taken together, the results of this study show that the brain's activity is a step ahead of the actual buying decision. Or at least, the *pre*-purchase activity of certain areas of the brain can be used as predictors of buying behavior. Shoppers are making decisions to buy products at the speed of their neural circuitry. Some of these decisions are happening at a completely subconscious level, before our brains have had a moment to 'think' about the outcome.

You know that expression, "you don't have a second chance to make a first impression." Well, studies like these make it true on a "neuroeconomics" level. In some cases, shoppers aren't doing all of the mental gymnastics about the outcome of their 'to-buy or not-to-buy' dilemma. They are reacting based on a set of old instinctual emotions and doing very little thinking at all.

Shopping:
The Agony
and the Ecstasy

Why Credit Cards Hurt So Good

I hardly ever use cash to buy anything anymore.

It's not that I don't have any, but that I make a conscious decision not to carry it. Not because I am afraid of spending it all when it's in my pocket (though that seems to happen from time to time), or that I'll get mugged and have to fork it over, but because I would simply rather pay with plastic.

I would have also never thought that I would do all of my banking online and hardly ever step into the bank branch a mile from my home to make a deposit, transfer funds between accounts, or make a withdrawal.

On special trips out to the farmers' market, a jazz festival or some other cultural event in the countryside, I'll use the ATM, get enough to cover the afternoon, and then be on my way.

This has, from time to time, caused a problem or two when the shopkeepers or merchants I've patronized accept cash *only*. But really, they are a dying breed. Even the small-time taxi guy with three cabs in his fleet plugs a credit card 'swiper' into his cellphone and, presto, we're paid up and the receipt is emailed to me. Easy... and I pay at the end of the month when my credit card statement arrives.

The prevalence of credit cards and other forms of electronic payment isn't just about offering convenience to the customer, though convenience is definitely part of the reason they are increasingly being used. Credit cards also don't activate the part of the shopper's brain that acts as an alarm system for 'feeling the pain' of handing over the cash. The insula, as we have seen in the previous chapter, is a key player in 'loss aversion' and the avoidance of pain. The Knutson study showed that things such as high prices get the insula activated, triggering the brain's predictors for anticipating loss and the brain shuts down any further consideration of the product we are looking at.

Lost sale.

On the other hand, retailers *can* do something to inhibit the insula's activation, such as lowering prices, giving customers gifts with purchase, or offering painless payment methods. These actions connect to the limbic area of the shopper's brain, easing the way to making sales and a shopping experience rich with dopamine. When retailers do this, they capture more sales and conversion rates rise.

Neuroscientists have conducted a number of studies on insula activation and believe that *anticipation* of physical pain gets the insula in the game and that it is therefore connected not only to loss *aversion*, but loss *prediction,* as well. If we think it's going to 'hurt,' we simply stay away.

The use of fMRI machines has made it possible to see that the insula plays a role in processing everything from facial expressions of disgust and fear, reading scripts that are sad, to perceptions of threats, to sensations of extreme heat or intense cold, to the pleasure of eating chocolate. [75] The emotions we feel, the things we think and the behavior we exhibit as a result are, not entirely caused by, but definitely all linked to, the insula. Most retailers know intuitively that keeping shoppers happy is a key feature of building deep and lasting relationships with them. I would hazard a guess though; few know the neuroscience that is the basis for treating the customer right. Insula activation is one area of the brain that can make or break a shopping trip.

Deeply rooted emotions are hardwired into our brains. Some of these emotional responses that customers may have during shopping experiences are due to somewhat rigid and reactive brain structures that aren't likely to change anytime soon, not when their wiring has been built up over a few hundred million years.

Keeping insula activity at bay is exactly what using credit and debit cards do because they defer the pain associated with paying at the time of the transaction to some point in the future.

A growing reliance on digital connections between retailers and customers makes this more significant in an age of tech-enabled shopping places. You might say that we are more disconnected from the direct embodied experience of shopping places *and* we are also increasingly disconnected from the reality of having to hand over the cash when we buy. More and more, we take buying with plastic for granted. We often don't give it a second thought because it's very much like the idea of acting on impulse; we simply aren't doing too much 'thinking.' We are operating instead from a 'feeling place,' the insula, and avoiding the feelings of anticipated loss or pain.

Paying with credit or debit cards is an incredibly effective way to keep happy emotions in the foreground of the shopping mind, at least while the purchase phase is unfolding. Customers may have a whole set of other, potentially negative emotions once they get home. But, in the moment of actually making a purchase, credit and debit cards are handy tools.

The idea that they can get it now and pay for it later is *very* attractive to consumers. Given the opportunity, we will avoid anything that signals pain. However, once the bill comes at the end of the month, that 'what did I do?' feeling shifts the positive effect of paying with plastic to feelings of regret and sometimes, shame.

Credit card and debit card use has increased exponentially over the past few years and is directly connected to our climbing debt levels as well as our growing propensity for excessive consumption. [76] It is estimated that using cash in consumer transactions dropped by about a third from 31% in 1974 to 20% in 2000. Credit and debit cards are replacing cash as the preferred mode of payment. [77] In 2011 shoppers used credit cards for 29% of point-of-sale purchases and that number is expected to grow to 33% by 2017. Gift cards and prepaid cards were used for 6% of purchases made with plastic last year. Only 7% of transactions were made with a paper check, and paying by check is projected to drop even further. [78] Plastic card purchases comprised 66% of all in-person sales, with nearly half of those, or 31%, being made with debit cards. The average American carries 4.4 cards in his/her wallet and one in ten has more than 10 cards. [79]

Using plastic may be convenient, but it also promotes more impulsive decisions when it comes to buying things. After reacting impulsively to something, you will often hear a person say, "I don't know what I was thinking." And that's just the point; they weren't thinking; they were acting from a brain area that is a more impulsive and reactive rather than the brain areas where clear reasoned cognition takes place – up in the prefrontal cortex.

While credit cards have been around for some time, other forms of electronic payment such as debit cards, "near field communication" (NFC), and smartphone apps are going to eventually make the shopping world cashless. The benefits of having the ability to pay with the easy swipe of a card, the touch of a button or the wave of a smartphone can be supported from both the customer and retailer's points of view. This issue will become an important aspect of creating effective shopping environments in the years to come. A cashless payment system will have a tremendous influence on the cash-wrap experience, often a negative part of the customer journey.

Mobile phones are also increasingly being used, adding to the shift to alternate payment systems that make buying increasingly easy. Recent studies established worldwide mobile payment transactions to be valued at $171.5 billion in 2012, up a whopping 62% from $106 million in 2011. The expectation is that global mobile transaction volume will average 42% annual growth between 2011 and 2016. Projections now have the mobile transaction market worth $617 billion with 448 million users by 2016.[80] Statistics such as these, point to the fact that some of the traditional aspects of the shopping experience, including standing in line (or queue) at an in-store checkout counter, will indeed be a thing of the past.

Filling the void in the customer journey shouldn't be too hard, since in many cases, the checkout experience of queuing up at an enormous cash-wrap counter is often the worst part of the shopping trip. Customers will welcome the change as they become increasingly predisposed to shorter and shorter wait times for anything they do in a more fully digital-enabled economy. An inability to delay gratification will fit like a glove with the insula's propensity to have us avoid anything that signals the pain of loss, be it loss of money or loss of time.

This change in shopping process facilitated by technology, and embraced by the insula, will provide more shopping time to the customer. Freeing up useful hours of our day has always been the promise of technology. And so, if we add a few precious moments back to our day through use of technology, we can move the newfound free time to our growing list of to-do's, or ... more shopping.

As retailers seek to maintain shopping trip length and not simply give up time saved in their stores to competitors, they will want to design environments that can capitalize on a few extra minutes of dwell time. As technology grants the customer (and sales associate) a few extra minutes in shopping process, that time can be turned towards engaging the customer in ways that foster their relationship to the brand or retailer. Providing the customer with the opportunity to learn more about the brand or the product assortment, to be entertained, or to be offered customer service amenities to fill these moments of captured time, may also add to the customer's basket. If not directly influencing additional sales, this extra time can be used to influence the customer's perception of the experience. Technology applications, such as mobile checkout, can facilitate the shopping process, allowing retailers naturally to process greater numbers of customer transactions. And, from the customers' point of view, they leave the store with a sense of satisfaction that their precious time wasn't squandered by waiting in line at the cash-wrap counter.

While not all customers will like to have the time they may have saved in the shopping process spent in the store, the sales associate who is attuned to the customer's needs may find a window of opportunity to introduce something new. Promoting novelty through getting the customer's brain into a creative emotionally connected mode, while decreasing perceived or anticipated pain, is an opportunity to be captured when a few minutes are freed up in the shopping journey. One of the benefits to the technological evolution in stores is that it gives brands more 'soft selling' time to connect to customers, when they can take a moment to teach brand ideology, create community and foster relationships. Calm shopping brains are more receptive shopping brains.

By creating easy and painless payment opportunities, retailers avoid the internal cognitive conflict and resulting negative emotional effect that comes from the price/preference differential. Customers buy now and think later. With a little bit more time on their hands, retailers capture an opportunity to craft experiences that focus customer attention on positive, connected, right-brained activities. Getting customers to experience more positive types of emotions needs to continue to be the goal.

With increased use of in-store technology, retailers are going to be able to facilitate faster transaction times (and presumably process more purchases in a given time frame), reduce queuing, and cut down on physical infrastructure. Cash-wrap counters have already started disappearing and eventually store fixture counts will reduce in response to deeply curated assortments. More importantly, they will also be able to gather important customer information through the digital information attached to the customer's mobile-device account.

With increased information about customers in their stores, retailers will turn this data into actionable tactics that will directly affect assortment planning, store layouts, technology integration, buying and merchandising, stock levels, and shipping processes. Changes to all of these will serve, hopefully, to make customer experiences more efficient, relevant and emotionally satisfying.

Since the insula never took a class on accounting and economics, and isn't so good with interest rates and finance charges, customers will likely be apt to make more purchases, putting off the pain of immediate payment with cash, until the bill comes at the end of the month. In the excitement of the buying moment, paying with plastic literally inhibits the insula.

When you consider payment with a debit card, both the immediate pain of paying in the store with cash goes away and so too does the delayed pain of getting the bill at the end of the month. Even though debit cards are immediately charged to the customer's bank account, the fact that people buy more when using both credit and debit cards, suggests that "it is not discounting of delayed payment but, rather, it is the abstract and emotionally inert nature of card payments that reduces the pain of payment."[81]

Either way, the insula loves the shopping trip when credit cards are the method of payment. If insula activity is mitigated, customers will buy things that, in the end, aren't even good for them.

Using the Card Even When You Know It's Not Good For You

One would assume that most people are interested in a long, healthy and productive life. If this were true, then one would also expect that people would make choices about what they put in their bodies from the grocery store and avoid spending money on food that is 'unhealthy.'

Imagine a scenario where customers are given a choice to buy food that is either healthy or unhealthy for them versus items that are more typically considered as healthy choices. Now add to this picture that they are given the ability to pay for what they load into their shopping cart by credit card or cash. What do they choose to do? Will the deferral of pain by paying with plastic override their good sense to make healthy choices? Will they pay with cash but buy less? Will they buy nothing at all?

In a multiple-phase study to investigate purchasing decisions, researchers found that despite shoppers' being aware that certain foods were unhealthy, they would buy them more frequently when using a credit or debit card. [82] The brain's impulse control went out the window and their baskets were filled with more cookies.

Conversely, shoppers only able to pay by cash tended to curb their impulsive responses and reduce the number and value of unhealthy choices.

Given that many shoppers have trouble regulating their impulsive responses, the researchers suggested that cash payment could be used as a self-regulation tool and that cash-only payment systems could have a substantive degree of relevance for consumer welfare. The thinking is, that if people were only able to pay with actual money in their wallets, they would be acutely aware of the 'pain' of paying with cash, and would be more likely to make better food choices and not give in to their impulses.

Imagine a store that says *cash only 'cause we're trying to keep you healthy.'* Given that the retail business is one of selling stuff, one would be inclined to think that the motivations of some retailers might not be so altruistic. The above idea is a great tag line, but I suspect that it would be left in the boardroom. More likely you'd see, '*It's a healthy choice and easy to buy. So use your card and give it a try…*'

We all think that we are able to 'keep it together' in the shopping aisle but studies are pointing out that self-control is not entirely, well…under our control. Holding impulsive desires in check can be made easier or more difficult by seemingly unrelated contextual factors that influence both visceral and emotional responses. These emotional feelings lead people to put things in their shopping cart, even though they know that they are putting their health at risk.

You might think that one of the reasons why shoppers buy more on a credit or debit card is because they don't pay attention to the price of the products they are choosing as much as when they are counting out the dollar bills at the check-out counter. It turns out that customers using plastic forms of payments don't have 'price blindness' at all when they are making product selections. In fact, when asked to estimate how much they spent, those who used credit or debit cards reported spending *more* than those who used cash. In fact, their estimations of how much they had spent were pretty close to the actual total price of their shopping baskets.

According to the Thomas study these results suggest that the painlessness of paying by credit card is not due to 'price neglect.' "Even when participants pay attention to price, paying by credit card reduces the pain of payment."[83] So, despite the fact that we *know* better, we don't *do* better and before you know it, we are loading those delicious cakes into our cart. Providing customers with a way to mitigate the pain of a purchase through the use of digital technologies – credit or debit cards or some other mechanism – will lead to more and higher-value purchases.

Our society is increasingly connected with technologies and digital media that facilitate access to, and the purchasing of, more products than ever before. This is the new normal: easy access to abundance and 'no pain – easy gain' shopping.

However, even though customers in the Thomas study willingly purchased more of things that were clearly unhealthy than they should have, they also just as often reported regret from doing so. This was especially the case with impulse purchases. So, when people are given an easy path to purchase, they will not, generally, be overtaken by indiscriminate spending. The thrill of putting off pain is short lived and often regretted later.

More than simply putting off the pain of a purchase, customers are looking for more *in* the things that they do buy. In our contemporary culture a strange paradox exists that even though people have more today than they have ever had before, they are less and less satisfied. "The paradox of prosperity is that while living standards have risen steadily decade after decade, personal, family and life satisfaction haven't budged. That's why more people – liberated by prosperity but not fulfilled by it – are resolving the paradox by searching for meaning...The most striking feature of contemporary culture is the unslaked craving for transcendence."[84] So, as customers load their shopping carts with products, they are increasingly thinking about not just what the products will *do*, but what they will *mean* in their lives.

Mirror-Mirror

It's Saturday morning.

The work week has been long. You satisfied customers and brought home the bacon and this will be a great day to just relax. You go downstairs, and start to make the house special of pancakes and hot coffee. Clutching your favorite warm mug, you take a moment to breathe.

A while later, the kids are up and at the computer, playing in a virtual world, creating new otherwise impossible realities. After a short time of quiet, you hear "I wanna turn...let me play" and the energy begins to change.

Tension is injected into your moment of peace.

Soon enough, the voices are raised, an argument is fermenting, you are called in to mediate, and grumpy faces stare at you.

You try your best to hold on to your peaceful feeling, but the more you are exposed to the negative emotions, the more your happy and relaxed feeling wanes.

You are in the boardroom.

You are prepared and alert, ready to give the presentation of your life and you are sitting across from a group of folks who aren't communicating very much. No smiles. They must have seen a number of presentations before yours and they look like they'd rather be someplace else.

You try to create small talk but get monosyllabic answers, and the guy at the end of the table lets out a big yawn. He doesn't try to hide it and you see clear across his back teeth.

You're not tired, but you yawn, too, trying to conceal it with your hand.

You are feeling increasingly uncomfortable and the door swings open. A big guy walks in apologizing insincerely for being late, and with a frown he says, "Let's get going. I don't have a lot of time!"

The parking lot is hot and you are making your way between the cars to the front of the store. The swish of the automatic door slides the glass panes aside and you step into the air-conditioned space. It feels good to be out of the heat.

A sales associate greets you and with a smile says, "Welcome to the *coolest* place in town! Is there any thing I can help you with today?" You get the pun and smile.

She continues to have an open look about her, makes eye contact, the smile isn't forced, and she genuinely looks to be enjoying the fact that you came in today.

You feel welcomed and calm, and ask where to find something. She points you in the right direction and you are off to the back corner of the store feeling welcome and happy.

Each of these scenarios is an example of how the *affect* of others *affects* how we feel. If you are around people with 'bad energy,' you might feel down, anxious and maybe a bit depressed yourself. And if you are hanging out with people who are joyful and open, chances are you'll feel the same. Our brains are tuned in to other people's emotional states and they can directly change the way we feel. This capacity for empathy comes by way of brain structures called 'mirror neurons.'

In the mid 1990's, an Italian neurophysiologist and professor at the University of Parma was studying the frontal and premotor areas in monkeys' brains. Giacomo Rizzolatti and his colleagues were monitoring a single neuron and watching what happened when a monkey picked up and ate a peanut.[85] What they discovered was that the neurons fired when the monkey reached out and grasped a peanut. They also discovered that the same neurons fired when the monkey simply observed another individual (in this case the researcher) doing the same action. As the monkey sat idle and simply watched the researcher carry out the action of picking up the peanut, its brain exhibited neural firing patterns that were as if it were doing exactly the same thing.

While Rizzolatti and his colleagues monitored the neuron they thought was responsible for the movement of the monkey's arm and hand to reach for and pick up the peanut, they concluded that there was a clear connection between the motor and the visual perception areas at the back of the brain.

More significant, however, was the activity detected in these 'mirror neurons' when the monkey simply watched the same action being carried out by someone else. Rizzolatti also discovered that in order to activate the mirror-neuron system, the action the monkey was watching had to be *goal directed*. In other words, the neurons would not fire when the researcher waved his hand or pushed something away or did something that didn't seem to serve some purpose.

Even though Rizzolatti had come across a significant neural system, his research paper was originally turned down for publication by the journal *Nature* because according to its editors, Rizzolattti's research was "very interesting for physiologists but had no broad interest for the public."[86] Subsequent publications of the discovery of mirror neurons by Rizzolatti put the neuroscience community on the path to one of the most important areas of study in our understanding of imitation, learning, language development and empathy in humans. It is now widely accepted that the mirror neuron system plays a critical role in all of these aspects of human behavior.[87]

In subsequent years, brain-imaging studies by Marco Iocoboni (and others, including Rizzolatti) would confirm the presence of these types of neurons in humans with some key differences between what occurs in the human brain versus that of a monkey.

While in the monkey's brain, activation of the mirror-neurons occurs only in connection to actions that are goal directed, in humans, these neural structures are able to create inferences about subsequent behaviors. In other words, human mirror neurons don't only code for 'what' the observed individual is doing, but also 'why' they are doing it. Simply watching someone else's behavior allows us to infer intent. Human mirror neurons are able to tell what others' facial expressions and body actions mean and how others are likely feeling.[88]

Mirror neurons don't just help us imitate other people; they are largely responsible for our feelings of empathy, as well. These remarkable neural structures send signals to the limbic region of our brain, and they don't work alone. Mirror neurons are also connected to dopamine neurons. Their connection to the area of the brain that is responsible for feelings confirms that we do feel more pleasure when around calm and joyful people because our pleasure center is kicked into gear by the mirror neuron system. This system is keenly tuned in to the full range of emotions including joy, anger, sadness, anxiety, fear and disgust.

This is extremely important when we think about feelings and empathic connection between people. That we can simply watch someone carrying out a behavior and learn how to do it by putting together neural firing patterns – this, then that – is interesting. In addition, by watching others we are also able to understand the future outcome of some sequence of actions. That is, we can infer intent. 'Reading' these actions, be they body movements, or facial expressions, and coming to some conclusion as to what the person in front of you is likely feeling, or about to do, are indispensible to social interaction. The studies by Rizzolatti and others point to a now widely held understanding that mirror neurons are tied to our ability for empathic extension.

'Monkey see, monkey do' has evolved in humans to 'human see, human feel.'

The way our brains encode the actions of others, whether facial movements or body gestures, helps us understand the emotions of those around us. To empathize with others, our brains connect behaviors we see in others with the emotions we are witnessing. "In the human brain, this empathic resonance occurs via communication between action representation networks and limbic areas provided by the insula."[89] The areas of our brain that are wired to understand actions and behaviors of people around us, are connected to areas that are wired for understanding emotion.

Mirror neurons, in a way, create an energy link between the person carrying out a behavior – who effectively telegraphs a message – and a person watching who receives the message. This is the 'flow of information and energy' that was described by Dr. Daniel Siegel in his definition of the concept of mind earlier. When we see others' behavior, we pick up on their internal state. Something magic seems to flow between two people, like radio waves. My brain activity and subsequent feelings influences those I am in contact with and the reverse.

We have all heard the expression about getting a 'vibe' from someone. Our perceptual senses pick up signals from other people and our mirror neurons activate areas related to motor function and emotion, so that our brain matches the internal state of those we are exposed to.

Our brains 'resonate' with other brains.

Now, coming back to the world of store environments... It's not just that genuinely happy greeters are an asset at the front door, but that the customer journey can simply not afford to have a scowling face or disaffected response to a question along any part along the path to purchase. Customers won't even think about it; they'll simply just feel bad or sad, or angry, or anxious, or scared or whatever emotion is projected towards them.

Want to crush a great customer experience?

Have sales associates not care and let them show it on their faces or in their body language.

The power of mirror neurons in the shopping aisle cannot be understated. The affect of others around us is contagious, and as we shop, the energy of the entire group can rest in the emotional feelings of a single individual. Enthusiastic sales associates beget enthusiastic customers. Enthusiastic customers influence those around them. So, keeping customers engaged and happy as they move from area to area within a store is extremely important. These transitions are like emotional handoffs among teammates on the sales floor.

While we might assume that these are best done between live people, our ability to infer another person's intent and emotional state can equally be done from pictures of other human faces. The importance of lifestyle graphics within shopping places is a key feature to maintaining the positive affect of shoppers as they move throughout the space. If these visual cues to shoppers include images of happy faces, all the better.

Reading Faces and Feeling Emotions

As far back as Darwin's assertion that human emotions are encoded into who we are through our evolutionary biology, scientists have sought to determine if the feelings we show on our faces are cross-culturally similar and if we all draw on the same well of facial gestures to show emotions.[90] For some time it was believed the emotions demonstrated by facial expressions were determined, if not molded, by exposure to certain cultural influences.

American psychologists Paul Ekman and Wallace V. Friesen developed a system that outlines the way we move our faces in expressing emotion. Each of the facial movements that happens as a result of muscles contracting and relaxing in a person's face is called an 'Action Unit' (AU). All facial expressions can be broken down into various action units and each of them has been categorized insofar as they relate to specific emotions. When we look at each of these individual movements, some of them only appear fleetingly across someone's face. These are called micro-expressions. Other body movements also send signals as to whether a person we are looking at is happy, sad, angry, etc.

Ekman's work on facial gestures and emotions demonstrates that there is a list of basic emotions that *all* humans display. While it may be that in some cultures, the display of these emotions is mediated by cultural rules – who can show what feeling to whom and when it is appropriate to do so – we nevertheless all seem to have them built into our neural circuitry. Across cultures, there are six basic internal human emotions that are expressed by the same facial movements: happiness, surprise, fear, disgust, anger and sadness.

The original compendium of human facial expression created by Ekman was called the "Facial Action Coding System" (FACS) and included taxonomy of every human facial movement that is tied to our emotional expressions. A recent update to Ekman's original work was published in the early 2000s and was renamed "Facial Expression, Awareness, Compassion, Emotion" system (F.A.C.E.). [91]

Great customer experiences are in large part reliant on great customer service. Yet the astounding thing about many of our shopping experiences is that they are rife with people who haven't quite got it that they are in the customer-service business. Sure, they are all selling stuff, but the emotional content of the sale is where the money is.

Tuning in to what customers are exhibiting in their facial expressions and knowing a little bit about how their brains are likely to react is a great idea. Even more so, sales associates' being aware of their own emotional projections is an indispensible tool to engaging customers and promoting positive shopping experiences.

Want to have a great set up for a winning experience? Have a smiling greeter or happy sales associate, or even a picture of a happy, smiling face on a big graphic, and you'll have the customer's brain primed for a more enthusiastic shopping trip. Activating mirror neurons systems in customers to get them in the mood can be initiated by projecting an open, welcoming smile, free of defenses and a bad attitude. Happy shoppers are generally spendthrift shoppers, or at least they are increasingly likely to part with their cash (and more so with their credit or debit cards) when they are surrounded by positive emotions.

This of course becomes problematic when you consider that increasingly, customers are buying through smartphones, tablets and other digital interfaces. There are a host of challenges when the goal is to impart a positive feeling to customers when what they are looking at is a small screen and not engaging in a person-to-person, embodied interaction. The question of how a retailer creates positive emotion in a shopper through a digital interface is becoming a focus of store development, since the shopping public may first interact with the brand digitally rather than going to the store.

This becomes even more complex when we consider that screens of various sizes have the physical challenge of being able to get images of faces in high enough resolution that the customer can see the detail of emotional expressions. All screens are not perceived equally and each of them requires special attention so that the emotional content that potentially triggers the mirror neuron system is enhanced.

Some of the smaller interfaces, such as handheld devices, are simply not as effective at making the resonant emotional connection between brains due to their limited screen size. Text-based messaging is more effective on these devices, whereas larger digital interfaces such as tablets, desktop computers and large-format digital interfaces are able to better activate the mirror neuron system because the screen size affords better detail and larger images of facial features.

If empathic connection requires the exchange of emotions, is it enough simply to see a poor-quality image of a face on a small screen?

Would video chat with a virtual sales associate help connect customers to sales associates and the brands they represent?

Mirror neuron studies indicate that humans are wired for making inferences about another person's next move in an interaction. While a still image of a smile on a screen or in-store graphic initiates mirror neuron activity, the image is not tied to actions – the graphic is only a snapshot of a moment in time. A still image is not perceived as a movement that occurs in a sequence of events that allows customers to 'connect the dots' and decipher the whole picture. It is, however, enough to get positive feelings flowing.

When we see happy faces, those neurons that code for happy are activated but they're just one part of the equation. Actions are another important aspect of the mirror neuron system. Those actions come in the form of facial expressions and body 'language' that are delivered to the observer in a sequence from which the observer creates meaning. Context is key to our understanding of intent.

How the face-to-face, embodied interaction happens in shopping places is a determinant of customer satisfaction. In a world where actual visits to the store are only one of the options available to customers, and we can hypothesize that trips to the mall or main street may become less frequent as customers buy from the palm of their hand, retailers bear an increasing burden to send the right message. Everything in the store is important when crafting great customer journeys, but nothing is more important than the connections between the brains of customers and those of the sales associates or people charged with representing the brand.

Corporations that inculcate in their employees with a culture of connection, from the C-Suite to the sales floor, will be more likely to activate more mirror neurons in the brains of their customers, leading to positive experiences. Sam Walton of Walmart had two rules about treating customers well: "Rule#1: The customer is always right. Rule #2: If the customer happens to be wrong, refer to Rule #1."[92]

If retailers are looking to defuse a disgruntled customer, empathy is required. Mirror neurons play a role in solving the conflict. If the customer sees defensiveness, anger, defiance or a blank stare, the situation is likely to head down the wrong path. If on the other hand, the customer sees openness, accommodation and genuine concern for the customer's point of view, then the situation is likely to defuse in a short time. Customers want to be heard, not held at arm's length.

The picture they see in the sales associate's body language and facial expression telegraphs a message of cooperation and solidarity or, the drawing of a line in the sand. If anger or frustration or sadness is met with anger, frustration or sadness, a feedback loop starts between brains that spirals positive experience into a vortex of negative emotions.

When we project feelings of positivity, it's a conscious decision on our part. And it's contagious. Using the knowledge of the mirror-neuron system requires a sense of introspection – self-awareness – so that people are aware of the changes that are happening inside themselves while they are in relationship to others.

If shoppers have made the effort to get to the store, retailers had better make it worth their while. With increasing pressure on price point as a differentiator, and a growing mindset about things becoming less and less costly, why shop the store when an online mega-retailer will always have it for less?

Customer experience will not be based simply on getting a good deal, even though the prefrontal cortex loves the challenge of working out the price/preference conflict. If customers find themselves standing in the store they'll likely be there for something else – connection through embodied experience. How they are engaged will set up their brains to have experiences that are fulfilling or disappointing. The influence of price will never go away entirely, but it will become more secondary to delivery of authentic experiences imbued with emotional content that resonates between buyers and sellers. Mirror neurons are a key feature to connecting to the emotional side of the customer. Projecting joy, appreciation, and openness will, in turn, activate those feelings in consumers as they engage in shopping places.

This, That or The Other Thing – Why Choice is Highly Overrated

When my two boys were toddlers, we used to watch a series of animated videos called *Veggie Tales*. Each episode was an amusing take on biblical stories, full of laughs and high on learning morals. We watched one particular episode, "Madame Blueberry," a number of times, committing the songs to memory and the message to heart.

This tenth tale in the *Veggie Tales* series uses an adaptation of the title character's name from *Madame Bovary* by Gustave Flaubert published in 1856. In Flaubert's novel, Emma Bovary tries to escape her boredom with provincial life through a series of adulterous affairs and living far beyond her means. Not exactly biblical, I know.

Veggie Tales' "Madame Blueberry" drops the salaciousness in favor of acquisition of 'stuff' as a means to happiness. With the subtitle "A Lesson in Thankfulness," this clever and sometime hilarious animated video conveys the message that material possessions from "Stuff Mart" will never truly make us happy, not even when the house you own in a tree is so overloaded, it bends under the weight and is finally catapulted, along with all the stuff, across the valley. Instead, the Madame Blueberry tale promotes the idea that we need to be thankful for what we have. See? Biblical after all.

Lovely story, and lots of memories with my kids.

Many retailers have lived under the impression that giving customers selection beyond comprehension is a good thing. 'Customers need choice, and if we have more of it, they are going to love shopping with us.' Or so they think. Granted, many retailers have developed empires on providing an assortment that extends as far as the eye can see, but the assumption that the customer can actually absorb it all and that it makes for a better shopping experience is simply off the mark.

In fact, more is not better. It's just more.

And, it's often not better. It's worse.

Furthermore, all that stuff is simply too much for the human brain to absorb.

Having 25 types of peanut butter to choose from in the grocery aisle doesn't make choosing which one to buy any easier, nor does it increase the satisfaction with the chosen product at all. In the end, it is more likely to have the outcome of compromising the shopping experience by creating confusion and leading to decisions full of regret.

Most people think that while walking shopping aisles, they are perfectly capable of making rational decisions about what to buy. It's not hard to imagine that when shoppers have a vast array of choices, they set to work comparing the alternatives and evaluating the pro's and con's of one choice over another. Except, that isn't what happens.

Shoppers are actually incapable – on a brain level – to keep in mind all of the possibilities that confront them while trying to pick one jam over another, or decide which of the 25 types of peanut butter will go with their choice of fruit spread. Should it be smooth, chunky or maybe *extra* chunky, salted, without salt, organic, sweetened with high-fructose corn syrup, with fluffy stuff or a swirl of jam already added to the jar, or made just from crushed up peanuts? And what size to get, and should it be in a glass jar or plastic? And what is almond butter about anyway? Would that be a good alternative? After all, your spouse's friend swears by it.

Okay… now choose…quickly.

What happens? Most often, paralysis.

Thinking about what to do often puts the prefrontal cortex into a loop of cognitive dissonance, making effective decisions tough at best and impossible more likely. It isn't that we don't like choice. In fact, research suggests that we initially like the idea of lots to choose from, but in the end too many choices make the process of deciding much more difficult.

American culture has thrived on the ideology of Freedom - freedom of speech, religious affiliation, political party membership and the 'freedom to choose' anything. Yet, given increasing choices, we often waver, get confused, freeze, and regret not having selected more wisely after we finally do make a choice.

Our culture has grown ever more reliant on acquisition and abundance to quell the latent fear of not having enough, believing that bigger is better and more is mollifying. Except that it isn't. If it were, one would expect increasing satisfaction in the studies mentioned earlier, not less satisfaction than ever.

David Meyers calls this "The American Paradox" and points out that despite the fact that we are more affluent and have the privilege of abundant choice, that "the divorce rate has doubled, teen suicide tripled, juvenile violence quadrupled, prison population quintupled, the proportion of babies born to unmarried parents sextupled, cohabitation (a predictor of future divorce) has increased sevenfold and depression has soared – to ten times the pre-World War II level."[93]

But wait a minute. If we have access to more than we could ever possibly need, how could these statistics possibly be true?

There are surely intricate socioeconomic, political, religious, technological and cultural influences woven into this staggering rise in dissatisfaction with life's little pleasures. Looking at the issue on a brain level, there are a number of studies indicating that abundant selection in the shopping aisle creates more problems for customers when they are trying to make good choices, and that they have less satisfaction in the choices that they do finally make.

You're standing in the grocery store looking across the ten feet of shelving that holds jams and jellies. You like a good peanut butter and jelly sandwich when you're snacking at night and now you are about to select from the vast assortment of certainly delicious flavors that your local grocer has for you. Left and right, up and down, you look. What do you select when there is so much to choose from?

Sheena Iyengar of Columbia University and Mark Lepper of Stanford University put grocery store customers and college students to a similar set of choices. In a series of experiments, she and her colleague tested what they referred to as the "choice overload hypothesis" – that "although the provision of extensive choices may sometimes still be seen as initially desirable, it may also prove unexpectedly demotivating in the end."[94]

To test the hypothesis they created three studies:

- **Study 1: Jam in a grocery aisle**
  In an upscale grocery store, customers encountered a tasting booth that displayed either 6 ("limited choice") or 24 ("extensive choice") flavors of jam. Dressed as store employees, researchers invited passing customers to sample jam from their station, which either had 6 selections, or in another condition, 24 selections. Customers were allowed to taste as many jams as they wanted and were given a $1 discount on their purchase of any jam manufactured by the company they were using as test products.

What the researchers wondered was whether or not the number of selections displayed affected the customer's initial attraction and subsequent purchase of the displayed product.

Of the 242 customers who passed by the display showing a selection of 24 jams, 60% of them stopped at the tasting station. In contrast, of the 262 customers who passed by the display with just 6 selections, only 40% stopped to try a sample. Not necessarily taking into consideration environmental factors that might have captured the customer's attention, such as lighting conditions, color variations in the surrounding environment, location in relation to traffic flow, etc., the more that was displayed at the tasting station, the greater attraction customers seemed to have towards the product.

One would think that, given the wide selection of products in the condition where there were 24 flavors to choose from, there would have been more sampling of the products and more subsequent purchases. But this was not the case.

Not only were the amounts of jams sampled (about 1-2 flavors) the same regardless of whether there were 6 or 24 selections, but people bought far fewer jams when given a choice of 24 than given a choice of 6 flavors. Only 3% of the customers given a choice of 24 jams subsequently made a purchase versus 30% given a much-reduced selection of only 6 flavors.

While greater selection may initially attract the customer, too much choice has a negative impact on the customer's willingness to buy.

- **Study #2: Writing essays**
In the second study, the researcher's subjects were students in a psychology class at Stanford University. They were required to watch a movie and then were given the option to write an essay for extra credit about what they had seen. Overall, 65% of the total class chose to do the extra assignment.

Of those who chose to do the essay, 70 students got a list of 6 essay subjects and 123 students got a list of 30 essay subjects. At no point were the students told that they would be graded on the essay assignment; rather, it was explained that by simply completing essay, they would receive the extra credit. This removed their motivation to have to do well on the writing of the essay in order to get the credit.

Did the number of essay subjects to choose from have an impact on the number of students who completed the work? You bet.

Of the 70 students who got the limited list of essay subjects, 74% turned in the assignment. In contrast, of the 123 students who got the extensive list of essay subjects, 60% turned in papers. Not only did the students with fewer choices turn in more papers, they actually produced better work.

- **Study #3: Choosing chocolates**

  In the third study, subjects were asked to choose from an array of chocolates in both limited-choice and extensive-choice scenarios.

  The researchers tested the hypothesis that when customers have a few options to choose from, they set to work trying to figure out which one of the various options is best for them, by implementing a strategy of optimization. They use a set of rules to 'optimize' the outcome by trying to select the 'best' one. When customers are faced with multiple choices they begin to think through a series of tradeoffs and try to create a set of rules to help simplify the problem. They struggle through the choosing ordeal by trying to find the option that is merely 'satisfactory,' rather than being the 'best' of all of the options.

  Prior to carrying out the experiment, the subjects were asked to predict how satisfied they were likely to be with their stated preference – whether they expected their choice to simply be 'satisfactory' or 'among the best.' In addition, after the subjects had made their choice, but before they had sampled the product, they were asked to provide feedback on how they felt about the choice-making process – did they enjoy it, find it difficult, or frustrating? After they had chosen, they were asked to share their feelings about whether or not they were satisfied with their choice.

  The researchers found that the number of products displayed did not have any effect on the strategy that the customers used to choose. In the case where they had limited choice, they did not tend to choose based on finding the best of the selection – to 'optimize.' And, there was no strategy used to simply 'satisfy' when the customers had an extensive selection. Also of note was that there were no differences in the reported anticipated satisfaction, whether or not the customers had more or less to choose from.

  As in the findings from Studies #1 and #2, customers who had an extensive choice reported more enjoyment in the decision-making process. But, they also reported more frequently that they found choosing more frustrating than those with a limited set of options. Interestingly, in what seems a contradictory set of feelings, customers could find extensive choice enjoyable *and* more overwhelming. In other words, while they liked the idea of having a vast selection, they also found the choosing process more difficult.

  When asked to rate their overall satisfaction with their eventual selections, customers given the limited set of options were significantly more satisfied with what they chose.

  So, customers liked being offered a wide variety of chocolates to choose from and, at the start enjoyed the process more. However, despite this initial enthusiasm, when given a broad selection, they proved to be less satisfied and harbored more regrets about the choices they finally made. Furthermore, when given the option to be compensated for their participation in the experiment with chocolates or money, they were more likely to choose money over more chocolate.

Having more choice did not enhance their satisfaction, but rather promoted a sense of regret of not having made the best selection after all of their deliberation about what to choose.

You would think that the idea of abundant choice, and the freedom to choose from all of it, is so deeply ingrained in our culture that retailers would likely meet a lot of resistance if they were to tell customers that they were going to take stuff away from them and slim the selection down. That is not what is happening in the design of new store concepts. Shoppers are overloaded before they ever get to the store and are expressing their concerns about there being too much to choose from and that they need help to navigate all of it. While this move to decreased footprints and curated selections is beginning to catch on, many retail formats are still about 'bigger is better' – even though, when customers have it all, they like it less.

Customers are so predisposed to seeing retail shopping places jammed with merchandise that they would rather blame their poor experience on disaffected salespeople, out of stock items, high prices and that they couldn't find a parking spot. If retailers solved for these issues but *still* provided extensive merchandise choices, customers' decisions would still be hijacked by a brain overwhelmed by merchandise.

Every time shoppers have to make a decision about what they will purchase, they are aware that one choice precludes another. Buying the product in their hand means that they give up any inherent values that the product they leave on the shelf had to offer. This can be tough going when the number of products increases and the differences between them are subtle.

The feeling that you are 'leaving something on the table' when choosing one option over another is the economics term, 'opportunity cost,' the loss of potential gain from other alternatives when one alternative is chosen. Virtually every choice we make has an opportunity cost tied to it. We are always giving up something to get something else. What we hope when making a choice in the shopping aisle is that the opportunity costs don't outweigh the benefits of the choices we do make.

Now, consider the dilemma of choice in the stores with abundant selections. Even more dramatically, imagine making a choice from a seemingly endless array of online retailers. Forced with the mind-bending task of having to evaluate the potential opportunities (and their related costs), customers shut down and often don't choose at all. The cognitive conflict becomes too much and, in the end, it is easier *not* to decide, or to defer making a decision for another day. When customers have to start evaluating the trade-offs between getting 'this, that or the other thing,' *all* of them become less appealing.

When (and if) customers do make a decision to buy something while having an extensive selection to choose from, they are often struck with cognitive dissonance or 'buyer's remorse,' that nagging feeling that the item left behind just might have been better. This is why the subjects who made choices from a limited set of options in the Iyengar and Lepper studies exhibited greater satisfaction with what they chose, and those who had multiple options felt worse. With each item left on the table/shelf/rack, opportunity costs mount. Thinking about all of the other flavors of jams and chocolates that they did not taste got the best of them, and their satisfaction levels diminished.

As choice increases exponentially in a digitally connected multichannel world, satisfaction in the choices we make will undoubtedly decrease as compounding opportunity costs pile up.

When people are given extensive choice they are forced into performing cognitive gymnastics. To-choose or not-to-choose, and then to-buy or not-to-buy – all of this gets the prefrontal cortex crunching all of the possible outcomes of the choice. When confronted with multiple choices to make, we go to work on determining the costs of possible outcomes, and it takes time and mental energy.

Recall for a moment the way the brain processes information when seeing a product that has piqued its curiosity. While the old mammalian brain (the insula and other more primitive structures in this area) is determining if the thing you're looking at is something to be feared or likely to produce pain, the prefrontal cortex area is also running the numbers and wading through the potential costs and benefits of one decision over another. With its higher-level executive function of weighing all of the costs and benefits of a particular conflict, the prefrontal cortex gets particularly busy when it has to choose between multiple options. In some cases our brain simply throws in the towel and chooses not to do all of that work.

Faced with too many choices, the customer's brain starts to take short cuts to avoid the burden of having to decide. Those short cuts may include deferring to an 'expert.'

When sales associates are nearby, they are often engaged in the decision-making process with the presumption that they have a vast amount of experience. Sales associates should know the pro's and con's of one product over another, thereby reducing the mind-bending calculations the customer has to go through to make the best choice. Also, engaging the sales associate in the decision process shifts some of the responsibility of making a bad choice from the customer to someone else.

It might be that the internal discussion going on in the subconscious mind of the customer is something like, "If it isn't any good, I can shift the blame and not feel so bad about myself."

Avoiding regret over making a bad choice by shifting the responsibility for making the decision to someone else, such as the sales associate, also becomes a rationale for making one choice over another. Think about "phoning a friend" on the game show *Who Wants to be a Millionaire?*, where you get to solicit the opinion of someone else who might know the answer to the million-dollar question. If they don't, they will distribute the shame and regret of not going home with a boatload of cash and the contestant won't shoulder the entire burden. In many cases though, calling on the expertise of the sales associate is a solicitation simply to have someone else help you get through the cognitive clutter of too many decisions.

Deferring the decision until some other time, not making one at all or shifting the responsibility of future regret for having made the wrong choice to someone else, are all part of the psychology of choosing when in a state of 'merchandise overwhelm.'

Consider recent statistics by the Pew Internet & American Life Project about use of cellphones in stores during the 2012 holiday shopping season that raise interesting issues related to what exactly cellphone users are doing with their phones while shopping. [95]

When shopping for holiday gifts for their loved ones, nearly six out of ten cellphone owners were using their device to solicit support from friends and family in making decisions about what to buy.

46% of cell owners used their phones while inside a store to *call a friend or family member for advice* about a purchase they were considering.

28% of cell owners used their phone while inside a store to *look up reviews* of a product to help decide if they should purchase it or not.

27% of cell owners used their phone while inside a store to *look up the price* of a product, to see if they could get a better price elsewhere.

Not surprisingly, the demographic reaching out for help in decision-making the most was done by young adults with 78% of cellphone users between the ages of 18-29 dialing a friend. This may be attributed to a number of factors, including insecurity and uncertainty about making a decision when one is younger and the pervasiveness of social media and the need to be 'liked' in one's social network. But, there is also the very real possibility that for these young minds, the sheer volume of options available in stores (and through their digital interfaces) is adding more and more confusion to the buying process, and not making it easier or any better of an experience.

Already overloaded with the amount of content that they process each day, younger shoppers are in a state of digitally induced ADHD. Immediacy of access and messaging, communications under 140 characters, and exposure to digital screens everywhere are all likely to have their brains in a state of high alert. Adding multiple choices in the shopping aisle can't help younger shoppers make a better decision; it just adds to the noise. While our brains are great at accommodating an amazing amount of stimuli, they simply weren't built for the onslaught they now face in the course of a typical day.

The value of "phoning a friend" is indeed a positive attribute to the social aspect of shopping. Including a wider range of opinions in the buying process also supports the overwhelmed brain in making a decision. Nevertheless, it is worth noting that younger customers are searching for support in buying decisions *out-of-store* through their mobile devices rather that turning to *in-store* sales staff, presumably the 'experts' in all things about the brand. Unfortunately, sales associates are not always the experts they should be. Often, they are reduced merely to part of the stock replenishment, merchandising and display system rather than acting as brand ambassadors, style mavens and trusted allies.

Faced with increasing difficulty to make a good choice, we look for help, don't buy anything, or buy with only partial commitment to the idea that what we are getting is the right thing.

This is even more likely when return policies allow customers to bring back almost everything they buy within a certain time frame. Customers may allow themselves to be only partially committed, and make half-hearted choices that lead to less satisfaction that can be ameliorated by an open return policy. Both the rational part of the brain that is stymied by choice overload and the emotional part of the brain that would prefer not to feel regret look for the easy way out.

Today you can return almost anything you buy, which sometimes leads customers to make decisions that neither optimize nor satisfy, but seek just to get the confusion over with.

From the customer's point of view, this practice might be considered to be good customer service – *'Can't decide? Then buy two of them, take them home, try them out, and if you don't like them, bring them back.'* The problem still remains that the retailer is not effectively helping the customer through the buying process by reducing the amount of stuff they are exposed to. Furthermore, flexible return policies make for nightmares in inventory management and other retail operations.

If customers have trouble making effective choices from 30 different types of jams, or chocolates, and being satisfied, what are they going to do when they can get a seemingly infinite number of goods purchased from the palm of their hand and delivered to their front door the next day?

Considering the increasing availability of virtually any product via our ubiquitous digital devices, it only stands to reason that things are likely to get harder, not easier, from the point of view of customers being able to make choices that they are happy with. With too much choice being a demotivation, retailers need to become expert curators. They must reduce selections and understand that they can't be everything to everyone. When they try to offer 'the biggest selection ever,' they may initially be attractive, but eventually they overwhelm their customers' brains with too much to think about.

Despite the fact that the customers say they want abundant choice, the retailer needs to know better and have carefully made buying decisions based on a mantra of 'fewer and deeper.' Customers will have the same feelings of enjoyment based on the *volume* of goods (fewer SKU's but more of each) and more satisfaction in the selections they finally make when their brains are not forced into choice overload. In addition, they will carry less regret over the choices they made, feel happier in the long run and likely return more often.

Both feeling decisions and thinking decisions are made in the shopping aisle. That is to say, customers make choices about what they want based on intuitive, emotional limbic brain processing *as well as* reasoned, cognitive processing in the prefrontal cortex.

The degree to which they use either of these has a lot to do with the amount of selection to choose from, as well as how busy these areas of the brain are in the moment of decision making. Whether a customer is buying on emotional impulse or higher-order rational cost-benefit analysis depends a great deal upon what decision-making resources are available in the moment they are exposed to products and asked to choose.

Stanford University researcher Baba Shiv put subjects to the test of choosing between two different options while they were more or less compromised with a memory task.[96] He gave students either 2-digit or 7-digit numbers to remember then told them they were to go to another room to recall their numbers and engage in additional tasks. On their way to the other location, they were to choose from two different snacks on a table in the hallway – chocolate cake or fruit salad.

Shiv was interested in determining to what degree choice was influenced by emotions that are the result of actively engaging in a task while trying to make a decision rather than those emotions that were the result of background conditions such as being tired or a shopper's general mood.

The study by Shiv was, in some respects, similar to the studies where subjects were engaged in trying to figure out what to choose from an extensive selection of jams, essay subjects or chocolates. In the earlier studies, extensive choice triggered an overload of cognitive process that rendered decision making difficult and resulted in less customer satisfaction. In the present study, Shiv would overwhelm the brain not with more product, but a simple memory task and would watch what subjects would do when given just two products to choose from.

Would choices be made from the part of the brain more governed by 'lower-order' emotional reactions, like some of the more automatic responses that are the result of our older mammalian limbic brain being reactive and impulsive? Or, would decisions about what to choose be the result of thoughts that come from higher-order cognitive processes involved in taking the time to deliberately think through a problem and arriving at well-reasoned decisions?

The types of choices presented to the subjects was significant in that it was presumed that the cake was associated more to intense positive emotions but less favorable thoughts (people loved the taste but knew it was less healthy) and fruit salad was associated with less favorable emotions but more positive thoughts (people may have still liked the taste but believed that it was a more healthy choice).

Shiv and his colleagues discovered that when subjects' brains were busy at work trying to remember the seven-digit numbers they were more likely to choose chocolate cake. While the prefrontal cortex was busy crunching away at the memory task, the subjects had less cognitive resources to think their way through the choice problem and made decisions based on emotions (impulsivity). The memory task the subjects were asked to do essentially overrode their ability to choose what was otherwise 'good' for them, and they gave into to a choice that fed their potential for being impulsive.

Conversely, when the subjects had the relatively easy task of remembering 2 digits, they tended to choose fruit salad as their snack. In this case, the researchers concluded that more cognitive resources were available to weigh out the options and make a decision based on thinking the problem through. Subjects chose more healthy snacks and were not swayed by the impulsive desires of the limbic area of their brains.

While it seems obvious that customers can get overwhelmed by too much product to choose from, they are also swayed in their decision making process by simply having too much to think about while considering what they want. In fact, these two conditions are not dissimilar. In each case the brain is being overloaded with *thinking*.

Knowing that customers are likely to choose quickly based on impulse rather than rationally thinking through the problem of choice when they have too much going on in their heads, might lead retailers to think they can implement a strategy such as, *'Always give customers more than they can deal with. Overload their circuitry and they will choose faster, thinking less and innately reacting more. Thus, we're likely to move more goods!'* Except that this will also quickly lead to dissatisfied customers, who will have the feelings of regret that are associated with making hasty, ill-considered, choices.

Adding more into the store for the customer to engage, or consider more, does not add to the shopping experience, but serves to undermine long-term positive feelings about the trip.

When trying to choose, less is invariably more.

Less confusion, *more* satisfaction.

An interesting part of the Shiv study dealt with the way the snack choices were presented to the subjects. In part of the experiment, the snack choices were presented as 'real' slices of cake and bowls of fruit salad while in others, 'symbolic' representations in the form of pictures. The idea at play in this phase of the study was that presenting the choices as photographs was likely to reduce the vividness of the options and the intensity of the positive emotions towards them would be changed. In other words, seeing a picture of a piece of chocolate cake would not be as effective in stimulating desire as seeing the real thing.

While the subjects who had to remember – 7 digit numbers invariably chose chocolate cake more often (since their cognitive resources were constrained), when they were shown pictures of cake versus the real thing, their choices of cake dropped by 20%. People reacted more positively to the real deal versus a scrumptious picture of it.

This, of course, has implications on the merchandise presentation that is done through digital interfaces. In our digitally connected world, handheld devices, tablets, desktop computers or environmentally placed digital interfaces will have an effect on how products are represented to a buying audience. But, regardless of the screen size or its resolution, symbolic representations are not ever likely to capture the emotional brain's attention as well as the real thing.

Given that there is an increasing propensity to search for and buy products online or from in-store digital interfaces, retailers will have to understand that those products with a largely hedonistic component, are things that customers will want to touch, smell, or taste while in the buying process. Product categories that do not necessarily have a deep emotional aspect to them and are purchased more on a cognitive level, based on their utilitarian features, will remain good candidates for the online channels of the retailer's business. In these cases, customers will shift from decisions based on emotions to cognitive-mediated decisions.

There is a lot of hype about augmented reality in the shopping experience. While it helps to begin to bridge the divide between embodied and digitally manufactured experiences, studies like those by Baba Shiv point out that, as the song says:
" Ain't nothing like the real thing baby,
Ain't nothing like the real thing."

Left Brain –
Right Brain

11

To really understand the shopper's brain, we have to look at how the two halves not only make a whole, but how they are responsible for the very different aspects of the way we behave, perceive the world, take part in decision making and finally, buy, whether we are in the store or on our mobile phones.

While the left and right sides of our brains are connected through a structure called the corpus callosum, they have very different takes on the world around us. To kick off our exploratory glimpse into the gray zone, we can remember that left is defined by three L's – Logic, Linear Thinking, and Language.

Language is a fascinating piece of this discussion because it demonstrates a shift in how we have come to interact with and understand our world. In the history of human development, language is actually very new. As we have evolved, we've relied more on non-verbal communication far longer than we have on spoken, or even more so, written, words.

For more than a couple of millennia, what we now attribute to the left-brain has been characterized as 'rational' or 'intelligent' and the right side of the brain is where empathy, emotion, intuition and context live. A look at language sheds light on the emergence of a school of thought about utopian society based in rational thought and a split of the logical and emotional aspects of the brain where the latter has often been marginalized.

If we believe that shopping has always been a social enterprise, then considering how we create shopping experiences that engage the right hemisphere is critical in an age where both the formal structure of language, and the way we use it, is changing in response to the pervasiveness of communicating through the Internet and digital media.

For brands hoping to communicate their message to shoppers, traditional pathways are no longer sufficient. How brands and retailers have communicated with customers in the past is quickly becoming outdated. A younger generation of shoppers is maturing and relying less on face-to-face communication and traditional formulations of syntax. They are instead morphing language to accommodate multiple channels of communication, all operating at the speed of light.

Life Before Written Language: Communicating in Pictures, Emotions and Gestures

We have come to rely so much on language that we are quite likely to forget that, as a form of communication between humans, language is a relatively new 'invention.' For most of our human evolutionary history we have used facial expressions, body gestures, sounds and pictures to express ourselves.

Despite being the subject of scholarly discussion for a long time, we aren't exactly sure when humans developed spoken language. To try to understand when language developed, scholars turn to archeological evidence, the differences in language among contemporary societies, communication between other animal species, notably the great apes, and now to neuroscience and what we know about how the brain works.

While determining the origins of language may continue to take some time, there is no doubt that a precursor to communication with words was communicating with images. As recently (in terms of human evolutionary history) as 20,000 years ago, we were still sharing significant stories about the meaningful aspects of our primitive societies through carved figures, drawings and paintings.

Lascaux, in the Dourdogne region of southwestern France, is famous for its Paleolithic cave paintings. Because of their size, quality and sophistication, they are considered to be the Sistine Chapel of the prehistoric world.

The impressive works of art are far from the main entry to the cave system, suggesting that they may have been used more as sacred or ceremonial meeting places than for the mere fun of artistic expression. Nearly 2,000 images depict human figures, horses, bulls and other animals that the artists would have found and hunted in their surrounding area. The Hall of the Bulls has images that are as much as 17 feet long – impressive when you consider the tools these primitive artists had to work with and the conditions under which they carried out their craft.

The representation of ideas through pictures has never abated. It's too ingrained in our way of communicating the things that matter in culture and it's fundamental to the fabric of social groups. Hundreds of millions of years of pre-language evolution has endowed our species with the remarkable ability to perceive and infer meaning from those things we see around us, especially in the facial expressions of our fellow humans.

As we began to have greater facility with representing ideas through pictorial and sculptural means, developing our communication from guttural sounds into a defined spoken language offered a broader and more detailed way to communicate the complexities of thoughts and social structures. Eventually, pictures used to represent ideas were augmented with verbal descriptions and it wasn't long (evolutionarily speaking) before we developed a way to record these spoken concepts with symbols. After a few thousand years of using scratches and shapes, humans eventually developed a method to write what we spoke.

Jumping forward to the land of the Pharaohs and the years around 3400 BC, writing had developed into representing language through symbols. Archeological discoveries in Egypt suggest that one of the earliest forms of writing may have been hieroglyphics. The written Egyptian language was a development of other primitive forms of illustrating ideas with symbols or "glyphs" that directly represent objects or ideas.

Only special people were chosen by the upper echelons of the social system to become scribes, who also held an elevated position in ancient Egyptian society by way of their knowledge of writing. Hieroglyphics were hard to learn and time consuming to create, but a step closer to a fully alphabetic language. The Egyptians used this form of writing for about 3,500 years most predominately during the years 3000 – 1300 BC.

The interesting part of hieroglyphics is that even up to about 3,000 years ago, our way of communicating with each other was imbued with pictures, or symbols that represented words and/or whole ideas. It would take another couple thousand years for the development of a truly alphabetic language that provided individual symbols for sounds created in spoken language.

The early Semitic languages spoken by workers in ancient Egypt are considered to be among the first alphabetic languages, though they were based on consonants. These simple forms of written language called 'abjads' did not account for sounds we now consider as 'vowels.' The Greeks adopted the Phoenician abjad form of alphabet, adding vowels that better suited their language, and consistently assigned letters to both consonants and vowels on an equal basis.

By about the second century BC, a bona fide written alphabet including symbols for all of the sounds of the Greek language, including consonants and vowels, was complete. In fact, the word 'alphabet' derives from the names of the first two letters of the Greek alphabet, 'alpha' and 'beta.' Soon after, the Romans adopted this Greek idea. They changed many of the letters into the forms we know today, and spread their alphabet throughout the Roman Empire.[97]

From this point forward, only a little over 2000 years ago in our human evolutionary history, we begin to see a growing reliance on the written word as a means of expressing human experience. Up until then, our visual-spatial-embodied experience was primarily the way for us to express ourselves. Up until then, understanding and representing the world in pictures reigned supreme.

The Rise of Rationality – Plato and Domination by Reason Alone

There's no doubt that language, whether spoken or written, is an indispensible part of human experience. Without it, our lives would not be as rich. Imagine our lives without poets, playwrights, lyricists, and authors of all genres of literary expression. Imagine a day without email, texts, social networking and blog posts. Imagine our outdoor environments without billboards, digital signs and advertisements.

Words are powerful.

Words are among our unique abilities that separates us humans from the animals. While animals can certainly be noisy and use sounds to communicate, they don't 'speak' nor do they form complex thoughts the ways humans do, built on the combination of memories, emotions and language based in words.

Language and a complete alphabet helped religious and civic leaders, poets and philosophers record the laws of the land and our most nuanced thoughts so that all could share in the content. With writing coming into its own, the spread of culture and ideologies would no longer be dependent on ritual enactment and oral traditions alone.

During the handful of centuries prior to the start of the epoch of the Common Era (otherwise know as *Anno Domini*, or AD), Greek philosophers were creating scholarly written works that would set the foundation of western thought. Being philosophers, and therefore big *thinkers*, Socrates, Plato and Aristotle, imagined a perfect society ruled by reason alone.

Rule-by-reason is an interesting philosophical concept that might do well on the planet Vulcan. However, it is totally counter to our innate predisposition to be connected to other people through empathic relationships and to experience the world in an embodied way. We are both thinkers *and* feelers, and each of these modes of processing the world around us needs the other.

From the point of view of the philosophers, the intuitive, emotional, relational brain seemed to keep getting people into trouble. It has been considered for millennia as being unpredictable and more akin to those behaviors exhibited by creatures below humans on the evolutionary totem pole. After all, according to the early philosophers, we had risen to the top of the heap because we could think big thoughts. As the most advanced species on the planet, we could talk about thoughts, carry on debates, and by the second century BC, even write them down.

Recording our thoughts is mostly under the control of our linear, rational, linguistic left brain. It is important to remember that language, both written and spoken, is processed by the left *and* right sides of the brain, but each hemisphere is predisposed to process the words we hear, read and write differently. The left side takes care of the 'meaning' of the words, their structure and context to one another. The right side takes care of the 'feeling' or emotional content of the words through understanding the tone, or prosody, the rhythmic and intonation qualities of language.

Back in the days of Plato (and ever since then) emotions were considered the uncontrollable, more primitive, part of who we were. Common among the intelligentsia was a school of though that went something like this: If only we could find a way to keep unpredictable emotions and impulses at bay and employ our rational minds to reason our way through all of life's conundrums, all would be good in the world. To Plato, emotions were more vice than virtue and the sooner we could create a society ruled by reason, the better all of humanity would be.

After all, this was still a time when ancient cities were established based on recreating the celestial geometries on the earth.[97] The stars didn't change and their constancy was a counterpoint to the chaos surrounding us earthbound souls.

Back then, the basic idea was that if we could define the arrangement of city streets by transcribing the geometry of the stars onto the ground, maybe some of the stasis of the heavens above would wear off down below and we would find more predictability in a generally unpredictable world. Anything that would give better explanations for the inconsistency in our lives and not allow for the unpredictability of emotionally based behavior was considered to be not just better, but the lofty goal of human development.

Except, you can't have balance when you've only loaded one side of the scale. Any 'ideal' society based on rational thought alone would likely not work, because left needs right, yin needs yang, Fred needed Ginger and logic needs emotion.

That said, our schools, workplaces and retail businesses have been structured around the idea that rationality would lead us to success. Logical processes led by lots of words and numbers were considered to be more reliable than emotion and intuition. For years, the spreadsheet has been the final word and differentiation by price point made you standout as a retailer.

Plato, the philosopher, was naturally what could be considered a 'cerebral-centrist.' For him, it was all about the head being the governing part of the body. He was, of course, right to think this way since without the brain we don't exist. But despite his leanings towards rationality being the road to righteousness, he also recognized that where irrational thoughts lurk in the shadows, seemingly uncontrollable emotions could burst forth, causing mayhem.

While Plato believed that we would be better off living a life governed by rational thought, he also conceded that we could not likely survive if we did not have rationality's counterpart of emotions. Emotions were the second-class citizens, vestigial elements of evolution which could not be fully jettisoned, but had to be assigned to the margin while the heavy lifting of rational thought hoisted us to the next evolutionary level.

One of the challenges of living Plato's way – thinking through every problem and seeking the best rational response – is that it takes longer on a brain-processing level. Our brain gets overloaded pretty easily. For example, when the number of choices exceeds seven options, our brain becomes less effective at remembering, choosing and acting. While it seems entirely counterintuitive, thinking a little less and feeling a little more tends, on the whole, to give us more satisfaction with the choices we make.

The Split Brain

While Plato was working through the philosophy of the ideal human society based on the reign of rationality, Hippocrates (whose life overlapped Plato's by some 58 years) was becoming the master of medicine. As far back as 400 BC he was aware that the brain was the seat of rational thoughts *and* unpredictable emotions:

"…Men ought to know that from the brain, and from the brain only, arise our pleasures, joys, laughter and jests, as well as our sorrows, pains, griefs and tears. Through it, in particular, we think, see, hear, and distinguish the ugly from the beautiful, the bad from the good, the pleasant from the unpleasant … It is the same thing which makes us mad or delirious, inspires us with dread or fear, whether by night or by day, brings sleeplessness, inopportune mistakes, aimless anxieties, absent-mindedness, and acts that are contrary to habit. These things that we suffer all come from the brain."[99]

As early as the fourth century BC it was understood that each side of our brain seemed to be related to different behaviors. Hippocrates wrote about his observations of people with head injuries on one side of the head leading to functional impairments of the opposite side of the body: "… if incision of the temple is made on the left, spasm seizes the parts on the right, while if the incision is on the right, spasm seizes the parts on the left."[100]

As far back as Hippocrates' time there was awareness about the contralateral aspects of the brain, that is to say, the right side of our brain controls the left side of our body and the left side of our brain controls the right side of our body. However, there was no detailed understanding that each side of the head was unique in its own right and that the left and right hemispheres were interrelated but, in large part, independently responsible for certain cognitive functions, especially when it came to things such as language processing. It would take centuries for the story to unfold about the dominant functional modalities of the left and right hemispheres.

In the early 1950s, psychobiologist and Nobel laureate, Roger Sperry studied the effect of separating the two hemispheres of the brain by cutting the corpus callosum, the bundle of nerves that acts as the bridge connecting the left and right sides.

The early studies in Sperry's lab with cats and monkeys demonstrated that if the researchers taught a task to one of the hemispheres in the animals while the corpus callosum was intact, the skill could transfer to the other hemisphere. But if the hemispheres were divided, this transfer of information did not happen. It was as if the divided halves of the brain were in their own worlds with no awareness of what the other side was doing. Each had its own perceptions and learned independently of each other.

This technique of separating the two hemispheres by cutting the corpus callosum had been used to treat epilepsy, where people with the condition have debilitating seizures that begin in one hemisphere and continue into the other hemisphere. It was thought that if the connection between the right and left sides of the brain were severed that the electrical cascade would not be able to travel from one side to the other and seizures would stop. Multiple procedures proved that with no bridge between hemispheres, seizures don't occur and people are restored to functional lives.

These individuals became know as 'split brain' subjects.

Research scientist Michael Gazzaniga continued the initial studies that Sperry had done and looked more closely at what the effects of this approach to treating epilepsy had on the patients' overall functioning. Results from the initial studies showed that after the corpus callosum was cut, the patients seemed to be getting on just fine. They no longer had seizures and seemingly suffered no adverse side effects.

Or so they thought.

Using the advantage of how the eyes are wired up to the brain, Gazzaniga conducted a number of studies to see how the 'split brain' was processing information after the corpus callosum was severed. With this research, scientists began the process of acquiring a detailed understanding of which side of the brain does what.

Gazzaniga knew that spoken and written language were processed largely on the left side of the brain in what is known as Broca's and Wernicke's areas. It was also common knowledge that the optic nerves from the right and left eyes cross over in an area called the optic chasm. The nerve from the right eye goes to the left side of the brain and the nerve from the left eye goes to the right side of the brain.

What do the processing of language and how the eyes process information have to do with each other? And, how does visual processing relate to the shopper's experience? To answer that question we first need to look at what happens when you uncouple the left and right brains from each other. A little removed from the mall, but it'll soon make some sense.

It turns out, since the left side of the brain is the location of the speech center, depending on what information gets to that side of the brain, split brain subjects will or will not understand what they see, are able to name, or whether they see anything at all.

If a picture of a spoon is presented to the right eye of a split brain subject, therefore processed by the left brain, and you ask, "did you see anything?" the split brain subject would quickly say, "a spoon." If, on the other hand, you show the same picture of a spoon to the left eye, meaning that the right side of the brain was processing the information, and ask, "did you see anything?" they would say, "no, I didn't see anything."

The subjects with the two halves of their brains disconnected through cutting the corpus callosum, not only were unable to verbally describe something by using the speech centers on the left side of the brain, but from the point of view of the right side of the brain, the object simply didn't exist at all. Or, at least initially, this was how it appeared to Gazzaniga.

Another experiment would prove that the right side of the brain did in fact 'see' it, but since no information was getting to the speech center on the left side of the brain by crossing through the corpus callosum, the split brain subject was unable to *verbalize* what the right brain 'saw.'

To verify if the right hemisphere was 'blind' to what the left eye was seeing, Gazzaniga prepared another test using the eyes as well as the hands. Remember, the right side of the brain controls the left hand and the left side of the brain controls the right hand. If the split brain subject's hands are kept out of sight, the left side of the brain has no idea what the left hand is doing and the right side of the brain has no idea what the right hand is doing.

What would happen if you showed the split brain subjects something to the left eye – which would be processed on the right side of the brain – and gave them a way to respond by hitting a Morse code key with their left hand (also controlled by the right side of the brain)?

The result was that when these subjects saw a flash of light that was processed on the right side of the brain, the left hand hit the Morse code key, but they *said* they saw nothing.

The split brain subject's right brain saw the light flash, and hit the key with the left hand, but the information needed to *verbally* respond to what it had seen never made it to the left-brain language-processing centers.

In another experiment, when a picture of an object was flashed to the right side of the brain (by only showing it to the left visual field), the left hand, which was kept from view, could select from a tray and pick up the object that was the same as the image that the right brain had seen. When asked "what is in your hand?" or "did you see anything?" the split brain subjects could neither describe what they were holding or verbalize that they saw anything at all.

From the studies done by Michael Gazzaniga, it was becoming clear that the right side of the brain was better at *visual spatial skills* and the left was better at *language understanding and formation skills.*

With continued study over the subsequent years, it is now widely accepted that the two sides of our brain are unique in their processing abilities. They do not, however, work entirely independently of each other; rather, they rely on the sharing of information between themselves to complete our understanding of the world around us.

Understanding of the attributes of each side of the brain augments how retailers and the retail designers create shopping places that are engaging on either an intellectual (rational) or an emotional level. A further look at what the left and right brain has to offer in terms of our understanding of environments will begin to point to what will be required in the future as stores become simply one of many customer touch points in a digitally connected world.

Left and Right Hemispheres – Which Side Does What

It seems somewhat ironic that to understand the workings of each side of our brain and how they communicate to form a complete representation of the world, scientists had to disconnect them. When separated, the two sides of the brain are very much in their own worlds, with individual experiences unbeknownst to the other. But when connected to each other via the corpus callosum, the two sides share information while remaining different in their capacities to deal with various sensory inputs. While they are capable of working independently of the other, as in the case of the split-brain subjects, they need each other to render full human experience.

From the Sperry and Gazzaniga studies, and more recently through the use of fMRI, a clear picture has begun to develop about the functional proclivities of each of the brain's hemispheres.

- **The left hemisphere:**
  The left hemisphere is a serial processor and deals with stimuli in logical sequences. This *then* that, *then* that, *then* that…

  The left side of the brain is markedly better at language understanding and speech formation. This is, of course, expected since the language centers of the brain located in Broca's and Wernicke's areas have been understood for some time to be on the left side of the cortex.

The left is adept at linear sequential information processing, such as decoding the meaning of language (whereas the right is better at understanding the feelings connected to the sequence of words).

The left is also good at those things considered as behaviors that are more intellectual, thought out and rational (whereas the right hemisphere is more intuitive and experiential).

The left side of the brain is considered more linear, rational, analytic, logical, and is 'all about the details.'

It is a master mathematician and excels at figuring out the meaning of groups of symbols in text.

- **The right hemisphere:**
  The right hemisphere is a parallel processor and can deal with multiple stimuli simultaneously. This *and* that *and* that *and* that…

  The right side of the brain is great at dealing with faces, focusing attention and taking in the big picture when making perceptual distinctions.

  The right side of the brain is more 'feeler' and 'empath' (whereas the left is more 'thinker' and 'logician').

  The right side is non-verbal, meaning that while it plays a role in language understanding, it is responsible for decoding the emotional content of language by seeing facial expressions and hearing the intonation of the voice.

  The right side of the brain is non-linear and more holistic in the way it understands the world. It sees the big picture. It is a context decoder and simultaneously processes a vast amount of perceptual information. The right brain loves seeing the world in patterns and pictures.

  Most of all, the right brain is the artist and poet and excels in relationship born out of empathic extension.

Because of the left brain's bent towards the logical, it has been aligned with the rationalist Platonic vision of society ruled by reason and has, therefore, been considered the dominant hemisphere. The left hemisphere's dominant position is also likely due to the location of the language centers, upon which we have grown so inextricably tied in all forms of culture and business. Language, it turns out, has promoted the alphabetic mind, predominantly run by the left side of the brain.

Given that spoken and written language is a defining feature between humans and the other creatures roaming the earth, it has held a prominent position in the development of our societies and businesses. It's no wonder that we have spent the better part of 2,000 years trying to assign dominance to the left hemisphere because of its tendency to be more rational and focused on 'intelligent behaviors.'

The right hemisphere, being more emotive, artistic, spontaneous and relational has been thought of as something that, while necessary, needed to be controlled and not to be taken as seriously.

The Language of Texts, Emoticons and Communicating Ideas

When sales associates and customers communicate, the dialogue between them is a key feature of the path to purchase. The exchange may be short or long, as little as an approving look or an involved description of why a particular product is best for the customer.

A well-delivered validation often transforms a hesitant shopper into a committed customer through effective communication. The relationship-building piece that comes as a result of communicating in shopping places promotes confidence in the brand and commitment to buy. The emotional aspect of communicating through language is key and this is very much the world of the right brain. It's not just *what* is said but *how* it is delivered that matters.

The left brain will process the factual words, 'that fits you' and the right brain will embrace the emotionally laden 'you look beautiful,' with rising intonation, an expression of sincerity and a body language of approval. The second of these two communications sends more than simply the information about fit. It affirms the customer's beauty or style and implies a host of other benefits that will come when the consumer wears the outfit in public. By a simple turn of phrase that is based in relational content, the customer sees herself in a context of other women out on the town, imagines her appearance among the others, feels herself to be desirable, and brings out of long-term memory a wealth of other imagery about what it means for her to feel beautiful, vibrant and validated.

Words matter. Not just because of the *information* they convey, but more because of the *feelings* they engender in the person to whom they are directed. A comment about fit is fine, but a compliment that fills the customer with emotion makes the experience memorable.

This is the right brain in action.

The way we as a culture are using language and its written manifestations is changing and becoming simplified. Thanks to email, texting, tweeting and other forms of digital communication, we are seeing an interesting reversion of a rich history of the word to a simplified version that is more akin to "Special English," used by the Voice of America broadcasting service. With only 1500 words, Special English reduces the English language to a very limited set of words able to relate ideas and experience to a non-English speaking audience. The totality of the English language has as many as 1 million words. Today's lexicon is under a drastic revision to a form that expresses thoughts in 140 characters, if even *that* many, per text.

As the digital world evolves, the divide in the use of language as we have known it, and that which is evolving due to the use of the technological communication, will continue to grow. English will be good to know, but the language of the younger shopper will be that of the digital world.

New forms of speaking are evolving: 'code and text-speak.' Programmers and the language they use (code) will be what begin to create both a young shopper's world on the Internet and in embodied everyday life, though these two worlds eventually will evolve to become one and the same.

Listening to my two teenage sons talk, you would think they are already in a college computer-programming course. They frequently share thoughts on their favorite computer games in language lifted directly from the programming code used to create the digital gaming worlds they play in.

The degree to which you can manipulate computer code will be an indication of how deftly you can surf the flow of change or simply ride along with the changing tides of ones and zeros.

There is something intriguingly creative about the development of a new form of communicating as we see it now in youngsters fully immersed in the digital world. In addition to code-speak, another truncated form of language acts as a shorthand between members of a younger generation, conveying thoughts and feelings in a more expeditious manner in a world where things move at the speed of light.

Why use all those words when a smiley face gets the idea across? It is certainly more relevant to the younger shopper. Emoticons, acronyms and text-based icons that convey emotions are in a way becoming contemporary society's hieroglyphics. Digitally created text-speak and emoticons are clearly easier to produce than engravings in clay or stone tablets, but are in some sense a promotion of communicating in symbols or pictures more than letters and numbers. One could argue that this is either a good or bad thing depending on whether you are a writer or a painter. The key feature to this discussion is that good or bad, the way people are communicating and telling the stories of their lives is changing. And it is changing quickly.

Brands, as well as the shopping places created to embody them, need to keep in lockstep with the evolving ways people are sharing the stories of their lives. This changing mode of communication is fundamentally re-writing language-based communication and re-wiring the brain.

While not entirely going away, language as we have known it will morph to accommodate a younger generation's new communication tools that facilitate connection through digital devices. Handwritten letters are going the way of the past (if not already gone) and are being replaced with messages that convey the gist of the sentiment being shared between two parties in acronyms, abbreviations and other means of texting-shorthand.

With a reductionist mode of speaking and writing emerging, it is likely that stores will develop more into incarnations of the Missouri state motto of being a "Show Me" mentality. Talk less and show more. In terms of right-brain engagement, picture-based, contextual-relational-emotional content of 'showing and doing' retail experiences are far more effective than left-brain engagements, and they build more long-lasting body memories. People have deeper and more memorable experiences when they actively participate rather than simply hear or talk about something.

When customers use a truncated form of language, without the subtleties that our rich history of the lexicon has to offer, it begs the question of how to get the brand message from sales associate to a customer who is not likely to be as adept at putting full sentences together as we might have been in the past.

Not only will the younger generation be less facile with the use of traditional forms of language, they are likely to have shorter attention spans as well. They will have developed a new way of speaking and it will be the retailers' job both to figure out this "newspeak" of a sort, and provide content that is understood by the emerging shopper. If retailers use words at all, they might likely be graphically arranged to create attractive visual images. Consistent with this idea is the rise in use of the "infographic," where limited amounts of pertinent text is arranged is visually compelling ways with pictures, icons, and graphs. The strategy of combining fewer words with more pictures to get the ideas across is a direct play to the time-starved individual who needs the facts, quickly, as well as a younger generation for whom short text blasts and pictures are the favored form of communication. Regardless of the method of transmitting the message, accessing the emotional content within the context of the brand experience will be a key driver to promoting sales.

We know that more is conveyed through facial gestures, body language and the rising and falling of the voice than simply the words alone. The intuitive, holistic, poetic views of our beloved brands are largely the workings of the right side of the brain. Delightful in their effects, emotions have often been considered mere entertainment aside the true dominant left hemisphere's calculation and linguistic ability. Nevertheless, the emotional connections customers have to brands are extraordinarily important in making shopping experiences memorable and they are masterfully coordinated by the relational right brain.

In a world that has evolved through eras of revolution – the agricultural, industrial, information ages – we now find ourselves on the precipice of an era of unprecedented change that embraces ideas, new thinking, new communication modalities, new technologies and an overhaul of past attribution of value to those proclivities of the left brain.

In a paradoxical twist, more information, more choice, and more 'friends' will be available, yet shoppers will become quickly disaffected unless 'more' means 'more *relevant.*'

More relevant will mean that whatever 'it' is, it will need to have greater intrinsic value to the shopper. Otherwise it will still be 'less.' Shopping places will have to give customers the opportunity to engage in a personal way where they take part in opting in and creating the experiences that they want because the experiences are at once connected to a larger social structure, and unique to the customer's personal preferences.

More relevant also means that the brain won't want to have selection beyond reckoning. It means understanding that while infinite selection is indeed available, the retailer has curated a set of options that satisfies the individual's specific personal profile.

The rally call will likely be, *"when I shop, I want the retailer to 'know me' and have the best (limited) assortment that makes it easy on me to choose."*

To 'know me' is to be attuned to the shopper and to engage in an authentic relationship. To attract him/her not just with selection and good price points, but to appreciate fully that connection is built through empathy and the sharing of emotion between the retailer or brand and the shopper.

To 'know me' means to open the conduit to the right brain and share in the making of experience.

To 'know me' means to be tapped into the side of the customer that ultimately matters – the side that has lived long before our intellectual superiority has had us believing that the way to transcendence was through pure reason and not through the body's connection to the world.

If you take classes in meditating, you discover that quieting the mind means shutting off the internal dialogue that our left brain is so used to having. Instead of the internal chatter, you focus on the body's sensations to develop an awareness of the environment around you. You connect with the right brain to the space you are in where pictures, patterns and emotions rule experience.

Whereas in the past, businesses and institutions may have run on a left brain approach to getting things done in a linear, logical, sequential way, the next generation of shoppers will want value to be delivered through *experience.* They will look to the more esoteric characteristics of the shopping places they visit and products they buy, such as the beauty in design rather than the mere utility of a product and its price.

Abundant choice and attractive prices are simply the entry ticket into the retail performance. Nowadays, everybody expects things to be less expensive, verging on free. There is an implicit assumption that products should deliver on their promises to do whatever they are supposed to do. Utility is a given or the products shouldn't exist.

People love a good deal, especially those deeply discounted prices that make the insula less anxious and the nucleus accumbens along with other structures in the pleasure center, happy. But that is not enough to keep customers coming back, since the dopamine rush of repetitive rewards diminishes once the brain understands the pattern.

For the past century or so, the way we have done business has been very linear and reliant on the numbers to give us what we think is the truth about what happens in the shopping aisle. Except that the truth of the shopping experience isn't found in the numbers only, but in the *brain biology between people* interacting on the sales floor. Numbers don't lie, but they don't tell the 'full truth,' either.

In the coming years, the way we will do business will be very *social* – more right brained, emotionally connected and focused on the social network of customers that include touch points far beyond the sales floor. There will be an expectation that the communication of brand ideology and emotional content born out of interaction between customers, will be as easy as a text punctuated with a smiley face. Fast, simple, to the point and above all else, validating.

Your Shopping Brain in an Omni-Channel Digital World

Continuous Partial Attention and the Re-wiring of Your Brain

Never before in our human evolution has change occurred with such unrelenting speed. The rate at which our brains are accommodating the flow of information and energy is unprecedented. Stimuli are bombarding us from multiple sources, not at the speed of hearsay along the old trade routes, but at the speed of light over a globally interconnected technology superhighway that has expanded the store to every corner of the planet.

How does the shopper's brain keep up?

How does the store keep up?

Retailers are trying to stay current but can't help but struggle to redefine shopping experiences that are in the midst of the largest upheaval in their history. Regardless of retailers' best efforts, they're lagging behind. It's hard to keep up when, running as fast as they can, the finish line seems to be getting pushed further and further away.

Technology is advancing ahead of our ability to fully appreciate the effects that it will likely have on all aspects of retailing and our society in general. While research studies are illuminating some of the effects of this technology-driven change – the drop in empathy among college graduates, for example – we are still trying to get our collective arms around the implications on culture and shopping.

Dystopian views abound regarding the decline of society and the emergence of an automaton nation. With the number of people you see glued to their smartphone screens, one might think that this view has plenty of traction already. And while a digital apocalypse is great for alarmist sci-fi movies, I am nevertheless hopeful. Despite what I see around me, I am optimistic about our innate human nature to be driven to connect in empathic relationships, and that technology will serve better to promote relationships than to tear us apart from each other.

Technological advances are shifting shopper's expectations about how and where they will relate to the brands they love and stores they shop. The growth in smartphone adoption across the planet and increasing channels to provide products to customers brings the store to the customer rather than the other way around. This change in *need* states, and the way shopping cultures are addressing them, is less evolutionary than revolutionary in that change is moving quickly, with no guarantee of outcomes that provide better experiences (though that is, of course, the perennial hope). Trying to keep up with the pace of change will require both looking into a virtual crystal ball *and* taking a leap of faith.

The long-range outlook on all of this, and other evolving methods of communicating and doing business, will impact the creation of shopping places in ways we cannot yet fathom.

Everybody with a smartphone today becomes an omni-channel shopper and the marketplace becomes not just the store, but every street corner. Retailers continue to find inventive ways to capture customers' attention and get products into their hands whenever the need arises. In a retail marketplace where customers are continuously bombarded with thousands of images each day, it gets increasingly difficult to capture their attention. Completely rethinking how to get in front of customers is reshaping the way retailers are reaching out. Digital technology is affording them access where in the past they had none.

At home, in the store, on the street, in the car, virtually every location now is an opportunity to connect to a customer. Once the store, and maybe a catalogue, were the extent to which customers could connect to brands. Mobile technology and wireless communication have completely changed that paradigm, so that now we talk about omni-channel retailing.

Whereas in the past, catalogue and in-store experiences may have promoted slightly different points of view for retailers, today's high-tech customers are expecting that all avenues to retailers should remain consistent and seamlessly integrated. And this is where omni-channel retailing strives to find its sweet spot. Omni-channel retailing concentrates more on a seamless approach to the consumer experience through all available shopping channels: mobile-internet devices, computers, brick-and-mortar stores, television, radio, direct mail, catalogue and so on. Of course, getting all of these different avenues of selling goods and services to align in terms of how they deliver customer experience is an extraordinary challenge.

Nevertheless, the retailer's goal now is to reach out and engage customers in very untraditional ways.

Often considered to be the Walmart of Korea, eMart embarked upon a campaign to capture shoppers with the use of QR codes. With more than 141 locations throughout South Korea, eMart struggled with capturing customers during one of the busiest times of the day: lunch hour.

Their goal? Drive sales increases for one hour of the day – between 12 and 1 pm.

Their solution? An ingenious sculptural panel that would create QR codes with shadows cast by the sun only between those hours; eMart called it the "Sunny Sale."

Scanning the QR code created by shadows jumped the customer to the "Sunny Sale" website where they could download special offers and coupons. "Sunny Sale" customers could make purchases from the eMart smartphone app and products were delivered to their homes.

Boasting a 25% increase in sales during their target time of the day, eMart demonstrated that in an omni-channel marketplace, ingenuity can be used to capture customers' hearts, minds and wallets, even if for only 60 minutes when the sun is shining.

The ephemeral quality of this promotion highlights the idea that in a digitally driven world, shopping experiences may become more transient, lasting only a few minutes and then moving on to some other location or disappearing forever. This idea of 'here today, gone in the next minute' also plays into customer's 'fear of loss,' and 'opportunity cost' discussed in previous chapters. When promotions are dictated by the passing of the sun, a sense of urgency develops in the shopper's mind about not missing out on something great. The fleeting nature also drives purchasing behavior in concepts such as pop-up shops and flash sales on the Internet. The "Sunny Sale" promotion clearly shows that the store doesn't have to be anywhere, or equally could be *everywhere*. This, of course, forces us to move our thinking from being *omni-channel to omni-present*.

An omni-channel shopping world doesn't just provide multiple access points to goods and services, but plays directly into long-held emotions that are powerful motivators influencing buying behavior.

Retailers and store designers will need to better understand the emotional need states of the digitally connected customer and find ways to speak their language in an ongoing effort to forge more relevant relationships. As digital technology progresses, becoming ever more woven into the fabric of society, it must be leveraged to enable better relationships through mindfully integrating them into the customer experience map. The ubiquitous adoption of mobile technology has dissolved the boundaries between stores and shoppers. While we have come to believe that access anywhere is simply a given in today's retail marketplace, providing access to a website doesn't necessarily mean increased sales. Many mobile apps or websites simply don't capture the customer's need for emotional engagement or their love of novelty and play.

Adoption of digital technologies and their integration into the shopping experience is occurring with analytics of the evolving customer, the supply chain and store operations. The shopper is moving quickly with a growing inability to delay gratification. Retail operations are not as proactive and forward thinking as they need to be to serve this emerging customer, and significant challenges remain when retailers, both big and small, are considering integration of digital technologies across the store chain.

An investment of significant time and resources is required to get ahead of the customer on the technology growth curve. With technology today being outmoded tomorrow, one highly charged and relevant question remains about across-the-chain implementation of digital technology applications: What will be the cost of implementing an omni-channel platform? When many retailers look at the costs of widespread implementation of technology solutions, they simply determine that technology is not where they are going to put their money. It's not that they don't see the potential, but that their capital is held captive elsewhere in the supply chain. Overhauling the back-of-house infrastructure is an enormous undertaking, especially when 'doing it right' means creating a seamless, digitally integrated customer experience that ties into customer relationship management, e-commerce, in-store experiences, supply chain and inventory, and a host of other operational issues.

The creation of shopping places, and the relevance of the store in general, is trying to keep pace with a customer who is shopping from a broader field of available retailers with similar products at competitive prices. In addition, how today's shopper can shop any retailer's assortment has opened up multiple access points. The store is no longer the only place to shop, and going there is not, as we know, a necessity when anyone with a smartphone has far more computing power in that device than NASA had available when they sent men to the moon.

Customers have enough options available to them to make the act of buying easier than it has ever been. Customers can buy online and pick up the items in the store, or buy online and return to the store. They can also buy in store from a smartphone or self-service kiosk and pick up after a brief wait, or opt for home delivery. These are part of an increasing set of options all geared to making shopping experiences more accessible, and to address the needs of the digitally enabled contemporary customer.

Omni-channel retailing serves to meet customers wherever they are and whenever they want to satisfy a need. The message to the customer needs to be tweaked in every channel to capitalize on the advantages each channel has to offer.

Truth be told, for the retailer, the omni-channel customer also is a more profitable customer. More places to connect to the brand imply more likelihood that the customer will make a purchase. Odds are in favor of retailers netting more sales if they are casting widely on the Internet and elsewhere.

One of the significant challenges for retail place making in an omni-channel world is that customers have increased knowledge about the product offering before ever entering the store. Shopping begins long before many customers cross the retailer's threshold. Digitally enabled shoppers have done their homework, and they are often in a position to usurp the knowledge of the sales associate.

These days, when tech-enabled and educated customers show up in the store they aren't necessarily looking for more information than they have likely uncovered through hours of Internet searches. They are often looking for validation, connection and support as they wade through the plethora of options and information at their fingertips. The tech-enabled sales associate is, to be sure, better informed and more agile given an ability to search through inventory with digital devices of their own. More than these left-brained aptitudes, though, the sales associate still provides a personal touch to the sale, which has always been key to the right-brain aspect of the shopping experience.

This, of course, puts a burden on the in-store staff to be on its game and educated with as much information about the product offering as possible. In-store technology has the capability to empower sales associates with additional knowledge about both products and, in addition, customer interaction strategies that support the in-store selling process.

The ability for sales associates to be empowered with digital technology in the store is becoming a requirement as customers now expect associates to be able to access information while in a discussion in the shopping aisle. A new pressure is being put on sales associates to be both a master of what's on the shelves in the store as well as the content they can access online. Fully 45% of customers expect sales associates to be knowledgeable about the entire inventory online. And, almost 70% of customers expect that store associates have mobile devices strapped to their hips in order to perform simple and immediate tasks, such as looking up product information and checking inventory.[101]

When customers are in a store talking to sales associates, not only do they expect the list of tasks just mentioned, but that associates are also able to check or reserve inventory in a nearby store, and know various return policies and much more. In short, omni-channel, mobile-enabled customers want sales associates to be 'omni-potent.'

When an item is out of stock in the store, sales associates now need to be empowered to 'save the sale' by taking the item out of inventory from some other store or a distribution facility, to ship directly to a customer's home. If a sales associate can ship an out-of-stock product to a customer's home, "a staggering 45% of consumers are very likely to take them up on the offer," as long as the product is being shipped to their house for free. If the customer has to pay for shipping, the portion of customers willing to take the sales associate up on the offer drops to just 12%. [102]

If the omni-channel customer has made the effort to come to the store, when they might well have been able to get what they wanted through some other 'channels,' the experience had better deliver. Retail leaders know that store employees give customers a reason to come to the store. The interaction between in-store staff and the customers has long been one of the cornerstones of a shopping trip.

In-store technologies do not function in a vacuum; they need to connect to the larger whole of the brand experience. They are but one piece of an integrated network of brand connection points.

The effects on the brain of living in a digitally connected, omni-channel world are already making themselves evident. The younger generation, whose vulnerable growing cortices are being wired to fit a new normal of how we communicate and enter into relationships with each other, is the most affected. What will be the effect on the brands they adopt into their lives?

Every day we can see how the proliferation of digital technology is changing the way we interact and shop, but we can't see into the heads of all those exposed to a constant influx of digital content. If we could, we may come to the realization that the shopper's brain has been forced into a state of constant partial attention – a digitally induced sort of ADD. Product and service choices *and* different shopping channels abound. Each of these can get the brain working overtime, never mind combining one brain with another as customers interact in-store or online.

The earlier that children are exposed to hours of digital content each day, the more their young plastic brains are fundamentally re-wiring, which, in turn, is changing their capacity relate to others. The more screen time we have, the more likely it is that the brain develops neural pathways favoring communication that is based on quick spurts of visual content at the expense of more traditional face-to-face interactions. Young brains are pruning away neural connections between the ages of two and twenty at a rate like no other time in our evolutionary history. What they are exposed to during those crucial years sets in place who they are and how they communicate with the world around them.

We have already seen in an earlier chapter, with the experiment by Gary Small on subjects who performed Google searches, that the brain can be re-wired in a few hours, creating neural pathways that were otherwise inactive. Of course, Google searching is not a bad thing – it's just that any form of repetitive behavior creates patterns in our neural circuitry that shape thoughts, beliefs, emotions and skills. The idea that we are continually *paying partial attention to multiple stimuli* has the brain on high alert. We used to think that multitasking was an admirable trait. Getting many things done at once and keeping it all together seemed enviable. Today's multitasking has become not only ineffective, but a depleting, exhausting, sense of 'never-enough.' Multitasking puts the brain into overdrive. We actually lose focus, perspective and motivation, not to mention productivity. If retailers are trying to create a resonant message with their customers amidst all that mental clutter… they have their work cut out for them.

Continual bombardment with things that need our attention draws on our cognitive resources. Humans just weren't built to be able to maintain a state of constant monitoring of our environment for long periods of time. If you have ever spent an extended period of time on your computer working, playing games or surfing the Internet, you may well have felt a bit spaced out, fatigued, and maybe even irritable and distracted. The result is a sort of digitally induced stress state. Under this sort of stress, our brains send out signals to the adrenal glands to secrete cortisol and adrenaline. In the short-term, these chemicals increase energy levels and enhance memory. However, when we are under chronic stress, "they actually impair cognition, lead to depression, alter neural circuitry in the hippocampus, amygdala and pre-frontal cortex – brain regions that control mood and thought."[103] The more shoppers are exposed to in an omni-channel marketplace, the more they are likely to feel negatively and unable to make clear-headed buying decisions that enhance their satisfaction with the experience.

The world of omni-channel shopping is both a blessing and a curse. It provides convenience to potential customers through offering goods and services anywhere, any time they want. However, it also adds extraordinary selection opportunity to the equation, which as we have seen, doesn't always result in better experience or more satisfaction with the choices finally made. It seems natural, then, to assume that, given abundance in both the array of products available and the multiple ways to buy them, that in an omni-channel shopping world we are simply adding to the noise in the customer's head in the name of providing convenience.

And yet, across the age spectrum of young digital natives and older digital immigrants, people continue to go back to the digital font for more. Hours are spent surfing, blogging, posting, texting, and otherwise just putting it out there and then… waiting for a response.

Continually reinforcing a neural pathway for Internet-based communication modalities is changing the actual physical structure of the brain. We are equally reinforcing the need for validation and feeding the pleasure center that comes by being 'liked,' or responded to by not one individual, but the hundreds of social-network friends.

This may remind you of the rat from the experiment, sitting in the corner repeatedly pressing the bar while the pleasure center ran the dopamine loop. A similar thing happens to humans who eventually get used to the constant state of posting and waiting, of always having too many things going on, and who seem to thrive on perpetual connectivity and validating feedback. Social networks serve to validate them and the degree to which they believe that they are intrinsically of value is seemingly in the hands of other people. We are walking a fine line of outsourcing our very sense of self-worth by a growing reliance on just how quickly, and from how many, 'friends' or 'followers' get back to us with a response to a text or social-network post.

Those people are all fired up. All the time.

Neural circuits are being set in place, getting used to rapid-fire digital environments, and as they do so, those pathways that have traditionally carried the responsibility of dealing with slower and face-to-face communication are being pruned away and replaced. The omni-channel shopping-brain is continually in a state of thinking through a series of dichotomies; as information and choice increase, attention and decision-making ability decrease; as empathy declines, narcissism increases; as abundance rises, satisfaction diminishes; as digital content takes over our environments, the less able we are to decode it; as shopping opportunities abound, we garner convenience at the expense of engaging in meaningful embodied connections.

In an omni-channel retail world, the shopping brain is going to need help. Stores will have to provide experiences that are fast, captivating, efficient, relevant, informed, and emotional – all without overwhelming the already overloaded brain.

10^n Screens

While on a business trip, my colleagues and I were collaborating on a project that extended the workday well into the evening. We were looking for a quick dinner before heading back to the design studio. Ducking under the big awning to get out of the rain, we entered through the doorway into a lively environment that smelled of rain-dampened clothes, cold beer and spicy tacos. The environment was activated by clamorous conversations and the sounds of sports games. Above our heads, hanging from the ceiling was a constellation of television screens.

I started counting.

Screens covered the wall area above the bar and around the entire perimeter of the space. They hung from the ceiling on circular steel structures with a screen pointing in every-which direction. The bathrooms had them above the urinals. There were screens mounted on the wall at the end of every booth. The only available surface for more of them would have been in the bar counters and tabletops.

At last count before our table was ready, 73 screens.

The glow from the ceiling was matched only by that from the multiple points of light casting a blue-white glow on patrons' faces from their cellphones. With that much visual content bombarding patrons in the space, I thought it would be tough for my brain to find calm amidst the clatter. While attending to conversations raised above the noise, reading their menus and looking at the multitude of screens, I wondered what more their brains could possibly take in from their phones?

It occurred to me that despite an enormous amount of inconsequential visual noise, staring at a cellphone might well allow for focused and selective attention. Or maybe it was just the irresistible allure of an incoming text.

Places such as this sports bar also lead me to question the degree to which people are able to understand the content of messages and what the retail designers are aiming to accomplish when they so overload the customer's brain with visual content. This sort of approach to painting the environment with the broad brush of digital media is generally ineffective, and doesn't yield the positive results we think it does. On a brain activation level, it puts people on alert trying to encode the overwhelming amount of information.

In a world that used to be dominated by only three screens – computer, phone, and TV – shoppers are now exposed to more screens than they could possible count. And of course, they don't 'count'; they just tune them out because most of them are just the visual noise of the environment. With all of these access/touch points to the brands we buy, one questions how much the brain pays attention to each of them, and to what degree the message on them is dependent on variables such as screen size, dwell time, location/context, etc.

Omni-channel access means that customers are exposed to different-sized screens, in different locations, for different lengths of time. Retail place makers need to develop an acute awareness of how the customer brain processes visual content, and that different screen formats require different design thinking.

It's a given that location-based digital media is going to be one of the key features of shopping environments. We have seen it in movies for some time from *Blade Runner*, to *Minority Report* to *Avatar*. We will interact with screens with the wave of a hand, a turn of the face or a glance of the eyes long enough to have our facial features or retina scanned.

As mobile technology is redefining the interpersonal communication paradigm, screen form factor is also in the midst of an upheaval. The omni-channel experience has, at its core, the principle of everywhere-access. That, of course, means screens will become ubiquitous, and their forms and functions will be as varied as the places we will interact with them.

What we have come to expect from digital content in our environment – in the form of wall-mounted plasma screens – has begun to morph to include brilliant high-resolution, multi-story displays that are defining features of places such as Times Square. Smaller screens embedded into seatbacks and contemporary versions of Flash Gordon's wristwatch are also already available. We understand these applications. They are not too far from our in-home TV or personal computer. But now, the applications of screens are changing to include the interactive, transparent, glass-touch panels that we see – and which were once *only* seen – in the movies.

In today's real-world shopping places, glass can be embedded with liquid-crystal displays so that showcases, and eventually storefronts, can be either clear or opaque with digital images that scroll across the surface.

Glass panels are not a recent technological development. In a restaurant application from the late '90s, simple LCD technology was used in the bathroom doors at "Bar 89" (now closed) located in SoHo, New York. The sheet of liquid crystal sandwiched between two normal panes of glass would change between opaque and transparent. When electric current was applied to the sheet, the crystals arranged themselves into a neat parallel formation that permitted the passage of light, making the bathroom door transparent. When the customer entered the bathroom and flipped the switch, a voltage change occurred in the LCD layer and the molecular array of the crystals changed into a naturally random pattern that dispersed light, creating visual privacy.

A few years later, in December 2001, the luxury brand Prada hired the renowned architect, Rem Koolhaas to design a $40 million SoHo flagship. In a building housing a downtown version of the Guggenheim Museum, Prada and Koolhaas created, if not a great store, at least a showpiece whose value in industry chatter and publicity well outstripped the store's construction cost.

The store became known for its bold architectural articulation, punctuated by an enormous zebrawood, veneered 'wave' scooped out of the interior. Its museum-like interior set aside open space as a feature to be considered as luxurious as the Prada product with its foray into emerging technologies was arguably far ahead of its time.

Koolhaas introduced a number of technological flourishes. The spacious fitting rooms included RFID-enabled closets, cameras that gave rear views when trying products on, embedded video displays playing fashion shows, and LCD glass in the fitting room doors. The glass panels switched between clear when not in use and frosted with the touch of a floor-mounted button. The doors became a fascination and easy interactive entertainment. Eventually, through excessive use, the doors ceased to operate in the way that they were intended. (Some twelve years later, in stores designed for an entirely different customer, Aeropostale Inc., a co-ed specialty store chain geared toward teens, re-introduced the LCD fitting room door.) And "so it goes" with many technology applications that are introduced into stores; infrastructure costs, content production, maintenance, and ultimately obsolescence end up being significant hurdles to their long-term application. Despite the emergence of a new set of needs and in-store expectations defined by the omni-channel customer, most retailers are conservative in their commitments to integrating digital technology fully into the customer experience.

Since the Prada flagship in SoHo, glass has come a long way. It can do much more than simply frost over to become a privacy panel. Transparent LCD glass is ushering in new change to the storefront. These 'window-screens' are capable of playing full-color video. Virtually any digital content can be played through a simple surface, turning sheets of glass into Internet-accessible touch computers as well as virtual portals to another world.

Transparent LCD glass is finding its way into the faces of large refrigerated cases or in smaller display windows of convenience and grocery store applications. Today's "C-stores" can introduce transparent LCD glass doors to the faces of large refrigerated cases or in smaller display windows.

Some applications are clunky, constrained by size limitations and high costs are problematic when you start to consider chain-wide application, *but all of it is doable*. It's not hard to imagine both handheld transparent glass displays as well as entire walls. This is not the work of science fiction; it's available today.

As we are now experiencing, there will hardly be a place left open in our built environment that isn't full of digital imagery that supports selling and buying opportunities. The challenge is understanding *when and how* to use the omni-channel, multiple-screen approach to retail place making.

There are places I now expect to see the application of screens that sell – billboards on the side of the road, my living room TV, my computer, and my phone, are a few examples. I have even grown accustomed to seeing them in the back of a taxi, at the gas pump, the airplane seat, the shopping mall, the sales floor and the fitting room. Beyond this, I am now exposed to them at bus stops and on subways, on elevators and escalators, in the mirrors above sinks or mounted to walls and even above urinals in restrooms. Wherever I can see, and possibly touch, there is likely to be exposure to advertising and an opportunity to connect to, and buy from, some retailer.

The big question is whether or not it will matter to the shopping audience or just become part of the visual static that blends together, not capturing customer attention. How does it all stay relevant to the shopping brain that is exposed to it all?

Well, it all depends on the screen's ability to capture the brain's attention. The relevance of brand messaging in the digitally enhanced world can be tied to some simple truths about what matters to the brain's perceptual systems.

We have already seen that the brain is a pattern recognizing apparatus. It reads and decodes patterns looking for variations and getting excited about finding them and even more so when there are rewards attached to the interruption in a pattern we think we have figured out. So, from the visual perception point of view, whether one screen is any more attractive than another has everything to do with how it is positioned in relation to other elements in the visual field.

Anything that breaks from the surrounding pattern either in detail, color, light output, or motion (real or implied) will attract the eyes and light up the visual processing areas at the back of the head. In a field of a hundred screens, if all of them are playing the same content (or even if each of them is displaying different content), the blank screen that isn't working is the one that will attract the shopper's attention. Before the brain is able to decode all of the various inputs from the other 99 screens, it will be drawn to the one that is different.

If it is blank, not only does the retailer have an IT problem on their hands, but they've also missed a great opportunity to convey a brand message to a customer whose attention they have inadvertently captured. The brain seeks out novelty, and if it comes via a change in the visual field through interruptions in the pattern language of a place, then the retailer has made the first step to making that point of contact relevant.

The next step of retaining the shopper's attention is somewhat more difficult only in that it requires an understanding that not all screens are equal in terms of the content they can provide. Not because of anything to do with the technology per se, but because of the innate way our brains 'read' the content of a visual stimulus. Different-sized screens are better at conveying different types of messages.

Faces vs. Facts and Figures

In previous chapters we looked at how we have become acutely attuned to 'reading' peoples' facial expressions and from them, inferring intent. This ability has come to us over millions of years of evolution and is one of the aspects of our neurobiology that has likely played a significant role in the development of cooperative social groups. Before words, we used facial expressions and body gestures a great deal to communicate.

The ability to pick up on the emotional feelings of others from the expressions on their faces is something we all share. Mirror neurons cement this ability into our neural circuitry and make it something we don't think about, but simply react to on a visceral and emotional level. It is not surprising, therefore, that when we think of images in shopping places, those graphics showing smiling faces connect us to the right-brain emotional content of the brand message.

On the other hand, signs touting '50% Off' connect us to the left-brain prefrontal cortex that deciphers the value proposition through a cost-benefit analysis, or to the limbic area, which is tied to pain prediction and evaluates price as a precursor to perceived pain. The deeper the emotional connection, the more profound the connection between customers and the brands they buy. While you could argue that pain perception leads to emotion, too, it is a deterrent to positive experiences and is not the kind of sentiment you want in either the shopping aisle or online.

No one likes to pay more than is necessary for something. However, as we have seen, if they do it with a credit or debit card, they are likely to do it with greater ease and even less regard for their well being. But, avoiding the negative emotions that come from 'buyer's remorse' or 'cognitive dissonance' is a *post-purchase* mitigation of emotions. Instead, what retailers want to do is to engage shoppers in the buying experience with processes that produce *real-time* positive emotions – good feelings while customers are right there in the aisle or on the website.

Smiles are easy to conjure up, and they set the customer on a positive path to purchase. Trying to motivate shoppers into making a purchase with pricing structures and payment plans is effective in the short term, but not so much when the goal is to build long-term relationships with customers. With the positive emotion of authentic connection, shoppers are primed to enjoy the experience and be more open to receive the brand message.

The core idea for retailers and their marketing divisions is to *'embrace the face'* as a key component of their brand positioning.

Looking at how to evoke that sense of 'feeling good' while connecting to the brand through a mobile device or other digital interface calls into question just how far you can get in drawing emotions out of the shopper through a screen of only that size. The format of the presentation (size of the screen) has a great deal of influence on the type of message you can push to the customer and in turn how they feel in response to what they see.

The eyes don't differentiate between the visual input from a cellphone or a large, touch-PC in a store or the TV in your living room. It's all just visual stimuli. The eyes capture content. They don't interpret it. The brain, however, processes the information in different ways, depending on the nature of the content and the size of the image it perceives. While we can access content across various platforms – TV, computer, tablet, and smartphone – to think that a single production of an advertisement for some product can be simply repackaged to play across each of them with equal effectiveness would be a mistake. This is not just because bandwidth or wireless connectivity may not allow content to stream fluidly, but also because the brain doesn't see the content on each of the various screen sizes the same way.

Recall from the previous chapter the "facial action coding system" developed by Paul Ekman: virtually every human emotion can be broken down into a series of facial movements. We have the uncanny ability to perceive facial movements that happen in the time frame of milliseconds. This ability goes beyond face-to-face interaction to virtually all other forms of media, be they print or digital images. If you see an image of a face displaying a sad, happy or angry look, your mirror-neuron system activates centers in your brain that process sad, happy or angry emotions. It's automatic, so there is little you can do about it.

Since we are geared to seeing faces and having them cause a reflected sense of emotion, they become indispensible in connecting in an omni-channel environment. There is a challenge, though, about how well we can actually see facial details on various screen sizes and what effect this has on cognition. As it turns out, there is "...a very interesting correlation between emotional engagement and form factor."

"The brain seems to have a very good engagement with emotions as long as the form factor or size of the face expressing emotion is the size of a normal human face."[104] As the shopper connects to brands and their stores more frequently through a screen, getting to the emotional side of the shopper's brain with happy faces becomes more difficult as screen sizes become smaller.

It used to be that the television was great for longer advertisements when viewers could see large images. Emotional stories were easy to tell in commercials that were a minute or more in length. With today's shift to mobile technology, the viewing time of an ad on a digital device has been reduced in size to a few square inches and in time to a few seconds.

Further complicating the delivery of content that captures the emotional side of the shopper, is that the smaller the image of a face, the less detail we can see. As detail is lost to our perceptual system, activation of neural pathways involved in emotional engagement drops off.

Counteracting the decrease in engagement with images of happy faces, however, is that the customer on a digital device has actively opted-in and their *focused attention* is heightened. When people choose to look at their mobile devices, they are making a conscious decision to engage versus simply being in a place where video screens are on the wall as part of the ambient visual environment. In those cases, the video screens are more digital wallpaper than attention grabber. Since people choose to look at their smartphones, the right form of content delivered in those precious seconds can be guaranteed to receive the viewers' full attention.

This then leads to the question about what sort of content is more effective when the retailer has the customer's focused attention, but screen size is a limiting factor in conveying emotion with facial expressions.

Because smaller devices are not as effective at evoking emotion, they should instead be more geared to delivering messages that are based on the viewer's capacity for focused attention. Like the patrons of the sports bar described earlier, online shoppers look to the phone's screen when they get a text or email notification or a call. In that moment, their attention is laser sharp, the environment fades into the background, and the retailer has them long enough to get them to consider an offer. Novelty (an interruption in the environmental stimulus pattern) in the busy bar will capture attention despite all of the 'noise.' Once the retailer has the attention of the shopper, the retailer is able to impart messages that will be embedded into memory.

Of course, as retailers or brands use targeted messages – "push notifications" – their frequency needs to be considered. While the interruption in pattern may get attention, unwanted or untimely solicitations may be a nuisance and turn customers off.

What should the message be, and how should it be formatted?

In general, if you can't see faces with clarity and in detail, people pay less attention and shift to other sensory cues such as reading a bigger image, body language, listening for sounds, paying attention to smells or trying to touch something. If faces are not effectively portrayed, then emotions are not fully activated. If emotions are not called into action, then the people will be less likely to remember the face and the content of the message. This becomes an endless loop that makes emotional content delivery less effective. Smaller interfaces have this inherent challenge.

If, however, the messaging is about facts and figures, includes fast-paced image presentation of new arrivals or product promotions, is in a text-based format, delivered in short burst of information, it is better understood on smaller screens.

This approach is more in line with how shoppers use their handheld devices to communicate by texting. Text-based ads are successful when the length of the messages is 20-60 characters in length for the initial message and no more than 160 characters when sending a full-length message. [105]

On smaller screens, the most effective messages are short in length using a limited number of words that impart the sense that action is required on the part of the shopper. 'Buy Now,' 'Sale,' '50% Off' and 'New' are all simple words that trigger the neural networks that enhance the likelihood of motivating action that leads to a purchase. Calls for action that get shoppers to react quickly to take advantage of some offer are both consistent with how people use text communication and play on the psychology that 'if you don't get it now, it's gone forever.'

Beyond simple, action-oriented, word-based messages, handheld devices have sound and 'motion' built into their circuitry. If you can't capture attention with short, verbal messages and colorful motion graphics, smartphones ring, of course, and vibrate as well. Imagine your favorite retailer sending you a message that has its own ringtone while the phone shakes, rattles and rolls to the beat. All possible and all capable of getting the shopper's brain to pay attention and go shopping.

Smartphones were originally an effective development away from simply using the mobile phone for voice communication. Interest in having devices that provide rich, multimedia content in a format that provides users with larger screens to view movies, read magazines and play games, brought about the tablet. This was great, except that people had to have two devices, one for speaking with others, and one for reading, watching and listening to streaming content.

It is interesting to note that personal digital devices with larger screens are being provided to the market. Smartphones and tablets are growing both in screen dimension and resolution, to provide what seems naturally more attractive to the brain – larger faces and more detail to decode emotions.

Taking these devices to the next step is like remaking the Reese's Peanut Butter Cup commercial, which showed peanut butter and chocolate coming together in humorous scenarios. Today's technological "two great tastes that taste great together" are bringing the functionality of smartphone and tablet together in one, palm-sized digital device.

'Phablets,' which combine the benefits of both smartphone and tablet, are emerging and defining yet another form of connection in the omni-channel shopping market.[106] Boasting screen sizes of seven inches, the phablet is the next generation of crossover devices providing phone functionality and the ability to capture emotions through larger screens. Bigger screens mean bigger faces and more brain activation to trigger emotion. And the shopper's right, relational brain is lovin' it.

Shoppers have more opportunity to connect to their favorite retailers than they have ever had in history. The number of customer touch points is increasing at an exponential rate. Even if an individual were an anomaly in contemporary society, and did not have a handheld device that could connect to the shopping sphere, they could likely simply look around and there would be a way to reach out and touch something to connect them to the world of internet shopping through a digital interface. Omni-channel access is part of the way shopping is done. It is not going away.

In the meantime, delivering brand content that is relevant is lagging behind customer adoption of the technology. Providing 'chatter that matters' should be another rally call for a new generation of brands that hope to stay up to date and out in front of shoppers. Knowing what matters means following young shoppers closely enough to become sensitive to their habits that are evolving quickly away from any recognizable traditional shopping practice. Every paradigm, that is, but their innate desire for engaging in meaningful connections.

So strong is this human quality, that the revolution in communication through social networks has skyrocketed. The shopper's social network, of which the retailer has to become a part, is a key connection point because it is driven by relationships. Finding engaging ways to embed the brand in the customer's social network profile requires retailers and brands to rely on *authentic empathic connection fostered through rituals, storytelling and play*. And, embracing neuroscience is a way to trigger emotions that form the basis for positive long-term memories.

Retail place making – whether it is on the Internet, through a phone or phablet or in the bricks-and-mortar store – is, in the end, about engaging the emotional brain.

The left brain wants to know how much things will cost.

The right brain will seek to understand the big picture and embrace the spirit of the brand.

Given that people have always sought to extend themselves beyond their earthbound existence, the shopping place will serve to engage the part of the brain and consciousness that allows them to transcend. Technology that supports relationship and the connection to big ideas, not more product, will continue to drive the creation of shopping experiences in a world of multiple customer touch-points.

PART 03

Technology and Transcendence

13

Shopping-A-Go-Go

Shopping in an Age of Distraction

All good relationships rely on good communication. Communicating relevant brand stories, articulating what the brand is about and what it truly believes in, are fundamental in capturing the attention, minds and loyalties of customers.

If within a few seconds of entering the store, customers cannot *make sense* of the environment, they will quickly become disoriented, unsure about the depth of the assortment and whether the retailer has what they have come in to get. While it's true that discovery is an important aspect of the shopping experience, confusion is a deal-breaker.

The same can be said with the 'softer side' of the brand expression. The intangible, sometimes esoteric, components of brand ideology have to find the customer by way of clear, authentic and relevant communication.

Typically, these resonant brand stories have unfolded in environments built on embodied, whole-brained engagement shaped by storytelling and play. Today, the smartphone is changing the communication game, the way we experience environments and the brain. By June 2014, there were more than 1.2 million apps for iPhones alone [107], and more than another 1.3 million apps for Android mobile devices. [108] The most recent statistics on cellphone use are providing surprising information about what customers actually use their phones for.

Recent studies continue the widely held assertion that the U.S. market is well behind the Japanese and EU countries. But, Americans are catching on and catching up – quickly. Despite the attention apps receive in the media, mobile phone app usage is still dwarfed by people's use of handheld devices for accessing the Internet by way of a browser.

By May 2013, 91% of American adults were cellphone owners, up from 65% from 2004. The majority (56%) of these cellphones were smartphones, highlighting the increasing trend towards communication devices that allow for sharing rich, image-based content, such as photographs, video and other forms of media to users through one device. [110]

The use of the cellphone as a way to stay connected is literally taking over every part of our daily and nightly lives. So strong is our need to stay connected to our principal social groups that an estimated 67% of cell owners find themselves picking up their phone to check for messages, alerts, or calls *even when they are fully aware* that the device is *not* ringing, pinging or vibrating.

We seem to be unable to put the phone down, and if we do, it is never too far from our sight or reach. Fully 44% of cell owners say they sleep with their cellphone next to their bed because they wanted to be sure – while they were out cold – that they didn't miss any calls, texts, or other updates during the wee hours of the night. Just who is actually calling while they are asleep, or why they should interrupt the pleasant dreams and REM cycle to return a text, is another story.

All of this (over)use has some avid cellphone users thinking they just can't make it through the day without their trusty handheld buddy. Remember when we used to send letters and wait for a written response? That could take weeks! There was a certain pleasure in writing, feeling the texture of the paper at your fingertips, and even the sound of the paper as you folded it into the envelope. No doubt, email and text are a far cry from that type of body memory. They are, however, indispensible to our communication today.

Most of us now recognize that growing feeling of impatience when the waiting time for a response to a text grows beyond a few *seconds*. Yeah, we forget that the signal has to bounce off a satellite or two before making its way back to Earth and finally into your phone.

The state of continuous partial attention that is very much a part of the younger generation's daily life is certainly causing a sense of technology burnout. The brain, while initially loving the excitement and novelty is being bombarded with 'new' every moment of every day. The long-term effect is that adrenaline pumped into the bloodstream, making one slightly hyper but able to react quickly to a threat, results in a tired, dizzy, foggy state of digital exhaustion.

Despite the fact that we know all of this is likely to not be good for us, individually and as a culture, 29% of cell owners describe their cellphone as "something they can't imagine living without." [111]

At this point, it should be clear that being digitally connected affects our neurophysiology and our psychology. We have already looked at the fire together-wire together relationship between perceptions, behaviors, thoughts and experiences forming connections in our neural circuitry. If we are repetitively surfing from one thing to another in an attempt to stay connected to all of the stimuli in our digital environment, then our brains are being rewarded through continually seeking something new and our ability to focus on a task wanes.

While our brains love all of this novelty, we are reinforcing neural connections that are geared towards jumping from one thing to the next without really absorbing the experience and learning from it. Young digital natives are training their brains to be distracted. A new generation of shoppers is continually challenged with parsing its attention among multiple connection points to social networks, video and music, digital media sources, games, activities and school work.

Most of us would agree that homework ranks pretty low on the list of enjoyable pastimes when you are a teenager. Given the entertaining draw of online media resources and the pleasurable hit of dopamine derived from the validation of being 'liked' by 'friends' in your social network, trigonometry and Tolstoy just don't fire up the pleasure/reward center in the brain.

In our present omni-channel world that a younger generation is so intimately connected to, it is not surprising that they are often doing two or three other things while trying to get their homework done. A Kaiser Foundation study on the influence of media in kids' lives found that half of the students between the ages of 8-18 are using the Internet, watching TV or using some other form of media while trying to get through the 'three R's.' The study found that 31% of them do this "most" of the time and 25% do this at least "some" of the time while they are trying to reinforce what they have been exposed to while at school. Regardless of what a young student may say, doing math homework and playing music with the Internet browser open is not relaxing, easier or effective.

Smartphone use in daily life is not an 'either/or' proposition; it's an 'either/and' one. According to Showtime and a Kagan Research Study, in 25% of all U.S. households nationwide (nearly 23 million), PC's and TV's were in the same room (now you can add the cellphone, and tablet to this, as well) and viewers in nearly 80% of those households watch TV and surf the net at the same time.

There is no question about the alluring quality of the Internet and equally what is to be shared, and learned from the innumerable websites, each with possible links to yet other content sources. In writing this book, the Internet was indispensible at bringing the world's knowledge to my fingertips *and* for years I have had a cellphone that is most often turned on and within reach. The problem is that there is no down time.

The unfortunate irony about this tsunami of digital connections is that, similar to choosing among 24 jams in the shopping aisle, more connection is seemingly *not* making us any *more* satisfied with our communication experiences. Like the eventually underwhelming effect of addictive behaviors, we want more but, as we increase the exposure and frequency, the effects diminish as the body habituates, only reinforcing the need for more. Interestingly, neuroscientists liken the attraction to digital content less to drugs and alcohol than to food and sex, each of which can be joyful and essential to survival but counterproductive (and even life threatening) in excess.[112] In any case, a vicious cycle ensues and we are locked in a digital world that takes us further away from what we really want, which is to fulfill a yearning for profoundly meaningful relationships and experiences. And, in the absence of such meaning, we get, well, anxious.

In a state of digitally induced, constant partial attention people are understandably more prone to be stressed out.

If we know that part of the brain's ability lies in recognizing patterns – shapes, sounds, experiences, etc. – to determine whether or not something is potentially dangerous or safe, then it's likely that the brain's lower order functional areas are on high alert when it spends all day continually responding to an overload of environmental stimuli. The continuous bombardment with digital media is an assault on cognitive resources and the areas of our brain that respond with instinctual emotional reactions.

From the evolutionary point of view, it made a lot of sense to pay attention to alerts in our environment, such as the sounds or sights of predators rather than continuing to add more sticks, mud and skins to the walls of the shelter. Interruptions in the patterns of sights and sounds of our environment signaled the potential for a predator to be lurking nearby. When something like this occurred, signals shot out across our ancestors' brain, focusing their attention and getting them to be alert. Areas of the brain that were related to the fight, flight or freeze systems, shot adrenaline into the body, prepping them for reacting quickly. But this didn't happen all day long. Returning to the present, we have evolved, but not that much, and this chronic stress of our age is creating a stress-reactive brain.

Messages and alerts come in to our mobile devices all day long to notify us of activity among the hundreds of 'friends' in our social networks. We get newsfeeds, podcasts, push notifications from retailers, and emails, texts, and other messages from colleagues, clients, friends and family. We listen to music, watch video downloads, take pictures and edit them for rebroadcast to the Internet. So, it is not surprising that, in a contemporary world, the rings, pings, chirps, and vibrations coming in on the cellphone can override the task at hand, sleep, even good old-fashioned play. Taking time to center ourselves and get focused, while we hold back the rush of potential distractions, happens in an emotional "Catch-22" where we both seek out the validation that comes from being wanted through our social network, yet at the same we feel unable to appreciate it fully because we're quickly moving on to the next text, tweet, app, phone call, or photo.

All of these alerts cause anxiety. And, they are supposed to. That's the way our brains developed to get adrenalin coursing through the blood stream to make us ready for 'fight or flight.' The system may be a few million years old, but it is still at work today. And, it is making us jumpy as well as exhausting us.

You may think that all of this points to a love-hate relationship with our phones. But scientifically speaking it's just a love-love connection. The thing is, people *love* their phones.

No, seriously, we actually do *love* our phones. Love as in best friend, new puppy or a person with whom we are having a meaningful relationship. The mobile phone has become, not just a method of communicating with other people, but truly a 'significant other' in our daily lives.

In a study conducted by Martin Lindstrom in collaboration with MindSign Neuromarketing, subjects were exposed separately to audio and video of a ringing and vibrating cellphone.

Not so surprisingly, their brains lit up in *both* the visual and auditory areas, indicating that if they only heard the sound, they imagined the phone's image in their mind's eye, and that if they saw the video of the phone ringing, they 'heard' it too. Our brains are triggered in multiple functional areas in response to stimuli and bring together mental images of things we are exposed to so that we get a holistic view and respond accordingly.

What was also very interesting about the Lindstrom study was that the insula also lit up. You'll remember that the insula is responsible for processing a number of perceptual inputs, such as perceiving and anticipating loss and pain. It is also happens to be tied into feelings of pleasure, compassion and...love.

According to the Lindstrom study, "The subjects' brains responded to the sound of their phones as they would respond to the presence or proximity of a girlfriend, boyfriend or family member. In short, the subjects didn't demonstrate the classic brain-based signs of addiction. Instead, they *loved* their iPhones."[113]

We already decorate our phones with rhinestones, cool covers, and colorful protective cases adorning them with personality. Soon we'll be naming them, personalizing the AI voice to our favorite historical figure, movie star, or just someone sexier than 'Siri.' And, you just know, that in the extreme case, some people will have their phones accompany them to the hereafter, as the Pharaohs did with their treasures.

At the 2013 Academy Awards, the Oscar for best screenplay was awarded to a film entitled *Her*. In this comedy-drama, the principal character played by Joaquin

Phoenix falls in love with an intelligent operating system (OS) called Samantha (whose voice is played by Scarlett Johansson). This OS has a witty personality and uncanny affinity for being a perfect match for Theodore who is coming to the end of a painful divorce from his real-life wife, Catherine. Constantly available, and always interested, the relationship between Theodore and the disembodied voice of Samantha grows as she provides support in an undemanding way and appears to become more 'human.' In case you haven't seen it yet, I won't tell you how it ends.

We may not develop intimate relationships with operating systems in the way that Theodore did in the movie *Her*, but mobile devices definitely become shopping companions, eventually providing more than simply directions to the store and product information. Eventually, we will come to see the world *through* our devices as they move from our hand to other forms of wearable technologies that allow us to more holistically interact shopping environments where real-life experiences are combined with digital constructions.

Smartphone Adoption – Who's Got 'em?

There have been a few seismic shifts in the retail industry that parallel the influence of mobile technology. It's not just that mobile devices are adding a new way to access the brands we love to shop, but that as consumers, we are changing to a mobile economy faster than any *retailing paradigm shift* we have seen in the past few hundred years.

It's not just that we can shop anytime, anywhere, but that the very core of the shopping experience, the social imperative, is being completely rewritten with the power of consumer connectivity through social networks. The need to connect and the power of the enabled consumer to do so from any place on the planet is an old idea that is being completely redefined.

According to some mobile-market studies, mobile devices, as a form of communication between people and the brands they love, are being adopted at a rate that is faster than their acceptance of PC's in the early '80s. Since Apple's launch of the iPhone in 2007, smart mobile devices are being adopted 10x times quicker than PC's were in 1980s, 2x as fast as consumer adoption of the Internet in the 1990s, and 3x faster than that of the recent social network explosion. [114]

We used to think of the triumvirate of PC, laptop and phone as our three primary screens. With advances in smartphone technologies, the handheld device is becoming the preferred go-to option for Internet connection. The smartphone is just one of many screens, but it will likely become *the* primary screen when customers want to connect to retailers. Mobile's use, both in and out of the store, is not just part of the shopping process, but poised to become the single most influential part of the entire path to purchase.

Mobile devices can go anywhere, are often less costly than a typical PC or laptop, and combine multiple functionalities in one device, which feed into our collective desire for convenience. By the end of 2011, more than one third of Americans didn't have traditional landline telephones.[115] An increasing number of consumers are turning to mobile phones to access the Internet and forgoing the purchase of a home-based computer altogether.

Access to the Internet is a key driver in cellphone use. In fact, it is for many the only means to access the information superhighway. By June 2012, 31% of current cell Internet users reported that they mostly go online with their cellphones rather than using their PC or their laptop computers. This translated to nearly 17% of all cellphone owners who can be considered as individuals who, when they want to surf the web, access the Internet solely through their cellphone.[116]

Consumers see their devices as integral to their lives.

In fact, half (54.6%) of smartphone owners say that they use their device for *all* aspects of their life. Their smartphone is not just a part of their life; it *is* their life.[117]

At least as a method to connect to the Internet, their smartphones are much stronger objects of their affection than their PC's have ever been. It is not too hard to understand why – 'convenience' is the cellphone's middle name. A significant number of individuals (64%) who access the Internet through their cellphone only, report that due to convenience and ease to carry, their phones go everywhere with them. For a culture that is always on the go, carrying the laptop can become a heavy load and it does not inherently have a connection to the Internet but relies on finding access Wi-Fi hotspots to get online.

The trend to dumping landline phones is mirrored in the PC world in that many of the individuals who access the Internet exclusively through their cellphones say that they have no other form of web-connectivity. They are forgoing PC's and laptops altogether and relying on their handheld devices alone. Moreover, 6% of those who browse the Internet exclusively through their cellphone say that they don't have access to a computer and 4% say they have no source to access the Internet other than their cellphone.[118] With the growth of tablets in the mobile market, we might well see a future where the desktop PC goes the way of the landline telephone as a preference grows for convenient portable devices.

Smartphone ownership is highest among young adults, especially those in their 20's and 30's, though every major demographic group showed an increase in smartphone ownership from 2011 to 2013. Despite greater costs, 77% of 18-29-year-olds with an annual household income of less than $30,000 were smartphone owners. When household income climbs above $75,000 a full 90% of 18-29 year olds are smartphone owners. It appears that even though greater household disposable income provides increased opportunity for smartphone ownership, a huge majority of less affluent youngsters makes the other necessary economic sacrifices to have them.

Not to be left behind in the young adopters' wake, 87% of those in the 30-49 age bracket whose household incomes are above $75,000 are also smartphone owners. Taken together, almost nine out of every ten cellphone owners between the ages of 18-49, with household incomes of $75,000 or more – are smartphone owners.

When it comes to choice of platform – either Android, iPhone, or Blackberry systems – ownership increases seem to be in those platforms that provide access to mobile apps, easy internet browsing ability and screen size that renders better experiences with advanced image quality. Smartphones based on the Android operating system showed significant growth between 2011 and 2013, with 28% of cell owners holding Android devices (a 15% increase since 2011) while owners of Apple's iPhone represented 25% of the smartphone population (an increase of 10% from 2011).

White, non-Hispanic, owners are essentially equal in their iPhone and Android ownership rates (27% saying they own iPhones and 26% owning Android devices). African-American, non-Hispanic, owners of smartphones are more likely to be holding Android devices (42% have Android based smartphones versus 16% who have iPhones).

And finally, when it comes to education and income levels, those with college degrees and with household incomes greater than $75,000 per year are more likely to be iPhone owners (38% of college grads have iPhones versus 29% who carry Android devices – and 40% of those with household incomes of $75,000 or more are iPhone owners versus 31% who own Android devices).[119] Whether it is on an iPhone or Android device, there is a growing preference for viewing digital content on larger screens with better resolution, as well as a change from pushing buttons to touch screen interfaces that you touch, pinch, swipe and drag content around with your fingers.

Keeping Up with the Jones'

The ways we communicate are changing and doing so at a pace that is hard to keep in front of or predict. In fact, most retailers, while believing mobile's primary benefit is to enhance the overall value of the brand, are in large part holding back on putting their money where their mobile stats are. Not because they do not see the value in mobile as a strategy that will drive increased value to both their business as well as customers, but because they, too, see the tide shifting so quickly that they are hesitant about committing the resources when technology and user preferences are continually undergoing change.

This is no longer the Tortoise trying to catch the Hare. Everybody is trying to catch up to a fast-moving chameleon.

While there are some retailers who see the proverbial writing on the wall and are gearing up to compete, the movement is not entirely in full swing across the retailing landscape. With a little less than "one-quarter of retailers preparing to deal with the complexity of mobile application deployment, it also points out that most retailers fear that devices and platforms are destined to change too quickly. This is what is keeping retailers on the sidelines from enacting more exciting mobile projects." [120]

Unwilling to stick their necks out, many retailers are simply adopting a wait-and-see mentality instead of fully thinking towards something completely new for their customers in the mobile world. Not wanting to be completely left in the dust of the mobile revolution, they are instead implementing strategies that are taking what they already have as a PC-based e-commerce platform, and modifying it to accommodate the mobile-enabled consumer.

There are, of course, leaders who are willing to jump in from the fray and incur costs while trying to implement new digital strategies. A good example is Jeff Bezos, Founder and CEO of Amazon.com, in his acquisition of *The Washington Post* newspaper. While *The Washington Post* may not come to mind as a 'retailer' in the typical sense (as we often simply think apparel, home goods, cosmetics, electronics, etc., when the word 'retailer' is bandied about), it does, however, sell a product – news information.

Probably more than other businesses, the publishing industry is directly in the eye of the communication paradigm-'shift storm.' As part of the publishing industry, the '*Post*,' along with countless other news organizations, has suffered with the rise of the Internet as a method of dissemination of news and current events. While newspapers are folding all over the country, Jeff Bezos purchased *The Washington Post* in August 2013. In the face of uncertainty about the continued viability of an industry that relied on actual paper and delivery door-to-door by the friendly neighborhood kid with freckles, he is perhaps ramping up to change the face of the newspaper world. While the eventual fate of the *Post* is uncertain, its survival will require yet another complete rethinking of the news-reporting paradigm that will be nothing short of a reincarnation for the medium.

While the lesson of *The Washington Post* is not directly about retail stores in transition due to communication methods changing, it *is* about how brands will need to change the way they *share their message with customers*. The stories in newspapers, magazines and other print-based business are crafted to follow a mission statement and brand positioning strategy like any other retail business. How stories are disseminated is what differentiates one publication from another. From masthead to editorial to articles and advertising, the entire publication, whether it is a daily, weekly, monthly or 'minutely' as in the case on online blogs, is all packaged as visual content that projects an image of the brand. As readers move to mobile, the entire print industry is being forced to redefine how they package their 'product' and keep it relevant for their customers.

While the print industry is actively changing customer expectations about how they get their information, retail is no less affected. If customers aren't reading traditional sources of information as much as they used to in preference for digitally based publications, they are likely not being exposed to the same advertising methods they may have become accustomed to. Fewer eyes on pages of magazines, newspapers and other print sources means a shift toward capturing customer attention to sell brand, products and services to webpages, social network sites, mobile applications, and digital signage placed throughout the environment.

What is intriguing about Jeff Bezos buying *The Washington Post* is that a master of Internet-based business and *product* distribution is taking over a business about *information* distribution.

Apps and Traps

There is no question that allowing customers to experience goods and services from the palm of their hand, wherever they are, provides added value to the brand in general. Looking for the mobile world to stabilize (which may not happen for some time as new technologies seem to emerge almost daily), many retailers are taking what they, and their customers, already know from their e-commerce platforms and extending to mobile devices. At the very least, it provides a new channel for their customers to access the brand and there is an experience of familiarity if the mobile platform mirrors the typical online store.

Extending the e-commerce platform to mobile devices seems reasonable, though not so daring as rethinking the shopping paradigm completely for a digitally enabled customer. There are some common sense assurances about this as a strategy; customers may know the retailer's web-based store having shopped there before, and they are, therefore, more likely to understand the brand and merchandise presentation approach. They are familiar with accessing and navigating around websites, and paying online. If they do all of the same things but on a mobile device, previous learning from their PC at home is transferred to the mobile experience, and the assumption is that shopping and buying from the palm of your hand is not burdensome. In this case, the mobile platform is a transaction-enabler, not necessarily a relationship-builder.

The downside to simply providing an e-commerce platform optimized for a mobile device through a browser is that retailers cannot take advantage of geo-location that comes through the use of mobile apps.

When we consider apps specifically designed for smartphones with GPS location capability, retailers stand to gain a huge amount of information about customers while they move along the shopping journey. Location-based marketing tied into the specific location of customers through their smartphones allows for shaping experience in real time, pushing customer-specific content to their devices while they are moving through the aisles or walking along the street.

Knowing where the shopper is, on the street or in the store, ties directly into understanding behavior patterns that influence product (or service) presentation along the customer's journey. If interaction opportunities are strategically placed, retailers and brands gain considerable information about where, and how, their customers engage with content.

Since information about mobile phone location can be acquired by their use at specific places, retailers can determine if customers are tuned in to messaging they have placed along with roadside signs, subway and bus stops, on the street or in a store. Any place the customer takes out a mobile device and engages with some brand-related content – scanning a QR code, using an augmented reality app or responding to a text/push notification – is an opportunity for the retailer to learn more about where the customer is at a certain point of time, how they are paying attention, and to what. Every time that Yahoo (or any other search engine) asks you to allow your location to be determined, your mobile device (to which you are attached) is tagged in a place in time.

The more that retailers are able to determine when and where their customers are throughout the day, the more they are likely to want to provide messaging that may be relevant to them in that moment. Location-based media/marketing will become extremely powerful as mobile enters full adoption with consumers. With the objective of providing marketing/advertising messages, or opportunities to buy from mobile devices while in the car, subway, taxi, or walking along main street, location-based marketing will become the norm as retailers and brands seek to target individuals rather than huge swaths of the shopping population.

Smartphone Adoption – What Are They Doing with 'em?

Traditional retail models have assumed that the experience starts and ends in the store. While advertisers and marketers have worked in the service of retailers to extend brand awareness beyond the sales floor, embodied experience needed to happen someplace physical. We know that this paradigm has changed and the path to purchase is as varied as the customer on his or her route. One thing is for sure: mobile is a growing beyond being simply part of the pathway and instead turning into the global superhighway, crossing the retail landscape. Enabled with their smartphones, consumers are more in control of when, where and how they shop than any other time in shopping history. Today, a mobile connection to the retailer or brand permeates the shopping experience. It is as significant a part of the decision-making and buying process outside the store as it is when customers are walking the aisles.[121]

Given all the talk about how retailing will benefit from customers holding a mobile device all day long, those users engaged with the mobile device for shopping are fewer than one might expect. A seemingly slim 6.5% of shoppers reportedly use their handheld device to access retail sites.[122] Don't let this lull you into thinking mobile devices are not significant as a platform to shop. The ripple is growing into a tidal wave. And, it's coming to shore – quickly.

If mobile-enabled consumers are not all flocking with their mobile phones to the stores they love to shop, what are they doing with all the connectivity they have? Given that upwards of 80% of smartphone Internet users are going online every day, what could they *possibly* be engaged with, if not shopping?

For the most part, mobile is supporting the social experience we have relied on to drive the development of our social structures and culture over time. So strong is our need to connect that even when customers are standing in the store, they are reaching outside of its four walls to connect with others. Across age, gender, race and economic standing, most of a consumer's time is spent browsing sites that provide a social connection.

In today's digitally enabled mobile market, nearly three out of every four American adults are social network site users. The boom in the social network platform has seen staggering since 2005 when only 8% of adults accessed them. By May of 2013, 72% of adults were 'friending' others and checking in on them almost every day. Thinking of it another way, this is a market that has grown 900% in eight short years.[123]

Not surprisingly, the highest percentage of Social Network Site (SNS) users is among those between the ages of 18-29. The young adopters are followed by the 30-49 year old set, of whom, 78% are users of social network sites. Not to be entirely left out of the craze, seniors are catching on. While only 43% of them admit to using social network sites, the number of seniors who say they use social networks tripled between 2009 and 2014.[124]

Entertainment and social networks top the list of preferred mobile activities, with upwards of 76% of mobile users reaching out to a social-network friend before they do anything else with their mobile device.

The motivation to stay connected to current friends is a key factor driving consumers to use social networks. Two-thirds, or 67% of SNS users say that they connect to sites such as Facebook, Twitter and LinkedIn to keep up with what is going on in their friends' lives. Also, 64% of SNS users report that the main motivation to access their social network is to connect to family. With the use of SNS being so prevalent when users first pick up their phones, we are seeing an interesting transition to a social scenario where staying connected to one's SNS 'friends' is becoming more important than maintaining connections to immediate family members.[125]

While only 5% of consumers who access social network sites say that the *main* motivation for doing so is to follow celebrities, athletes or politicians, it turns out that about 41% of SNS/Twitter users follow individual artists, musicians or other performers. [126]

It is not hard to qualify artists or musicians, or these otherwise creative individuals or groups, as those who establish the current aspects of a society's cultural content. They are the modern sages, witch doctors and yentas of the old marketplaces from whom we learned about cultural myths and morals. They are a significant part of the cultural structure of a society along with political, business and religious leaders. They sing, dance, write and make art to describe the intricacies of our contemporary relationships, instigating dialogue that gets us beyond ourselves. Historically speaking, rituals enacted by these individuals provided the mythical and mystical content into our lives, giving meaning and context to those things that were not fully understood. It is not so surprising that SNS users find themselves going back to the spiritual well, as it were, to find out what the poets and oracles of the day are saying about the world.

In Part 1, I explored the idea that old marketplaces were much more than a place to find the necessities of the day. The marketplace was the cultural schoolhouse where we learned about ourselves in the greater context of our world. Social networks such as Twitter and Facebook are no less a part of how we determine who we are in relation to our family, culture, nation and cosmos. In fact, they are speaking to this need, to such an extent that their emergence as a prime communication medium is growing yearly at astonishing rate.

Interestingly, this might speak to the lack of relevant and meaningful connections we have in general with the world around us. We apparently have more than ever, but it appears to mean less. Despite the fact that we live in a world of opportunity and abundance, there seems to be a pervasive desire for transcendence. We have always looked beyond ourselves to make sense of our world and this aspect of human nature is no less important today.

The challenge we face is that the endless loop of social network indulgence is fed by a basic yearning we all have to connect with others. Our interest in forging new relationships, our brain's delight over novelty, the emotional psychology of validation, our desire to be entertained and to learn and our innate response to alerts in our environment, are keeping us glued to the mobile device in our hand.

We could argue the pro's and con's of the influence of social media in our lives, whether we are communicating more and connecting less, but the fact remains that a new generation of shoppers is in large part finding what it needs as a social experience by not actually having to get together with other people. It is not just that young shoppers visit their friends' SNS pages online, but they are also visiting their favorite brands' fan pages as well. Brands and retailers have become another node in this intricate web of social relationships that weaves together our work, home, spiritual, and sociocultural lives. Brands and retailers share the significance of connections between family members, workmates and friends. With more than 90% of consumers between the ages of 18-29 checking each other out through social network sites, retailers cannot afford to stay out of the social networking game. [127] Providing access to the brand, store and special offers through the social network channel is a critical part of retailing that will only grow in prominence over the next few years.

Research conducted by WSL/Strategic Retail suggests that two-thirds of SNS users who 'fan' social media pages are choosing to follow brands and retailers. This surpasses the number of users who follow celebrities and TV shows, which are followed by about half of SNS users. "We may think everyone is following the Kardashians on Facebook, but in fact, Walmart is the greater social media 'celebrity' with more than double the number of followers as the Kardashian family's most popular member, Kim," said Wendy Liebmann, CEO of WSL/Strategic Retail. [128]

The growth of social media use among retailers and brands continues to grow. Name a product, store, service, sports franchise or musical group and you'll find them on Facebook or Twitter. Specialty-retailing analysts at UBS have highlighted the big players in the retail business who are not just visible on social media sites, but are actually making sales and growing their brand from it. [129] The leader of the pack with more than 45 million Facebook fans is L Brands Inc. This retail powerhouse is a conglomerate of some of the most successful brands we know and is run by perhaps one of the greatest retail visionaries of our time, Les Wexner (Founder, Chairman & CEO). With its stable full of retail thoroughbreds such as Victoria's Secret, Bath & Body Works, Pink, La Senza, and Henri Bendel, it's not a surprise that L Brands also has the most Twitter followers (4 Million) and the second most followers on Pinterest and Instagram (1.8 million).

Included among the highest followed retailers on Facebook are Abercrombie & Fitch (19 million) and Gap Inc. (15 million). While Lululemon is not as strong as the other leaders on Facebook, it has the highest number of followers on Instagram and Pinterest, with more than 19 million followers and the highest number of Twitter tweets with 56,000.

Can a retailer or brand create a mythic quality about itself that aligns with that of the artists' and musicians' power at shaping culture? No doubt about it. The brands we all love to shop are also the brands we love to talk about on social networking sites, and in doing so they take more than their fair share of time in the cultural discussion.

Beyond the pull of their social network, 73% of consumers turn to their handheld devices to find out what is going on in the world around them. By accessing location-based services that provide information about weather, the ability to search local maps and source reviews about local businesses such as restaurants, they are always connected to a dynamic flow of content that keeps them current. Not unlike going to the Agora in years past, consumers go next to their mobile devices to find out more about the world outside of their immediate surroundings. As a result, 63% of mobile owners use their device to access news sources including entertainment, local and national news. [130]

Shopping on the Go – On the Mobile Device

When consumers pull their phones out and don't immediately text, tweet, blog, post, 'friend,' or 'like' something, and instead they think about shopping, how do their smartphones come into play?

Given that as many as a third of smartphone users spend at least three to four hours a week shopping on mobile sites, it stands to reason that an increasing number of retail transactions start with the smartphone as the source of information. [131]

The top three activities consumers engage in with their mobile device before they either enter the store or buy a product from the palm of their hand are:
- locating a store or determining store hours (86%)
- browsing or looking for a product or service (81%)
- reading customer reviews of the products they are considering (69%) [132]

Future shoppers will be more aware of their options as they turn to their mobile devices to search for products and then compare them against other retailers selling within the same category. As many retailers generally offer the same categories of merchandise, finding a point of differentiation from their competition will become increasingly more difficult.

Offering experiences that are different from the next store will require some inventive thinking and a change to understanding how to craft a relationship with consumers, who are more informed, but more distracted, and now have more options than they have ever imagined, but are disaffected and growing disinterested. Building brand loyalty with customers will rely on getting into the head of the digitally driven customer to make sure that store design and product offering are tied to creating customer experiences that touch the shopper's emotional nerve center.

While demographics play a role in the degree to what and how consumers are buying, there are in general three main consumer product categories that seem to be topping the list of all mobile sales.
1. The most prevalent category, representing about 65% of mobile purchases, is in the 'packaged'/downloadable entertainment media category, such as music, books, games and movies. [133]

Consumers are going to the smartphone first to buy items that bring entertainment and fun into their lives. We yearn for playtime. Music, games, books, and stories, which in our contemporary society are delivered by way of video, are deeply ingrained into who we are. This, of course, is entirely consistent with what shopping should be all about. Going to our smartphones first to engage in fun and to experience the esoteric qualities of our culture from today's contemporary minstrels, storytellers and magic makers, is still what seems to engage us.

For most of us, technology is magic. We don't know how it works, but that thing in our hand somehow grabs information off of invisible radio waves that move through the air around us and images appear. If what we hold adds to our delight by enabling us to play music (deeply rooted in who we are as a species) or games (which enliven our propensity for play as a teacher of culture and empathy) or video/movies (which as a visual storytelling medium, is also intricately tied to our social evolution), then bring it on!

On all counts, our emotional selves love this.

2. Once entertained, mobile consumers turn next to apparel, shoes and jewelry as the objects of their fancy. Approximately 30% of all mobile purchases are clothing and the accessories that make the little black dress look even better.

3. Rounding out the top three consumer shopping categories on mobile devices are consumer electronics in the price range up to $250. While consumers are adding CE products to their mobile shopping carts that exceed the $250 price tag, it is more typical that men will buy more, and at greater prices, than women when shopping this category. Men tend to be gadget hounds, as they are more than twice as likely to buy big-ticket electronics items than women. Nearly a third of men bought electronics items over $250 compared to 15% of women who did so in 2012. Women, on the other hand, are far more inclined to use their mobile device to access social networking sites.

Mobile-Enabled Customers in the Store

In the hands of today's consumers, the mobile phone is a contemporary vehicle that provides a greater context to who they are and where they fit in the world around them. In many ways, nothing has changed for a few thousand years, and in other ways we are a world apart from visiting the local market to get the eggs and the news of the day.

A significant challenge for retailers in this mobile-enabled paradigm is that customers are no longer in the dark about the merchandise stores sell. With seemingly unlimited resources at their fingertips, today's customers are smarter, or at least more informed, than they have ever been in shopping history. This poses a problem when they enter a store and may well know more about the products on the shelf than the sales associate does.

If the core of the shopping experience is based on the social relationship between the seller and the buyer, sales associates are finding themselves at an information crossroads when talking with today's customers. Not only is the language that customers are using changing under the influence of social networks, texting and email communication, but their interest in talking with sales associates, *at all*, is also waning.

There is a two-fold challenge at hand:

1. The brains of younger consumers are being re-wired through continual Internet use. The result is that they may be less interested and perhaps less able to engage in meaningful conversations and profound, empathic, interpersonal relationships. Especially with sales associates whom they may perceive as unnecessary in their shopping experience.

2. Today's customers are coming to the store with better, and many times superior, knowledge than the sales associates have about what they are selling. It is coming to the point that many smartphone users say "that they prefer using their mobile device rather than interacting with store employees for simple tasks…73% favor using their smartphones to handle simple tasks compared to 15% who favor interaction with an employee."[134]

There are many complexities to address when dealing with the mobile-enabled customer, but none will scuttle the sale quicker than not being able to make an emotional connection through intelligent, relevant and engaging communication. Sales associates must be armed with more than standard information and product knowledge. A retailer's mobile strategy needs to put better tools in the sales associates' hands by way of in-store Wi-Fi and devices that support their ability to search, not just inventories, but detailed product information beyond what is available to customers.

Retailers recognizing that the store is more than a place simply for making transactions will also recognize that their sales associates are a key component to the selling process. My wife's friend drives 35 miles from her home for her dog food instead of going to the grocery store 5 miles away. Why? She likes the store and the service she gets while there. She feels that the sales associates understand her and how much she loves her dog. The experience she has with the shop owner more than compensates for the added cost for the products she buys, and the longer time she spends in the car coming and going.

If customers come into stores at all in the future, they will do so for engaging and interesting interactive experiences. While sales associates cannot halt the evolution of their customers' brains, they still have a good chance at remaining relevant if they can learn to communicate the way their customers do, and make sure they know more about the assortment than the shopping public does.

The reliance on virtual friends has become so prevalent, that once inside the store, customers are using their phones to ask for help and validation from their close social-network friends. They have come to rely on the opinion of a greater number of individuals rather than trusting their gut or turning to a sales associate for support on making a decision.

Not surprisingly, when customers were asked about their cellphone use in a store in the 30 days prior to an interview with researchers, 38% them said that they used their phones to call a friend while in a store to ask for advice about a purchase. [135]

In addition to asking for advice from someone other than the sales associate about a purchase, 25% of the customers surveyed said they used their phones to look up the price of a product online while in the store to see if they could get a better deal somewhere else. Continuing their search for more information to help make a decision, 24% of these shoppers stood in the aisle and looked up product reviews of what they were intending to buy.

One of the largest assaults on the world of retailing is the transformation of the retail place from a place to see, try and buy, into simply a showroom to get up close and personal with products only to leave the store and buy them online. 'Showrooming' as it has come to be known, has the retail world in a tizzy. Conversion rates are dropping away since shoppers, many times, have no intention of actually buying in a retailer's store. More and more customers are there just to check stuff out, maybe learn more about what they are looking to buy, and then leave to get it elsewhere.

The obvious question to be asked is, "If customers are in the store and they physically experience what they want to buy, why aren't they doing it, then and there?"

Part of the answer is of course that they can indeed get it cheaper online and have it delivered to their house as soon as that afternoon or the next day. So they have saved a few bucks, but is that it? Have shoppers become more cost conscious than they have ever been? Not likely. Buying goods and services at what is perceived to be a fair (or cheaper) price has always been a driver to the retail exchange. No one willingly wants to pay more for something than what they perceive it to be worth.

The missing link to keeping customers in stores is 'connection.'

The genius in Apple's Genius Bar is that it is based on the fundamental drive to connect. And, it's even better when the person who you are connecting to understands you and your individual problem, knows more than you about the products and services the company has to offer. The 'oracle' (the Apple staffer who stands behind the Genius Bar) seems to be empowered to make decisions on the spot that are in your best interests and can deliver sage advice along with a solution in real time face-to-face, one-on-one. Furthermore, giving customers the ability to schedule an appointment is an explicit recognition of the fact that customers are hard-pressed for time and would always prefer to be in control of their lives and shopping experiences. For customers, being able to craft self-directed shopping experiences makes their in-store time unique to them and therefore inherently more relevant.

Instead of getting up in arms about the idea of showrooming, retailers may do well to look at customer interaction protocols, and build in-store experience strategies around remarkable, person-to-person service that is simply not available through a digital interface. Studies are continuing to show the critical importance of in-store personal connection in remaining relevant, and viable, in the world of retail. And yet, despite the fact that shoppers are likely in a state of merchandise-information overload when they arrive at the store, a study by TimeTrade shows that an overwhelming number of them (93%) still can't find the right person to help them through the buying process. This leads to 90% of them simply leaving the store. On the other hand, "when helped by a knowledgeable associate, more than 93% are more likely to buy. And even better, nearly 85% are likely to buy more."[136]

A growing reliance on social media connections is giving shoppers more personalized and 'trustworthy' advice from their network of online friends than what they are generally able to find on the sales floor. Multiple online sources also provide immediate access to information about product, price and availability at the various competing retailers. This may lead one to question the relevancy of the sales associate altogether and whether or not the idea of 'customer loyalty' is simply a thing of the past. If better product knowledge and lower prices are to be found outside the store, how does the store survive?

While it may not come as a surprise to some, people, not product depth and low prices, give the bottom-line a huge push into the black. When retailers connect to customers immediately upon entering, and line up the right sales associate with the shoppers' need states and help them through the buying process, sales increase. When shoppers have everything they could need online, the reason they make their way into the store is driven by wanting to connect to knowledgeable sales associates and to be engaged in the social experience of shopping with others. The TimeTrade survey again shed light on what seems obvious: "80% of the retailers survey reported that sales increase by 20-50% per transaction when shoppers get the attention and insightful recommendation they need and deserve."[137]

This is the social imperative of the shopping experience. It has been this way from the first exchanges years ago and remains a core feature of great shopping experiences today. And, it will remain this way into foreseeable future. However, the way it will happen will morph to meet the needs of the tech-enabled customer with digital access to a global marketplace. The way young customers communicate in every other aspect of their daily lives is under tremendous change. They see the world differently, as did every generation before them. The key differentiator is the integration of digital technology into their lives and the resulting change in both communication and their interpersonal neurobiology.

Mobile technology is not the end of stores. But, retailers will have to embrace change that is nothing short of revolutionary in order to keep in lockstep with the changing needs of the Millennial and the generations of shoppers to follow.

14

Mysterious Millennials

Who, What, When, Where and Why?

If you are a retailer, you probably think you know your customer. But do you know Millennials?

Over the past few years, the generation of Americans between the ages of 18-29 has received a lot of attention. By some accounts, they are considered disengaged, entitled, suffering from a lack of empathy and perpetually with head down gazing at the glow of a phone in their hand. While some think that these attributes are appropriately placed, they are in no way a complete view of this otherwise diverse group. There are as many differences in the Millennial Generation (also known as Generation Y) cohort as there are between the generations in general.

Why consider Millennials in a book about creating right-brain shopping places? Several reasons, actually.

- As a consumer group, they pose significant challenges to creating engaging retail experiences that meet their needs. Their changing lifestyle habits are redefining priorities, which are reshaping the requirements for providing engaging and relevant shopping places.

- They are a generation of shoppers coming into their own as consumers with a lot of clout. By some estimates, their projected spending will grow to $1.4 trillion annually by 2020 and represent 30% of total retail sales. [138]

- Their communication habits are re-crafting the manner in which brands share their narratives. In terms of retailing as a storytelling medium, they are redefining how the customer needs to be engaged in compelling stories across multiple customer touch points.

- They are a watershed generation at the forefront of a long future of consumers who will have never known a time without digital technology being a major influence in everything they do, including shopping.
- Their brains are being re-wired through their use of technology and the old rules of engagement will not apply.
- And, if shopping places don't remain relevant to them, Millennials will conveniently get what they need and want through their smartphones.

What *makes* a Millennial? Let me try to assemble a profile to give you a better idea of why he or she may be a big deal as a future customer.

For starters, this is not a one-size-fits-all generation. The Pew Internet & American Life Project published one of the most comprehensive studies of the Millennial generation in February 2010. [139] The study, called "Millennials – A Portrait of Generation Next. Confident. Connected. Open to Change," describes a generation both similar to and very different from any generation before it. Born between 1978 and 2000, they are complex in their contradictions and unified in their ubiquitous use of technology. The following paragraphs draw on the findings of the Pew Center's research, providing some interesting and perhaps alarming statistics about who Millennials are, what they are about and how they are likely to change the world of retailing as we know it.

Millennials are individualists who value independence. They see themselves as being defined by their affinity for, and increased power from, the Internet and digital communication world.

This segment of the American population is more racially diverse with 61% classified as non-Hispanic whites. Racial and ethnic minorities make the other 39% of this cohort. This is only marginally higher than Generation X (born between 1965-1985), wherein 38% are ethnic and racial minorities. Just 27% of Baby Boomers (1946-1965) and only 20% of those Americans over the age of 65 are racial and ethnic minorities.

Millennials may be better educated than older generations, boasting more than half (54%) with a college education. But, they are less likely to be working. National economic factors such as the Great Recession (2008-2010) proved to be bad timing for Millennials, many of whom would have just been entering the work force but remained in college.

Millennials are generally considered to be more liberal in their points of views on marriage, sex, lesbian, gay, bisexual and transgender issues than older generations.

Although about 30% of Millennials rank having a successful marriage as one of the important priorities in their life, only 20% of 18-29 year olds are actually married, and only slightly more than half (12%) of those are married with children at home.

Individuals between the ages of 18-29 make up a large part of the first-time marriage group, but are twice as likely to be single parents (8%) living with their children than Baby Boomers (4%). While they are more likely not to be married (in comparison to individuals of the same age about 20 years go) – and if they are, to be raising kids alone – they still value being good parents. In this they're not significantly different than the older generations who say that getting parenting 'right' is one of the most important things in their lives (52% of Millennial parents feel this way as do 50% of parents over the age of 30).

In terms of priorities other than being a good parent and having a successful marriage, Millennials see 'helping others' and 'having a home' as things that are most important in their lives (21% and 20% respectfully).

Moving down the priority list, only about 15% of Millennials see leading a 'religious life' or being in a 'successful career' as one of the most important aspects of their lives. While these two aspects of their lives don't rank high as the *most important* of 18-29 year olds priorities, 28% of them see religion as *very important* and 47% see a successful career the same way. Either way, religious affiliation is lagging behind career in terms of life's most important priorities.

Self-Expression

Even though the Millennial generation plays the leading role when it comes to the pervasive use of online video sharing sites such as YouTube, Vimeo and Vine, as well as image-sharing sites such as Instagram, Flickr, Snapfish and Pinterest, they do not see themselves as interested in fame. This seems to fly in the face of their enormous use of such sites and their propensity to post 'selfies (a self-taken personal photo intended to be shared). Self-expression is a key feature of the Millennial, but it takes on many forms.

More than any other generation they are more likely to have a personal profile on a social networking site, where they sometimes divulge more than would be considered appropriate by older adults. Despite the fact that many of the 18-29-year-old set share considerable personal information online with their social network friends, the issue of privacy for the Millennial generation is still somewhat of a concern. Some studies that we will look at in a moment suggested that they don't mind giving away private information as long as they get something in return for it.[140]

Millennials like to look good and they are into adorning their bodies. In fact, nearly 40% of them have a tattoo. Fifty percent of those who are 'inked' have between two and five tattoos. But surprisingly, 72% say that their tattoos are not visible to the public. Millennial men who have tattoos are significantly more demonstrative with their body art than are young women. However, one in ten women says that her tattoo(s) is (are) visible depending upon what she is wearing.

Along with the popularity of tattoos, piercings are big with Millennials. Close to 23% of them have a piercing someplace other than an earlobe, which is about six times as many as adults over the age of 30 with piercings. While men have more ink and show more of it in public, Millennial women have more piercings (35%) in places other than their earlobes than young men (11%).

While we can look at tattoos and body piercing as suggesting that Millennials are people whose personalities are more adventurous, risk-taking, and have an anti-establishment mindset, it is likely more than this.

Tattooing has moved into the mainstream with TV shows such as *Miami Ink*, from which tattoo artists have become celebrities. This is not what most of society would have thought about the idea of getting a tattoo, or the tattoo 'artist,' a generation or two ago. No longer suffering the image of something that is done by drunken sailors and unsavory characters, the social stigma of body art is fading – unlike the art itself, which remains for life.

The prevalence of adorning one's body with indelible works of art seems consistent with a younger generation for whom re-making their images for social networks is a large part of their lives. Online social network performances and changing the appearance of whom they project to the world are two sides of the same coin. Altering one's body with ink seems entirely consistent with the sensibilities of a generation who has crafted one, or more, personalities to live online.

Techsters

All generations have some collective experience that helps define who they are and what makes them tick. These shared cultural events become what define age groups over the centuries. The Millennial generation is truly unlike anything that has come before.

If you ask people between the ages of 18-29 what makes them unique, they will likely say that they get tech. They are the always-connected generation.

Not unlike generations who shared experiences of Industrial Revolutions, World Wars or Great Depressions, technology's influence on the Millennial generation isn't something that they had a whole lot of control over. It just so happened that what was evolving in the techno-sphere coincided with their development through teenage and early adult years.

Whereas individuals in older generations try to accommodate technology into their lives, for Millennials it is a given. With the Internet becoming available for general public use in 1992, the youngest members of this group would not have even been born yet, and will not have known a time without the it. The oldest in the group would have been in the second grade of elementary school and their grade school years would have coincided with adoption of personal computers and going online.

While adults over 30 years old may have had an 'opt-in' view of emerging technologies, for Millennials (and the following generations) technology is not something they try to adjust to or fit into their lives – it *is* their lives.

Being connected 24/7 gives them more than simply a bottomless well of information and entertainment; it draws a line in the sand that puts them, along with their tech tools, on the opposite side of an informational divide from older generations. Digital technology, and the gadgets that are used to engage with it, are perceived as commonplace.

For the most part, people of all ages find technology has made their life easier. However, more Millennials (74%) than Gen X'ers (69%), Boomers (60%) and those of the Silent Generation, individuals born between 1925-1945 (50%), feel that technology has made their day–to-day existence more manageable. [141]

Having grown up digital, most Millennials will naturally say that technology simply makes lives easier and helps them be more efficient. After all, throughout most of their childhood and teenage years they have had their parents telling them about the world before mobile digital technology, when things took time, lasted forever and the lives lived now were only to be found in the musing of futurists. Imagine them taking pictures with film and waiting (a whole hour!) for the film to be developed, or going to the library to flip through card catalogues to find a book. For Millennials, those are throwbacks to the Stone Age.

There used to be a time when the only access to a store (apart from the few catalogue companies such as Sears, Roebuck & Company, for example) was, well … the store.

Because this age group has an ease of use with all things technological, they are very fluid in their buying habits. Moving across various platforms throughout the day, they present opportunities to retailers who know how to engage them across the multiple customer journey touch-points.

If you looked at Millennials as young adults in the workforce and charted their use of technology throughout the day, they might well have a smartphone or tablet nearby in the morning when they wake up. If they are driving to work, their phone (unlike the car radio) can display a roadmap with an indication of where traffic is moving slowly as well as giving them weather and maybe news or sports scores.

Once at the office, they may write reports on a desktop computer while also surfing the Internet and constantly checking their phone.

As they go out for lunch they are bombarded with digital, place-based media screens of all sizes from billboards to digital menu boards.

Walking back from lunch they text a friend, call mom, and buy movie tickets from their smartphones.

After dinner they may watch some TV while texting a friend or updating Facebook to arrange meeting the following day.

And as they wind down for the day in bed, they may read a book on a tablet or e-reader.

At each of these points of the day, they are either being solicited or marketed to in some way, and they are likely to be buying something. While the focus here is on Millennials, it is important to remember that this pattern of being connected is not unique to them. Gen X'ers and Boomers (as well as older generations, though to a lesser degree) are following similar digital use behavioral patterns.

And, another thing. There is *no such thing as waiting* for the Millennial. They assume everything to work at the speed of the Internet. They place a premium on speed, ease and efficiency in almost everything they do. This equally translates to their interactions with sales associates, whom Millennials seemingly have less tolerance for being slow or uninformed about the retailer's assortment, or their inability somehow to intuit their shopping needs.

Because they move across platforms throughout the day, there is an expectation of a consistent and seamless brand experience from one device to another. If they are in the store and didn't download the discount coupon at home, they expect to be able to get it on their phone while they are standing in the shopping aisle. No questions asked and no hassle incurred.

Loyalty, Trust and Value

Given the fact that the Millennial shopper moves from shopping channel to shopping channel with greater frequency than any other generation, you might assume that they are less loyal. While they may be more distracted, like multiple options and want immediate gratification, they are far from being without loyalty.

That said, loyalty comes at a cost.

When entering into an exchange, both seller and buyer give something up in order to get something that benefits them. For the retailer, those are goods and services in order to generate revenue. For the Millennial shopper, part of the exchange is dealt with in 'social currency,' personal information and the opening of a one-to-one marketing door where the retailer has more direct access to them. The retailer (or brand) also provides *increased value* through incentives/rewards/loyalty programs where they offer discounts, special offers and promotional opportunities to customers who say 'yes' to giving them personal data.

But loyalty is not a prerequisite to all customer/brand relationships. Some relationships may be purely transactional, left-brain processes. They don't require anything but knowledge of the price of products and the expectation that they will serve the function for which they were bought.

Other relationships engender loyalty, where the exchange between buyer and seller becomes a more right brain, emotional process. In these cases, a sort of covenant is entered into between the brand/retailer and the customer that transcends utility at a price. Some brands/retailers and the products they sell are imbued with more than simply the ability to get the job done. They have an emotional component in the mind of the customer that goes deep and acts as the cornerstone to the relationship.

When retailers or brands look to foster loyalty among their customers, they must *build a sense of trust, provide value, and open the communication pathway to the free exchange of information.*

When there is the feeling of trust between people in a relationship – the sense that someone looks out for another's best interests – loyalty is exchanged. One's willingness to follow a leader, a brand or a retailer is based on the *feeling* that the leader is going to make decisions with the integrity of the relationship in mind.

Call it an implicit, unspoken brand promise. When customers enter into emotional relationships with retailers and brands, trust between the parties is crucial to how things play out.

To ensure the loyalty of the brand faithful, brands and retailers need to continually work on providing the customer with value. That said, value cannot simply be considered as better prices for the products retailers sell. In a world with continuing price pressure, and the availability of similar goods and services in abundance from numerous retailers, customers will continue to look for more than low prices as a motivator to buy from one retailer over another. For a retailer or brand to sustain a customer's loyalty, the perceived value that the customer receives from the relationship must *increase over time*. And, it can't simply be dependent on price.

While 'value' is in part determined by financial considerations, it is not the same as 'price.' We tend to see value and price as being synonymous, if not intimately linked, when in fact they are very different things. When we hear the expression 'great value' it is typically assumed to imply 'low prices,' but this is not necessarily the case.

Let's instead think of value as a *proportional relationship* between the 'function' of some product or service – how it satisfies some need or want – and the 'cost' (not to be confused with price to the consumer) of the product or service – the sum of all activities it takes to provide it to the customer.

The value equation might then be seen as:

$$\text{VALUE} = \text{FUNCTION}/\text{COST}$$

Generally, higher costs to satisfy some function are reflected in higher prices to the consumer, though there is not necessarily a direct relationship between cost and price, and the two may vary widely. For example, let's say that an average mid-range fashion accessory, call it 'Handbag #1' (where name recognition is not a factor in the consumer's choice), may cost 'x' to produce and be made available to the retailer.

Handbag #1 may typically be priced at '$2x$' to cover costs of production and provide for the retailer's profit. In this case, the product would be priced at 200% more than its cost (to bring it to market).

In another case, 'Handbag #2' is produced at slightly more than Handbag #1's cost of 'x,' say '$x+\$100$,' because it has better leather and reinforced stitching (each of these elements adding to its cost). But, Handbag #2 is made for a luxury brand whose name *cache* allows Handbag #2 to be sold for much more than Handbag #1. In this case, we may see that its price at retail may not be '$2(x+\$100)$' but '$10(x+\$100)$.' In the case of Handbag #2, its price is *ten* times its cost.

The cost-price relationship isn't linear and is influenced by a multitude of factors. Materials and manufacturing processes attribute real numbers to cost. Brand name can attribute almost any number, assuming the retailer has a market of buyers willing to pay whatever the price, independent of the product's cost to the retailer in making it available.

If we drive costs up through product design, manufacturing, shipping and a host of other factors between a product's inception and its delivery to the customer, without also increasing its function (the things the product does for the consumer), we *decrease* its value. Increasing costs also likely increase prices and with no added attributes to the product's end-use, consumers spend more for less.

Now think of the customer-brand relationship in terms of the value equation. For brands to sustain loyalty in their existing customer base, and grow it among new recruits, the value of the relationship must increase over time.

While customers want to have consistency in the fundamental tenets of the relationship – the rules of engagement as it were – they want the relationship to *grow*. This is the *consistency of change* that is a fundamental aspect of the brand-customer relationship.

The key to increasing perceived value over the term of the relationship is to either reduce the cost (and as a consequence, possibly reduce the price as well) – everything that is to be done to get the product or service to the customer – and/or increase the function of the product – what the product or service does for the customer.

The challenge in seeing value in terms of a relationship between functions provided at some cost lies in the way we think about 'functions.' We can see functions both in terms of their objective utility – what the thing does from a physical point of view – *wash clothes in the case of a washing machine or provide shelter in the case of a house*, as well as seeing functions in terms of subjective emotional experience – how using this product or service makes the customer feel – *feeling refreshed and presentable in clean clothes, or empowered if the house is large, well-appointed and in an exclusive area, or feeling safe if buying new, reliable car versus an old clunker form a used car lot.*

When we think of the value equation from the point of view of function as a *subjective emotional experience*, how buying a luxury product makes us feel as opposed to getting some no-name bargain basement product, we tap into a *part of customer experience that transcends price.*

A juice bar on a busy main street shopping area near where I live sells hundreds of smoothies every day for $7 or more. Each drink is chock full of natural ingredients and things that are supposed to make you feel great. There is always a line along the order counter all the way to the front door. Customers wait because these drinks are fresh and great tasting, but more so because Animo Juice is selling their customers health in a cup. Taste is one thing but, making lives healthier (and presumably longer), is something for which most customers will pay a little extra. While it is not overtly built into the Animo Juice marketing platform, my favorite of their offerings, "Animo MD," gives me far more than utility and great taste; it portends to give me a new lease on life.

The same goes for a luxury product. This difference in perceived value is not simply because one item is more or less expensive than another, but because the item may have all sorts of ideological attributes associated with it, such as perceived status or group belonging.

If we look at the idea of cost as part of the equation that determines value to the customer, we need to look at it also in terms of the non-tangible 'personal costs' – such as emotional commitment and how much effort the customer needs to put into getting the product or service. These include traveling to the selling place, time spent searching the aisles, waiting at the cash-wrap counter, and increasingly, doing product research online.

If the customer is putting out a lot of effort (personal costs) to satisfy a need or want and not deriving more emotional satisfaction, they are likely to perceive a decrease in value.

As the customer-retailer relationship develops, customers need to continue to get more for less – more satisfaction for less cash, emotional or physical outlays. Better experience – more service at lower prices *and* less hassle – grows relationship value, which in turn supports the development of loyalty.

When we think about Millennial shoppers' perception of value, their use of technology has made them expect the relationship, as well as the exchange of goods and services, to be *easy*. Anything that slows the process or that requires too much output of energy or resources undermines the value they think they are getting. Something may be priced low, but if it's a hassle and can't be bought in a few easy clicks, then it likely will be passed over. For Millennial shoppers, ease-of-shopping, facilitated with seamless technology integration across all platforms, is extremely important in determining perceived value.

When Millennials shop and perceive the relative differences between retailers and the products they sell to be similar, they determine their loyalties based on expectations of getting *added value.*

Generally this means that in Millennial customers' minds, their long-term commitment comes with benefits and incentives that keep the relationship value evolving. "Over three quarters of U.S. Millennials (78%) rate loyalty and rewards programs as 'very' or 'somewhat' likely to make a difference in their purchase decisions."[142]

Loyalty programs have been around for years, and as a method of maintaining commitment to the brands they love, customers often receive price incentives (discounts), which allow them to get more for less. In return the brand/retailer gets the promise of return business.

Remember, decreasing price is an *insula activity inhibitor. That means anything that reduces the perceived pain of an excessive price tag is a delight for the brain and an increased motivation to buy and stay connected to the brand.*

This of course brings into question the continuing validity of price as a means to keep customers buying and loyal to the brand. With the e-commerce world continuing to offer a host of options for shoppers to buy (often at lower prices than those items that are bought in-store), price as a differentiator between brands and retailers becomes less of a key driver in maintaining relationships with customers.

The Great Recession has made fickle consumers of the Millennial generation and they are even more price-conscious than older shoppers. With less cash in their pockets, loyalty is swayed by what they can get while not having to go broke to get it. Millennials are more likely to feel and act more loyally to a retailer or brand if they offer *rewards for commitment.* "Fully three fourths of Millennials are likely to purchase more from, feel more connected to, and tell their networks about brands (and retailers) that offer reward incentives."[143]

Abundance in products and services, and our ability to access it in an ever-increasing number of ways, will not put aside shoppers' interests in getting perceived value as a function of low prices. Price will never completely go away as a motivator (or detractor) to buying behavior. It will, however, become less relevant as a *differentiator* between brands and retailers. Despite the sweet notion that the 'the best things in life are free,' we still pay for the stuff we want. Rewards in the form of discounted prices will likely not go away, but rather will be overshadowed by providing 'enhanced experiences' in exchange for loyalty.

So, if determining value based on reduced price, a left-brain mediated process, is less impactful as shoppers have increased choice at better prices at every swipe or click, what drives profound commitment if not *everyday low prices*?

Relationship – based on emotional bonds, independent of price-point consideration.

Powerful, embodied experiences – through immersion in brand experience that engages the senses and the brain in ways that provide novelty through mindful integration of technology into built environments.

Merchandising and selling approaches – promote interaction with real and virtual displays that are innovative not for their looks but because they change the way to shop a category of products.

Perceptions of value are often not a dollars-and-cents thing, but very much part of our non-tangible emotions and a set of beliefs we have about what the product will do for, or give us. And, in many cases we pay for the esoteric qualities of a product when we line up for a $5 coffee drink or shop for a $5,000 handbag, not necessarily because it's a better cup o' joe or that the handbag magically organizes all our stuff, but because of how we *feel* with the cup in our hand or the bag on our shoulder.

Pablo Picasso put the value equation this way:

"VALUE IS NOT INTRINSIC; IT IS NOT IN THINGS.
IT IS WITHIN US; IT IS THE WAY WHICH MAN REACTS
TO THE CONDITIONS OF HIS ENVIRONMENT."

When we consider that customers' perceptions of value often does not reside in the thing they buy, but in their *feelings* about having one product over another, or receiving good service over poor service – we begin to shift our thinking to better address the needs and wants of virtually all shoppers, not just Millennials.

This aspect of perceived value is very much the providence of the right brain, where consideration of the larger contextual implications of buying one product over another are more profoundly processed. The right brain thinks of a purchase decision in terms of the big picture, how a purchase fits in a larger whole of more subtle relationships between the products we buy and the meanings they hold for us. Whereas, the left-brain will think about what the product *does for us* – utility, the right brain will think about what the product *means to us* – emotion.

If we want to get at the emotional centers of Millennials (as well as all other shoppers) we need to give them experiences that connect them to a greater whole, a collective mind set, a shared sense of community.

Since our emotional right-brain loves being in community processing all of the intricacies of the relationships, using the power of social media is a windfall for retailers who can craft content and delivery mechanisms that are relevant and unique to young shoppers.

It won't be enough for retailers to communicate *what* the prices of products are or how many they have in stock. In addition, retailers will have to tell customers *why* buying this or that product, at any price, will be a good reason to engage in spending precious time in the retailer's store, on their website, with their app, etc. When retailers move from selling '*what* they do' to a position of '*why* they do what they do,' they engage the shopper's right brain in processing contextual relationships and generating meaning.

Push-me, Pull-you

While there is a strong collective mindset between Millennials that helps to establish identity by association to the larger group, they also want to be seen as individuals in the shopping aisle. When shopping, they want respect and attention that is appropriate to their individual needs. With their propensity to be adopters of technology as a means of communication, meeting their needs will undoubtedly require brands and retailers to become as facile with the digital world as they are.

A shift in the communication paradigm with Millennials will act as one of the cornerstones to the retail store's longevity as a place to exchange goods and services. Without a fundamental rethinking of how retailers and brands communicate with the emerging culture of digitally enabled shoppers, the relevancy of shopping places, as we know them, is treading on thin ice.

This places the onus on the retailer to provide personalized attention that addresses individual needs in some other way than the traditional sales associate paradigm. In this case there is a huge benefit to creating relationships with 'opt-in,' location-based marketing, directly created for individuals, based on data collection from smartphones tagged to databases of the customer's personal profiles. Within a couple of years there won't be a Millennial without a smartphone – *the* conduit for retailer-shopper communication while shoppers are both in and out of the store.

As customers open themselves to the push of content like new product information and discount coupons, they get what they ask for, when they ask for it. The key feature to the Millennials' acceptance of information being sent their way is that they have opened the door, though not unhooked the chain from the latch. They want to control who comes across the threshold.

This is not too different than the expectations of other consumers who have legitimate security concerns. It seems that Millennials, though, are generally less concerned about the operators of a retailer's rewards program being loose with their personal information. Only 14% of Millennials (versus 20% of older shoppers) voice concerns about who knows what about them.[144] It could be that the younger shopper generation is simply more used to sharing information online since they have grown up aware of the trade for access paradigm; they get the *quid pro quo*.

'Opting-in' to loyalty programs implies an acceptance that customers also have content pushed their way even when they might not have specifically asked for something to be sent to them in the moment. Opting-in is the authorization to an open-door policy that allows retailers and brands to craft messaging that is sometimes entirely unexpected, but assumed to be welcomed by the customer nevertheless.

Easy access to any product stokes the fires of instant gratification. Being able to have *promotional offers* immediately *in situ*, rather than downloading them at home and needing to go to the store to redeem them, will become an *expectation*.

Real-time promotions that come to shoppers' digtial devices while they are standing in the aisle are a play directly to the brain's love of novelty and are very much like the spinning wheels of a slot machine. Getting an unexpected reward offer while in the shopping aisle (assuming having opted in to the retailer's program) is something the shopper's brain loves.

More than the predictable reward of the store's dependable merchandise assortment or everyday low prices, a push notification for 20% off the outfit you are standing in front of right now because you are a loyal shopper is something that gets the dopamine rushing in the pleasure center three to four times more than a typical shopping trip. Millennial or member of an older generation, we all love the rush of a good deal, especially when we don't expect it.

Assuming retailers can parse the data quickly enough to have individually relevant offers ready to fly through cyberspace to the shopper's smartphone, there is still the sensitivity of the retailer being perceived as overstepping boundaries and being invasive. There is a fine line between connecting with value offers that satisfy customers' rewards-based needs, and their feeling that an intrusive retailer is watching their every move. This delicate marketing *pas de deux* must be mindfully danced by large corporate brands that may be mistrusted by Millennials anyway.

TMI OMG ;)! – Information Sharing and the Relationship

When looking to increase relationship value in the minds of Millennials, we need to continue to look for differentiating elements to their mindsets from other generations.

Connection to the wealth of information on the Internet and their reliance on social networks to vet brands/retailers and the products they sell arms these young shoppers with information establishing a point of view that makes them more discerning in the shopping aisle. With a laptop or smartphone in hand, they have become used to accessing a broad array of product and price options, and have clear expectations of getting quality and value from both the relationships they engage in and the products and services they buy.

Information is a defining feature of the evolving customer-retailer relationship. With the exchange of more information between the customer and brand/retailer, trust and loyalty grow with the implicit understanding that transparency and authenticity are important drivers in the exchange. One of the key challenges in this new communication paradigm is to be able to cut through the digital chatter and provide value to the individual shopper in a personal, focused and relevant way.

Smartphone adoption among Millennials is less a techno-trend than a fact of contemporary living. Connection to the flow of content available through the Internet is shifting cultural behaviors as well as building trust and loyalty based on access to information and transparency. It might have been in the past that the retailer held all the cards and older generations took pricing structures at face value, but not anymore. Millennials are quick-to-the-draw with the phone at their hip to price-check and comparison shop on the spot.

Whereas older generations might have trusted their gut more when making buying decisions, Millennials determine the veracity of a retailer's pricing claims and adherence to the brand's ideology by social network consensus. In fact, they think nothing of snapping a photo of a product in the store to post to their social media network or send a text message as part of their decision making process. Embracing this ritual can help a retailer connect with a customer's mindset and build affinity as well as sales.

'Power to the people' in Millennial-speak means that retailers or brands may live another day with a thumbs up 'like' or suffer the castigation of a network of tens of thousands of individuals if they misuse the privilege of the customer-retailer relationship.

While one might be lead to believe that Millennials are somewhat cavalier with the exchange of personal information, freely sharing pictures of themselves and details of their social lives on the Internet through their social networks, they are likely to be more circumspect when giving away personal details to corporations who want to use it for marketing to them. It turns out that "U.S. Millennials identify rewards and incentives, data security, and ethical use of data as their top requirements for brands that wish to collect and use customer data for marketing."[145]

That said, Millennials are more willing than older generations to offer up personal details as long as they feel the information is not going anywhere else, *and* if they feel that in giving it away there is something in it for them.

Providing personal information is part of the exchange for the Millennial shopper. In a seemingly paradoxical bit of thinking, they are at once concerned about the abuse of their personal information (albeit less concerned than older generations) while, at the same time, collectively accepting of the practice of divulging personal information when opting in. They are more willing than older shoppers to share personal information with brands and retailers who will give them rewards in the form of promotional offers such as price discounts.

Half of Millennials, versus 37% of other generations, will offer up personal information to join a reward program and more than a third (36%) of them will fill in the blank boxes on a website registration page versus just 22% of older generations.[146] The Millennial mindset is, 'I give you information about me and you give me rewards, incentives, and promotional offers.' Level of commitment is based on a 'what's in it for me' point of view. Furthermore, the Millennial expects the reward quickly. Reduced attention spans are making instant gratification an expectation in the new retail economy.

In the Millennial generation, personal information is part of the currency that drives the value equation. They know that whatever they want is going to have some price. If part of the price tag is an exchange of data that includes personal preferences, then they are more willing to play the game than previous generations, as long as the brand or retailer delivers on their end of the deal. If the retailer/brand is sloppy in minding the information that is given them, Millennials are quick to shut down the relationship.

The (Anti-)Social Network - 140 Characters, Emoticons

In the *Forbes* youngest billionaires survey of 2013, five of the world's richest young adults were Millennials. Among them, they have a combined worth of $25.9 billion. Three of these five were students who from a dorm room at Harvard, developed a new way for people to create personal web profiles, join together in social groups and communicate about their lives. Thanks to Mark Zuckerberg (30 years old, worth $13.3 billion), Eduardo Saverin (30 years old, worth $2.2 billion), and Dustin Moskovitz (28 years old, worth $3.8 billion), the world of interpersonal communication has Facebook, and 1.5 billion people have added their personal profiles to the world of social media networks.

By founding Facebook, these (now) thirty-something's have re-shaped the future of interpersonal communication. Their 'invention' consistently ranks among the main activities that most Millennials, Gen X'ers, Boomers and even some of the Silent Generation participate in every day.

Today, Facebook is the social networking leader. As of April 2014:
- Facebook had 1.28 billion users with 128 Million daily active users in the U.S.
- Over 66% of Millennials have a Facebook account.
- A teenager has an average of 300 'friends' on Facebook.
- Facebook users share 48% of all selfies shared on social media sites.
- Facebook 'Like' or 'Share' buttons are viewed 22 billion times every day. The average daily number of 'Likes' is 4.5 billion.

- Over 350 million photos are uploaded to Facebook every day.
- Every time users log on to Facebook, they are potentially exposed to 1500 pieces of content. [147]

A significant proportion of these connections is binding individuals in the Millennial generation together in both the virtual and physical social network. [148] Every day when the sun rises, 50% of Millennials roll over and turn to Facebook to say good morning. [149]

The rise and influence of the social network should not come as a surprise to any of us. The fact that it has grown to connect billions of users is a testament to our evolutionary drive to be in relationship. It satisfies the very core yearning we all share – the need to connect with others in meaningful relationship and establish a sense of group belonging, from which we derive context and meaning about what it means "To be" in the world.

Social media sources, such as Facebook, drive content to our computers in pieces, 'friend(ly)' morsels, and along with them we are exposed to a trail of other posts. The right brain is in its element when it sees the big view of where a single post fits into a larger conversation. The right brain, being all about context, thrives on understanding the big picture. More than the left side of our cerebral cortex, it is focused on drawing together a broad view of the world, seeing it holistically. It isn't so much interested in the individual pieces that make up the whole of experience but the overall feeling borne of our assembling a larger worldview.

Pinterest and other image-based platforms such as Instagram are perfect for right brain processing because they display groups of images as collections of 'picture feelings' that have narrative and subtext. These are things for which the left brain's linear, sequential, assemblage-of-parts understanding of the world is ill equipped. The left brain doesn't get the narrative, story, subtext and inferences that are the subject of much of what passes between enabled devices on the social network superhighway.

The value of the social network for sharing images cannot be understated. Our brains love pictures and our emotional intuitive right brain is a master at dealing with all that is implied in them. Social media users that share images are both the creators of new content and the curators of content that already exists. In either case, they are assembling picture stories and relying on a long, evolutionary history of humans explaining their world in images.

The right brain loves stories and the weaving of complicated narratives with multiple players. In the woven world of nodes and ties of the social media network, the sinews that draw each of the individuals together are the stories they tell. The wonder of the stories that emerge across the net of connections is that they are in a state of dynamic change. They are created when they are first told, but as they spread, they are modified through re-telling as comments are added from individuals far and wide. The ties of the social network resonate with the chatter of novel, dynamic, captivating and emergent stories for our right brain. Pictures deepen the message.

Images and video are a key social currency online. Nearly half (46%) of adults online create and post pictures and videos. Also, 41% of adults online assemble images or videos that they have found on the Internet and *re*-post them.[150] When it comes to Millennials, an overwhelming number immerse themselves in the ritual of posting images. In general, the younger generation is the creator of its own content. More than two-thirds (67%) say that they have posted images and 33% say they have posted personally taken videos to websites.[151] In total, 69% of Millennials have shared pictures or videos they have taken themselves. If they are not sharing content they have created themselves, Millennials are sharing content created by others.

The emerging generation of shoppers is one of content creators and curators.

Young adults are big users of image-sharing sites. Pinterest, while dominated by women overall, has more users who are Millennials (16%) than older age groups. The smartphone app Instagram is used by Millennials three times (27%) more than Boomers (8%). In fact, far more Millennials use Instagram than the sum of all people over the age of 30, with the percentage of Internet users between the ages of 30-65+ equaling 18%.

Facebook has been a social network leader since shortly after the medium was invented. As Facebook has grown, so too has the influence of images as a way to tell a story on the Internet. It's not surprising that, seeing this trend and noticing Instagram's position in the thick of it, Facebook decided to snatch them up for a cool billion dollars. Instagram continues to grow in popularity, allowing account holders to post visual content as a principal form of communication. As of March 2014:

- Total number of monthly active Instagram users is 200 million.
- Year over year growth for Instagram mobile is 66%.
- Total number of photos shared is 20 billion.
- 60 million photos are posted every day.
- Every second, 8500 photos are 'liked.'
- Every second, 1000 comments are made on posted photos.[152]

Sites such as Instagram and Pinterest have become so popular as a way to share visual stories online that retail stores are adopting a store-design strategy that mimics the scrap-book-like pages that users create of their favorite things.

As our digital culture moves to more image-based social networking platforms, retailers are rushing to fill the holes in their marketing platforms and connect to customers. Many retailers and brands are working to figure out just how to leverage this powerful tool.

Whole Foods Market has been an early adopter and one of the fastest growing brands on Pinterest since launching an account in 2011. As of May 2014, Whole

Foods has increased its activity on Pinterest with pins on 59 boards (up from 22 in 2011, a 37% increase), 3,513 pins (up from 700 in 2011, 20% increase), and now has 187,748 followers (up from 14,421 in 2011, a 7.68% increase).

For the marketing director of Whole Foods Market, Michael Bepko, the push to 'pin' is pretty simple, "It allows us to curate images from across the web that really speak to who we are as a company, images that reflect our core values and essentially communicate the essence of who we are."[153]

The sharing of a set of carefully curated and impactful images on Pinterest amounts to creating a digital inspiration board. As such, it expresses shared interests between individuals and the brands they love. It becomes a place where customers can express their emotions and more importantly their *aspirations*.

Curiously though, on the 59 boards that Whole Foods Market actively uses to pin content, you'll hardly find any of their product. Instead their marketing team scours the social-network sphere, reading other writers, searching for images and content that support the brand's point of view of itself. "Pinterest allows us to share the images that move us," says Bepko.[154] Presumably, as the brand gets enthusiastic about the images that express what is true to its core values, customers, who have adopted it as a place they love to shop, will get excited, too. For Whole Foods Market, using social media is about being relevant to the community of followers on the social-media site. For them, relevancy is born out of using this digital medium to create emotional connections around things that they and their customers have common interests in.

While some retailers and brands, such as Whole Foods Market, understand that the key to the game is relationship, many of the relationships that social-media-using customers create with brands are often more transactional than they are personal. They 'friend' or 'like' a retailer or brand as part of a trade-off. This kind of connection, which is fueled by the *quid pro quo* paradigm, is short lived. When retailers and brands move *beyond* using the social network to facilitate transactions – providing a promotional coupon and finding a way to solicit a thumbs up 'like' for some post – the relationship moves to another level, one in which the retailer or brand has become a more meaningful part of the customer's life.

The brilliance of the social network lies in its ability to draw us together in worldwide communities of likeminded individuals who opt-in to relationships that support their *raison d'être*. While the 65+ age group is catching on with increasing use, social network sites are the lifeblood of a generation that prefers expediency in communicating in the same way that they expect things to happen quickly in almost every other aspect of their lives. Going slowly *and* truly being present, in the moment, is a challenge for younger generations since their early, or even earliest life experiences, have shaped their brains to expect fast as the new normal.

So retailers find themselves running to try to catch up when instead they should be running, like a good wide receiver, to the place where the football *will* be thrown to. The wide receiver's path down the field plots a course through the opposition, but with the clear intention of getting to the spot where the ball *will be*, such that the receiver catches the football in an open-field sprint towards the end zone.

Creating a strategy to embrace the future of retail shoppers requires a deep dive into what are now emerging as drivers behind the buying motivations of young shoppers, including a better understanding of brain science and what activates the emotional brain, an awareness of emerging technologies and how to seamlessly integrate them into the path to purchase, and an appreciation of the power of social media as a tool for connection, not just communication. To be ahead, retailers and brands need to *think ahead* – beyond the three-year cycle of their store concepts – putting into place, *now*, the strategies to solve for *future problems* they don't yet know exist.

The key is not to think just about what all this new-fangled technology and communication paradigms *do* and how they do it. This would continue to be a very left-brain approach that simply leads to regurgitation of what we already know. Instead, we need to think in a non-linear way, not about cause and effect but *context and experience* – to think about what it all *means*. Thinking contextually is done with mastery by the right brain. The right brain thinks outside itself, connecting to the other, whereas the left-brain is singularly focused on itself and what it already knows.

It is not so surprising that many businesses lack innovation because, in general terms, business of all kinds have relied on the rational, left-brain world of operational processes and spreadsheets that know nothing beyond themselves. To open up opportunities for creating new places to engage shoppers, we have to step beyond the narrowly focused formality of operational systems and pricing structures, to allow the right brain to engage in broad flights of imagination in a world of possibility.

The data that retailers and brands collect on existing customers and other target markets is geared, presumably, to 'get in the head space' of the shoppers they want to attract. From the retailer or brand point of view, when they shift to seeing future customers holistically as the sum of the demographic data, in-store shopping habits *and* personal online profiles, they will be better able to craft more profoundly engaging experiences. This is a shift in mindset from seeing people as numbers and data points to considering them as individuals who, nevertheless, have an affinity for, or direct association with, some subgroup of the shopping population.

Strategic thinking about capturing new customers, and engaging existing ones, are skills the right brain does well. So, retail design, merchandising and marketing strategy sessions might consider putting the spreadsheet aside, temporarily, and allow for tangential creative discussions to develop that promote consideration of what the customer *feels*, not just *thinks*. Retailers and brands have got to 'know them' as more than an outgrowth of their demographic data.

How do retailers do this?

They practice empathic extension.

Simply put, they put themselves in the position of the shopper.

They imagine experiences through the customer's brain. When they do, they make better-informed decisions about how to cater to their customer's needs, whether they are connecting to them on the street or in the mall, on their smartphones or tablets.

Chatter That Matters – Communicating with a Millennial

Store designers and retailers alike, who are able to connect to the younger generations of shoppers, are learning TSL – "Twext-as-a-Second-Language."

Texting and tweeting are looking more and more like how new shoppers will engage with each other and the brands they love. Millennials 'out-text' every other demographic in the U.S. On an average, they send and receive about 67 texts a day (1,831 texts a month). This is almost double the amount sent and received by even the most avid texters of the older, Gen X group. [155]

Email is not going away, but Millennials prefer texts and tweets for quick blasts of easily digestible messages. Recently, a growing number of young consumers are using Twitter where the efficiency of communication is further reduced, as we all know, to sending messages with a maximum of 140 characters.

By February 2012, nearly one-third of the individuals between the ages of 18-29 who were connected to the Internet used Twitter, up from 18% in May of 2011 and 16% in late 2010. [156]

What many adults see as an evolving, truncated communication method may continue fundamentally, and maybe irrevocably, to change both the way the generation after the Millennials communicate with each other as well as re-wiring their young and impressionable cerebral cortices.

Should this change in written language be a concern? Not really, says linguist John McWhorter, who in his TED Talk, describes texting as a natural evolution in the use of language, like the emergence of a new dialect. [157] In fact, we shouldn't think of texting in the same way as other forms of writing at all. If we do, we fall into the possibility of disregarding texting as a stripped-down form of writing that demonstrates a degradation of the skill that we have for a long time regarded as one of the defining abilities that makes us human.

Along the evolutionary path, written language as a way of communicating has come only recently to humans. Pictures, dance, song, and gestures preceded spoken language, which may have been in use for as many as a hundred thousand years before writing entered the communication scene. Written language has transformed over the years. No one spoke quite like Shakespeare wrote, not so much back in Elizabethan England and certainly not these days. Language morphs, across time and across cultures, and spoken language's extension in the writing of words changes as well.

In a way, texting is closer to the speed and tempo of spoken language than the way we have typically have written our thoughts. McWhorter explains that linguists have shown that when speaking, we typically express ideas in word groups of 7-10 words. In this regard, texting is very similar to speaking in that it occurs in short packets of 'words.' Instead of writing out long speeches with complex formal language structures, as might have been done in the past, thumbs flying across the digital keyboard on the smartphone are creating a new type of language. "What texting is, despite the fact that it involves the brute mechanics of something we call writing, is fingered speech...now we can write the way we talk."[158]

So, with this in mind, we need to see texting less as 'writing gone wrong' and more as the emergence of a new form of language. In this regard it is a wonder in the making. With texting, we are seeing the development of a new language whose adoption is akin to bilingualism In fact, texting can be seen as a huge asset since studies have shown that bilingualism has cognitive benefits.

Recent studies on the benefits of being bilingual highlight that as bilingual individuals use one language, the other is active at the same time.[159] Hearing parts of words as they are spoken activates the brain's system to guess at a whole host of other possible matches to the initial sound before the word has been finished. Your brain is working in double time as it processes in both languages since "auditory input activates corresponding words regardless of the language to which they belong."[160]

Being bilingual (or multilingual as in the case of my wife's grandmother who could speak six languages) is great for the brain and staves off cognitive decline. It is not only great exercise for 'ye olde' neural network, but has also been associated with better memory, visual-spatial skills and even helping us be more creative.[161]

Older generations might not like the truncated form of communication that Millennials are increasingly using, but that may have a lot to do with a generational bias towards how we learned to communicate. As individuals text, they don't forget the 'other' language; it is being activated, causing the brain to light up in all sorts of ways, including those seldom-used creative centers that could use a little exercise, by forming small, new words to represent big, old ideas.

From the point of view of customer engagement, texting is becoming increasingly important as the new language. Texts will continue to facilitate communication between retailers/brands and the customer. Messages that distribute promotional offers and new arrival announcements are best suited to the format of the smaller smartphone screen, and can arrive in text form while shoppers are in the aisle or anywhere else.

We'll have to wait and see whether texting replaces written language as we know it, or influences spoken language, creating new words, changing syntax, and influencing grammar, or will simply get adopted into the way we speak as a dialect.

In either case, @TEOTD we might A2D about txtg & its fx.

B4YKI we'll be BFFs LOL sayin BTDT growin our brain

OMG LOL

OAO;)!

(Translation: *At the end of the day we might agree to disagree about texting and its effects. Before you know it we'll be best friends forever, laughing out loud, saying 'been there done that, growing our brain.' Oh my God. Laugh out loud. Over and out!*)

Millennials Like Going to the Store

Everyone likes a good deal.

The growth of online auction sites such as eBay and travel sites such as Priceline are testament to the pursuit of value at a cost the customer helps to curate. These online companies give the customer an opportunity to name their own price for the rice cooker they want or the airline ticket to Tahiti. In either case, bids can start at a penny.

Millennials are no different than other generations in welcoming the lowest prices possible and they are wide adopters of online shopping, looking for both deep discounts and convenience. It may, therefore, be fairly common that this young group of consumers spends up to one hour a day checking out online retail sites with 45% of them surfing the web for digital shopping deals. Somewhat more surprising, *Millennial men report shopping online more than women*, with 20% of them compared to 13% of their female counterparts spending more than two hours a day shopping online.[162]

Why? Because there is a lack of compelling brand stories and in-store experiences that cater to the sensibilities of men of all ages. In addition, men have a general propensity to embrace technology more than women and find the online experience more appealing. Men gravitate to expediency when shopping. The online experience is in this sense a good fit for Millennial males, whose options are few when looking for in-store experiences that authentically cater to their needs.

While a couple of hours a day of shopping online may seem like a lot of time, it blends into the Millennials' total daily screen time as part of their general online activities. They can be writing a Facebook post, texting a friend, looking at a YouTube video and finishing up schoolwork, all while perusing a retail website and buying shoes. In their connected world, multitasking with digital media is an evolved skill. Shopping can, and often does, get folded into the big picture of online experience. When you consider that for Millennials, shopping is simply part of their daily entertainment, two or more hours can go by pretty quickly.

Young shoppers enjoy easy access and instant gratification, and the world of online shopping offers both. Looking for a good deal, they are more likely to engage in online shopping activities than older shoppers and they frequently include online auction sites among the places they go on the Internet. In fact, according to one study, 40% of Millennial males and 33% of females reported that they would ideally buy *everything* online rather that ever going to the store.[163]

While this statistic may seem alarming, what it also highlights is that the larger proportion of Millennials (60% of males and 67% of women) still *like* going to the store. The idea that they are *all* about the Internet is, for the time being, a myth.

This, of course, would be welcome news to retailers, but it shouldn't keep them from getting onboard with an overhaul of how they do 'business as usual.' Retailers must continue to find ways to make the in-store and the online experience equally as interesting and engaging. As far as experience goes, the online world has a way to go to provide the visceral type of full-bodied experience that the real-world store does. This won't take too long as emerging technologies are getting closer every day to delivering emotionally engaging online experiences that light up areas of the shoppers' brain as if they were actually participating in in-store shopping.

As online shopping experiences evolve, they will have to move beyond obvious perks, such as keeping the process simple, no shipping costs, easy returns and peer reviews. If shopping is a social event built on relationships between participants, then jumpstarting the process by using social media, texts, blogs, and live (video) chat, is a step in the right direction towards building relationships, especially with younger shoppers for whom digital communication is the norm. However, all of these leave out a significant aspect of how we have all evolved a profound need to be in physical relationships, face-to-face, with each other. Until the online shopping world evolves into holographic environments with somatosensory qualities that make shoppers feel as though they are 'there,' physical brick-and-mortar stores will host the most profound expression of the customer-shopping experience.

And so, of course Millennials like to go to the store. It delivers more profound sensory experiences that engage their bodies as well as their young, novel, experience-seeking minds.

It is part of the Millennial mindset to associate shopping with socializing and feeling good. This is as it should be; partly because of the historical nature of shopping as a social paradigm, partly because they are more connected to the social sphere than any other generation, but also because shopping's social quality can be seen as an extension of every part of their day.

When in-store shopping is combined with other leisure activities, it becomes more attractive. Mixed-use developments that combine shopping, work and other social activities, such as dining out, are increasingly preferable to these young adults as places to live. [164]

In contrast to the older generations who kept work and family generally in separate buckets, the boundaries between work life and social life blur for the Millennial. Fielding texts or updating Facebook is something that older generations typically find out of place at their desk in the office or in a restaurant.

As we have seen, Millennials share a lot about themselves through their online social networks and they are more prone to do so than older generations. Sharing is part of the way they connect both in between visits to the store *and* while in the shopping aisle. It is natural for them to reach out and text a friend whenever they feel the urge.

Sharing is both a social activity as well as a broadcasting of where they are at a point in time and, therefore, a determinant of association to a group. There is a subtext of sharing with friends, including where you are and what you are doing, placing you in a context that projects an image of belonging. If I am posting on a social networking site or texting selfies from some place, it says a lot about who I am, whom I hang out with and what my interests and affiliations are and what brands I love.

The 'shareability' of the in-store experience is a key factor for engagement with a retailer. Despite the access to e-commerce sites, Millennials *like being in the store* and they like it even more when they can share it with friends. While they may be shopping in the store with a BFF, they are also very likely to be extending their perception of the experience to multiple connections beyond the walls of the mall.

This of course means savvy management of the social network by the retailer or brand. It's a big effort to be continually out in front of the chatter, grabbing attention and creating interesting content. It does, however, pay off if the company providing experience is able to insert itself into the flow of the dialogue.

For example, I recently stayed at a boutique hotel in New York well known for its trendy design, atmosphere with uber-cool status and…tiny rooms. While checking out, I posted a photo of the entryway and tweeted:

"Welcome to the xyz Hotel NYC.

Ok, the rooms are the size of a match box, but it's still cool after all these years."

A day later I received a comment on the tweet:

"@DavidKepron very cool David!"

The hotel had mined the Tweetasphere and sent me a tweet back, letting me know that they thought the photo was cool. Now, you might say that a day was too long to respond; that'll change I am sure, but that they cared to get involved in what I had to say was a good move.

Despite the small rooms, I'll be going back.

While we might think of older generations as being more practical, for Millennials, it's about the fun of the game. Millennials enjoy 'fun-with-friends' experiences, more than older shoppers. This is partly because they are still young and partly because they have grown up in a gaming world. They truly are about having a good time, social networking and social shopping.

This is exceptionally good news for retailers who know how to engage them in meaningful social interactions while in (and out of) the store. And, while the method of socializing may be different than on the silk trade route of years past, in the end, it serves the same purpose of connection.

What is important for Millennials is that the experience delivers a sensory rich and fun-filled adventure. If a shopping experience delivers on these qualities, they are likely to get online and share with a wider audience. The immediacy of capturing the moment with their smartphone and putting it out there is a key element of their experience of a place or event.

As attentions spans contract with extended use of digital devices, it is becoming commonplace for Millennials to expect that everything changes – quickly. Watch a teenage girl with her phone as her thumbs move in what is now called 'swipe-texting' – where the fingers never leave the keyboard screen but slide quickly across the projected keyboard. It's not just that the speed with which she 'types' out text messages seems unnatural, but the speed with which she is fielding incoming messages is dizzying. When you can get this amount of content in a moment, it is not surprising that the speed with which they become bored with shopping environments is also increasing.

Retail places need to keep up. Not just with the information that a sales associate must have in his or her hands to attend to the well-informed new customer, but the entire business model needs to alter, providing in-store experience on a schedule that is in keeping with expectations of young shoppers.

Zara did it with apparel.

Whereas many apparel retailers commit a large proportion of their inventory to designs six months in advance, Zara only lines up about 15-25% of a season's fashion line that far out. And, it locks down about 50-60% of the line by the start of the season, which means that they have a lot of opportunity to design on the fly, while looks are coming off the runway during the various fashion shows. If pink floral is the new thing at the latest show, Zara's designers get to work creating merchandise, essentially overnight, that can be manufactured and available in stores in two weeks.

Fast fashion is in keeping with fast everything else. Shoppers like it because the in-store appearance changes frequently, providing novelty for the brain. And, as evidenced by Zara's example, shoppers come back to the store more often – as many as 17 visits per year in Zara's case – when other major brands are trying to capture a handful of shopping trips per customer over the same period.

That Millennials are accustomed to change should be obvious. The history of retail is about change and the success of one retailer over another has often been predicated on who could watch emerging trends and have the perspicacity to see customer needs of tomorrow and fulfill them today. Those retailers who have flourished, crafting innovative solutions to old selling problems, have been those who moved purposefully into the flow of change. They understood the customer's need for novelty and had the vision to focus their point of view not in the present but in the expectations of what the future of shopping (for what they were selling) might hold. It isn't even thinking 'out of the box' that makes some businesses great; it's thinking that there simply is no such thing as a box to begin with.

There is a difference between being in the eddy of the river, spinning around your own center, and throwing yourself into the white water.

IKEA dove in and changed the way we shopped home goods.

Sephora made a splash with a new way to sell cosmetics.

Starbucks "poured itself into it" creating the '3rd place' around the coffee experience.

And Apple went adventure rafting in the whitewater of change, completely redefining the consumer electronics store.

New store formats, such as Story in the Chelsea area of New York, embrace change and the new generation of shoppers by putting the idea of transformation front-row-center as the entire retail strategy. Rachel Shechtman, the founder of Story envisioned the store as a magazine, with a new issue arriving on the newsstands every four to eight weeks. Magazines, like stores, rely on great visuals and compelling stories to engage their readership. This retail concept gives its customers a new visual feast and merchandising story to 'read' by completely redoing the environment. Story doesn't change *some* of the product; it changes *all* of it, along with the entire interior.

It's a business model based on the idea of change that caters to both our right-brain's love of novelty and the Millennial's short attention span and propensity to be quick to boredom.

In Story, the idea that the virtual online world is in a constant state of change is made real as part of the physical, built environment. To be sure, the change-out of the entire assortment, as well as a complete redesign of the store interior every couple of months, is a big exercise. Nevertheless, it is a concept that is perfectly in line with what is happening online.

Perhaps the most significant of the challenges at hand when we consider how to address the needs of the Millennial in the shopping aisle is that there is no longer simply a generation gap based on ideology, life experiences, morals and values. There is in addition to these, a growing chasm in *how the brains of teens and young adults work versus those of the older age groups*. With a growing reliance on digital technology to communicate, younger generations are likely re-wiring their brains and pruning away those neural connections that are responsible for things such as embodied empathic connection.

When we view the communication chasm between teens and adults as something that is not solely based on generational ideologies, but the result of a biological redefinition of our brain structures, we are talking about a "Brain Gap," as Gary Small has suggested – not simply a Generation Gap. [165] If the brains of younger generations are simply unable to process information to allow them to communicate with 'older' brains, there will be a neurophysiological differentiation between the generations' brains resulting in a gap not easily closed. This isn't quite like two species trying to talk to each other, but it does feel like a new branch on the evolutionary tree is beginning to bud. And, it isn't going to take a few million years for the limb to develop either. It is happening in the blink of our evolutionary eye – in the span of a generation.

How do we stop this?

Well, we can't stop the revolution but we can re-frame what is happening. We can change our point of view from seeing a train careening off the tracks to viewing it more like *Chitty-Chitty-Bang-Bang*, a magical car that could fly. The fictitious, vintage racing car that Ian Fleming (better known for his James Bond novels) created as a children's story, avoided traffic altogether by folding up its wheels and simply flying off. When we are better able to appreciate future shoppers and the context within which they are making buying decisions, we are more apt to meet their needs. But it means getting out in front of what we know and thinking about what we'll likely need in the future.

The Greek philosopher, Heraclitus, was quoted as saying, "the only thing constant is change." Even change has changed over the years with its cycles becoming shorter. We are now in the midst of yet another paradigm shift where the retail platforms we have been accustomed to are being turned on their heads to try to address the demands of a new generation of shoppers.

Millennials are a bridge generation.

They are born of a world without technology in everybody's hand but will usher in a time where shoppers will never have known a moment without it. They are not like their predecessors, and the generations growing up behind them will be interacting in a digital world that may only vaguely resemble the stores of today. That means retailers and brands need to continue to adapt to the dynamic landscape of their customers' lives at whatever speed they unfold in front of them.

In the store design landscape, as well as in our lives, technology can draw us together as part of our evolutionary imperative to be in relationship. It can equally keep us from each other if we only interact through the screen. In the making of relevant and engaging shopping places, digital technology is an extraordinary tool in the retailer's and store designer's toolbox. It's a tool not for its own sake, as we often see today, but in the service of growing and strengthening the retailer-customer connection.

CHAPTER

15

The Shopper's
Mind Extended

Connected World – Connected Brains

Most of us think about the technology we use and our brains as being independent from each other. We don't necessarily see the digital devices in our hands and our brains as part of a connected, functional unit that extends out across the world via the Internet. Brains and bytes are part of a system of interacting, communicating, imagining, creating, and learning that all work together.

Neuroscience's discovery of mirror neurons in humans has led to an understanding that we are wired to 'read' facial expressions and body movement to infer others' intentions. Simply seeing images of other people's faces can trigger neurobiological reactions in our brains that influence the way *we* feel.

It is then hard to deny that the media we are exposed to via our devices also influences our neurobiology and therefore our emotions and connections to others. The more we integrate technology into our ways of communicating with each other, the more our brains become wired to the binary world of digital devices. This cognitive comingling with technology is a dynamic interplay between our brain and the digital world around us.

The relationship between the brain and the natural, built and digitally driven environments is truly collaborative in the making of experience. The world around us shapes the brain and, in turn, the brain shapes the experience of the world.

A key driver in the making of shopping experiences in a digitally driven world is the dynamic nature of this '*give-and-make*' of experience.

Remember, Dr. Dan Siegel's definition of mind was "...*an embodied and relational process that regulates the flow of energy and information.*" The power of digital technology, especially its use through social media, is that it has the intrinsic ability to extend one shopper's mind to a multitude of others, and in doing so, draw collective minds together. While the brain may be embodied in our skull, the influence of the Internet and digital media extends the shopper's mind to the world.

The relational mind thrives when connecting to other individuals. It used to be that we would come to understand ourselves in the context of a larger whole through going to the marketplace to buy the eggs and hear the news of the day. Understanding who we were also came from the sharing of stories with our immediate social groups, family and friends and spiritual leaders.

Today, and more so in the future, the market in the town square has been extended to a global marketplace, and the concept of 'family and friends' has been redefined to include a multitude rather than a handful of close social relationships. As technology has enabled us to connect across a vast geographic and interpersonal landscape, we have moved from close-knit, and embodied groups of like-minded individuals to a multidimensional, digitally connected, cognitive network.

As our communication network has evolved through the use of digital technologies, the one-on-one relationship with a shop owner has been supplanted by digitally mediated social networks of brand loyal customers who connect to each other at the speed of the Internet. The conversation about the store/brand is happening more and more *between customers* than it is between individual customers and the brand. The collective mindset of customers is a powerful force in establishing brand identity. Because customers' minds are connected, the *perception of brand experiences* and the emotional impact of them are shared across the extended cognitive network.

Positive or negative customer impressions are influential in shaping the brand since the *collective* perception of a brand experience has the possibility to make it true. The brand, under the influence of collective customer perception, can become how it is perceived, rather than what it really is. It is therefore imperative that the brand stays in the flow of the *customer conversation as an influential storyteller*, feeding content into the digital flow of energy and information in the shopper's extended cognitive network.

As the integration of technology into our lives continues unabated, we will see the emergence of two seemingly paradoxical tracks with respect to the nature of digital communication and brand experience:

1. On the one hand, we will continue to see the cognitive coalition between loyal adopters of the brand (made possible via the single shopper's mind being extended to the global shopper network) drawing the extended shopper's

network together as a unified whole. This global conglomerate of like-minded brand adopters shares a *collective* energy and emotional connection. As a group they shift and swerve like a school of fish, driven by their collective affinity for the brands they love (or love to hate).

2. On the other hand, the *individual* within the matrix of comingled minds will be increasingly provided with brand experiences that are uniquely crafted to cater to their personal preferences.

Our ability to capture increasingly detailed information about individuals and their buying behaviors is providing retailers and brands with the predictive ability to determine what customers will need and likely buy on their next shopping trip. With the tool of predictive analytics in the hands of brands and retailers, the focus of attention can be the individual shopper rather than massive market segments built on demographic similarities. It is possible that the idea of mass marketing will be replaced by marketing to *individual customers on a massive scale*. Customers may aggregate into groups, where variations between them are slight, but it's more likely that with detailed information about individual shoppers, retailers will want to message specific content to individuals to enhance the relevancy of what it is they are offering.

If we consider retailing as a complex system, the individual parts (of which shoppers are an integral part) influence the creation of emergent properties generated by the system. Disturbances in customer relationships and experience in one part of the system can be sent cascading through the network of digitally connected shoppers, resulting in a mind-storm of negative consequences.

The shared perception of a brand or retailer does not start at a single moment in time when all members of the network simultaneously become sentient. It starts with the individual shopper, who, in turn, reaches out across the digitally enabled global retailing landscape to influence others. Minds connect, emotions are shared, relationships are fostered and loyal customers are born. In a shopping paradigm where customers' minds are connected across a global social network, experiences that don't meet with a shopper's needs or expectations produce a shift in the matrix, creating brand detractors more than return customers.

What customers share is *e-motion (energy in motion)*, not the mere facts of things such as stock counts or price points. And, when customers do share left-brain details of cheap prices or abundant choice, they do it with enthusiasm of how 'great it was that they *got a deal*,' how 'the choice was *amazing*,' or how 'helpful the sales guy was.' In the end, they share the emotional consequence of experience, not the dry details. Our communication goal is ultimately about the right brain's search for joy, a sense of belonging and pleasurable experiences.

We will have reached a significant watershed when technology is part of the very fabric of the products we create, sell and buy, and we can manipulate our environment with computers automated by our bodies and minds. The effective future of embedded technology will be when it is wearable and eventually part of who we are.

The revolutionary speed with which we are moving to a man-machine merge seems to be on an exponential growth rate towards "The Singularity," the day when humans and computers blend in a seamless integrated whole. While this idea of merging and human capabilities was considered science fiction a few years ago, remarkable developments in technology and neuroscience today allow people who have no use of their limbs to control robotic arms with their *minds* so that they can pick up and drink a cup of coffee and perform other rudimentary tasks. [165-166]

Imagine, you haven't had the use of your arms and legs for years after an accident left you paralyzed. You do, however, have the use of one of the most remarkable 'machines' in the universe, your brain. Electrodes are placed into the motor area of your brain and, through a series of practice trials moving objects on a screen as in a video game, neural activity is recorded. These neural impulses are turned into a series of commands to a robotic arm that can be activated simply by thinking of what your arm and hand would do if you reached out to touch and grasp a cup on a table. The robotic arm reacts to neural signals and responds as if it is an extension of the actual body.

The convergence of digital technologies with the human mind is well underway. That a thought can move a machine is remarkable. Connecting the brain to machines is still not as fluid as we would like, or imagine it could be, because our real-life experience is held in comparison to how we see it as fully realized in movies and TV programs. But, in a short time this will become commonplace.

Even as digital technology abounds, what many retailers have not (yet) quite figured out, is what makes sense when trying to use technology to engage customers in a way that really means something to them. This is not just *what* to put on screens that customers have in front of them, but whether or not the screen itself is distinguishable from the rest of the visual environment.

As customers are exposed to multiple screens in all sorts of formats across their daily journeys, ubiquitous digital exposure makes every touch point blur with the next and as it does so, shoppers experience a decline in the messaging impact due to habituation. It all just looks the same after a while. Relevant messaging – chatter that matters – is the elusive brass ring.

"Technempathy"

As we think about the integration of technology into retail places today, we are more likely to see, in our mind's eye, a sea of screens – in our hands, on the wall, a building, the back of a seat, a bus stop, and so on. There is no question that ubiquitous digital computing will be part of our everyday life, but it won't be simply the digital wallpaper we see today.

The goal of technology integration in the creation of retail places is of course to help sell goods and services. The underlying premise, however, should be that technology is best used when it benefits the relationship between shoppers and retailers or brands.

In the hands of marketers and advertisers, technology is a vehicle for the distribution of creative storytelling. Its format and location enhances brand awareness and inspires shoppers into action, if not just getting them to consider one product over another. With screens everywhere, brand marketers are being forced to create messaging approaches that attract shoppers, hold their focus and activate the shopping journey in inventive ways that remain engaging. Moreover, they are being challenged with the creation of content that does not lose its efficacy as it is translated between increasingly varied distribution channels, form factors and customer touch points.

In the hands of sales associates, technology facilitates the buying process and serves to support the in-store relationship between sellers and buyers. Tablets and handheld scanners are becoming commonplace as a method to do away with the cash-wrap counter, but keep the face-to-face connection between brand ambassador and customer. Huge stock inventories are being replaced by technologies that allow you to be in the store but buy from a warehouse and have it shipped to your home. Don't have a million SKU's on the sales floor? No problem. Go to that touch screen and access the entire inventory, not just of the store you're in, but the entire store chain.

In any scenario, technology works best when serving a relationship.

Having the right marketing message at the right time in the right location is about crafting and delivering a message that triggers positive emotion and desire that initiates or supports the relationship.

Having the best, up-to-date information in the hands of the sales associate is about their having more knowledge than the customer, in order to help educate and demonstrate expertise and grow trust in the relationship.

Having access to wide inventories in easy-to-navigate stores or web-page layouts is about making shopping simple, supporting the overwhelmed, time-starved customer, and playing the role of ally and advocate to build loyalty in the relationship.

Technology can do more than provide digital wallpaper.

Despite the research that suggests that technology is disengaging us from each other and making us less empathic, we have a choice to use it in a way that can bring us together. It can be used to 'show me some love' and enable more meaningful, connected relationships between all aspects of the retail business and customers.

I've been looking for a term that recognizes the seemingly dichotomous points of view about what is often seen as technology's potentially negative influence on culture and its ability to extend the mind and draw people together.

A term that is less about what will *be done* than what will *be necessary*, in the future shopping mall and in our lives.

A term that is the marriage of technology and empathy, the coherent union of left- and right-brain capacities.

The use of technology needs to embrace, be infused with or be in the service of – "Technempathy."

How might we define Technempathy?

"Using the power of technology in the service of empathic extension."

When used in crafting shopping experiences that engage the emotional, empathic, intuitive, creative, relational right brain, technempathy helps to foster meaningful relationships between customers and retailers and the products or services they buy from them.

Right now, technempathy is about harnessing technology to enhance the empathic connection between people. It is an enabler of, or a conduit between, two or more people in a relationship. While the sales associate with the tablet in his hand is, for the most part, directing the conversation on the sales floor, the technology doesn't play any direct role in mediating the relationship. It is a tool and does what it does well – crunches numbers, searches databases and hopefully provides better communication and connection between the parties to a pending transaction.

The tablet isn't 'aware'; it doesn't 'know' anything other than what it has access to in a database. In a way, it is very left-brained in that it knows what it knows, and has no interest in seeking out more than what it is provided with by its programmers. It codifies, systematizes, and is interested in representing semantic structures rather than writing poetry. It is certainly not emotionally connected to anything and it doesn't make inferences or predictions. (At least not yet.)

Emerging technologies will allow Technempathy to develop such that our digital devices will move out of their third-party peripheral position in the making of shopping experiences and place them directly into the flow of our brand experiences and buying processes. Shoppers' technology will 'know' about them because it will follow the digital trail left behind when accessing the world through their devices.

Technempathy will include the act of engaging in customer relations mediated by another individual but enabled by technology. It will also mean that digital devices will themselves be able to 'read' a shopper's emotional need states by employing algorithms that decode facial expressions and a shopper's physiology. The device will then crunch the numbers of our digital backstories and offer up suggestions that are relevant to real-time need states.

The Millennial generation is ushering in a new propensity to share details about themselves to a broad audience. In general, they are more likely to find the sharing of information with others across the global social network less objectionable than the older generations. That said, virtually all age groups are adopting the use of digital technologies and the Internet as a means to get connected and share their lives with each other.

As access to greater amounts of information, services and products continues to grow, the cognitive and emotional loads on individuals will also increase. Shoppers will become increasingly accustomed to sharing both their cognitive and emotional loads with other people in their digital network. They will also look to brands and retailers to keep them from becoming overwhelmed and to help them make the tough decisions in the shopping aisle.

Our relationship with personal technology devices will continue to deepen. What we might perceive now as a disconnect between humans and machines, will eventually fade as our digital devices become part of who we are, both figuratively and literally. Along the way to this man-machine merge, our machines will be 'learning' with us. Computers are a long way from being aware in the conscious sense, but algorithms will continue to parse the details of the digital trails we leave, and they will become better and better at predicting our next moves.

As customers connect to each other and retailers online, they share details of their experience. There is data that captures buying history – the what, how many, how often and at what price parts of the shopping experience. And, there is data that comes from the sharing of emotional content derived from the shopping experience that is shared through blogs, emails, texts and social-media posts. In either case, the exchange is between people, each of whom can read facial expressions as well as the subtext and inferences in the written content of post-shopping blogs, texts or emails. In the sending and receiving of these messages, shoppers 'feel' the experience of the other person, all thanks to our highly attuned emotional right brain.

As this sharing of experience occurs today, the personal computer or handheld device is simply a conduit to connect people. It is external to the person-to-person relationship. As we hold our mobile phone, it really doesn't play any role in understanding the emotional state of a user or participate in crafting experience. While technology enables communication, it isn't an active participant in the relationship between shoppers and the retailer or brand.

Machines, however, will continue to be made 'smarter' and they will be able to learn along with us. Moreover, they will begin to sense our body state – nervous, scared, happy, sad – and help shoppers make buying decisions more effectively. As we continue to operate in a world of overwhelmingly abundant choice, we may increasingly turn to machines to help us make decisions in the shopping aisle.

The ability of a digital device to 'read' your physiological vital signs – heart rate, body temperature, whether or not you are sweating or breathing deeply, and your inner emotional state, is something we are already seeing in some smartphones. Our digital devices will offer suggestions for products you may need or want, or services that might enhance your mood, or rattle the steering wheel to wake you up and suggest a place to pull over and rest. They may also make choosing easier by culling down the assortment by combining your digital shopping history, predetermined personal preferences, and 'awareness' of your mood in the moment.

Moving increasingly to our digital devices to make purchases, we will find ourselves in a shopping world that places computing systems in the role of helping us decide.

The history of our digitally enabled shopping behavior, and the likelihood of making a purchase, will not only be predicted by a shopper's 'click stream – "…the path the a visitor takes through one or more websites," but from a combination of factors. [167] While the 'click history' of online shoppers provides data as to where the shoppers went, what they looked at, for how long, and whether or not they bought anything, it doesn't take into account the emotional state of the shopper.

The ability of the computer device you are using to be able to read your facial expressions, and predict, based on the look on your face, whether or not you are likely to buy something, will be increasingly used in the path to purchase. Technology will begin to *interact with*, not simply *react to,* shopper's need and wants.

Facial recognition systems are gaining traction as a way to understand customer feelings in the shopping aisle. Undoubtedly, some people will find it creepy that a machine can read your facial expressions, get a sense of how you're feeling, and then offer a series of product choices to match your mood. San Diego-based Emotient secured $6 million in venture capital funding in March 2014 to further develop facial recognition software/apps to use in retail applications. [168-169]

Emotient wants to help retailers use its emotion tracking and analysis software to gather more accurate information about how customers are feeling when interacting with merchandise, sales associates and the store in general. The software has been able to detect seven major emotions of those coded by Paul Eckman (joy, sadness, anger, fear, disgust, surprise and contempt). They are also able to determine a customer's overall affect (positive, neutral or negative) as well as more advanced facial expressions such as frustration and confusion.

With studies indicating that the present generation of college graduates is lacking in its ability of empathic extension, this might be a saving grace on the sales floor if the present trend of hiring the retail sales force from among the college age population holds. Can't tell if a customer is getting confused, frustrated and annoyed? Well… we've got an app for that!

This of course extends to any place where a camera can capture a facial expression. So, applications on the go with customers' mobile phones or wearable technologies are a natural fit as well.

In the world of online shopping, where sales associates are physically disengaged from direct customer interaction, the ability of retailers to read the emotional disposition of shoppers helps to maintain a core aspect of customer interaction – empathic connection. Granted this connection will be made between shoppers and a computer, but the basic tenets are the same – reading facial expressions to infer the other's emotional state and then to offer advice, products and/or services that are appropriate to the individual's need states. This can still be considered as a form of empathic extension that customizes the experience to individuals. It is a preemptive sales tactic that creates positive memories and long-term relationships.

Emotions we feel affect brain chemistry, which in turn affect the heart, the nervous system and a host of other physiological processes in our bodies. These changes are evident through our faces in the movement of facial muscles and provide insight into the states of our bodies and minds. If we can read shoppers' facial expressions, there is evidence to suggest that we can likely infer their emotional states and potential buying behaviors.

Nearly a decade ago researchers from Stanford used computer-mounted cameras to record the facial expressions of individuals browsing and buying products online. [170] As shoppers browsed through a series of web pages, their facial movements were recorded and computer algorithms determined correlations between a multitude of facial movements and future buying behavior. With computer algorithms determining emotional states of shoppers through their facial expressions, the researchers found that they were able to predict, at a level far greater than chance, whether the shoppers' browsing session would lead to purchase. In addition, it turned out that the more the shoppers were "highly involved" – meaning the more emotionally involved they were in the buying decision – the greater the accuracy of predicting whether virtual window shopping would lead to a purchase. The more emotional shoppers were about the activity, the more it showed on their faces and the more easily the computer algorithms could predict that they would, or would not, buy.

In addition, the researchers found that "products that invoked amusement in people showed markedly higher prediction rates than for non-humorous items." [171] The study suggests that, while we might try to keep a 'poker face' to hide our true emotions, humor can lead to "a moment of 'leakage' in facial expression where the individual temporarily loses cognitive control of the face and true expressions 'leak' to the surface, thus allowing the face to display his/her genuine thoughts or feelings." [172]

When people are shopping, the likelihood that they will buy or not can often be sensed and predicted through a careful observation of changes in their facial expressions. When customers are encouraged into emotional states (hopefully more positive feelings than negative) or when they are making 'hedonic' buying decisions, their facial actions don't contradict their true emotions, and the ability of predicting their next move becomes easier.

We like to have fun when we are buying. No surprise!

Studies such as these at Stanford provide a window into another one of the potential uses of technology to predict buying behavior. They highlight the coming era of computer-human-interaction where our devices are not external to the process of shopping, but are *integral to determining shopper's emotions* and presenting product and service options that are relevant to how they are feeling while walking the shopping aisles or clicking through a website. When technologies such as facial recognition systems are used more frequently in the shopping journey, we will likely see changes in the crafting of customer experience maps because they will use technology in dynamic, interactive relationships with shoppers.

Augmented Cognition and Adaptive Interfaces

Most of us share the feeling that we don't like being 'sold to.' We don't like the pressure of being made to feel that once we are in store we've got to buy something. We don't like the feeling of the hovering sales associate. It can feel like an invasion of our personal space. Equally, despite retail's long history of the 'pile 'em high and watch 'em fly' attitude to merchandising, we don't really enjoy the process of shopping with a huge amount of choice, and we're less satisfied with the things that we finally buy when we have had to choose from a large selection.

One of the key benefits of having our digital devices 'interact' with us in the shopping aisle is that they will presumably change the nature of the engagement from hardcore selling to suggestive assistance. As our digital devices continue to learn about our buying histories, and algorithms are implemented that help predict buying behavior, we will increasingly see brand experience strategies created that are focused on a customer's individual needs. Marketing and merchandising approaches will move from selling to supporting individual shoppers by simplifying buying decisions in a world of infinite choice.

An important aspect in this migration to a supportive selling approach will be a search for *simplicity*. Engaging shoppers in the buying process, and keeping them from merchandise overload, will increasingly rely on the support of computers to make choosing simple. Instead of increasing the cognitive load by providing yet even more options, we will look to technologies that can cut through the clutter and strip away everything that is unnecessary, unimportant or simply uninteresting.

Augmented cognition is yet another step closer to the blending of man and machine. 'AugCog,' as it is referred to by researchers, is a field of study that is at the intersection of human-computer interaction, psychology, neuroscience and ergonomics that aims to create 'relational' human-computer interaction. The basis of this more dynamic mode of interacting with computers is a human-computer interface that measures the real-time cognitive state of the user. Depending on the cognitive load, emotional arousal and the ability of the user to continue to demonstrate focused attention, the computer interface adjusts itself. It sets priorities and then curates the flow of information and energy being conveyed to the individual using it.

"The technologies developed over the past decade in measuring brain activity and various facets of cognition are serving as the basis for managing the way information is presented to the human operators of complex systems."[173] If the amount of information being directed at users is putting them into a state of cognitive overload, the computer is capable of reducing the flow of content so that individuals can remain effective in a number of tasks.

Big Data is about following the digital trails of shoppers' online buying behaviors. It combines our digital back-story with other variables, such as demographics, to provide suggestions about yet another item to put into the basket. It is a digital archeological dig that unearths history with the intent of providing a suggestive up-sell and/or predicting future buying behaviors.

Augmented cognition, on the other hand, aims at creating adaptive interfaces that change in real-time to meet the needs of users *in the moment*. It captures data in the now, and modulates the interface/environment to best serve individual users and enhance their effectiveness at performing a task.

In the studies performed by DARPA, subjects were "…operators of complex systems..," namely simulated war aircraft in mock battle conditions. While we wouldn't consider shoppers wandering through aisles of merchandise or surfing online shopping sites as being under siege, we can think of them, not as operators *of* a complex system, but operators *within* a complex system.

As I have explained earlier, retailing is a massive complex system. It has multiple constituent parts, each moving in relationship to each other with sometimes unpredictable, emergent properties. If we think about the number of things in the virtual or bricks-and-mortar-shopping environment that customers are being asked to attend to, it is no wonder that their ability to make effective buying decisions is compromised. Granted, they are not being shot out of the sky along with a multi-million dollar aircraft. And as we well know, the consequences of a negative shopping experience can send ripples through the interconnected complex system of digitally enabled customers.

Over the past few years, developments in cognitive science have shed increasing light on how we decide and why we buy one product over another. As we are more immersed in a world of digital distraction, the innovative technologies being developed will transform the human-computer interaction paradigm. Our computers will become sensitive to the capabilities and limitations of the human side of the man-machine relationship and be enlisted to make it easier to shop. Facial recognition systems and adaptive interfaces are already in use in cars. Dashboard-mounted cameras can sense emotional states, levels of fatigue or distraction and play a role in driver safety by implementing vehicle-collision avoidance systems. Systems also keep drivers from backing into other objects by alerting them to their relative proximity to something else with chimes that increase in frequency the closer they get to each other.[174]

When it comes to using facial recognition systems in the shopping aisle, there is the potential to determine, at the onset of the shopping trip, the emotional state of the shopper, and predict buying behavior. Preliminary steps in this direction are being developed that draw together a shopper's social media network, personal profile and 'like' history to provide offers in-store that are specifically target to the individual customer.

Applications such as "Facedeals" are 'check-in' apps whose use is authorized through your Facebook account (though not associated with Facebook).[175] The technology captures facial-image data and provides in-store promotional offers to customers who are registered with the program. Using custom-designed cameras, faces are identified when entering the store and personalized deals can be sent to their smartphones in the moment, anytime while the customer is in the participating retailer's store.

It won't be long before camera technology and decoding algorithms will be able to move beyond simply tagging an image of a shopper's face to a personal profile. Eventually, cameras will capture micro-facial movements and get a sense of how shoppers feel as they cruise through the front door and down the aisle. With the kind of data in hand that determines emotional state, it is not unreasonable to assume that retailers will create environmental digital signage that can be modified to present targeted messages that are more relevant as shoppers scan the environment and the product assortment.

In the near future, shopping places may evolve to change more than signage or offer in-store, real-time promotions to smartphones. As technology is increasingly embedded into our environments, decoding the emotions we express while we shop will become an important factor in the way we interact in our digitally driven culture. As technology interfaces are enabled with the ability to detect emotional states, digitally enhanced environments may morph, changing lighting, colors, environmental graphics, and the merchandise presented to customers. Virtual shopping assistant avatars, created to match personality profiles, may well respond to shopper's needs with personalized/individual attention.

The Shopper Ecology and the "Buyosphere"

For most of the years of my career in the retail-design field, the store – square footage, ceilings, floors, walls, lighting, materials and finishes, product densities, etc. – was the focus of our creative attention. The store was the singular place where customer interaction would unfold. There was no significant online retail experience, and pop-up shops were not in yet vogue. You could shop from a catalogue and on TV via QVC and HSN, but you couldn't buy stuff from the Internet through your cellphone. And, your social network was your immediate family, some friends and a few coworkers. In fact, our view of where we exercised our prowess as retail architects was a very narrow slice of the retailing experience.

In comparison to today's multidimensional network of global experience opportunities, the retailing landscape of twenty years ago was the 'flat' earth that dropped off on the other side of the ocean. People had no idea that we would someday see far beyond the walls and edges of traditional retail places.

Over the past decade, we have gradually seen stores being replaced as the only place of customer–brand/retailer interaction with multidimensional brand/retailer ecologies. These intricate ecosystems include all of the aspects of the brand across multiple channels. Facilitated by technology, all of the aspects of these brand ecologies are in a dynamic relationship that continually moves, adjusting to various inputs.

In the retailing industry today, the great a-ha moment is to realize that the retail experience world no longer exists on a single plane. Customer experience is evolving beyond what the retail industry has been calling 'omni-channel.' There is no edge to the retail world. Instead, we must think of the retail world as more like the brain; it folds back in on itself creating a layered, integrated whole.

If, as I suggested earlier, our brains connect and share experience via the mirror-neuron systems, then, in some manner, all customer brains in a brand's ecology are collectively engaged in understanding and creating the experience of the brand. Any customer in a brand ecology, with the help of digital technologies, may be able to connect to all customers. At the same time, an individual can be both the consumer of the brand's ideologies and products as well their creator. Collective customer perception creates the reality of the brand ecology. Moreover, as social networking ties customers together over the Internet, individuals become brand/retailer promoters, playing an instrumental role in the definition of brand ecology. They help to shape the relationships between customers and the brand, and in doing so, shape the brand presentation across the ecology.

The linear left-brained 'the retail world is flat' mentality is being replaced by an integrated, right-brained system of nuanced relationships between all customers in a brand ecology. Whereas we considered the store as the single touch point for customer experience in the past, in the new paradigm, we now have an intricate web of persons, places and things. The retail world is no longer a two-dimensional landscape, but a three-dimensional, interactive, multi-layered sphere of interdependencies.

Instead of thinking about an omni-channel retail landscape with distinct distribution avenues, we must consider the brand experience to be the function of a new dynamic system that is less linear and more multidimensional. The Buyosphere is truly a complex system. Customers and their brains are complex systems within complex systems.

Individual shoppers incorporate many brands and retailers into their daily lives. In doing so, they reinforce the idea that they, as customers, are parts of interrelated brand ecologies and play a role to influence how a vast network functions. As individual brand ecosystems evolve in the future, they will be designed to help customers focus on where their innate skills and true desires are best used – in the connection of personal, empathic relationships, and participating in the making of experience.

When individual brand ecologies combine through the interrelationships built between networked customers, the Buyosphere is born.

What's the Big Deal with Big Data?

Digital Life-stream

Every time we interact with the digital world to surf the web, post a picture, text a friend, pay a bill or buy a present, we take a step towards digital immortality. Even if we don't live on forever, our digital past-life potentially can. Given that many people don't erase emails, texts, social network posts, buying histories from online stores and other digital interactions, all of this information exists, out there in 'the cloud' someplace. It is searchable and able to be filtered to provide retailers with a wealth of information about their customers.

All the ones and zeros we leave behind are a Hansel-and-Gretel trail of virtual breadcrumbs that are stored, aggregated and likely processed by computer algorithms. The data that is collected and parsed into chunks can be used to illustrate, to those who have access to it, what you like to spend your time on, who your friends are, what restaurant reviews you read last night and practically anything else that was enabled by a device connected to the Internet.

Okay, so not all of this data is supposed to be available to everybody. It was suggested earlier that the fair exchange of information between shoppers and brands/retailers is based on an opt-in mentality and the assumption that once personal information is given away, that it is kept safe from prying eyes who mean to use it for ill-gotten gains. We want this to be the case every time we exchange information about ourselves. Notwithstanding the sharing of information among individuals on a social network, which users give away freely, there is information that is made accessible in the digital world that, while we expect it to be held in safe keeping, nevertheless finds its way into hands of others and is used without our awareness.

Nevertheless, there is an increasing ease with which information is shared among younger Internet users.

The divide between the 'real-life-us' and the one created through our digital life-stream is beginning to close. As technologies are increasingly integrated into our lives, our actions and experiences become an intricate weave of data points that enrobe us.

In the shopping world, digital interactions can be processed with various computer algorithms providing information about what we might like to buy, in addition to the things that we already have in our shopping cart. Computer code crunches the numbers, providing companies and individual shoppers with our digital histories, which are both a reflection of, and used to shape, attitudes, shopping behaviors and our digital identities. As information about our activities and preferences is reflected back to us in the form of advertising, marketing, promotional offers, and products or services, we begin to see ourselves in terms of our reflected digital self. The more we see ourselves in digitally reflected terms, the more we are likely to find our attitudes and behaviors shifting to suit the persona we see in the digital mirror.

You might think that we could keep our digital personas and real-life selves distinct, and that doing so would be a function of our level of awareness of what is 'playacting' in the digital sphere and what is real-life behavior. However, while we may think that we can keep these two identities separate, the reality is that the more we engage in behaviors and thoughts related to our digital activities the more our neural structures are changed, wiring them into our new neural network, making them real. The difference between who you think you are online and who you are in real life becomes less clear. Because neuroplasticity inherently means that our brains adapt and physically change in response to our experiences, keeping the two things separate is more difficult than we might have thought, if not impossible.

So, all of our relationships, whether they are with real people or virtual social networks, help to define us. Who we connect to online through our use of social networking sites, the brands we buy and the retailers we shop, all contribute to our sense of self. Each of these relationships provides context to our lives by our simple association with them.

The context-building nature of shopping places such as the Agora, Ponte Vecchio, or the Mall of America that engaged us in embodied relationships will continue to migrate to the digital context of the Internet and its e-commerce sites and social media networks. As we become increasingly connected to our digital life-streams, the meaning of our lives given to us through the context of where we stand in the big digital picture will not vie for our attention; it will simply be perceived as being more relevant.

As opposed to the real life around us, our digital life-stream can be created to reflect who we 'really are' or some other persona that we 'aspire to be.' In either case, that persona becomes real to us if we choose to experience the world around us through it.

The data generated by us and collected by others as we move through the digital world feeds back into our lives, influencing our relationships with other people, as well as our perceptions of ourselves. The challenges of the Internet and social network communications are in the nature of the 'other-ated' validation that we receive from the continuous feedback loop of being 'favorited,' by 'likes,' 'thumbs-up,' and re-posts of the content that we shared. As our digital personas are validated through content that we provide for others to review and comment upon, the positive (or negative) reinforcement substantiates their relevance to our audience. The long-term viability of who we become online rests less in our own hands than in others upon whom we rely upon for feedback in our digital ecosystem.

Within the context of the relationships that make up individual shopper's ecosystems, the big deal with 'Big Data' is that information from all of our digital activities can be used to help predict buying behavior. Retailers and brands will ask for us to provide information, or mine the data we leave behind in the digital shopping world to learn more about our behaviors. Their virtual archeological digs will unearth 'digital artifactoids' about us that will provide insight into our needs and wants.

If retailers and brands can get a better sense about what you are likely to do in the shopping aisle, they will be better able to craft product offerings and experiences that are more relevant and engaging. This will completely redefine aspects of traditional retailing, such as assortment planning. The data captured on previous shopping trips will point to a set of preferences that can be used to better define what retailers will make available to shoppers the next time they are in the store, or on the company website or mobile app.

In an economy that relies on connection and the fostering of empathic relationships, having one's own curated assortment will be seen as inherently more valuable since it will be perceived as having been assembled uniquely for 'me.' The perception that the brand/retailer took the time to find out about 'my unique needs and wants' will promote a deeper sense of being taken care of – that the retailer is 'looking out for me.' It will validate our need for personal connection and will be a part of how retailers and brands will express empathic extension in our future shopping places.

In an effort to reduce the potential of immense assortments overwhelming customers, retailers are experimenting with new formats that introduce technology as a vital component to becoming better curators and helping customers navigate the store.

Hointer is a Seattle-based company whose aim is to revolutionize the way we buy apparel. The Hointer concept is the brainchild of Nadia Shouraboura who happens to know a bit about technology, delivery systems, and Internet sales. She was employee number ten at Amazon.com and spent more than eight years as Amazon's Technology Vice President of Worldwide Operations, in charge of supply chain and fulfillment. You can bet that during those years she learned a thing or two about getting the right product into the hands of customers efficiently.

Entering Hointer, the first thing that you notice is that the thousands of units of jeans in a typical apparel store are reduced to single pairs of each style, each with its own eTag, a unique QR code. After selecting a style and wash you like from those displayed, you use your mobile phone to scan the eTag, select from a series of size and color options, and press a button on the mobile app which initiates the back-of-house fulfillment system that delivers your jeans to a fitting room nearby.

The jeans arrive in the fitting room through a chute. Those that fit, you keep. Those that don't, you put into another chute and they are returned to the warehouse. Touch-screen technology in the fitting rooms allows the customer to interact with the warehouse or sales associates to deliver different options if the first choices don't work out.

According to Shouraboura, the Hointer system "allows customers to focus on playing with the product, or trying on, or learning about the product instead of doing boring things like lugging it around or digging through piles."[176] Which, of course, is exactly the point when you are introducing technology into retail places. The technology becomes part of the backdrop to a place that engages the customer in play. Technology cannot be an end to itself, but rather it needs to be a vehicle that supports relationship building, engagement and experience making. And this has always been the challenge of purely online shopping experiences. "When you go online, you see a picture, you see a description, you click and you're there. It's very convenient," says Shouraboura. "But it's not memorable. It's not amazing. In store, you can really explore the product. Quite a bit of it will be helped by technology, and quite a bit will be through design and other inventions."[177]

Another great example of how retailers are addressing the specific needs of their customers comes by way of the consumer electronics company, Crutchfield, in their "Discovery Store."[178] In 1974, when Bill Crutchfield founded his company, bankers and suppliers were very skeptical that he could open a mail-order business, selling car stereos to do-it-yourselfers. With vision and tenacity, Crutchfield grew his offering into a successful online retailer of consumer electronics, never knowing that he would one day be inducted into the Consumer Electronics Hall of Fame, taking his place alongside Thomas Edison.

Crutchfield's strong belief in connecting with his customers and using their feedback to craft better experiences has been a hallmark of the Crutchfield company. The Discovery Store is as much an evolution of the Crutchfield business as it is a laboratory for experimentation on how best to sell consumer electronics in the 21st century. Addressing the digital age and all that it portends head-on, Crutchfield has crafted a store that establishes a new paradigm for the selling of consumer electronic products.

At Crutchfield's Discovery Store, there are "intelligent interactive fixtures" that help customers find what they want from an assortment that numbers in the thousands. Except, not all, in fact very little, is actually on the sales floor.

Store fixtures display a careful curation of the best, or most popular, products from each of the categories that Crutchfield carries. Sixty-five touch screen interfaces and interactive technology systems, linked together by more than 20,000 linear feet of cable, allow customers to find out more about the products they like and select from a vast array of options that are housed in the in-store stockroom or a few miles away at their principal distribution center.

As customers approach the intelligent fixtures, motion sensors recognize that a shopper has approached the interactive screen and change it from a branded video loop to content specific about the category. When products are lifted from display platforms, large touchscreens come alive with detailed information and selection options. Customers can search by brand, size, style, price, features, and more – it's as easy as using your phone or tablet.

In the unlikely event that customers have difficulty finding what they need, they can have a discussion with a highly knowledgeable sales associate, or if customers are more self-directed, they can link to customer service agents in a call center in a live video chat. True to Crutchfield's industry reputation for having excellent customer service, sales associates are never too far away with mobile tablets connected to the Internet and inventory system to help find answers.

Both the Hointer Store and the Crutchfield Discovery Store have work to be done to fully realize the potential of supporting the customer while shopping in over-assorted retail places that put the brain into cognitive overload. In these initial efforts, they focus on using technology in ways that dovetail into the digital habits of a new shopper. As they develop, they will need to continue to connect back to the shopper with engaging activities that support our need for environments that enhance a sense of place and other key features of experience such as play and storytelling. Nevertheless, these retailers are vanguards for new thinking about how to engage 21st-century customers in relevant ways.

The ability of retailers and brands to comb through data laid down from previous experiences in our digital life-streams as well as data that comes from technologies such as real-time facial recognition systems will make retailers and brands really good at combining the past and present to craft experiences that matter.

Data will become one of the most valuable currencies in the digitally driven Buyosphere.

Predictive Analytics and the Predictive Power of Dopamine

The crystal ball work that is done with data collected from shopper's digital histories is called 'predictive analytics.' Statistical analysis of our data trails and computer modeling algorithms seek to find patterns in our transactional data to point out potential risks to businesses and offer opportunities to shoppers to make the experience of shopping more enjoyable and relevant.

Because customers will become increasingly at ease with the use of the Internet, their expectations about how experiences, products and services should be delivered will change. Shoppers already understand that as they go to various websites throughout the day, advertising is targeted directly at them and it's consistent from website-to-website. They notice that many of marketing messages presented to them seem to be directed to their individual needs. This, of course, is not coincidence, but rather targeted messaging that is created from analyzing a series of web searches, Internet purchases, and digital communications that customers may have engaged in recently. Gathering digital information and offering opportunities for products or services in real-time will be increasingly important, especially with a generation of shoppers for whom 'now' means right now, in the moment where they are standing in the aisle, at a shelf, trying to decide. Using predictive models to manage the customer relationships in real-time will become the norm.

The idea that our digital histories are held in gigantic databases is like imagining that there are other versions of ourselves – avatars of a sort – digitally constructed, in suspended animation within the digital realm. Except that they are not wholly separate from us; they are intimately connected to us because they mirror, albeit digitally, our experiences.

The cautionary tale in this story is that relying exclusively on 'avatar analytics' will promote manufactured shopping experiences that are good at predicting needs and wants based on transactional history, but not good at providing experience that comes about serendipitously – those chance encounters with people, places and things that we could have never anticipated.

When retailers and brands continue to refine their manipulation of data and use it in the service of manufacturing simplicity in a world of digital distraction, will curated experience be death of novelty? Will everything we do in shopping places be constructed to satisfy our individual needs and wants to the extent that there will no longer be any discovery or fun in the process?

This is the dichotomy in the use of predictive analytics; we will be able to know what individual shoppers are likely to need, want or do, based on their digital life-stream, and provide shopping experiences crafted to their unique needs. But, as retailers make shopping 'perfect' for them, they will run the risk of boring their customers unless they are also creative at introducing moments of discovery and novelty into the experience as well.

Using predictive analytics in creating memorable shopping moments is like Wolfram Schultz's monkey-and-juice study from an earlier chapter. You may recall that after being exposed to a repeated pattern of stimuli, the monkey's brain came to expect/predict the arrival of juice and released dopamine into the brain prior to the actual arrival of the rewarding squirt of juice into its mouth. The monkey's brain learned the pattern and began to predict the reward ahead of time. When the juice didn't arrive as expected, the brain took notice of its prediction error and reduced dopamine production until it began to learn a new pattern, upon which, dopamine production increased. As prediction of the pattern became easier, dopamine production again leveled off. Dopamine reached peak production only when the monkey was experiencing something new.

The same is true of us, and potentially, purely predictive-analytic shopping. In a sense, the brain becomes 'bored' with what it already knows. What it really wants is novelty and new experiences. The challenge with predictive analytics, therefore, is to avoid providing experiences that are, well, predictable.

Using Big Data to get a sense of what the customer may do in the future is great since it helps decision-making in a complex retail environment of abundant choice. On the other hand, relying on it to continually present the shopper with the 'best' set of options in every circumstance runs the risk of creating shopping experiences that verge on the banal.

Because the use of predictive analytics may have weeded out everything that 'doesn't matter,' it is possible that a shopping trip of curated products or services actually makes the experience less interesting. Removing the unexpected, the interruptions in the pattern as it were, is like holding on to the expected pattern of the ring of a bell and delivery of juice in the Schultz study. Unless the predictions of future shopping behavior are comingled with other seemingly tangential opportunities, then removing choice also removes exploration and the novelty our brains are designed to seek out.

If a shopper buys new shoes, the predictive power of computer algorithms may suggest that she should buy new shoelaces, shoe care products, other shoes or even associated products in the fashion accessories category such as handbags. She might expect to see these up-sell options being offered to her. On the other hand, along with those items, the algorithms could suggest a podiatry appointment or foot massage, or a ballroom dancing lesson, or a fancy restaurant, perhaps even a connection to a local running club and jogging routes. These adjacencies are not so predictable, though tangentially connected to the idea of a new shoe purchase, and help to introduce novel selection options.

Understanding Big Data and putting it to relevant use by employing predictive analytics is an extremely powerful tool in the brand or retailer's toolbox. If retailers and brands are to keep in step with shoppers' needs and wants in the future, they will come to rely on parsing Big Data into chunks that make it effective in predicting behavior and providing simplicity in the shopping aisle.

But prediction of buying behavior alone will not be enough.

As our ability to capture even more granular bits of information about customer habits grows, shopping places will have to provide excitement through exploration and novelty. This will require creativity, invention and intuition. In short, the right brain.

Sensors Everywhere – The Sentient Shopping World

The late Mark Weiser, widely considered as the father of ubiquitous computing, wrote an article in 1991 for *Scientific American* magazine titled "The Computer for the 21st Century." In his opening, Weiser provided a vision of integrated technology for the coming century:

"The most profound technologies are those that disappear. They weave themselves into the fabric of everyday life until they are indistinguishable from it."

"Ubiquitous computing is roughly the opposite of virtual reality," Weiser wrote. *"Where virtual reality puts people inside a computer-generated world, ubiquitous computing forces the computer to live out here in the world with people."*

Increasingly, we are moving to the integration of computing in our daily lives in ways that makes it an indispensible part of our interactions with the world around us. Computers are becoming smaller, faster, and able to store information in volumes that are unimaginable. Today we are surrounding ourselves with technology that we interact with directly. More than this, technology is being implanted into objects in our environment that allows them to connect to each other. Sensors are being embedded everywhere, from household appliances, to the vehicles we drive, and the communication devices we use to entertain us. Weiser envisioned the day when technology would find a place not alongside, but integrated with, humans.

Fifteen years ago, Neil Gross proposed an idea in a *Business Week* article, "21 Ideas for the 21st Century." In number 14 on the list, Gross explained that the world would be cloaked in an "electronic skin." He suggested that,

"In the next century, planet earth will don an electronic skin. It will use the Internet as a scaffold to support and transmit its sensations. This skin is already being stitched together. It consists of millions of embedded electronic measuring devices: thermostats, pressure gauges, pollution detectors, cameras, microphones, glucose sensors, EKGs, electroencephalographs. These will probe and monitor cities and endangered species, the atmosphere, our ships, highways and fleets of trucks, our conversations, our bodies...even our dreams." [179]

Thinking back some 25-30 years, the 'top technologies' used by the general public were devices such as fax machines, VCR's (video-cassette recorders) and cellphones the shape (and weight) of a brick. Personal computers were the size of an under-the-counter fridge, with only a fraction of computing power and functionality of a modern smartphone. As we envision the past, we would probably say that these 'high-tech' devices were enormous and cumbersome in comparison to what we take for granted today. What we will be carrying in our pockets a few years from now will make today's slim-profile mobile phones seem clunky and unsophisticated.

A step beyond a few years from now, we will be *wearing* our technology, embedded into the very fabric of our clothing, our glasses or contact lenses, and the human-machine merge will be further on its way.

In the meantime, we are seeing an increase in the number of sensors we have around us that do everything, including telling us our heart rate and calorie burn on a bike ride, our emotional state and that we should do yoga to Zen out, or that we need eggs and milk and that we can order them from FreshDirect from the face of the refrigerator, what the smog rating is in the atmosphere and that living in the valley is unhealthy, how dry it has been lately and then automatically turn on the sprinklers so the lawn doesn't dry out, and so on.

Objects are becoming smart, learning about our interactions with the environment and our personal preferences as we move though the digitally enabled world. Inanimate objects are developing sensing abilities, and they are being hooked up to communicate with each other. Digitally enabled sensing devices are becoming integrated into the larger social network of the Internet. They, like human users, are becoming nodes in a complex web of relationships.

For some time, humans were the sole users of the Internet. Not any more. Sensing devices around us are now sharing information back and forth, uploading and downloading data, making 'little decisions' on their own. Sometime between 2008 and 2009, the number of objects or 'things' connected to the Internet finally outnumbered the number of human users. According to a 2011 Cisco white paper, the "Internet of Things" was born at the point in time when "more things or objects were connected to the Internet than people."[180]

In 2003, the world population was approximately 6.3 billion people. At that time, it is estimated that there were about 500 million devices connected to the Internet. There was fewer than one device per person.

Over the past decade, we have seen extraordinary growth in ownership of smartphones, tablet-PCs, and other personal computing devices. As a result, "the number of devices connected to the Internet was brought to 12.5 billion in 2010 while the world's human population increased to 6.8 billion, making the number of connected devices per person more than 1 (1.84 to be exact) for the first time in history."[181]

In 2005, the "Internet of Things" hit another level when the United Nations' "International Telecommunications Union" (ITU) – a specialized agency for information and communication technologies – published its first report on the topic. In this report, the authors wrote, "A new dimension has been added to the world of information and communication technologies (ICTs): from *anytime*, *any place* connectivity for *anyone*, we will now have connectivity for *anything*. Connections will multiply and create an entirely new dynamic network of networks – an Internet of Things ."

How does the world of the Internet process all of the information being exchanged by millions of machines *and* people? It does so by introducing a beefed-up version of the IP – the communications protocol that provides an identification and location system for all of the computers accessing networks, and the thing that routes digital traffic on the Internet. In 2011, "IPv6" had its public launch and the digital floodgates were opened more than ever before. The new protocol allows for 2^{128} (approximately 34 undecillion or 340,282,366,920,938,463,463,374,607,431, 768,211,456) addresses or, as Steven Leibson put it, "we could assign an IPv6 address to every atom on the surface of the earth, and still have enough addresses left to do another 100+ earths."[182] So, we won't be running out of IP addresses for some time. Which means that more machines and more people will be able to connect to each other a long time into the future.

Looking ahead a few years, Cisco predicts that by 2015, there will be 25 billion devices connected to the Internet and by 2020 that number will grow to 50 billion. This doesn't mean that each human on the planet will be carrying a handful of devices on themselves, but that the number in integrated digital devices in the environment around us will grow substantially.

As more things come online, we can imagine that shoppers again will have to contend with more in their environment when trying to make buying decisions. Increasingly, objects in the daily lives of shoppers that are connected to the Internet will vie for a slice of their of partial attention. Unless, of course, they do what Weiser considered as the best-case scenario – that they simply disappear into the fabric of the environment and are removed from the visual clutter of our already overcrowded shopping places.

Sensors and mini-computing devices in our shopping experiences will become ubiquitous. This transformation is already on its way with Radio Frequency Identification (RFID), Near Field Communication (NFC), security/anti-theft systems, mobile/tablet checkout devices, etc. In-store technologies will be best used when they take on the heavy-lifting of computational process, decision-making from vast assortments, navigating densely packed sales floors and scanning through visually cluttered spaces. Technology will need to be integrated in the service of allowing shoppers to do what they do well: engaging in the community of like-minded shoppers, making relationships, and actively participating in the creation of the experience.

When sensors and integrated digital computing devices are part of the fabric of shopping places, they will be used to promote convenience and the shopability of the environment. In doing so, they will provide increased opportunity for engaging in right-brained connection and the extension of the shopper's mind across the Buyosphere.

Mindful integration of the Internet of Things into shopping places will make environments sentient. Stores will begin to 'think' for and with their human inhabitants. Both customers and technology devices will be co-creators of future shopping experiences. As the shopper's mind extends across the Buyosphere it will engage in relationships that include other shoppers, computing systems and in-store digital technologies as other nodes on the network.

The Buyosphere will continue to evolve into a complex system of systems including the blending of those that are both human and technological. Our ability to continue to gather the wealth of data that is being generated from all of these systems is now just slightly ahead of our ability to effectively analyze the streams of ones and zeros, looking for patterns. Gathering is easy – making sense of it all, not so much.

As we continue to get better at pattern recognition and predicting outcomes of the activities of shoppers across the Buyosphere, retail experiences will undoubtedly become more efficient. The design of shopping places enabled by ubiquitous computing will need to promote the ease of shopping as a counter-balance to digital (and consequently cognitive) overload.

We will continue to get better at using predictive analytics to provide shopping solutions crafted to individual needs and wants. When retail designers don't have to worry about cognitive overload in a world of digital distraction, we will shift customer relationship management to engaging shoppers in creative place making. The doors to innovative shopping places will swing open.

When we talk about sentient shopping places and a 'smarter planet,' we describe a collaborative relationship between what technology can tell us about various systems, how efficient they are, and how this information can support change. We can look to the retail network of systems and find ways to be more supportive of shoppers in the midst of making buying decisions. We can also monitor the nature of the Buyosphere to ensure that the impact on the global ecosystems is being less destructive. Feedback loops of integrated technologies can support customers in the shopping aisle as well as mediating production and delivery systems that drain natural and economic resources as products and services make their way to market.

Amassing data allows us to know more than we have ever known before about shoppers and the intricate interdependent system of systems that is the Buyosphere. As retailers and brands collect information, they are able to generate new insights into what will matter to future shoppers.

Shopper activity will change in a sentient shopping place. New forms of relationships will develop between shoppers and the retailers and brands they incorporate into the network of extended shopping minds.

Nearly a century ago, (in a 1926 *Colliers* magazine interview), Nikola Tesla, the Serbian-American inventor, electrical and mechanical engineer who is best known for his contributions to the design of alternating current (AC) – envisioned the future and predicted:

"WHEN WIRELESS IS PERFECTLY APPLIED, THE WHOLE EARTH WILL BE CONVERTED INTO A HUGE BRAIN, WHICH IN FACT IT IS, ALL THINGS BEING PARTICLES OF A REAL AND RHYTHMIC WHOLE … AND THE INSTRUMENTS THROUGH WHICH WE SHALL BE ABLE TO DO THIS WILL BE AMAZINGLY SIMPLE COMPARED WITH OUR PRESENT TELEPHONE. A MAN WILL BE ABLE TO CARRY ONE IN HIS VEST POCKET."

Prescient thinking.
We are moving well beyond that.

Blurring Boundaries – Digitally Driven Sensory Experiences

CHAPTER 17

Kiosks, Video Walls, QR Codes and the "Holodeck"

When digital technologies first entered the customer-experience journey, they were mostly found as freestanding kiosks and wall-mounted plasma screens. Malls, department and specialty stores, train stations and airports implemented them as a means to animate the shopping trip but they often served as no more than digital way-finding devices. Over the past decade, technology has taken a quantum leap forward, yet store environments lag behind. Screens abound, but they seldom fulfill their promise of augmenting the customer experience journey in a way that is relevant.

As new retail concepts are developed, brands will rely, in the short term, on mobile technologies and the social network to remain relevant and communicate their story. These devices, however, will seem clunky and hopelessly out of date as handheld devices are replaced by other, wearable technology that better integrates The Internet of Things and the extended shopper's mind.

Over the next few years, shoppers will begin to shed the cumbersome cognitive processes of cost comparisons, curating the assortment into segments that are easier to shop, and understanding the details of product specifications. Computer algorithms will be applied to the decision-making process so that retailers and brands can make shopping what it is at its best: a creative, social interaction that promotes emotional relationships and provides enriched experiences that build positive memories about the brand.

Retailers and brands will need to create environments that engage the customer with real-time personalized downloads, augmented reality games in real and virtual space, and immersive experiences at multiple touch points using traditional media, smartphones and smart ubiquitous computing – *all at the same time.*

The implementation of technology in stores today has evolved incrementally, providing mobile checkout as one of the latest modifications of the shopping process. With regard to technology that has shaped the experience of the retail place in terms of its architecture, fewer evolutionary steps have been taken despite the speed with which technology is moving. Today, the in-store kiosks that were often no more than way-finding systems or digital catalogues are fewer. Customers don't need a digital way-finding device. Wall-mounted video monitors, with endless video loops or social media feeds, as a way to connect to the tech-savvy customer base, have become bigger. They now cover entire walls, utilizing several, synchronized screens rather than being displayed singly.

While some of the digital media application on walls in stores is geared towards creating interior store architecture, it often comes as an afterthought rather than a leading design influence that shapes the environment and, therefore, the experience. In many cases, in-store media is not only expensive and a waste of resources, but a misreading of what the customer really responds to.

Technology that is part of the process of shopping, something engaged as part of the experience leading to a purchase, will enlist the shopper's body and mind in creating positive experiences that are part of the personal, brand and cultural fabric. In future stores, today's digital wall paper will be replaced by an interactive digital environment that is relevant because customers will actively participate in its making.

When I was growing up, the original *Star Trek* TV show introduced me to the idea that in the unimaginably vast universe, our little blue ball is but a speck. It would take the "Next Generation" series of the TV show to imagine that the worlds we inhabit could be digitally created in real-time.

When the crew of the Enterprise were cruising the universe and couldn't get off the ship, they really needed something like the "Holodeck." This 3D virtual environment, inspired by New York inventor and holographer, Gene Dolgoff, was a virtual reality wonderland in which *Star Trek: The Next Generation* characters could physically walk through fantastically imaginative, virtually created experiences.

The Holodeck was good science fiction *and* a very real possibility. When it was created over twenty-five years ago, this 3D holographic environment was delightful entertainment and considered something of the distant future. Today, many companies are working on Holodeck-like rooms and technologists believe that machines able to be called "Holodecks" could be only about 10-15 years away. [183]

A key feature of the Holodeck was the ability of the user to determine the nature of the experience. There were programmed environments and those that could be created to match a user's personal preferences. The virtual playground could be operated in two modes: a first-person 'subjective mode,' in which the user actively interacted with the program and its characters; and third-person 'objective mode,' in which the user remained outside the actual running of the program and did not directly interact with it.

Creating an immersive virtual environment by assembling digital images, sounds, smells and motion is underway. With enough computers working simultaneously, we can stitch together a 360-degree video image and fill the environment with directional sound technology, creating a pretty convincing virtual environment without the need for heavy, virtual-reality headsets.

LED technology is now providing designers the ability to create environments of 3D forms on which digital content can be played.[184] No longer are images constrained to flat screens with predetermined sizes and proportions. Digital walls can twist in a spiral, form spheres, and complex 3D objects. Developments in LED technology applications are a step in the direction of creating immersive shopping environments, where digital architecture offers endless possibilities to creating space that morphs either with pre-programmed content or content that can be created by people inhabiting the space.

The Holodeck shopping environment is totally feasible.

Well…almost.

The goal of having 3D objects in the environment that a user can pick up and manipulate (or purchase and remove from the environment) is a far-off goal. With the invention of 3D printing, this may not be as far-fetched as it sounds. Digital content is now being turned into everything from toys, jewelry, weapons, food, and even human organs.

Organs, creepy. Food, yummy!

At the 2014 South by Southwest Interactive conference, Mondelez International, the makers of Oreo cookies, tied together social media and real-time marketing that literally engaged customers on a gut level.

Specially created vending machines used Twitter trends to offer conference attendees "deliciously hyper-personalized and customized snacks based on real-time data collection."[185] "Snackers" could choose from a dozen varieties and the flavors offered were based on what the social media platform told them was trending in the moment. In a master stroke of marketing, the vending machine could print an Oreo cookie in two minutes, "connecting trending moments to the cookie itself."[186] This takes the idea of fast fashion developed by Zara where they move product from runway to the store in two weeks, down to a timeframe of two minutes. Granted, we are only talking about 3D printing a product that measures approximately two inches in diameter, but we have to believe that this is just beginning.

We are not yet at the stage of creating virtual environments that are entirely as user-generated as the Holodeck, nor are we able to 3D print a full product array of various types of merchandise, but we are inching closer and closer. While we can, through gaming, enter other worlds and 'inhabit' alternate realities and even take on alternate personalities, we are still doing so through an interface that sits on your desktop, in your lap or the palm of your hand. Even though these virtual environments are compelling, verge on addictive and can capture your attention for long periods of time, the screen, despite even the highest resolution and size, just isn't the same thing as actually standing *inside* the scene of a game.

Although virtual-reality headsets such as the Oculus Rift are able to provide wearers with compelling virtual environments, people who use them are still tethered to their computers and can't go too far in the virtual environment before the length of cable runs out. As virtual-reality gaming headsets develop, providing immersive stereoscopic 3D rendering, wide fields of view and ultra-low latency head tracking, they will take a huge leap when wireless technology provides unlimited physical movement away from the actual computer.

The brilliance of the Holodeck was that it could be a world of your own creation. And then you occupied it with your mind *and* body. Whether you manufactured a virtual world from your imagination or chose from a preset number of options, you were integrally involved in defining the nature of the experience. The individual established the parameters of the interaction, and, in doing so, it was relevant and engaging.

The Holodeck was not technology in an environment; it *was* the environment.

Today, holographic images are beginning to find their way into retail applications. Some stores have found that activating the storefront – when the store is closed – with digitally created holographic projections, captures customer attention on the street. Realistic holograms of models showing off the latest fashions are an inventive way to engage the window shopper.

At the Empreinte L'Atelier Lingerie flagship store in Paris, the intimate apparel retailer used holographic technology as a seductively surreal promotional campaign to mark the opening of its first concept store. Between May 23 and May 26, 2012, a model appeared after 9 pm each night, animating the window with a fashion show. Models wearing the Empreinte line of fine lingerie paraded in the store window before disappearing in a shower of stars. [187]

Speaking of stars, holograms will also be moving to your smartphone. Remember that scene in *Star Wars* (episode IV: "A New Hope" for you younger folks), where R2D2 delivers the plea for help from Princes Leia to Luke Skywalker as a projected hologram? Well, imagine images like that appearing above your smartphone. Amazon, which had been rumored to have been developing such a device for a number of years, launched a holographic smartphone into the market on June 18, 2014. [188]

There are a plethora of smartphone devices on the market. So, what will set the Amazon "Fire" smartphone apart from its competitors? Well, for starters, you can point it at virtually anything and it will recognize the object and allow you to jump to the Amazon website to buy it. And, it will incorporate glasses-free 3D technology. The phone "employs retina-tracking technology embedded in four front-facing cameras, or sensors, to make some images appear to be 3-D, similar to a hologram." Whether or not customers will really want images and information projected about their phones in 3-D is yet to be determined, though I thought the effect was pretty cool when I saw Princess Leia talking to Luke in the 1977 *Star Wars* movie.

While not truly holographic in the sense that images appear to be floating above the device, the phone's screen provides the illusion of objects and scenes having depth. Soon enough, some company is going to provide consumers with devices that render 3D objects that we can 'touch' and move around, as they appear to float in the air. Interactive holographic projections from your handheld device will move consumers from simply swiping a flat glass screen, to an experience closer to the Holodeck where they can manipulate 3D virtual objects in space. While that technology is developing, the Amazon "Fire" smartphone is nevertheless an indication of things to come and an intriguing step away from two-dimensional representations of our world on flat-screen, handheld devices.

As we become better at collecting data and using it to define in-store experiences, we will find that customers will be able to interact with shopping places in real-time, changing parameters of the spaces they are in. The customizability of in-store shopping experiences will become ever more popular. The ability for customers to create the environments they shop in – laying out the store in a way that is intuitive for them to navigate, playing the music they like, providing shopping assistants (virtual or real) who are created to meet the shopper's personality type, and curating the assortment to the individual shopper's needs – will be possible in future shopping places where technology merges with the customer's imaginative brain.

On our way to totally immersive digitally generated holographic-type shopping environments, we will, of course, have a series of intermediate steps. The defining feature of this shift will be speed of transition. The ability to have Holodeck-like experiences in 10 years will be a move towards a new shopping paradigm.

In 2011, Google started allowing users of their Google Maps application to get off the street and into stores. A new feature of Google Maps called "Business Photos" uses the street view technology for 360-degree views of the interiors of shopping places. The Google Business Photos website explains that, "with Business Photos, your customers can walk around, explore, and interact with your business like never before. Customers will be able to truly experience your business – *just like being there!*"[189] The experience is far from delivering the emotional right-brain connection that comes from truly standing in a store. Nevertheless, it gives customers the opportunity to have high-quality, in-store views that they can navigate in an individualized way.

While this technology is intriguing, it has inherent challenges of using 'still images' to represent a dynamic system. Merchandise *flows* through a store. New arrivals, promotions, visual displays and stock levels all change. While having every piece of merchandise in a perfectly folded stack is a better strategy than disorganization and visual clutter, in the real world, the sales floor is occasionally messy. Sometimes, not being perfect is preferable.

Most of all, people *inhabit* shopping places. They are an integral part of the shopping experience, bringing a level of dynamism to the store. I have never seen a store that is void of people (unless of course it is closed). Technologies such as the Google Business Photo experience belie the reality of shopping places – that they are in a state of constant change, energized and made real by the people who use them. Yet, shoppers in stores do not play a part of the Google Business Photo experience.

For now, Google Business Photos fall short on delivering these critical attributes of shopping in a real environment. A development to this in-store visualization tool may be to introduce augmented reality overlays that call out promotional offers, product information and the ability to pick something off the shelf and rotate it in real time. While using the Google Business Photos software is interesting in that it provides sequential views of the interior space, it doesn't really show what it might be like to shop there on a busy Saturday morning when the place is full of people, chatter and the sound of cash registers ringing.

Today these tools are static and provide a series of interior views that are somewhat predetermined, like a video game where the path of travel of the player you set up allows for a limited number of options. But that's not the way people move through space. From trip to trip, the customer may experience a retailer's store in many different ways, taking a different route through the place each time.

When this technology allows shoppers to use Street View to 'go through the door' of retail businesses as if they were walking main street on a Sunday afternoon, and interact with merchants and merchandise, then technology will be used to connect to shoppers in a relevant way. The technology will evolve from being a 'cool tool' into a usable shopping interface.

Personalized experience and exercising the free will to go where you want in a shopping environment are key features of empowering a customer. This is where virtual-reality and high-resolution, computer-generated imagery come in to play.

We can also now experience virtually constructed malls that shoppers navigate online. Despite the effort that goes into 'building' 3D virtual environments, they are, nevertheless, a poor approximation of the 'real' thing. The question might be asked, why even go to the trouble of building a virtual mall, which looks like something we have already experienced? Furthermore, how can we expect shoppers actually to enjoy the experience of pushing an avatar around on the screen to shop store concepts that they have gone to a hundred times, in the real world?

Are the virtual stores more captivating and fun than the real thing? Unlikely.

Unless significant innovation comes to how they are conceived, the novelty of walking through a virtual mall on a computer will dissipate pretty quickly as the brain's love of novelty is underserved by giving shoppers what they already know.

Virtual shopping malls that try to bring together the best of social networking with online shopping but provide dreary, 3D-shopping environments, lack a true understanding of what drives mall traffic. [190] It may be convenient to browse from your chair at home, but this alone will not allow the virtual mall to survive in the future when we have moved beyond the screen as an interface. Furthermore, retailers who jump on board to have stores in this virtual world, who do not also take an enormous leap beyond what they have in their real stores – in terms of design, assortment and customer experience – will capture neither the magic that virtual environments can provide nor the imagination of their customers.

With the exceptional ability we now have to create lush, 3D worlds, the virtual mall had better deliver what we are increasingly coming to expect from movies such as *Avatar*. To engage a generation of informed, sophisticated and tech-savvy shoppers in a virtual mall requires that retail designers (or in this case, virtual mall developers) cannot simply reproduce, in virtual space, what we already have in the real built environment. Instead, the developers of these places must hire gaming-oriented young graduates from the fields of computer graphics, as well as interior design, architecture, theatre, fashion, neuroscience, digital media production and interactive technologies to imagine worlds of creative possibilities beyond our typical experience.

Virtual malls don't have to live in a world with gravity. Why should they look like they have to?

Big Data gives the creators of shopping places the ability to understand customers' motivations in a more granular way than we have been able to understand in the past. In the future, retailers and brands will get even better at predicting their customers' needs and desires, as well as delivering environments that allow for customization of the assortment *and* the environment in which it is housed.

The Holodeck of shopping experiences may also run in 'subjective' mode in which shoppers create and directly interact with the surroundings. These shopping places of the future will engage shoppers in right brain, imaginative 'making.' They will not be a one-size-fits-all experience, but rather a 'smart' interactive playground that directly addresses our deep need for play, relationship and creating, which are the founding principles of our collective evolutionary past.

QR Codes, Augmented Reality and Avatars

As our relationship with technology evolves, we will find the merge between real and virtual worlds becoming more cemented into our everyday lives. Physical and virtual worlds will blend into a seamless net of physical and digital environments, media creation and online interactions. What is real and what is digitally manufactured will intertwine, influencing our brain's architecture as well as that of the physical environments in which we shop.

Digitally manufactured realities don't have to operate in a world where the rules of physical sciences apply. The inherent challenge in creating user-defined digital environments is that they are capable of becoming 'better than real.' I can't fly, but in my digital world I might be able to possess superhuman abilities that overcome my real-world limitations. Coming back to real life from a journey in virtual space may be a difficult transition for some when they remember that Newton's laws apply in the real world.

As we are able to create 'better than real' digital experiences, customer preferences for those things that extend their brains and push the limits of the laws of nature will be in direct competition with the design of the real world. A digital world can also have the ability to be more emotionally charged because it can expose us to situations that would not occur in our daily lives. It can be exceptionally appealing and even more satisfying when you consider that a virtual experience can allow us to do things that we normally couldn't. Furthermore, they can be crafted to be a perfect fit for the individual shopper, rather than one in which the individual needs to accommodate to a larger cohort. Customer experiences 'made for me' can be very alluring.

This should be seen as a call to action for designers of shopping places as well as the retailers and brands they serve. If an immersive digital shopping experience that is user-created is more captivating than the real in-store experience, then the need for relevant design will be ever more important. We will need to start enhancing our real, physical experiences in order for them to remain compelling and relevant. Otherwise, virtual constructions will prevail as the preferred form of experience, and the embodied world will seem mundane.

Far from being marginalized as part of the store-making process, the retail designer will become increasingly pressured to play a vital role in crafting customer experience that rivals virtual shopping worlds where anything can happen. We can already get products from concept to the shelf in a matter of days, why not environments that are able to change in real-time to adapt to the customer's needs?

Changing physical architecture is complicated and requires heavy machinery.

Changing the 'digitecture' can happen from the device in the palm of a shopper's hand.

If there were ever a time to understand the power of design in engaging the brain and creating captivating shopping places, that time is now and in the unfolding of the next few years.

As Mark Weiser suggested, ubiquitous computing will find computers embedded into our real world as opposed to virtual reality finding us embedded in a virtual environment. In the best-case scenario, we will see not an either/or – real vs. virtual – way of living, but one in which technologies support and augment real living. In a ubiquitous, computing world, displays are located wherever people may need them in the world around us: in tabletops, refrigerator doors, car dashboards, stove tops and shower stalls. Or in shopping places, in hangers, fitting rooms, shopping carts, mobile checkout tablets, security devices, shelf edges, graphic panels and products themselves.

In the short term, we will move to having blended realities, digital/virtual overlays, in our real-life environments. We are doing it now with QR codes and augmented reality applications that allow us to use our mobile devices to peer through the 'looking glass' of the screen in our hand to views of our environment augmented with interactive, digital content.

These are as simple as an in-store shoe display (Nike) or an interface to 'try on' virtual sunglasses (Oakley), or on the side of bus stops to order pizza (Dominos), or on subway stations to shop on your way home from work (Tesco/Homeplus), or catch butterflies for fun and discount coupons at a local fast food restaurant (ibutterfly).

While these applications are novel and engage shoppers in re-thinking how they can access products and services, they still stand outside full-embodied immersion in the experiences. There is no question that the number of print-to-mobile applications is growing for marketing retail brands. However, the smartphone or tablet acts as an interface through which the shopper sees content – at arm's length. Even though visual stimuli are a key component to memorable experiences, as we have suggested throughout previous chapters, fully embodied interaction is more profound.

The world of QR codes is often a 'flat' two-dimensional link to web content. And, as good as these pictograms are as a tool to engage people in locations other than stores, shoppers are collectively more engaged in immersive, 3D worlds.

QR codes on the side of a cereal box or in-store graphic, a shoe display or subway stop are all methods of augmenting the environment. Images are overlaid on what is in front of the observer. These applications are novel and gaining traction as a way to engage shoppers in unique locations. More inventive uses for QR codes have been implemented to make places interact with digital content while moving through built environments. They go beyond simply being a graphic application to being an integral part of the architectural expression of a place.

The Russian pavilion at the 2012 Venice Biennial designed by architect Sergei Tchoban, along with partner Sergei Kuznetsov, used QR codes in the service of place making, both in the real-time and in the virtual-otherworldly senses. [191-192] The floors, walls and ceilings of the Russian pavilion's rooms were tiled with QR codes, creating a textural overlay that filled the space with various levels of light and engaged visitors in actively participating in the making of their experience.

One of the key ideas behind the experience was the sharing of information. Rather than having the exhibit content presented as text on printed or digital panels as one might expect in many other museum-like experiences, in the Russian pavilion it was embedded in the digital content provided by reading the QR codes with iPads. The content lived beyond the space and had to be found by the individual by pointing handheld tablets (with QR code readers) at the wall (or ceiling or floor).

Stories became pieced together by scanning the exhibit space – illuminated QR code to QR code. The big picture was not immediately obvious, but rather uncovered along a path of discovery unique to each person. Since each visitor scanned the room in a different sequence, the story unfolded for each of them in an individualized way.

When visitors to the space walked through the exhibit, they fed their novelty-seeking right brain with continuous opportunities for learning. The architecture was experienced as a creative and collaborative process, made more profound through individual making. While not holographic, the interior of the pavilion shared some similarity with the Holodeck in that it blended digitally driven content and the real world. The spaces created by the Russian pavilion at the 2012 Venice Biennial provided a framework for experience and engaged visitors in making it their own.

QR codes are easily recognizable. It's hard to miss the black and white glyph on a page (and even more difficult when they are part of an entire building). They immediately let the shopper know that there is a component of what they are looking at that is digital and not immediately visible unless accessed with the QR code reader application on their mobile device. Furthermore, QR codes can be used to gather information about viewers that marketing teams can use to foster relationships with existing and future customers. They are easy to create and scan, and will continue to have a place in the making of shopping experiences as retailers and brands offer universal access to products and services.

In the 1890s the development of plate glass rapidly changed the retail landscape. Store windows which had, until then, limited the display of products due to their diminutive size, were being replaced with large plates of glass, allowing unobstructed views into store interiors. 'Window dressing,' as it was known then, was about to take a giant leap forward as both an art form as well as an occupation. The development of plate glass allowed the retail world to engage shoppers with a whole new approach to product presentation and the store window would become the stage.

The art of window dressing was developing rapidly and a salesman from Chittenango, NY, who had a passion for writing and editing, seized upon the idea of creating a trade magazine dedicated to the stories told behind the glass. In 1897, despite some financial hardship, *The Show Window* was published for the very first time, and L. Frank Baum began to hit his stride. Over the next few years, Baum brought the retail industry a trade publication bestowing the virtues of what we now call visual merchandising, as well as the manuscripts for two children's books – *Mother Goose in Prose* and *The Wonderful World of Oz*. Thanks to Baum, the 'wonderful world of window dressing' (not to mention the wonderful world of children's imaginations) has never been the same.

While off to see the Wizard, Baum wrote other stories. One in particular was titled "The Master Key." Penned in 1901, this short story previewed the invention of the Taser, an automatic translation machine, a handheld PDA with Google-like capability including live video streams, and a wireless phone.

The gadgets that Baum conceived in his novel were given to a young boy who inadvertently summons a "Demon of Electricity."

"...THAT YOU MAY JUDGE ALL YOUR FELLOW-CREATURES TRULY, AND KNOW UPON WHOM TO DEPEND, I GIVE YOU THE CHARACTER MARKER. IT CONSISTS OF THIS PAIR OF SPECTACLES. WHILE YOU WEAR THEM EVERY ONE YOU MEET WILL BE MARKED UPON THE FOREHEAD WITH A LETTER INDICATING HIS OR HER CHARACTER. THE GOOD WILL BEAR THE LETTER 'G,' THE EVIL THE LETTER 'E.' THE WISE WILL BE MARKED WITH A 'W' AND THE FOOLISH WITH AN 'F.' THE KIND WILL SHOW A 'K' UPON THEIR FOREHEADS AND THE CRUEL A LETTER 'C.' THUS YOU MAY DETERMINE BY A SINGLE LOOK THE TRUE NATURES OF ALL THOSE YOU ENCOUNTER."

Baum had a prescient understanding of not just future technologies, but of how people's minds connected through the flow of energy and information in the way that neuropsychiatrist, Dan Siegel, suggested decades later in his concept of mind.

"And are these, also, electrical in their construction?" asked the boy, as he took the spectacles.

"CERTAINLY. GOODNESS, WISDOM AND KINDNESS ARE NATURAL FORCES, CREATING CHARACTER. FOR THIS REASON MEN ARE NOT ALWAYS TO BLAME FOR BAD CHARACTER, AS THEY ACQUIRE IT UNCONSCIOUSLY. **ALL CHARACTERS SEND OUT CERTAIN ELECTRICAL VIBRATIONS,** WHICH THESE SPECTACLES CONCENTRATE IN THEIR LENSES AND EXHIBIT TO THE GAZE OF THEIR WEARER, AS I HAVE EXPLAINED."

In 1901, L. Frank Baum's set of glasses called "The Character Marker" were a preview of our later discovery of mirror neurons and the invention of augmented reality glasses.

L. Frank Baum's fascination with retailing and visual display did not wane. He edited *The Show Window* magazine for a number of years and it eventually became one of the retail industry's premier trade publications, *Display World*, and, ultimately, *Visual Merchandising and Store Design*, or *VMSD*. [193]

Increasingly, we are finding augmented reality (AR) applications allowing for the overlay of digital experiences on the real world. Lego has created an AR kiosk called a "Digital Box" that allows shoppers to hold up boxes of products and see the contents animated in 3D. Lego tractors and combine harvesters roll around farm scenes, trucks park in garages, planes fly and Lego firefighters roam the firehouse. [194]

IKEA's 2013 catalogue was full of AR experiences allowing readers to see 3D visualizations of furniture overlaid on either the catalogue page or in the rooms of their homes or simply to access further content beyond the booklet that arrives in their mailbox. [195-196]

In a remarkably fun and cleverly executed application of digital, out-of-home technology, Pepsi created the "Unbelievable Bus Stop," a virtual window into another world. The creative use of digital-screen technology was part of PepsiCo's integrated March 2014 campaign for the UK that brought together Pepsi MAX's "Unbelievable" combination of taste without sugar. With a window set up to provide a live-video feed of the street, a bus stop became a portal to photorealistic animations visible from inside the inside while waiting for public transit to arrive.

When people looked down the street for the approaching bus, high-resolution digital animations gave them fantastic views of enormous robots shooting lasers as they crashed down Oxford Street, Bengal tigers running towards them, and huge alien tongues appearing from a manhole cover to swallow up people on the sidewalk. The digital content was perfectly mapped to the environment and appeared as though it was part of the real-life scene. The effect was so realistic that video captured of waiting passengers showed them getting up from the bench to run from the charging tiger and other things approaching them. [197]

The overlay of digital content is in full swing and inventive applications such as these highlight the coming blend of realities in the shopping places we will experience. The idea that customers can shop both through their mobile devices and in store is being enhanced by the fact that they can now point tablets and smartphones at objects and/or places around them. The surrounding digital overlays are a captivating way to sell.

Many retailers are launching projects with the name 'Store of the Future.' Belk department store CEO Tim Belk launched a new vision of the Belk "Modern Southern Style." In the company video promoting a future view of Belk stores, we get a glimpse of a host of digital, interactive customer experiences, both in and out of the store. [198] Prominently portrayed is the idea of AR in which a customer uses her tablet to view products she wants to purchase for a special dinner. As she raises her tablet to her back yard, the place settings appear on her table. Another customer checks herself out in digitally enabled fitting rooms where a dress she wants to buy is made visible through AR.

In whichever format we are beginning to see more augmented reality applications, what is clear is that we are moving away from strictly interacting with AR content through a single form of interface, the smartphone or tablet, that is held in your hands. We will continue to create blended realities where information in the form of 3D visualizations will be displayed *on* the world around us. Eventually, digital visualizations will shake free of the confines of the screen and will be projected everywhere for shoppers to 'see' through means other than the mobile phone.

Wearing our Tech

Over the next few decades, emerging technologies will completely redefine customer experience. Change is in the genes of retail. It is an expected part of the experience.

Like an old-time steam locomotive, getting up to speed takes some time, but once momentum takes over, it is hard to stop from lumbering down the tracks. Our technology revolution has long since taken us from zero to sixty. We are now moving at breakneck speed in comparison to a hundred years ago, or even five years ago. But this train will not go off the tracks because inventive retailers and brands will forge new rails.

Plate glass reshaped store windows and allowed visual merchandising to perform a leading role in the theater of retailing. Plate glass storefronts transformed retail storytelling as well as shopping habits.

Google Glass will give shoppers a new view on the world, and digitally augmented shopping environments will have more layers of interaction, information and opportunity for creative place making. Wearable technology will revolutionize customer experience by changing the way people see the world, their expectations, and therefore, how they interact with the store as they shop.[199]

More than a century after L. Frank Baum foresaw a wearable technology that allowed for information to be projected on the world, Google has released the first generation of their 'spectacles,' not to a single lucky boy, but to anyone who wants them.

The retail industry is quickly approaching another watershed moment as we begin to wear our technology. If the mobile phone has been the big idea of this half-decade, then wearable tech will dominate the coming years leading to 2020. Wearable technologies will take the supercomputing power of smartphones out of your back pocket and project it on the world in front of you. The boom in mobile technology has usurped the personal computer as a way to connect, and while tablets and smartphones abound today, wearable technologies will eventually make the smartphones we now use seem like something out of the Stone Age.

Developments in smartphone technologies have solved a number of Internet connectivity issues. Companies that aspire to deepen our connection to the wearable tech world will benefit from things that have come as a result of the research and development of cellphone companies (such as Bluetooth). Wearable tech will ride on the coattails of cellphone technology developments and incorporate available technologies, giving this new generation of mobile devices easy connections to the Internet. While wearable devices will serve as the means to project content onto the world, they will pair with the smartphone in your pocket, which will serve as the conduit to the digital world via the Internet.

In an increasingly digital world, wearable technologies reduce the steps to connection. Instead of taking the smartphone out of your pocket, swiping to unlock it, keying in a phone number or web address or launching an app, we will move to voice commands and not lose the precious seconds in which we can capture an image of the moment. Wearable technology will fit well with the search for simplicity in our lives. In addition, it will provide retailers with a huge degree of flexibility in brand messaging and product merchandising, and provide shoppers with a completely new way of 'seeing' the experience.

New technologies like Google Glass are a step toward wearing technology that allows us to translate information, presented as an overlay on real experience, into immediate action.[200]

While Google is not the only company developing wearable technology, Google Glass happens to be the brainchild of the company that created of the largest and most powerful search engine the world uses.[201] The power of a worldwide search engine once only *at your fingertips* is now being placed *on your face*. This will prove to be one of the most important technological advances that interpersonal communications will have ever seen, potentially replacing the use of mobile phones altogether within the next 7 or so years.

Activated by voice controls and small touches of the frame of the glasses, Google Glass places an information overlay on the world you see in front of you. Visual content is beamed to your retina by a small prism that receives content from a tiny projector inside the lens. So, you see both the physical world and all the relevant data that you want associated with it at the same time. With Google Glass, the technology that you would have traditionally used in the form of a personal computer, laptop or mobile phone evaporates and you get all of that imprinted on the visual world in front of you.

Google Glass will take technology out of our pockets and put it on our faces, freeing up our hands and our ability to move more fluidly through the environment. The time between wanting information and having it easily accessible in front of us will come down to a voice command.

This is one of the great promises of wearable tech – a reduction in time between intention and action. With the emergence of the 'now' generation of users, reducing the time lag between 'wanting and having' will be a key driver in the success of delivering positive experiences to future shoppers.

The speed of the Internet and easy access to more information than ever before are accelerating everything and placing a premium on 'fast' when delivering on brand promises. The idea of "without-delay" really means that we want retailers to guess our needs and wants. The most forward-leaning companies will find ways of using mobile devices and high-power predictive computing to know what customers want even before *they* do! Geo-location and predictive analytics will provide what will look like mindreading, and will allow retailers to deliver context-based solutions to their customers' needs and wants as they think about them.

Wearable technology puts information derived from Big Data and predictive analytics into the visual environment of the user in real-time as part of on-going experience. It is summoned either by request or through geo-location applications that are part of the system's software. This technology allows individuals to interact with their surroundings while providing them with context-aware images that influence their opinions and choices. When retailers and brands tie Google Glass' augmented reality abilities with predictive analytics, they will be able to provide shoppers with compelling, individualized, visualizations while walking the aisles.

If shoppers can wear the technology, freeing up their hands and eliminating the view of the world through a small screen, it may signal a whole new way of 'looking' at in-store environmental graphics, way finding, price-point signage, promotional offers, visual display, product education, and interactions with sales associates. It might do away with sales associates altogether, providing AR avatars that are called into action when the shopper needs assistance. Assortment and adjacency planning will become entirely different when shoppers can see products as AR overlays on a perimeter wall display or a table at the front of a department. Music and branded video can augment the experience and be user defined or based on a set of curated choices that are preset through mining the customer's digital life-stream.

Buying a new set of cookware and need a recipe for pasta sauce, but don't want to open a cookbook and have the bubbling pot splash on the printed page? No problem. Ask your wearable tech to give you the recipe and have it float in the upper right part of your field of view while you slice, dice and stir.

Combining wearable tech such as Google Glass with sophisticated facial recognition software will allow for a whole new way to interact with others. While Glass will not be released to the general consumer with software to determine if someone is good or evil as in L. Frank Baum's "Character Marker," it is not hard to imagine that they will eventually be able to do something similar. While this may be a scary thought for some, imagine the kind of support this technology could give an individual with autism, for whom assessing other people's emotional states or picking up social cues is a challenge. These smart spectacles could read facial expression or other biometric markers and feed this information to the user, allowing him to mitigate awkward social interactions.

MIT Media Lab has merged wearable technology and facial recognition systems with a product they have developed called "Self-Cam," which is part of a larger Social Emotional Sensing Toolkit. Self-Cam is a wearable camera that analyzes the wearer's facial expressions and head movements, and reports back to them which of six states of mind the wearer may be conveying to others: agreeing, disagreeing, interested, confused, concentrating or thinking. "Self-Cam was useful both as a real-time self-awareness tool, where people thought about how they presented themselves, and as an off-line self-reflection tool, where video paired with mental state analysis provoked self-evaluation.[202]

This type of technology is a game-changer for both culture in general and shopping in particular. While Holodeck-like in terms of its ability to augment our real-life experience, it is a form of blended reality that keeps us in real life while enlisting the power of digital technology to fill in, or enhance, some perceptual and informational gaps.

The more shoppers can interact with digital versions of real-life products and learn more about a brand's products and services, the richer their in-store experiences will become.

It is very likely that we will see a split in customer experience typologies into those who provide blended reality interaction and those who do not. Retail places that allow this sort of interaction to happen will have a much more profound customer experience and competitive advantage than those who don't have this offering.

It is likely that by 2020, these types of 'glasses' won't be necessary. Instead, we'll have moved from wearing something on our head to simply having contact lenses that do the same thing. Already in development by a number of research labs and two research arms of Samsung, soft contact lenses are overcoming some of the problems that have made contact-lens displays impractical. Nanowires, organic conductors and graphene are made into conductive sheets by depositing solutions of the nanomaterials onto a spinning surface such as a contact lens. [203] For those who are more fashion sensitive and might feel wearing a set of glasses to be indiscrete, these contact lenses will provide a relatively invisible alternative. [204]

Feeling Through the Screen – Haptic Technology

Up until now, this discussion has focused on the use of technology in the visual realm of user experience. Keeping in mind that we understand our environments with more than just our eyes, there are other technologies that are engaging our other senses as well.

In conjunction with augmented-reality image overlays on real-life experiences, we are also seeing the development of gestural ways of interacting with digital content. X-Box One, perhaps the most pervasive gaming interface on the market, uses Microsoft Kinnect technology that tracks the user's body movements as well as capturing other biometric data. Today it is becoming commonplace to swipe, pinch, wave and poke at screens and the air to interact with the digital world around us.

Before we open our eyes as newborns we 'feel' the new world with the largest and most finely tuned sense organ we have – our skin. Despite knowing that we experience the world with our five senses, our computer-user experiences have been dominated by sight and sound, leaving out one of the most profound of our senses, touch/feeling. Increasing the sensory input of an experience increases the perception of reality and makes the interaction more profound. When we can *feel through the screen*, we will be able to deliver customer experiences that are more intense on a sensorial level and more profound because they provide better, body-based memories.

As mobile technology adoption continues unabated, the creators of digital brand experiences come up against the problem of not being able to engage the shopper fully, in an embodied way. Pictures can be beautiful, but touching, smelling, hearing and even tasting, round out experience. While we access more and more products online and through our devices, our brains want the satisfaction that comes from engaging all of the senses (recall the Baba Shiv experiment where real slices of cake and fruit were preferred over their photographic counterparts). As we access the brand through the screen, we fall dramatically short of really 'getting it' even if we create content to maximize the impact on the form factor we are using.

Researchers today are addressing the problem that our technology interfaces are typically smooth, touch screens with no sense of texture or temperature. Dragging your finger across a smooth glass screen is very different from feeling the texture of a fabric on your fingertips.

What if our screens could get us closer to embodied experience by providing tactile sensations?

What if a shopper could swipe fingers across the screen of a handheld tablet, and feel silk, or wool, wood or the rough texture of brick?

What if the glass surface of your handheld device was able to impart the sensation of warmth or the 'wetness' of water?

Even though scientists have studied the physiological and neurological components of touch for decades, computer scientists have lagged behind in transferring the understanding in the biology of touch to human-computer interfaces.

This is now changing.

Technology developments are introducing the 'touchy-feely' nature of experience into our devices. *Haptic* technology provides stimulation to our body by way of touch-capacitive sensors or a device's movement that delivers sensorial information either from the user to the device or the reverse. The term haptic comes from the Greek "haptesthai" meaning to touch/grasp/perceive. As an adjective, it means relating to, or based on the sense of touch. As a noun, usually used in a plural form (haptics), it means the science and physiology of the sense of touch.

Most of us have experienced a form of haptic technology at work with our mobile phones when they are set to vibrate with alerts and calls. The specific nature of the vibration could be tagged to an individual's profile in your contacts list, and identify who is calling, not by the number on the screen or preset ring tone but by how the phone jiggles in your pocket. These forms of haptics require small motors that vibrate, creating a feeling of movement.

Samsung developed a mobile phone in 2008, the "Anycall Haptic" that took the buzzes and jiggles to another level. Like other mobile devices on the market, the phone had a touch-screen display, but this one enabled users to feel clicks, vibrations and other tactile input. Beyond the buzz, it provided the user with 22 kinds of touch sensations.

We may also have experienced touch screens with digital buttons that combine the sound of a click and the sensation of their moving when touched. Designers at Nokia have also created a touch screen that makes on-screen buttons feel as if they were real. When users pressed the button, they felt a subtle movement replicating the push down and pop up. Adding to the sensation, users also heard an audible click. To do this, Nokia engineers placed two small piezoelectric (electric polarity due to pressure especially in a crystalline substance such as quartz) sensor pads under a screen, and designed them to move slightly when pressed. To make this convincing, the movement and sound are synchronized perfectly, giving the simulation of a real button moving when pressed.

We're increasingly turning to digital devices for communication and, in many cases, interacting with them requires the touch or swipe of a finger. Digital interfaces are getting better and better, both in the quality of images that they are now able to present and the lag-times that traditionally resulted between a touch and having something happen on the screen. While touch technology is getting better at providing immediate cause-and-effect, the things we touch, pinch and drag across the screen give us no sensory input that is related to what they are. *Everything* on the screen feels like glass.

Today, companies such as Senseg are re-imagining haptics, creating touch surfaces that have the feeling of various materials and finishes. Their technology uses an electrostatic field to turn touch screens into *'feelscreens.'* Senseg creates high-fidelity tactile interfaces with no moving parts. By passing an ultra-low electrical current into an insulated electrode, they can create a small, attractive force between the finger and the screen. As they change this attractive force over the surface, a variety of physical perceptions can be generated, including physical edges, contours and textures.

With no moving parts, the technology's response to touch is immediate and silent. The technology is scalable to different form factors from cellphones and touchpads, to larger interactive displays. What's even more interesting is that this haptic technology can be applied to almost any flat or curved, hard or soft, transparent or opaque surface, which extends the applications far beyond the touch screens we use today. [205]

In the future, haptic technology will allow us to feel 'through' the screen, connecting us in a more natural touch-sensitive way to our environment. Being able to feel through the screen will give us a more profound and emotional connection to the virtual world and each other.

The long-standing criticism about digital customer experiences being void of the ability to 'touch and feel' products may well be resolved with further developments in the use of haptic technology. Online shopping will take a significant turn towards being more 'real' when shoppers are able to 'touch' what they are considering buying. Haptic technologies may help solve some of the present challenges with online retailing by enhancing the shopper's ability to engage with product. It can also be enlisted in the service of connecting people with other people.

As technologies such as haptic computing evolve, they will support the dissolution of barriers to emotionally fulfilling and relevant shopping experiences. Shoppers will engage with technology that allows for a degree of physical interaction even when they are not in the store. We can expect to see the future shopping experience being a blend of all of these tech tools.

There is no way to stop the retail technology revolution. And, I am not sure we would want to.

It won't mean the death of stores. Far from it.

The idea of online shopping arrived on the scene almost as soon as the Internet became accessible to the general public. When the National Science Foundation lifted its restrictions on commercial use of the Internet in 1991, online commerce began to grow substantially. By 1995, adoption of personal computers was in full swing and Amazon, eBay and Yahoo were launched to meet the growing interest in shoppers going online and getting their stuff from some place other than the store. As e-commerce ramped up through the late '90s, the bubble grew, and it seemed as though every business were developing an Internet store. With the groundswell of e-commerce spreading into the early 2000s, many in the retail world predicted the death of the in-store retail experience. That, of course, didn't happen. Online shopping turned out to be just another way for retailers and brands to get their products and services into the hands of customers.

As mobile technology continues to evolve, it will simply become another way for shoppers to interact with brands and retailers. Choice will increase, both in products and services and how shoppers get access to them.

In the coming decade of retail place making, increasing importance will be placed on simplicity and bridging the sensory gap between seeing and feeling experiences, despite the fact that the 'bridges' may be digital constructions. The idea of making shopping easy has been a mantra for successful retailers for some time. F.W. Woolworth was quoted as saying, "I am the world's worst salesman; therefore, I have to make it easy for people to buy."

Simplicity will be a foundational strategy for retailers in an abundant world and it will be embedded into any emerging technology that finds its way into the customer journey. 'Making it *easy* to buy' will mean that retailers will seek to decrease the amount of work required to wade through all of the information that surrounds the shopper, and increase the amount of engagement between customers and the technologies that shape experience. Removing drudgery from shopping experiences and providing opportunity for delight through novelty will engage the right brain and make going to the store worth the effort.

Our shopping culture will move naturally towards simplicity by removing the barriers to interaction. Customers won't stand for anything that seems clunky, that takes too long and doesn't satisfy their needs in the moment. The pressure is now on, and will be greater into the future, to provide meaningful interactions in real-time wherever shoppers are – even more so if they have ventured to the store when they didn't have to.

In many of today's applications, our technology is like a game of 'monkey-in-the-middle' between shoppers and retailers. The 'connection ball' is being tossed back and forth between customer and retailer, with technology in between. The best-case scenario is for customers to talk directly with brands. To interact in an embodied way, the 'go-between' is not a device but a place…the store.

What we know is that technology interfaces or digital channels of engagement support the relationship between customers and retailers, but when they do, they often contribute to a growing disconnect between individuals and the brands they love. It is true that the Internet extends the shopper's mind and draws together the like-minded followers of a brand. Retailers and brands need to continue to search for inventive ways to support relationship and keep customers in stores.

Despite fears of disengagement and dystopian views that technology is leading us to our collective demise, it isn't going to happen. There are too many visions for the positive use of technology to engage customers in relationships that matter, for us to toss our hands up and feel powerless to make technology count with the right-brain experiences we all delight in.

Perhaps one of the most remarkable combinations of technology, empathy and customer participation that I have been exposed to was called "Pennies For Life" by the MicroLoan Foundation. In late February 2012, the MicroLoan Foundation ran a unique, and I might say beautiful, live digital event that tied together many of the themes of this book.

Through the foundation, people could donate small amounts (£2) to women in sub-Saharan Africa to help them establish businesses. People donated money from their mobile phones by texting to a number established by the foundation. As people made donations, an enormous digital billboard at the Westfield London shopping center depicted pennies flying into the screen to compose portraits of the supported female entrepreneurs. The individual donors were recognized for their contributions on the screen, for all to see, by a personal thank you. The Pennies For Life campaign was "a live example of small change here creating big change in Africa."[206]

In this example, technology drew people together using their phones to send a donation by means of a short text message and, at the same time, they directly modified the environment around them. From the mobile device in the palm of their hand, people were empowered to engage in social change, to connect to a cause bigger than themselves, to find context and meaning in a larger world, and to physically modify their environment.

This is Technempathy in action.

Another relatively easy, but incredibly impactful, use of technology was the "WestJet Christmas Miracle Campaign." In August 2013, WestJet "started brainstorming what 'giving' looked like at its best. We wanted to do something big, exciting and fresh. Fast forward three months and, with the help of 175 WestJet volunteers, three airports and Santa himself, we made a Christmas miracle happen for more than 250 guests on two Calgary-bound flights."[207]

Instead of having their boarding pass scanned by a gate agent, WestJet passengers were asked to put it into a machine, whereupon they had a discussion with Santa Claus. During the discussion, Santa asked them what they wanted for Christmas. Passengers responded with everything from new socks to a big screen TV. During the flight, the WestJet 'elves' went out and purchased everything that customers had asked for. Instead of their suitcases coming down the baggage carousel, gifts – wrapped with Christmas paper and bows – tumbled out before them.

Toy trains, socks and underwear, a warm scarf, an android tablet, and...a big screen TV were delivered to astounded customers.

The last couple sentences from the WestJet video go like this, "WestJetters would say it was more than just fun. Miracles do happen when we all work as one!...Merry Christmas to all and to all a *good flight!*"

WestJet gets it.

This, too, is Technempathy in action.

As long as we have a screen between us, we'll have experience at arm's length. For some, I can imagine this would be quite acceptable; the less interaction they have to contend with, the better. I suspect, though, that the overwhelming majority of shoppers want to be out in the social mix of other shoppers. It is our nature to be socially engaged.

As technology continues to influence the shopping experience, we may see a split in experience types: those driven by virtual interaction in a virtual shopping reality, those that blend ubiquitous computing and augmented reality overlays on real physical environments, and finally, good old-fashioned, face-to-face exchanges of goods and services. Which one of these will dominate the world of customer experience? It will likely depend on the retailer, brand, category or service. In any case, those that tap into the right brain, fostering an emotional connection with the customer will, no doubt, succeed.

Creating Right-Brained Stores in a Digitally Driven World

CHAPTER

18

'Making' is Intrinsic to Us All – Engaging Our Need to Create

We have long ago incorporated our need to create into the very DNA of our species. The wise man, *Homo Sapiens*, is also Man the Maker – *Homo Faber*. As young children, we loved to create, and we did so without self-consciousness. Children don't care if the proportion of the head is in scale to the rest of a stick-figure body. Forts made with empty boxes and a sheet thrown over a chair become imaginary worlds they inhabit. These acts of creativity are full of story. They have meaning and help to make sense of the world around them. While engaging in making, children live in the worlds of their work. These places are very much alive, and transcend time and place. They are *real*.

With our hands – carving wood, building a model, raising paintbrush to canvas, or pencil to paper, we tell stories. All acts of creativity are about stories, expressing ideas and creating meaning where once there was none.

In essence, making is magic.

Making is empowering because during the act of creating, we control and mold our world to our whims, dreams and visions. In making, we express the truest sense of who we are. Our creations are unique. They *are* us. The energy wielded by the hand in making is our life force. It is an extension of our mind. Our soul, physicalized. While we have changed in many ways over the centuries, that we seek opportunities to make, and find joy in it, has not changed.

The *creating* of experience, not just *observing* the unfolding of it, will be a game-changer for both the shopping world as well as the inner-world of shoppers. Digitally driven shoppers have an ever-increasing facility with crafting their everyday life experiences. Capturing the world around them as digital content to be edited and posted to social network sites is making each of us producers of our lives as digital docudramas. The mind is made through our experiences of the world and re-made through the digital capturing of life moments produced for publication to the Internet. Our self-perception, our mind's point of view on who we are, is created and reinforced by how we repeatedly see ourselves in relation to the world. As we create a digital storyline of our lives, our minds regulate the flow of messages that reinforce self-perceptions.

Understanding that the shopper's mind is both regulating the experience and actively creating it is a cause for pause. Our brains and the environment are continually in a sort of dialogue, exchanging information and energy to help craft experience in our minds. They are actually continually involved in the creative process of experience making, but many of these things happen below their perceptual radar.

Customers, in general, love being empowered. Having a say in what they are doing, trying and buying makes the experience more fun and more meaningful.

Nobel prize winning scientist Eric Kandel says the "brain is a creativity machine, which obtains incomplete information from the outside world and completes it."[208]

Seen in this light, retail places should allow for more 'making' in the store. If retailers and brands change customer experiences so that they are based on more than product depth and price, they will engage the customer in making the experience on his or her own. When people get involved in this sort of interaction it is intrinsically more relevant, validating, and empowering.

A number of retailers have discovered that allowing customers to create products fosters an innate sense of creativity, makes connections and deepens the relationship between the brand and the shopper.

Converse allows the customers to customize Chuck Taylor sneakers both in their stores and online.[209]

Nike has its "NikeiD" program that provides a similar creative opportunity.[210]

The entire brand platform of Build-A-Bear Workshop is built on the idea that kids can come in and select bears and related accessories to create their own, cuddly Teddy bear.[211]

And, online companies such as Threadless, engage the ingenuity of their artistic network to create designs that are printed on T-shirts after being voted upon by members.[212]

By *creating* the products we buy, we invest ourselves in the process and those products become more intimately tied to who we are. There is more than just a sense of ownership in the products that customers make themselves; these products become more firmly fixed in time and place, having greater context and relevance in their lives.

Engaging the shopping mind in the aisle requires that we seek out opportunity to connect and to become aware of each other's subjective experience. Shopping, whether in the palm of your hand, on a tablet, in a street, mall or country marketplace, needs to provide relevant information that allows for establishing context and meaning. Shopping places need to be designed in a way that is 'mindful' of customers as both separate individuals and part of a community connected through shared human experience.

Now imagine a shopping place where each customer creates part, or maybe *all*, of the shopping experience. This is customization on a grand scale and the mind is going to love it. While this is only happening today in small ways with the creation of customized products, it may well be that in the future, customers will be able to modulate the entire shopping environment. Allowing customers to have a say in how the environment unfolds along the shopping trip may also be a way for them to offset the feeling of being overwhelmed by an ever-increasing number product choices and places to buy.

Today, a generation of tech savvy young people engages in the process of making by way of an endless linking of ones and zeros. Digital life-streams are made and shared throughout the world at a speed and volume that we have not seen before in our human history. A continuously updated stream of data archives one's needs and wants, values, habits and aspirations, creating the story of one's life.

In a few short years, I have seen my sons' creative expression go from making puppets, picture books, stuffed animals and forts out of boxes in the real world, to constructing buildings and composing music in the virtual world. Media creation is becoming a lexicon that they are increasingly using to express themselves to their friends and the world through social networks.

There is now a generation of creative people, artists, architects, interior designers and visual merchants, who will mature into professionals who design shopping places but seldom draw on paper with a pencil or create a model with cardboard, X-Acto knife and glue. It is probable that the pendulum could swing so far in the direction of digitally enabled design that freehand drawing skills will fade from formal design education altogether.

Perhaps I am still old school in my thinking about creating. Personally, I prefer the 'old fashioned' way of creating, the practice of forming a direct body-to-object connection. I, of course, use the computer to model in 3D, but I always *draw first*. In drawing we go through the mental gymnastics of turning forms around in our mind's eye. We use the right brain and our visual-spatial abilities to rotate things and look at them from different angles. It is a skill honed by 'doing' with our own hands rather than a mouse or stylus.

In earlier chapters I explained how people have relied on images to impart meaning to others for longer than they have with written language. For some two thousand years, since the creation of a complete alphabet by the Greeks, left-brain rational thought and writing have made a serious play for dominance over our hardwired, right-brain capacity for understanding the world in pictures. Nevertheless, the power of the picture has never been usurped by the written word.

Despite the earlier assertion that bilingualism is better for the brain, one might wonder if the growth of texting signals the gradual end of communication in written terms and the re-emergence of picture-based communication as a principal form of sharing meaning between people.

It is hard to imagine that writing may vanish as we see an interesting cycle of communication styles playing out as technology facilitates the making of story with images. It seems as though we have moved from communicating with song and dance, to images painted on the wall of caves, to written words dominating communication, to a re-emergence of pictures playing a prominent role in how we communicate.

These days, we capture the 'performance' of our lives with handheld devices, to project ourselves and what we see around us to the world through video (moving pictures).

As younger generations become more adept at creating digital content on mobile devices for publication to social networks, we will see the emergence of savvy, media *manipulators* – not in the negative sense, but a creative one. The emergence and rapid adoption of applications that rely on pictures to communicate ideas are an indication of a renaissance of storytelling with images not words. Facebook may have bought Instagram for a cool billion, but Instagram is overtaking Facebook as a means to communicate between young social-networking technophiles.

Snapchat is an app that allows users to send and receive images that last for only a short period, then disappear forever from the digital world. Snapchat is gaining traction with a young audience that would prefer to communicate in images and not have them stay around to be mined by other people.

Flickr, Imgur, Snapfish, Vine and others are creating avenues for media makers to create and upload anywhere, anytime. In the context of our ever-evolving digitally driven world, it's hard to say how long the specific applications will be around, but they are a validation of the image as a profound means of communicating human thoughts and emotions.

Creating image and video content for publication to the Internet has become a key feature of our culture. Are we becoming more concerned with capturing the moments of our lives as postable images and video snippets, than we are in living them out while they are happening? Do we prefer to capture and archive our experience for distribution to a larger audience than to live it in the present?

As handheld devices with high-resolution image capability become ubiquitous, sharing our life stories in pictures is becoming embedded in our culture because it *feels* empowering. That feeling is promoted, in part, by the ease with which we can make images. Making image-based content for re-broadcast is also going to have a dramatic impact on the design of shopping places.

The making of images and video empowers shoppers with the ability to become *skilled storytellers*. When they see the world of experience through the screen of their mobile device and the pictures or video they take with them, they participate in its making and the re-telling of its story. As they capture, edit and re-broadcast images of their customer experiences, they directly participate in the telling of the brand story. Furthermore, they become an integral part of it.

Creative Collaborative Consumerism

Shopper-storytellers are now *influencers*. And they know it.

This sort of customer empowerment is not something to be feared or abated but to be carefully, intuitively understood and harnessed by retailers and brands.

A generation of technology users is becoming very comfortable with the idea of 'now.' For them, now is natural and waiting is wasteful. They expect things to happen in an instant because they have come to expect that cause and effect in the digital world have immediacy to them. For them, change shouldn't take generations, but should happen at the speed of the Internet. If they want change, it should happen right away, even if that means changing public policy or political leaders, national borders or the physical environment. While in the past, we may have expected change to be slow and deliberate, today we are seeing change at an unprecedented pace.

An expedited pace of change is affecting and influencing everything we do. Everyday experiences are being truncated as the immediacy of online experiences is determining the nature of our expectations. As our culture speeds up, the availability of goods and services, coupled with the delivery systems that satisfy customer needs, is re-setting the benchmark for what we think of as normal. A defining feature of the new, digital economy will be that 'normal' will be in a constant state of flux. It's a good thing that the right brain likes change and novelty, because that will be the predominant theme defining the nature of future, digital-driven shopping places and our lives.

Our life experiences are increasingly recorded as memories that are done in pieces – digital factoids that can be quickly stored and distributed – rather than in complete stories. We seem to experience life episodically rather than holistically. As experience unfolds in front of us, we grab the smartphone, record and hit send. It's impossible to be truly present during an experience if we are looking at it through the screen on our phone, and thinking about where this life experience snippet will be best posted in the future to our socially networked audience.

Of course, as life accelerates around us, we see that customers are naturally more impatient. Conveying brand messages needs to happen quickly as well. Transmitting relevant content to potential customers has got to keep time with everything else that is speeding by in their lives. Conveying a message to a shopper must get to the point and be uniquely crafted for the individual, rather than the masses, to remain relevant enough to capture and retain their attention.

With increasing use of mobile devices to create image-based content, we may also come to expect that our interaction with the environment should be as easily modified as a picture we take and change by the addition of a filter to re-color, add texture and lighting effects, and finally crop so we can post and distribute it. Editing images or video content for re-broadcast is equipping everybody with the ability to create mini-masterpieces and ideal portraits that, no matter how good they are, still express de-contextualized visual memory segments of our experience. When communication takes the form of postable pieces, a lot ends up on the cutting room floor.

In the emerging culture of media creators, it isn't enough simply to capture an image of the environment the way it is. Capture, *edit* and archive to our digital life stream, is the way we share our life images.

What does this imply?

People will increasingly want and claim creative control of modifying their environments as they participate in them.

They already control the telling of their life stories through the digital content they create and publish to their social networks. Stories can be rewritten and edited after they occur or even manufactured for the sole purpose of projecting a certain sensibility of one's self onto the digital world. Experience runs the risk of being scripted to fit a digital persona within an individual's social network.

We could see this need to edit experiences as simply adding a little personal touch, to 'make it your own.' But more than simply being an esoteric add-on, re-making the world in our own image gives us a sense of agency as well as the validation that we are part of a larger whole.

We activate the emotional, right brain's penchant for creativity and making meaning through the weaving together of contextual relationships between the differentiated parts of our daily lives. As we participate in the making of an experience, it is more relevant to us. Nothing will be more relevant than the things we create because they are uniquely about us. It behooves us to pay close attention to how consumers are using digital media in the service of emerging identities.

The ability to modify an experience through the editing capability available on our handheld devices could be extended to the modifying of *whole environments rather than images and video clips.* If customers can create personally curated experiences as they participate in them, they necessarily craft them to suit their unique needs and wants.

To some degree, this is already happening today with applications such as "Roqbot for Business," where customers are able to change the music playing in stores based on a set of personal preferences. Customers become in-store DJs. The Roqbot co-founders say that they want to put an end to boring background music and so, they are turning to their customers and online libraries of millions of songs to allow the customer to choose their own.

Those who have the Roqbot app can use their smartphones to check-in at their favorite retailer, see what's playing, make music requests, vote for their favorite song in the store's play list, and check out special promotions and new arrivals. That's a winning combination of technology, crowd sourcing and social interaction.

This doesn't mean that the sound system is going to be overrun by customers changing the music all day long, because the retailer can still pull together immense play lists that support the feeling the brand wants to portray in-store. Furthermore, Roqbot's approach is to offer continuous streaming of content so that the same music isn't played over and over.

Not surprisingly, the management team at Roqbot believes that the future of music in public venues will be social and mobile, so they've started by enabling users to publish their check-ins and music picks to Twitter, Foursquare, Last.fm and Facebook. If you want to add a song that's not in the queue, you can use the app's credits to buy it on Amazon with PayPal or your credit card. And that's where the startup's monetization aspirations come in.[213]

As the adoption of wearable technology increases, it will support the customer's desire for the creation of relevant personal experiences. AR overlays seen through wearable technology will not only be under the control of the retailer or brand, customers will want a say in what they are seeing in the shopping places they visit. They will want to actively co-create digitally augmented environments they'll inhabit or access on-demand media content that becomes part of the experience as they live it.

Before they walk about in Holodeck-like environments, they may stroll through environments fabricated with LCD glass panels that run digital media in the surface. It is possible that content from a shopper's handheld (or wearable) device could be pushed to the screen (glass wall) and the environment would be digitally augmented in real time to meet the customer's personal preferences.

Imagine a shopping world where the customer is able to create virtual Pinterest-like walls that capture both products that are in the store and those that are digitally projected into the space. Digital walls could become big picture books, telling stories of the customer's life. In real time, they could illustrate how the brand fits into the customer story. As well as providing additional content about the products/services, such interactive digital interfaces could incorporate social media networks that ground the shopping experience in personal relationships.

Wearable tech, such as Google Glass, may allow for additional content overlays of product options on actual merchandise displays or on walls of LCD glass that display images of the new collection. While walking the sales floor, customers may access a digital folder of fashion outfits they are considering purchasing. Whole collections of additional products could be projected onto surfaces in a shopping place, as augmented reality overlays and haptic technology could change wall-sized touch interfaces made of glass to be able to feel the textures of products. Entire structures of LCD glass could be modified with digital content created by either the customer or the retailer. What today is often no more than digital wallpaper could be changed in real time to interactive digital surfaces as customers walk the floor.

In future shopping environments, Big Data, predictive analytics, facial recognition systems, wearable and haptic technology and the co-creation of digital content will coalesce in what I call *collaborative creative consumerism*.

Shopping experiences will not be a one-size-fits-all solution based on demographics, but on the opt-in exchange of digital life-stream content and the collaborative co-creation of merchandise assortments, and the physical environments in which they are displayed. Customers will actively participate in and 'own' the stores they visit because they will have, in part, made them.

It's crucial to observe social media trends and how they are being ushered in, filled in, tuned in (and out). These observations can help retailers and brands prepare for the shopper-storytellers of tomorrow. Whereas in the past we might have thought of 'tomorrow' as some distant time in the future, tomorrow is right now. In a retail world that will be less and less about delivering relevant shopping experiences and satisfaction with price point and endless choice, retailers that engage the customer in creatively making a positive experience will have a competitive advantage.

Designers who create shopping places will have their work cut out for them. As the pervasiveness of digital content will continue to grow, playing a highly influential role in creating environments, it will challenge designers to be at the top of their game. They will need to be able to create shopping places that compete with the better-than-real digital experiences to which shoppers will become accustomed.

Capturing the attention, imagination and wallets of shoppers will be no small task. It will require the collaborative creativity of the masses. As the Internet enables the extension of the shopper's brain across a vast network, like-minds will form creative coalitions that will share 'energy and information.' They will provide feedback throughout the making of shopping places, from design inception to environments that will have the capability to change in real-time to meet the needs of the individual shopper.

Creative collaborative consumerism 'co-ops' the creative process, where designers, brands, retailers *and* shoppers are truly in sync as quick-change artists who will use traditional architecture and digital media to engage the creative right-brain in making relationships and relevant experiences.

The Market Segment and Brand of 'Me'

We've been used to thinking of activity, trends and statistics along a continuum of months, years and decades. For the first time in our history, we can break down the minutes and glean powerful information about what people do online in any given sixty seconds. It is estimated that every minute of every day:

More than 72 hours of video content is uploaded to YouTube.

347 blogs are posted.

More than 204 million emails are sent.

571 new websites are added to the Internet.

20 million photos are shared on Flickr, 104,000 on Snapchat, and Instagram users post 216,000 new photos.

Pinterest users pin 3,472 images.

More than 278,000 Tweets are sent.

More than 700,000 Facebook entries are made. In total, Facebook users share 2.46 million pieces of content.

Amazon generates $83,000 in sales. [214]

Every 60 seconds, our digitally driven culture continues to generate and share content at a volume that is millions of times greater than all of the books that were ever written in human history up to the year 2000.

Between 2011 and 2013, the Internet population grew 14.3% and now represents 2.4 billion people worldwide.

What is the world's population? [215]

7 billion (7,017,846,922).

Over a third of the world's population is connected to the Internet.

A digital connection provides access to, and connections within the Buyosphere, which draws together a multitude of shopper ecologies, creating an intricate web of relationships. Every digital touch point generates content that allows providers of goods and services to gather customer information and increasingly fine-tune their offerings. In a marketing and advertising environment that is laser-focused, the connections that retailers and brands make with customers will be inherently more profound, too, because they uniquely target individuals rather than large swaths of a population.

In short, customers will get used to being in the market segment of 'Me.'

This doesn't mean that retailers will become generalists, trying to provide everything they can in a broad range of categories. Instead they will become acutely focused on providing goods and services that *meet the needs of the individual customers*. It might be likely that the future will continue to see ever increasing specialization. Stores may continue to be reformatted into smaller footprints, each specifically tailored to a very small segment of the shopping population. Like pop-up shops, they may come and go, only trying to meet a particular need within a very narrow timeframe.

Big-box retailers, department stores, and category killers whose strategy has been to carry huge amounts of product in multiple categories, might face an interesting challenge as they try to compete for customers who become increasingly specific about what they want and from whom.

Customers' expectations about assortment depth, availability, delivery, costs, customer relations, and the entirety of the experience along the path to purchase will change. They will expect direct and clear communication that is informed, tailored to their individual needs. It will need to be imbued with empathy and a regard to their personal circumstances and their life story. A collaborative dance between individual customers and the providers of goods and services will be set in place that is a portrayal of the customer's digital life-stream and previous connections to the brands and retailers they shop.

At the same time, shoppers will be developing a growing awareness of marketing strategies at work in the Buyosphere. As individuals continue to develop digital content and share it with their 'followers' and 'friends,' they are forced into the role of being marketers of brand of 'Me.'

In a similar way that retailers and brands feel the pressures of remaining desirable by their customers, staying relevant and vital in an individual's social networks requires one to be continually on top of producing new 'product' for distribution to the group. Social networks, and their continuous feedback loops, quickly evaluate the relevancy of posted content and let the person who 'put it out there' know if it was worthy of their attention. A 'like-fest' is the social network equivalent to the sound of the cash wrap ringing up sales.

Despite being a maximum 140 characters, posting a tweet requires thought about content, what picture to use, what to write and whether anyone will care enough to 'retweet' or 'favorite' it. Either of these is a validation that feeds the emotional brain and fosters a motivation to keep producing content to promote the brand of 'Me.'

Feeding the social network machine makes us think about whom we are producing content for and why it matters to them. It puts the relevancy-shoe on the other foot and gets the customer-producer to become good at both empathic extension –

• *Will this post meet the viewers' needs and make them feel something?*

As well as awareness about marketing –

• *How do I package the message for maximum sell-through –'likes'/'favorites' and continued 'friendship,' or maintaining 'followers?'*

Selling themselves into their social networks makes individuals better marketers and as a consequence more savvy shoppers because they are more aware of what it takes to market the products of brand of 'Me.'

Millennial shoppers, and those coming up behind them, will be the recipients of both hyper-focused, brand marketing and advertising while being skilled marketers in their own right. Armed with more information than shoppers have ever had before them, and skilled at the selling of the brand of 'Me,' it will become a more complex process for retailers and brands to capture their attention and retain their loyalty.

For shoppers growing into the emerging digitally driven shopping world, experience will extend throughout all parts of their day. In the past, we thought of the store as the singular most profound customer touch point. Shopping was generally an *event* you *planned*; you had a need to be met, you went out to the store, satisfied it and went home.

Today, for the shopper living in a digitally driven world, customer experience is an ongoing phenomenon. From the time we are all awake until we are asleep, exposure to the Buyosphere implies *continuous experience.*

We now often consider the brand's access to the customer or the customer's access to the brand as occurring in various 'channels' – hence the term 'omni-channel retailing.' While the term allows for a common vocabulary among those in the retail business, there seems to be an implication that these avenues are simply a conduit for products or services. Looking beyond simply providing customers with more access to stuff or finding increased access to customers for themselves, retailers would do well to re-imagine the possibilities of providing places for great customer engagement when they think 'omni-*experience*' rather than 'omni-channel.'

In an omni-experience environment, the 'Me' customer segment and marketer will be connected to a world of global ubiquitous computing with continuous access to the Buyosphere where they will buy and sell without inhibition.

The Brand Performance Place

"ALL THE WORLD'S A STAGE,
AND ALL THE MEN AND WOMEN MERELY PLAYERS;
THEY HAVE THEIR EXITS AND THEIR ENTRANCES;

AND ONE MAN IN HIS TIME PLAYS MANY PARTS…"
— WILLIAM SHAKESPEARE, AS YOU LIKE IT

On November 19, 2013 Oxford Dictionaries announced that "selfie" was its international Word of the Year.[216] According to language research conducted by Oxford Dictionaries, the frequency of the use of the word "selfie" in the English language increased 17,000% in 2013 from the previous year.

We are growing a young culture for whom relevancy, and therefore self-worth, is found in becoming a social media *performance artist*.

When we create, we draw on the faculties of the right side of the brain, using intuition, inference, holistic and imaginative thinking to assemble pieces into content that has meaning. The things we create have meaning for us because they provide context, tell stories and make clear the relationships between the concrete – people, places, and things; and the esoteric and ephemeral – ideas. Making is meaningful to us. In a digitally driven world, what is increasingly considered relevant to an individual is what is made by them for re-broadcast to their social network(s). What is created for online distribution is a digital representation of one's life. An emerging challenge in a digitally networked world is that one's self-concept is being outsourced.

There is little indication that the present obsession with social media engagement is slowing. The content distribution modalities may be changing from text-based blogging to picture and video-based interaction. Form-factors for its distribution may be continually shifting, but these are simply an evolution of the same phenomenon of extending ourselves into a larger context to find meaning and validation. We are creating our digital life-streams and in their 'sharing,' we are becoming our own media broadcasting companies, our own with six o'clock newscasts, complete with late-breaking stories, entertainment reports, political commentary, fashion editorials, relationship segments, and weather advisories.

'Lifecasting' will continue to be a communication style with an emerging generation of digital media creators. The sense of empowerment that is a derivative of making one's life story, as well as the validation that comes from the continuous and immediate feedback loop that is the internet and social medial sphere, will have significant influence on the nature of shopping places. Retailers and brands will have to respond to a culture of Lifecasters.

This approach to future shopping places will be inherently more creative in its expression. It will need to remain fluid and continually evolving to meet the needs of individuals rather than the masses. And, to counteract the effects of 'better-than-real' digital experiences, the store, as a place for the expression of the brand, will likely evolve into an environment that meets Lifecasters head-on as a place for 'Brandcasting.'

As the influence of online availability goods and services continues to shape the shopping experience, the relevance of stores as a place for getting the 'stuff' we need, will continue to diminish. Same-day home delivery of almost anything that shoppers have accessed through their digital devices will indeed reduce the need to go to the store. 'Showrooming' will continue to grow as a shopping behavior, and enhanced, digital experiences may well create virtual shopping places that surpass real-life stores in their ability to take customers on a shopping journey that is physically impossible in the real world.

The store will become less storage facility for customers to buy from than it will be a distribution center for the retailer/brand to ship from. We may well see an inversion of the traditional space allotment of stores being mostly sales floor and little stock room. Existing and newly built shopping places will likely see significantly reduced assortments on a shrinking, sales-floor footprint, while the stockroom grows to accommodate store-to-home shipping policies and practices.

Product won't *completely* disappear from the sales floor. But, we will see a complete realignment of SKU count on the floor to what is available through digitally interactive means while the customer engages in the shopping place. Whether through a handheld device, adaptive touch interface or wearable technology, customers will have both abundance, should they want it, or curated assortments that are assembled uniquely for them as individual customers.

During the '70s and '80s, the shopping world saw the remarkable growth of a form of retailing almost identical to what today is called 'showrooming.' Started in 1934 by Harry and Mary Zimmerman as a five-and-dime store, Service Merchandise grew into a major, national chain, which, at its peak, was achieving yearly sales of $4 billion. The Service Merchandise retail model took the catalogue business and grew it into something that embraced the idea of customers interacting with merchandise, reducing product counts on the sales floor, and warehousing vast arrays of products. In the years leading up to the company's closing in 2002, customers actually *bought* product rather than just scanning it with a smartphone to find another place to buy it for less. However, as the new millennia ushered in vast vendor choice via the Internet, Service Merchandise finally succumbed to 'terminal showrooming.'

With Amazon now becoming ubiquitous in our vocabulary, time will tell whether or not this online 'catalogue' retailer's lack of a place to engage physically with the brand will be a significant part of their customer experience. For the time being, connection to the Amazon brand only happens online and with the deliveryman at the front door, or the proposed new drones, "Amazon Prime Air," which Amazon intends to 'launch' as a delivery system within a few years.

There is no physical place for the customer to interact with the Amazon brand and most of its real estate is tied up in distribution centers. Nevertheless, "for a company whose showrooms are all online, Amazon.com spends a staggering amount on bricks and mortar. The e-commerce giant has invested roughly $13.9 billion since 2010 to build 50 new warehouses, more than it had cumulatively spent on storage facilities since its 1994 founding, bringing the total to 89 at the end of 2012."[217] It was recently estimated that the 102 Amazon distribution centers up and running by the end of 2013 covered an approximate 70 million sq. ft. of space.

Today's common usage of the word 'showrooming' really isn't anything new. When retailers creatively embraced the original idea of showrooming, we moved to a merchandising paradigm where product became the star of the show. Not because of how many were loaded onto the shelves, but because there was something inherently special about each of the things that a retailer chose to have on the sales floor.

As the proportional relationship between sales floor and stockroom changes, what remains of the sales floor will become a brand performance place where customers live the brand experience by playing a role in the story. Ritual, story, play and empathic relationship will find a renewed position of importance at the forefront of experience, replacing abundant choice and price-point as key drivers to shopping at one retailer over another. Shoppers will have all they can imagine in terms of selection and the time they commit to being 'in-store' will become more significant as the brand performance place engages them in real-time making of unique experiences.

When shoppers evolve, *they* will be at the epicenter of brand immersion places where performance becomes key aspect of brand experience. The store is fast-becoming a stage for the brand to be enacted. Shopping will invite us all to light up our right-brain imaginative capacities in the brand performance place in which digital integration is active across multiple touch points. In the brand performance place, the director/animator/sales associate will be a facilitator of renewed shopping rituals.

Retailing on the Right Side of the Brain

As we move towards a digitally enabled retailing future, customers, retailers and retail designers will all have significant challenges as the shopping paradigm we know undergoes radical change.

Throughout this book, we've looked at a number of shifts that are taking place in our culture through the increased use of digital technology. Since shopping emerged as a coherent social paradigm a few thousand years ago, social movements, emerging technologies and cultural change, have swept the process and shaped shopping places. Yet, at its core, shopping has remained a key component to our expression as social beings. As such, it is an illustration of many of the things we are as humans – empathic beings who engage in play and ritual for the purpose of growing ourselves in relationship, and extending ourselves outside of our immediate experiences in order to connect to a greater context that gives meaning to our lives.

Perhaps because of its connection to language and speech, the left-brain has been considered the 'dominant' hemisphere. This point of view has had a strong foothold in our concept of the brain and how it works, since, despite our long history of using pictures to communicate, the left hemisphere started to do all the talking.

Over time, we have come to accept an entrenched prejudice that positioned the left hemisphere and its proclivity towards rational, linear thinking as a point of differentiation between humans and the rest of the world's living creatures.

The right side of the brain has often been considered as the color commentary to the left brain's play-by-play analysis. The left brain has been considered to be the side of us that attends to the serious business in our lives. The right side has been looked upon with a skeptical eye, perceived by many to be untrustworthy and emotionally unpredictable. But, neither one of these stereotypical and rigid views of the left *or* right hemisphere hits the mark exactly.

There are, in fact, significant differences between the left and right hemispheres. Each side of the brain sees the world in completely different and relatively incompatible ways.

The right side of our brain sees the world with a broad and open view, synchronously taking in all of that is around us. From the right side of our brain we experience the world as a live, embodied, complex set of interdependencies that may be dynamic and ambiguous, always changing and reforming, which deeply connect us to the world. The right side embraces ambiguity, novelty, and thrives in determining the contextual relationships between multiple elements that come together to create meaning.

The right brain is ideally set up to adapt to the digitally driven future. As digital content continually changes, spaces around us will become more dynamic, in turn providing customers multiple opportunities to engage in the process of creative making. Rather than reacting with fear and resistance to the evolving shopping place, the right brain will be engaged in playing in a place to which it is perfectly adapted.

The left side of our brain tends to rely on focused attention, seeing not the whole but the parts that comprise it. Its experience of the world is a representation of what has already been understood by the right brain. Our view of the world through our left brain tends to be relatively static and constructed from a series of fragmented pieces, which are grouped together into classes or lists. You like to-do lists? That's your left brain in action. Do you feel like you can't remember things unless they're itemized and categorized? Left brain at its best. Do you follow your GPS as a text list? Left. As a map with colored dots on a visually detailed map? Right.

Left doesn't care about context.

Left stares at bottom-line results, not the experiential process of progress. Left sees black or red, wide or small margins, profits or losses.

Right is emotional. Loves the variable and spontaneous dynamics of life, people, ideas and new experiences.

Despite the distinct differences between the left and right hemispheres, customer experience cannot be fully appreciated unless the left and right sides of our brains are fully integrated and working as a coherent whole. That said, if the objective is to create customer experiences that engage people on a more profound emotional level, overtures must be made towards the innate sensibilities of the right side of the brain.

Let's light the right.

The right side of our brain is a master at seeking out and determining context, how things fit together and imply meaning. Shopping as a social activity that serves to create meaningful relationships between people, places, products and brand ideologies is perfectly in sync with the very nature of the context-creating ability of the right hemisphere.

Our capacities to engage in empathic extension and to display, and to understand, emotion in others are largely right hemispheric functions and are core features that determine positive customer experiences. Beyond the simple utility of acquiring goods that satisfy our basic needs, the context-building quality of shopping is a key reason for why people do it.

There is no question that with access to increasingly powerful computers, digital content will become more and more pervasive. We are already at a tipping point where customer experience is being shaped by digital proliferation and our resulting chronic partial attention. With so much to attend to in the environments we experience, the key to successful retail shopping places will be the retailer's capacity to *truly and authentically capture a shopper's attention.* This will be no small task as a customer's cognitive resources are drawn away in efforts to attend to multiple stimuli.

Today's consumers are savvy. They are more apt to sniff out a trick, quick to detect insincerity of intent, and adept at filtering out who or what is the real deal. Perhaps, because Millennials, for example, have so much choice and have become virtually expert online researchers, they have become connoisseurs, in their own right, and resistant to the hard sell or the feeling of being hustled. They just don't like it. And they have no problem with letting retailers know – or steering clear.

Remaining relevant in a digitally driven shopping future will first rely on the retailer's ability to appropriately capture customer attention in a way that the customer fully consents to and enjoys. It will be hard won, but, when done, the retailer will able to convey brand stories that resonate with the customer's emotional right brain. The goal is to cement how the brand fits into the individual's shopping ecosystem and becomes part of the interconnected and interdependent nodes in a complex network of people and things that is the global Buyosphere.

Not all forms of attention are equal.

Conventional neuropsychology literature distinguishes five types of attention: vigilance, sustained attention, alertness, focused attention, and divided attention.[218] It turns out that the right hemisphere is responsible for every type of attention except for "focused attention."

It's not surprising that the left hemisphere's penchant for lists and seeing the world in bits and pieces implies that it has a dominance for seeing things in the details – which, of course, requires focused attention.

But, comparatively, the right hemisphere, with its broader, global view of the world, is able to attend, in different ways, to everything else. And, this is a good thing considering that our environments will become increasingly full of digital content vying for slices of our attention. In the world of digital proliferation, we will need to rely on the right brain's ability to attend to the larger holistic picture of our environments.

When walking the sales floor, the right hemisphere is attending to everything that is 'out there' right in front of the shopper. It is taking in the big picture, the holistic view, and making meaning from the multiple messages.

When shoppers use their digital devices to access a retailer's website, they attend to the activity and the form factor of the digital device in a different way. They focus their attention on the single screen in the palm of their hand. And so, it too is not surprising that the form and content of messages that can effectively be conveyed to customers through their handheld devices, are influenced by the way the left brain processes information that comes within the crosshairs of focused attention.

Form factor and the type of focus required to attend to a handheld device are better suited for the capacities of the left side of our brain. Messages can be short, to the point, and focus on price, features and benefits rather than emotional content and brand stories. If, on the other hand, retailers are trying to capture profound emotional experiences, then there will be no substitute for a shopping place that engages customers in full-bodied interaction which require the types of attention that are best suited for the right side of our brain.

We've already established that the idea of novelty – interruptions in perceived patterns – is the key feature to customer experience. We've also established that when we talk about customer experience, it is not 'out there' in the architecture, merchandise, lighting and displays, but *in the customer's mind and initially processed in the right side of the customer's brain.* Since the right hemisphere processes information with a goal of assimilating information into a global context, new experiences are processed first by the right brain before they get further processed by the left. "Global attention, courtesy of the right hemisphere, comes first, not just in time, but takes precedence in our sense of what it is we are attending to; it therefore guides the left hemispheres local attention."[219]

Inside a store, customers do not have to focus on every single element and build a mental picture of the details. The right hemisphere takes it all in and processes it so that it's understood, and then passes it off to the left hemisphere that attends to the details with its capacity for focused attention. So, quite ironically, when customers first enter a store, simply being in a new shopping environment has already captured their right hemisphere's attention, which gets to work, immediately coming to a gestalt perception of the place.

Because the right brain is interested in the big picture, it is naturally more interested in the whole rather than the individual parts. Its concern is with the *relationships between things.* It stands to reason, then, that our capacity for empathic extension is a feature of the right hemisphere. Because it focuses on understanding relationships, our right brain prefers the living and the personal to the mechanical. It will always prefer face-to-face interaction with an authentic and happy greeter at the front door to being directed by a kiosk. Even when a potential customer ventures beyond the front door and is offered opportunities to seek further information about products or services, the right brain prefers the human touch rather than in-store technology. This, of course, calls into question the value of using kiosks in the shopping aisle as a way to connect to customers. While retailers will say that a kiosk will drive up revenue, using them also drives the right brain out of the equation. The right brain wants a face-to-face interaction; the left brain just wants a deal. Or think of it this way – the left wants a reason to buy; the right needs a reason to come back.

If retailers believe that connecting to the customer's emotional center is a core element of their brand platform, then they must engage experiences that are less about utility, price point and depth of assortment and more about relationship.

They must teach their sales associates the power of 'embracing-the-face' and how projecting emotion is part of the interpersonal relationship between sales associates and shoppers. It relies on their attitude, body language and facial expressions. Emotion is a key driver of positive customer experiences. There is evidence that when it comes to emotional perception, in most of its forms of expression, it is the right hemisphere that is dominant.[220]

This is also true of the emotional content that is embedded into spoken or written messages. When customers understand the feelings behind the brand narrative, they are being engaged on the right side of their brain. If a retailer's goal is to connect to customers in a deep and meaningful way, emotional stories that paint the many hues of relationship onto a larger canvas will invariably be more successful than those that are built on value propositions with price points as a key theme. A brand is far more than a memorable logo. It is a tapestry of universal human emotions. The best ones sear both visual iconography and emotion into customers' memories.

The particular strength of the right hemisphere and understanding stories comes from its ability to put words together and understand the context, the subtle underlying messages that are implicit rather than explicit. So when it comes to understanding a joke or the moral of the story, the right hemisphere is very much responsible. Telling *brand stories* and delivering messages, whether in the shopping aisle, on a cellphone or on a roadside billboard, all play to the right side of the brain.

Whenever retailers use environmental graphics or other images that are non-literary in their form, they are asking the customer's right hemisphere to get involved to make sense of the underlying messages. This is particularly true when sarcasm, irony, humor or other indirect forms of communication are being used. Understanding the implied meaning of a brand message is a right-hemisphere skill. The left hemisphere sees the words, but doesn't always necessarily get the message. Telling brand stories is extremely important because they are, by their very nature, *a right-brain, transcendent phenomenon.*

Transcendent because only engaging the right brain's ability to see a global, contextual, picture of things, can assign shopping experiences that quality.

Transcendent because, while the left brain is fixed in the present and always references what it knows, the right brain is always embracing the unknown, the 'Other' beyond itself. In this way, the right brain and shopping are intimately linked. Shopping, like play, takes us outside of ourselves, connecting us to a larger contextual framework. When shopping, we incorporate other imagined realities. Without the right brain, the transcendent experience of shopping would not be possible.

How does transcendent experience fit into our technology-driven world? Because the right brain embraces the fluid, flexible, dynamic nature of things around it. The right brain is perfectly positioned to excel in the dynamic digitally driven future. Where the left brain is concerned with things it already knows, the right brain is concerned with the experiences it will have.

Understanding how people perceive, move through store space, seek out relationship, and buy because of their emotional response to environment, their internal state and their interaction with the brand at every touch point – opens up countless gateways to creating transcendent experiences. Not in spite of this digitally driven age, but because of it.

The possibilities are literally endless.

It requires us all to get creative, to innovate, to come up with fantastic, seemingly implausible ideas for memorable and meaningful connection, all based on our human nature of play, empathic connection and engagement. This is, in essence, a call back to our original selves, to the way we were designed, even while we journey into a future world of technology and change.

We all love to play. It's in our genes, remember? And that's another reason we love our devices. If cellphones required too much work from us, the kind that goads us into resentment, procrastination and frustration, we wouldn't be carrying them with us day and night, but rather forgetting them in a drawer.

Play requires our full attention. The best kind of playing and creativity change us from the inside out. The most successful companies and brands have undergone terrific change as they've grown through adopting a mindset of playful engagement between employees and with customers. Play is dynamic. So is change. And so is shopping.

But there are challenges, of course.

One interesting challenge with in-store technology is that is that it is generally used in a way that is *contrary* to how the right brain works. The right brain likes to engage in empathic relationships and imitate other *living* things. It's not so much interested in machines. Stories of human-like robots have been around for years, but we are a long way off from sentient machines that look, feel and act like humans. You can't bond with a piece technology; it simply doesn't work. People don't empathize and identify with machines. They empathize and identify with other people.

While product, price and place have driven customer experiences in the past, none of these things would have mattered if not for people. In the future of retail place making, the premium will be placed on people: what they create themselves as part of their own personal brand of 'Me' platform, what they create for others to be posted to social network sites as well as to online retailers that engage them in the creative act of making, and what they create as stores for themselves when they're not consuming products and services through their handheld or wearable digital devices.

There has never been a time in the history of shopping where customers are more empowered than they are today. Access to the Internet and increasingly powerful mobile technology has given today's customer knowledge and information beyond all previous generations.

Retail technology is not the point-of-sale system. Though, of course, POS is part of it, but, from the customer experience point of view, it's the last part that shoppers engage with and often the least enjoyable or pleasurable part of the shopping trip.

Retail technology is also not an in-store kiosk, accessible Wi-Fi, or a digital sign that displays a video loop, Twitter or Facebook feed. Well, okay, that's part of it, too, but the ways these things are provided in store are often disconnected from what the customer truly wants and how they use technology when they're on the go.

Understanding digital integration within retail experiences is about finding a way to use it to enhance the core of shopping, which is to bring the retailer and customer together in relationship that results in an exchange. This is why I believe the theory and practice of "technempathy" is so important. It implies a move from using technology for its own sake to a position of using its power to build relationship.

When seen as a tool to enhance communication, sharing brand stories and the building of interpersonal relationships with customers, technology takes on a whole new perspective – and purpose. From this point of view, it makes technology more than digital wallpaper that is often irrelevant to the customer.

The Store Will Never Go Away

Before writing this part of the book, my outlook about the retail world's future, and indeed our own culture, was rather mired in deep concern. Frankly, I was worried. I could fully imagine a dystopian future and I didn't need to see it in a sci-fi movie. I understood the studies demonstrating that a new generation of college students was less empathic. I understood the neuroscience of synaptic pruning and what was likely to happen to the physiological structures of our brains if new communication paradigms keep us from face-to-face interactions. I understood the power of social media and how it is changing us from living life to performing it for re-broadcast as episodic moments to an interconnected global network of 'friends.'

None of these conditions made me feel particularly comfortable.

It was easy to see disaster looming on the horizon.

And, yet, all the while, there were moments of hope.

There were examples of retailers and organizations doing great things, to forge meaningful customer relationships, make sustainable products, engage communities at a local level and to re-think the shopping paradigm in preparation for a new shopping future. There were risk-takers who stepped beyond the norm to engage the novelty-seeking, emotionally focused, holistically perceptive, aspiring, transcendent side of the shopper's mind. They seemed to understand that the bottom line was not a number in a spreadsheet column. Instead, it was about how much they cared for their customers, understood their true motivations, beyond the goods and services they provided for them. These retailers and brands understood that what customers really wanted was more than what they would carry home in their shopping bags, but something they would carry home in their hearts.

We have come to a watershed moment in the making of retail places. Technological advancements are moving faster than our ability to keep in step with the change they are inducing. And while there is cause for concern, it is not so much for being overwhelmed but for simply being left behind in the swift-moving current of change. The good news is that our right hemisphere is perfectly adapted to embrace the ambiguity and uncertainty brought about by change in a digitally driven retail future.

We may think we fear the unknown, but actually, we love it.

It's the driving force behind growth, innovation, creativity and change.

Retail design is not a department. It is not a group of people up on the second floor who make lovely pictures of places that customers will be unable to resist.

Retail design is a *behavior*. A mindset. A way of being and doing.

It's thinking about how you engage shoppers in experiences that are relevant and meaningful to them because you have taken time to appreciate who they are – to *get inside their minds* and better understand what motivates them both on their phones *and* in the shopping aisle.

Today's customers, and the digital world they live in, may signal a split on retail's evolutionary tree.

But, the store will never go away.

Shopping is too deeply entrenched in our culture as an expression of who we are as people, to have the store fade into extinction because the digital world is providing new methods to buy goods and services. In the face of remarkable technological advancement, *the store will become even more important* as a place of ritual, storytelling, and play. The brand performance place will retain its relevance because customers will share in its making.

Brands, retailers and designers must keep ahead of the pace of change and innovation. Not simply by *thinking* new things but by *doing* new things.

What exactly the retail store of the future will look like is uncertain, but the change that will come upon shopping and the places made to do it will not be incremental. The pace of change will require a rapid overhaul, and upend most of our perceptual biases about what it means to go shopping. While the nature of the shopping place will most definitely change, the core principles of shopping being a right-brained activity will not.

Customers have always owned their experiences because they have been created in the confines of their own minds. In today's digitally driven world, people, places and things are interconnected and customer experience is being projected outwards on the world around us as an overt expression of the dynamic relationship between shoppers' minds and shopping places.

This kind of change is more than history in the making; it's driven by radically changing capabilities for communication, and shaped by our ubiquitous human need for connection and meaning. This progress is moving faster than we can define it. One thing is certain, the balance of power has shifted from retailers and brands – who have held all the cards upon which customer experiences were built, to the customers – who have knocked over the house of cards, creating their own content and who expect experiences to be crafted and delivered in a more profound and relevant way.

As the shopping place spins in a tornado of change, there won't be any firm footing upon which we will stand – except that shopping, for millennia, has been about relationships between people.

Where we eventually land may be magical and it won't be a permanent place to rest. The whole complex system will soon be swept up and moved yet again. And, each time it touches down, shoppers will likely say:

"TOTO, I'VE A FEELING WE'RE NOT IN KANSAS ANYMORE.
WE MUST BE OVER THE RAINBOW!"

WELCOME TO THE RETAIL (R)EVOLUTION.

Bibliography / Works Cited

For an online version of these sources, please see retail-r-evolution.com.

1. International Council of Shopping Centers – ICSC, "2013 Economic Impact of Shopping Centers," www.icsc.org.

2. Bell, Catherine. Ritual theory, ritual practice. Oxford University Press, 1992.

3. Singer, Milton B., ed. Traditional India: structure and change. Vol. 10. Philadelphia: American Folklore Society, 1959.

4. Myers, W Benjamin. Shopping the Shopper: Retail Surveillance and Performances of Consumerism. ProQuest, 2007.

5. Grimes, Ronald. Beginnings in Ritual Studies. 3 Reprint edition ed: CreateSpace Independent Publishing Platform, 2010, p.41.

6. Grimes, Ronald. Beginnings in Ritual Studies. 3 Reprint edition ed: CreateSpace Independent Publishing Platform, 2010, p.35.

7. Lindström, Martin. Buyology: truth and lies about why we buy. Random House LLC, 2010.

8. Lindström, Martin. Buyology: truth and lies about why we buy. Random House LLC, 2010.

9. Lindström, Martin. Buyology: truth and lies about why we buy. Random House LLC, 2010.

10. McLuhan, Marshall. Understanding media: The extensions of man. MIT press, 1994.

11. Grimes, Ronald. Beginnings in Ritual Studies. 3 Reprint edition ed: CreateSpace Independent Publishing Platform, 2010, p.71.

12. Grimes, Ronald. Beginnings in Ritual Studies. 3 Reprint edition ed: CreateSpace Independent Publishing Platform, 2010, pg.70.

13. Grimes, Ronald. Beginnings in Ritual Studies. 3 Reprint edition ed: CreateSpace Independent Publishing Platform, 2010, pg.69.

14. Campbell, Joseph. The hero with a thousand faces. Vol. 17. New World Library, 2008.

15. Speer, Nicole K., et al. "Reading stories activates neural representations of visual and motor experiences." Psychological Science 20.8 (2009): 989-999.

16. Gernsbacher, M. A. "Language comprehension as structure building, 1990."

17. Pulvermüller, Friedemann. "Brain mechanisms linking language and action." Nature Reviews Neuroscience 6.7 (2005): 576-582.

18. Buckner, Randy L., and Daniel C. Carroll. "Self-projection and the brain." Trends in cognitive sciences 11.2 (2007): 49-57 and Vincent JL, Snyder AZ, Fox MD, Shannon BJ, Andrews JR, Raichle ME, et al. "Coherent spontaneous activity identifies a hippocampal-parietal memory network. " Journal of neurophysiology. 96(6) (2006): 3517–3531.

19. Zwaan, Rolf A., and Gabriel A. Radvansky. "Situation models in language comprehension and memory." Psychological bulletin 123.2 (1998): 162.

20. Pink, Daniel H. A whole new mind: Why right-brainers will rule the future. Penguin, 2006. See p. 83.

21. Huizinga, Johan. Homo Ludens: A Study of the Play-Element in Culture. Boston, MA: Beacon Press, 1971, p. 4-5.

22. Huizinga, Johan. Homo Ludens: A Study of the Play-Element in Culture. Boston, MA: Beacon Press, 1971. Print, p.1.

23. Panksepp, Jaak. Affective Neuroscience: The Foundations of Human and Animal Emotions. Oxford university press, 1998.

24. For more, see https://www.youtube.com/watch?v=q_AHfKD8XgE.

25. MacLean, Paul D. The triune brain in evolution: Role in paleocerebral functions. Springer, 1990.

26. For more, see http://www.wholefoodsmarket.com/about-our-products/quality-standards.

27. Rifkin, Jeremy. The empathic civilization: The race to global consciousness in a world in crisis. Penguin, 2009.

28. Sartre, Jean-Paul. "The Writings of Jean-Paul Sartre, edited by Michel Contat and Michel Rybalka." (1974).

29. For more, see http://www.learnoutloud.com/content/blog/archives/2012/07/charlie_rose_brain_series.html.

30. The White House. "Fact Sheet: Brain Initiative." April 2, 2013. Accessed from: http://www.whitehouse.gov/the-press-office/2013/04/02/fact-sheet-brain-initiative

31. White, J. G., et al. "The Structure of the Nervous System of the Nematode Caenorhabditis Elegans." Philos Trans R Soc Lond B Biol Sci 314.1165 (1986): 1-340. Print.

32. For more info on the Human Genome Project, see http://www.genome.gov/10001772.

33. For more, see http://www.ted.com/talks/sebastian_seung.html. Also see http://www.humanconnectomeproject.org and Seung, Sebastian. Connectome: How the brain's wiring makes us who we are. Houghton Mifflin Harcourt, 2012.

34. Alivisatos, A. P., et al. "The Brain Activity Map Project and the Challenge of Functional Connectomics." Neuron 74.6 (2012): 970-4.

35. Gershon, Michael D. "The second brain: the scientific basis of gut instinct and a groundbreaking new understanding of nervous disorders of the stomach and intestines." Harper Collins Goyal RK, Hirano I.(1996). The Enteric Nervous System. N Engl J Med 334 (1998): 1106-1115.

36. Emeran A. Mayer, MD. Professor of Medicine and Physiology CURE: Digestive Disease Research Center/Neuroenteric Disease Program UCLA Division of Digestive Disease UCLA School of Medicine.

37. http://www.sabonnyc.com/company/our-store-experience.html. Also see the hand washing ritual video at https://www.youtube.com/watch?v=sIRmx0J8ns0&feature=player_embedded.

38. Gazzaniga, Michael. Who's in charge?: Free will and the science of the brain. Constable & Robinson, 2012. See p. 44.

39. Gazzaniga, Michael. Who's in charge?: Free will and the science of the brain. See footnote 3 on p. 45.

40. Gazzaniga, Michael. Who's in charge?: Free will and the science of the brain. See p. 38.

41. Rose, C. "Part One of the Charlie Rose Science Series: From Freud to the mysteries of the human brain." (2006).

42. MacLean, P. The triune brain in evolution: Role in paleocerebral functions. Plenum, 1990.

43. Roth, Gerhard, and Ursula Dicke. "Evolution of the brain and intelligence." Trends in cognitive sciences 9.5 (2005): 250-257.

44. Lent, Roberto, et al. "How many neurons do you have? Some dogmas of quantitative neuroscience under revision." European Journal of Neuroscience 35.1 (2012): 1-9.

45. Gazzaniga, Michael. Who's in charge?: Free will and the science of the brain. See p. 31.

46. Sejnowski, Terry, and Tobi Delbruck. "The language of the brain." Scientific American 307.4 (2012): 54-59.

47. Sejnowski, Terry, and Tobi Delbruck. "The language of the brain." Scientific American 307.4 (2012). See p. 59.

48. More on the origin of this phrase at http://www.carnegiehall.org/History/History-FAQ/.

49. Petanjek, Zdravko, et al. "Extraordinary neoteny of synaptic spines in the human prefrontal cortex." Proceedings of the National Academy of Sciences 108.32 (2011): 13281-13286.

50. Nie, Norman H., and D. Sunshine Hillygus. "The impact of Internet use on sociability: Time-diary findings." It & Society 1.1 (2002): 1-20.

51. Vandewater, Elizabeth A., et al. "Digital childhood: electronic media and technology use among infants, toddlers, and preschoolers." Pediatrics 119.5 (2007): e1006-e1015.

52. Rideout, Victoria J., Ulla G. Foehr, and Donald F. Roberts. "Generation M²: Media in the Lives of 8-to 18-Year-Olds." Henry J. Kaiser Family Foundation (2010).

53. Small, Gary W., et al. "Your brain on Google: patterns of cerebral activation during internet searching." The American Journal of Geriatric Psychiatry 17.2 (2009): 116-126.

54. Small, Gary, and Gigi Vorgan. iBrain: Surviving the technological alteration of the modern mind. HarperCollins, 2008. See p. 19.

55. Small, Gary, and Gigi Vorgan. iBrain: Surviving the technological alteration of the modern mind. See p. 21.

56. Small, Gary, and Gigi Vorgan. iBrain: Surviving the technological alteration of the modern mind. See p. 25.

57. Konrath, Sara H., Edward H. O'Brien, and Courtney Hsing. "Changes in dispositional empathy in American college students over time: A meta-analysis." Personality and Social Psychology Review (2010).

58. Konrath, Sara H., Edward H. O'Brien, and Courtney Hsing. "Changes in dispositional empathy in American college students over time: A meta-analysis." Personality and Social Psychology Review (2010).

59. Konrath, Sara H., Edward H. O'Brien, and Courtney Hsing. "Changes in dispositional empathy in American college students over time: A meta-analysis." Personality and Social Psychology Review (2010).

60. Konrath, Sara H., Edward H. O'Brien, and Courtney Hsing. "Changes in dispositional empathy in American college students over time: A meta-analysis." Personality and Social Psychology Review (2010).

61. Sutherland, Stuart. Macmillan dictionary of psychology. Basingstoke: Macmillan, 1995.

62. Gazzaniga, Michael. Who's in charge?: Free will and the science of the brain. See pp. 58-59.

63. Doidge, Norman. The brain that changes itself: Stories of personal triumph from the frontiers of brain science. Penguin, 2007.

64. Bar-Yam, Yaneer. "General features of complex systems." Encyclopedia of Life Support Systems (EOLSS), UNESCO, EOLSS Publishers, Oxford, UK (2002). See pages on "Self-organizing patterns".

65. Schultz, Howard, and Dori Jones Yang. Pour your heart into it: How Starbucks built a company one cup at a time. Hyperion, 1997.

66. Siegel, Daniel J. Mindsight: The new science of personal transformation. Random House LLC, 2010. See p. 58. For more information on Dr. Daniel Siegel, see http://drdansiegel.com/about/biography/.

67. Siegel, Daniel J. Mindsight: The new science of personal transformation. See p 69.

68. Olds, James, and Peter Milner. "Positive reinforcement produced by electrical stimulation of septal area and other regions of rat brain." Journal of comparative and physiological psychology 47.6 (1954): 419.

69. Schultz, Wolfram. "Predictive reward signal of dopamine neurons." Journal of neurophysiology 80.1 (1998): p, 1-27. For a great summary of the predictive power of dopamine neurons, see Radio Lab: https://www.wnyc.org/radio/#/ondemand/91687 and http://www.radiolab.org/story/91687-seeking-patterns/.

70. Schultz, Wolfram. "Predictive reward signal of dopamine neurons." Journal of neurophysiology 80.1 (1998): p.2.

71. Gazzaniga, Michael. Who's in charge?: Free will and the science of the brain. See p. 46.

72. Chen, Ingfei. "Brain cells for socializing." Smithsonian Magazine (2009). Also see http://www.smithsonianmag.com/science-nature/brain-cells-for-socializing-133855450/#VvGXTYa2MQeZxJKR.99

73. Frank, Michael J., Brion S. Woroch, and Tim Curran. "Error-related negativity predicts reinforcement learning and conflict biases." Neuron 47.4 (2005): 495-501.

74. Knutson, Brian, et al. "Neural predictors of purchases." Neuron 53.1 (2007): 147-156.

75. Paulus, Martin P., and Murray B. Stein. "An insular view of anxiety." Biological psychiatry 60.4 (2006): 383-387. Also see http://koso.ucsd.edu/~martin/PaulusSteinInsulaReview.pdf

76. Humphrey, David B. "Replacement of cash by cards in US consumer payments." Journal of Economics and Business 56.3 (2004): 211-225.

77. Thomas, Manoj, Kalpesh Kaushik Desai, and Satheeshkumar Seenivasan. "How credit card payments increase unhealthy food purchases: visceral regulation of vices." Journal of consumer research 38.1 (2011): 126-139.

78. Javelin Strategy & Research, "Retail Point of Sale Forecast 2012-2017: Cash is No Longer King; Cards and Mobile Payments Likely to Rise" June, 2012.

79. "How We Use Our Credit Cards," UniBul Credit Card Blog, March 14, 2014, see http://blog.unibulmerchantservices.com/tag/credit-card-statistics/ also, for other credit card statistics see: http://www.creditcards.com/credit-card-news/credit-card-industry-facts-personal-debt-statistics-1276.php.

80. Gartner, Inc. May 29, 2012. See www.gartner.com/newsroom/id/2028315.

81. Thomas, Manoj, Kalpesh Kaushik Desai, and Satheeshkumar Seenivasan. "How credit card payments increase unhealthy food purchases: visceral regulation of vices." Journal of consumer research 38.1 (2011): 126-139

82. Thomas, Manoj, Kalpesh Kaushik Desai, and Satheeshkumar Seenivasan. "How credit card payments increase unhealthy food purchases: visceral regulation of vices." Journal of consumer research 38.1 (2011): 126-139

83. Thomas, Manoj, Kalpesh Kaushik Desai, and Satheeshkumar Seenivasan. "How credit card payments increase unhealthy food purchases: visceral regulation of vices." Journal of consumer research 38.1 (2011): 126-139

84. Pink, Daniel H. A whole new mind: Why right-brainers will rule the future. Penguin, 2006.

85. Rizzolatti, Giacomo, et al. "Premotor cortex and the recognition of motor actions." Cognitive brain research 3.2 (1996): 131-141.

86. A series of videos featuring Giacomo Rizzolatti discussing the subject of mirror neurons is available at http://www.gocognitive.net/interviews/giacomo-rizzolatti-mirror-neurons.

87. Rizzolatti, Giacomo, et al. "Premotor cortex and the recognition of motor actions." Cognitive brain research 3.2 (1996): 131-141 Rizzolatti, Giacomo, and Laila Craighero. "The mirror-neuron system." Annu. Rev. Neurosci. 27 (2004): 169-192.

88. Iacoboni, Marco, et al. "Grasping the intentions of others with one's own mirror neuron system." PLoS biology 3.3 (2005): e79.

89. Carr, Laurie, et al. "Neural mechanisms of empathy in humans: a relay from neural systems for imitation to limbic areas." Proceedings of the national Academy of Sciences 100.9 (2003): 5497-5502.

90. For more on expressions of emotions in humans and animals, see http://en.wikipedia.org/wiki/The_Expression_of_the_Emotions_in_Man_and_Animals.

91. For more on the Facial Coding Action System, see http://www.ekmaninternational.com/paul-ekman-international-plc-home/research.aspx.

92. For more, see http://www.wal-martchina.com/english/service/aim.htm.

93. Myers, David G. The American paradox: Spiritual hunger in an age of plenty. Yale University Press, 2001.

94. Iyengar, Sheena S., and Mark R. Lepper. "When choice is demotivating: Can one desire too much of a good thing?." Journal of personality and social psychology 79.6 (2000): 995.

95. Smith, Aaron, "In-store Mobile Commerce During the 2012 Holiday Season", Pew Internet & American Life Project, January 31, 2013. For more, see http://pewinternet.org/~/media//Files/Reports/2013/PIP_In_store_mobile_commerce_PDF.pdf.

96. Shiv, Baba, and Alexander Fedorikhin. "Heart and mind in conflict: The interplay of affect and cognition in consumer decision making." Journal of consumer research 26.3 (1999): 278-292.

97. For more on the history of the alphabet, see http://en.wikipedia.org/wiki/History_of_the_alphabet.

98. Rykwert, Joseph. The idea of a town: The anthropology of urban form in Rome, Italy and the ancient world. MIT Press, 1988.

99. Adams, Francis, ed. The genuine works of Hippocrates. Vol. 1. W. Wood and company, 1886.

100. On Wounds in the Head, in Hippocrates, trans. E. T. Withington (1927), Vol. 3, 33.

101. "Customer Desires vs. Retailer Capabilities: Minding the Omni-Channel Commerce Gap," Forester Consulting, January 2014.

102. "Customer Desires vs. Retailer Capabilities: Minding the Omni-Channel Commerce Gap," Forester Consulting, January 2014.

103. Small, Gary, and Gigi Vorgan. iBrain: Surviving the technological alteration of the modern mind. See p. 23.

104. "Can a Mobile Ad Make Your Cry? Not Likely" Dr. A.K. Pradeep founder and CEO of Nielsen Neurofocus.

105. Mobile Marketing Association – "Mobile Advertising Guidelines 5.0". See http://www.mmaglobal.com/policies/consumer-best-practices and/or http://www.mmaglobal.com/policies/global-mobile-advertising-guidelines.

106. 'Phablets' and Fonepads the New Tech Lexicon, Wall Street Journal, April 24, 2013.

107. Perez, Sarah. "iTunes App Store Now Has 1.2 Million Apps, Has Seen 75 Billion Downloads To Date", June 2, 2014. See http://techcrunch.com/2014/06/02/itunes-app-store-now-has-1-2-million-apps-has-seen-75-billion-downloads-to-date/.

108. See http://www.appbrain.com/stats/number-of-android-apps, appbrainstats.com, July 29, 2014.

109. "The mobiThinking compendium of mobile statistics and research – June 2012". See http://mobithinking.com/mobile-marketing-tools/latest-mobile-stats.

110. For more info, see http://www.pewinternet.org/Reports/2013/Smartphone-Ownership-2013.aspx.

111. Pew Internet & American Life Project, June 6, 2013. See http://www.pewinternet.org/Commentary/2012/February/Pew-Internet-Mobile.aspx.

112. Richtel, M. "Your Brain on Computers, attached to technology and paying the price." New York Times 1 (2010). See: http://www.nytimes.com/2010/06/07/technology/07brain.html?_r=1&scp=5&sq=richtel&st=Search. Last accessed 25th Sept 2010.

113. Lindstrom, Martin. "You love your iPhone. Literally." New York Times 1 (2011): 21A. See: http://www.nytimes.com/2011/10/01/opinion/you-love-your-iphone-literally.html?_r=0.

114. Flurry Research, August 2012.

115. "17% of Cell phone owners do most of their online browsing on their phone, rather than a computer or other device", Pew Internet & American Life Project, June 26, 2012.

116. "17% of Cell phone owners do most of their online browsing on their phone, rather than a computer or other device", Pew Internet & American Life Project, June 26, 2012.

117. Mobile User Surveys, Prosper Mobile Insights, 2012.

118. "17% of Cell phone owners do most of their online browsing on their phone, rather than a computer or other device", Pew Internet & American Life Project, June 26, 2012.

119. "Smartphone Ownership", Pew Internet & American Life Project, June 2013. See http://pewinternet.org/reports/2013/Smartphone-Ownership-2013.aspx

120. Kilcourse, Brian, and Rowen, Steve. "The Impact of Mobile in Retail, Benchmark Report 2012", RSR, December 2012.

121. Tablets are also growing in popularity with consumers devoting up a significant amount of time to them, with 31% using a tablet daily between 1 to 4 hours. Adobe 2012 Mobile Consumer Survey Results White Paper, see http://success.adobe.com/assets/en/downloads/whitepaper/20860_mobile_consumer_survey_white_paper_ue_v5.pdf.

122. For more info, see http://mobithinking.com/mobile-marketing-tools/latest-mobile-stats/d#usmobilebehavior.

123. Brenner, Joanna and Smith, Aaron, "72% of Online Adults are Social Networking Site Users", Pew Internet & American Life Project, August 5, 2013.

124. Brenner, Joanna and Smith, Aaron, "72% of Online Adults are Social Networking Site Users", Pew Internet & American Life Project, August 5, 2013.

125. Smith, Aaron, "Why Americans Use Social Media", Pew Internet & American Life Project, November 14, 2011.

126. Smith, Aaron, "Why Americans Use Social Media", Pew Internet & American Life Project, November 14, 2011.

127. Adobe 2012 Mobile Consumer Survey Results White Paper, see http://success.adobe.com/assets/en/downloads/whitepaper/20860_mobile_consumer_survey_white_paper_ue_v5.pdf.

128. For more, see http://www.csnews.com/industry-news-and-trends/technology/retailers-brands-have-most-social-media-followers#sthash.7TtBCxkr.dpuf.

129. Jackson, Lee. 24/7 Wallst.com, Retailers with the Most Facebook and Twitter Followers, April 1, 2014. See http://247wallst.com/retail/2014/04/01/retailers-with-the-most-facebook-and-twitter-followers/.

130. "In the Know About On the Go", Adobe Captures what Mobile Users Want, Mobile Marketing White Paper http://blog.larsbjorn.com/download/002647.AdobeCapturesWhatMobileUsersWant.pdf.

131. "In the Know About On the Go", Adobe Captures what Mobile Users Want, Mobile Marketing White Paper http://blog.larsbjorn.com/download/002647. AdobeCapturesWhatMobileUsersWant.pdf.

132. "Smartphone Use for Retail", Mobile User Surveys, Prosper Mobile Insights, July 2013.

133. See multiple resources, each with slightly different survey responses including Adobe: In the Know About On the Go - Mobile Marketing White Paper, Comscore, Prosper Mobile Survey Jan. 2013.

134. Accenture, December 6, 2012.

135. Pew Study: "In-Store cell phone use Holiday Shopping 2012".

136. TimeTrade: Industry Update, "The Retail Customer Evolution", TimeTrade Systems, Inc., 2014.

137. TimeTrade: Industry Update, "The Retail Customer Evolution", TimeTrade Systems, Inc., 2014.

138. Accenture – "Who are Millennial Shoppers? And what do they really want?" Outlook 2013, No.2 issue.

139. For more, see http://www.pewinternet.org/Presentations/2010/Feb/Millennials.aspx.

140. For more info on teens, social media and privacy, see http://www.pewinternet.org/~/media//Files/Reports/2013/PIP_TeensSocialMediaandPrivacy.pdf.

141. Pew – "Millennials: A Portrait of Generation Next" http://www.pewresearch.org/millennials/.

142. "Born This Way: The US Millennial Survey, Rick Furguson, aimia.com.

143. "Born This Way: The US Millennial Survey, Rick Furguson, aimia.com.

144. Aimia Study.

145. "Born This Way: The US Millennial Loyalty Survey, Rick Furguson, Aimia.

146. Aimia study.

147. For more, see http://expandedramblings.com/index.php/by-the-numbers-17-amazing-facebook-stats/2/#.U-pcEv1Ws8N

148. http://expandedramblings.com/index.php/by-the-numbers-17-amazing-facebook-stats/2/#.U-pcEv1Ws8N

149. For more, see http://zephoria.com/social-media/top-15-valuable-facebook-statistics/ (Source: The Social Skinny) and http://expandedramblings.com/index.php/important-instagram-stats/#.U22Ag15Enps

150. "Photos and Videos as Social Currency Online", Pew Internet & American Life Project, September 13, 2012.

151. "Photos and Videos as Social Currency Online", Pew Internet & American Life Project, September 13, 2012.

152. For more, see http://expandedramblings.com/index.php/important-instagram-stats/#.U-pdxf1Ws8M

153. Drell, Lauren. "What Marketers Can Learn From Whole Foods' Organic Approach to Pinterest," Mashable.com, February 23, 2012.

154. Drell, Lauren. "What Marketers Can Learn From Whole Foods' Organic Approach to Pinterest," Mashable.com, February 23, 2012.

155. Experian: The 2013 Digital Marketer, see http://www.experian.com/assets/marketing-services/reports/2013-digital-marketer-download.pdf?SP_MID=768&SP_RID=812481 "Life is the channel", Pew Internet & American Family Project: "Teens, Smartphones & Texting", March 19, 2012, http://www.pewinternet.org/2012/03/19/teens-smartphones-texting/.

156. Brenner, Joanna and Smith, Aaron, "Twitter Use 2012", Pew Internet & American Life Project, May 31, 2012.

157. McWhorter, John. "Txtng is killing language. JK!!!", see http://www.ted.com/talks/john_mcwhorter_txtng_is_killing_language_jk

158. McWhorter, John. "Txtng is killing language. JK!!!", see http://www.ted.com/talks/john_mcwhorter_txtng_is_killing_language_jk

159. Marian, Viorica, and Anthony Shook. "The cognitive benefits of being bilingual." Cerebrum: the Dana forum on brain science. Vol. 2012. Dana Foundation, 2012.

160. Marian, Viorica, and Michael Spivey. "Bilingual and monolingual processing of competing lexical items." Applied Psycholinguistics 24.02 (2003): 173-193.

161. Diaz, Rafael M., and Cynthia Klingler. "Towards an explanatory model of the interaction between bilingualism and cognitive development." Language processing in bilingual children (1991): 167-192.

162. Urban Land Institute and ULI Foundation, "Generation Y: Shopping and Entertainment in the Digital Age," May17, 2013. See http://www.uli.org/wp-content/uploads/ULI-Documents/Generation-Y-Shopping-and-Entertainment-in-the-Digital-Age.pdf.

163. DDB Worldwide, "DDB Life Style Study" Adweek. April 24, 2013.

164. ULI reports that 62% of Millennials prefer developments that combine shopping, dining, and office space. See http://www.uli.org/wp-content/uploads/ULI-Documents/Generation-Y-Shopping-and-Entertainment-in-the-Digital-Age.pdf.

165. Small, Gary, and Gigi Vorgan. iBrain: Surviving the technological alteration of the modern mind. HarperCollins, 2008. Also see Cathy Hutchison, a woman who suffered a stroke and did not have use of her limbs for 15 years, move a robotic arm to pick up and drink from a cup with a straw at https://www.youtube.com/watch?v=D6CCpfE2NoQ and http://www.washingtonpost.com/national/health-science/paralyzed-woman-moves-robotic-arm-with-her-thoughts/2012/05/16/gIQAd52hUU_story.html

166. See Tim Hemmes, a man who has been paralyzed for years, high-five his girlfriend by moving a robotic arm with his mind at http://usatoday30.usatoday.com/money/industries/health/story/2011-10-15/robotic-touch/50774398/1

167. Bucklin, Randolph E., et al. "Choice and the Internet: From clickstream to research stream." Marketing Letters 13.3 (2002): 245-258.

168. Emotient is a company specializing in facial recognition software for retail applications, http://www.emotient.com.

169. Kokalitcheva , Kia. "Emotient announce $6M Series B to Bring Facial Emotion Tracking to Stores," VentureBeat.com. March 16, 2014. See http://venturebeat.com/2014/03/06/emotient-announces-6m-series-b-to-bring-facial-emotion-tracking-to-retail-stores/.

170. Ahn, Sun Joo, M. E. Jabon, and J. N. Bailenson. "Facial expressions as predictors of online buying intention." Proceedings of the 58th Annual International Communication Association Conference. 2008.

171. Ahn, Sun Joo, M. E. Jabon, and J. N. Bailenson. "Facial expressions as predictors of online buying intention." Proceedings of the 58th Annual International Communication Association Conference. 2008. See p. 17.

172. Ahn, Sun Joo, M. E. Jabon, and J. N. Bailenson. "Facial expressions as predictors of online buying intention." Proceedings of the 58th Annual International Communication Association Conference. 2008. See p. 17.

173. St. John, Mark, et al. "Overview of the DARPA augmented cognition technical integration experiment." International Journal of Human-Computer Interaction 17.2 (2004): 131-149.

174. Bertozzi, M., et al. "Infrared stereo vision-based pedestrian detection." Intelligent Vehicles Symposium, 2005. Proceedings. IEEE. IEEE, 2005.

175. Facedeals by redpepper, an ad agency/media invention lab. See http://redpepperland.com/lab/details/check-in-with-your-face.

176. Persaud, Christine. wifi hifi, "Q&A with Dr. Nadia Shouraboura, CEO of Hointer, April 9, 2014.

177. Persaud, Christine. wifi hifi, "Q&A with Dr. Nadia Shouraboura, CEO of Hointer, April 9, 2014.

178. See http://www.crutchfield.com/app/retailStores/discoveryStore.aspx.

179. See http://www.businessweek.com/1999/99_35/b3644024.htm.

180. Evans, Dave. "The internet of things: how the next evolution of the internet is changing everything." CISCO white paper 1 (2011).

181. Evans, Dave. "The internet of things: how the next evolution of the internet is changing everything." CISCO white paper 1 (2011).

182. See http://www.edn.com/electronics-blogs/other/4306822/IPV6-How-Many-IP-Addresses-Can-Dance-on-the-Head-of-a-Pin-.

183. Hartley, Matt. "Star Trek-like holodeck may be closer to reality than you think", Financial Post, February 20, 2013. See http://business.financialpost.com/2013/02/20/star-trek-like-holodeck-may-be-closer-to-reality-than-you-think/.

184. LED lab and IC technologies. See http://ic-technologies.tv/custom-made.

185. Sloan, Garett. "Oreo Users Twitter to Make 3D Cookies at SXSW, Brand feeds passersby in real time, " Adweek. March 6, 2014.

186. Sloan, Garett. "Oreo Users Twitter to Make 3D Cookies at SXSW, Brand feeds passersby in real time," Adweek. March 6, 2014.

187. See https://www.youtube.com/watch?v=2LTXZZuedxQ.

188. Bensinger, Greg and Rusli, Evelyn M. "Amazon Preparing to Release Smartphone: Retailer Has Plans to Announce Phone by June, Begin Shipping by End of September," Wall Street Journal, April 11, 2014.

189. For more, see http://maps.google.com/intl/en/help/maps/businessphotos/. Also see http://www.youtube.com/watch?v=INg83kArY4g and http://www.pcworld.com/article/242697/google_maps_provides_street_view_look_at_store_interiors.html.

190. For more, see http://virtualeshopping.com.

191. For more, see http://thecreatorsproject.vice.com/blog/qr-codes-cover-every-inch-of-russias-pavilion-at-the-venice-architecture-biennale-2012.

192. For more, see http://www.speech.su.

193. The publisher of this book, ST Media Group International Inc., is also the publisher of VMSD magazine, and continues to venture off to L. Frank Baum's Oz in its monthly pursuit of creativity and magic making in the wonderful world of retail. For more, see http://stmediagroupintl.com/books/ and http://stmediagroupintl.com/brands/vmsd/.

194. For more, see https://www.youtube.com/watch?v=mUuVvY4c4-A or https://www.youtube.com/watch?v=WiPIWcgJgOE

195. For more, see https://www.youtube.com/watch?v=vDNzTasuYEw

196. For more, see https://www.youtube.com/watch?v=0dS5L7zHv74

197. For more, see https://www.youtube.com/watch?v=Go9rf9GmYpM

198. For more, see https://www.youtube.com/watch?v=uzo3pGpHvJM

199. For more, see http://www.google.com/glass/start/. Also see: "How Does Google Glass Work," by Techlife.com, http://www.techlife.net/2013/07/how-does-google-glass-work. html.

200. For more, see http://www.google.com/glass/start/. Also see: "How Does Google Glass Work," by Techlife.com, http://www.techlife.net/2013/07/how-does-google-glass-work. html.

201. Wasik, Bill. "Why Wearable Tech Will Be as Big as the Smartphone." (2014).

202. Teeters, Alea, Rana El Kaliouby, and Rosalind Picard. "Self-Cam: feedback from what would be your social partner." ACM SIGGRAPH 2006 Research posters. ACM, 2006.

203. Bourzac, Katherine. "Contact Lens Computer: Like Google Glass, without the Glasses" MIT Technology Review, June 7, 2013. Other electronic contact lenses have been developed for monitoring the eye pressure of glaucoma patients. See http://www. sensimed.com.

204. For more, see https://www.youtube.com/watch?v=GJKwHAvR4uI&feature=player_ embedded.

205. For more, see video interview about the technology and its applications with Dave Rice, VP, Marketing and Business Development, Senseg, Ltd., http://www.cnet.com/ videos/senseg-demos-prototype-touch-feedback-technology/.

206. For more, see http://www.penniesforlife.org.uk. Also see https://www.youtube.com/ watch?feature=player_profilepage&v=WYlLCXHoUc4 and https://www.youtube.com/ watch?v=VS3ThxPrlVo.

207. For more, see http://blog.westjet.com/westjet-christmas-miracle-video-real-time-giving/.

208. Kandel, Eric. "What the Brain Can Tell Us About Art", The New York Times April 12, 2013.

209. For more, see http://www.converse.com/products/custom-products.

210. For more, see http://www.nike.com/us/en_us/c/nikeid?cp=usns_kw_ AL!1778!3!34161626222!e!!g!nikeid.!c.

211. For more, see http://www.buildabear.com/shopping/.

212. For more, see https://www.threadless.com/make/submit/.

213. Empson, Rip. "Roqbot Raises $1.2M From Google Ventures & More to Turn Your Smartphone into a Social Jukebox," Techcrunch.com. June 12, 2012.

214. "What happens online in 60 seconds?" Qmee.com, July 24, 2013. See http://blog. qmee.com/qmee-online-in-60-seconds/ and "Data Never Sleeps" Domo.com. See http://www.domo.com.

215. For more, see www.internetworld.com.

216. For more, see http://blog.oxforddictionaries.com/press-releases/oxford-dictionaries-word-of-the-year-2013/.

217. Kucera, Daniel. "Why Amazon Is on a Warehouse Building Spree," Bloomberg Businessweek, August 29, 2013.

218. McGilchrist, Iain. The master and his emissary: the divided brain and the making of the western world. Yale University Press, 2009.

219. McGilchrist, Iain. The master and his emissary: the divided brain and the making of the western world. Yale University Press, 2009.

220. McGilchrist, Iain. The master and his emissary: the divided brain and the making of the western world. Yale University Press, 2009.